THE ANALYTIC THEIST

THE ANALYTIC THEIST

An Alvin Plantinga Reader

Edited by

James F. Sennett

WILLIAM B. EERDMANS PUBLISHING COMPANY
GRAND RAPIDS, MICHIGAN / CAMBRIDGE, U.K.

© 1998 Wm. B. Eerdmans Publishing Co.
255 Jefferson Ave. S.E., Grand Rapids, Michigan 49503 /
P.O. Box 163, Cambridge CB3 9PU U.K.
All rights reserved

Printed in the United States of America

03 02 01 00 99 98   7 6 5 4 3 2 1

Library of Congress Cataloging-in-Publication Data

Plantinga, Alvin.
The analytic theist : An Alvin Plantinga reader / edited by James F. Sennett.
p.   cm.
"Alvin Plantinga, a bibliography": p.
Includes bibliographical references.
Contents: God and analogy — The free will defense — The ontological
argument — Is naturalism irrational? — Reason and belief in God — Justification
and theism — A defense of religious exclusivism — Necessary being — Does God
have a nature? — On Ockham's way out — Advice to Christian philosophers —
Sheehan's shenanigans — Christian philosophy at the end of the century.
ISBN 0-8028-4229-1 (pbk. : alk. paper)
1. Religion — Philosophy. 2. Theism. 3. Philosophy and religion.
4. Christianity — Philosophy. I. Sennett, James F., 1955- . II. Title.
BL51.P55   1998
210 — dc21   98-18063
                           CIP

The editor and publisher gratefully acknowledge permission to reprint materials
granted by the individuals and institutions listed on pp. 368-69.

Contents

v

101002

III
DIVINE NATURE AND ATTRIBUTES 211

IV
CHRISTIAN PHILOSOPHY 293

Preface

This project began as an idea in the summer of 1993. I was a participant in a National Endowment for the Humanities summer institute at UC-Berkeley under the direction of Keith Lehrer and Nick Smith. The subject was "Knowledge, Teaching, and Wisdom," and one of our guest lecturers was Alvin Plantinga. While visiting with him and talking over some of his more significant work, I was suddenly struck by the fact that so much of that work is scattered hither and yon in a dozen different sources — a journal here, a book chapter there, etc. "How odd," I thought, "that no one has put all this important philosophy of religion in one place." I broached the idea of a collection to Plantinga that summer and received his endorsement to pursue it. But, as academic careers so often go, it would be over two years before I launched the project in earnest.

Now at last I am pleased to present this volume. I hope it will be a valuable contribution to the study of philosophy of religion and Christian philosophy in America. But more than anything it is a labor of love, presented with gratitude to one who has given so much to me and to Christian philosophers across this country. I testify to those contributions in some detail in my introductory essay, and will reserve the accolades until then.

As can be seen from the bibliography at the end of this book, Plantinga's published corpus is immense. Choosing a representative sample of that corpus was no mean task, as they say. Some selections were simple: no collection of his work would be complete without "Reason and Belief in God" or "Advice to Christian Philosophers." But beyond that the selection task was quite arduous. In choosing the pieces I did I was guided primarily by the desire to represent as adequately as possible Plantinga's immeasurable contribution to contemporary philosophy of religion in general and to the resurgence of Christian philosophy in particular. But I was painfully aware that there were many different ways this might be done.

vii

One problem I faced was that Plantinga's work ranges from the semi-popular to the laboriously technical. To make the right selections, I had to decide exactly what kind of audience I envisioned. For better or worse, I have selected these essays primarily with the scholarly audience in mind. They are not, for the most part, easily digested. They require intense study and reflection, plus perhaps some delving into related literature, for full appreciation.

However, I do not think one need be a *philosophical* scholar to benefit from this work. (For example, I selected Plantinga's less technical treatments of the Ontological Argument and the Free Will Defense in *God, Freedom, and Evil,* rather than his highly specialized and technical treatments of them in *The Nature of Necessity.*) Theologians, biblical scholars, and social scientists, among others, should be able to read and understand Plantinga's writings, and benefit greatly from them in their specific disciplines.

Two editorial notes. First, as I intimated above, I include a bibliography of Plantinga's work at the end of this volume. The entries in this bibliography are numbered consecutively. References to Plantinga's works in the introductory essay, editor's notes, and the section introductions are then made by using those numbers. Second, I have tried to stay out of the way as much as possible in this volume and allow Plantinga to speak for himself. I have kept the actual editing of the original texts to a bare minimum (with the exception of chapters five and nine, very large works that had to be excerpted to make it feasible to include them at all). On occasion, however, clarity requires my intervention with a short editor's note. These are indicated in the text by an asterisk (*) and appear at the bottom of the relevant page.

Many colleagues and friends across the country provided me with insights and suggestions regarding the composition of this collection and other dimensions of the project. I thank all of them profusely, though I could never pretend to name them all. I will offer special thanks to Paul Draper, William Hasker, Dewey Hoitenga, Philip Quinn, Tom Senor, Richard Swinburne, William Wainwright, and Nicholas Wolterstorff, who provided me with very helpful written comments concerning the structure of the volume and offered helpful words of advice regarding a project of this nature. Of course, I must say a very special word of thanks to Alvin Plantinga for making himself available to me as this project unfolded, for writing the Afterword, and for being the kind of philosopher, Christian, and human being that is worthy of the appreciation this volume intends.

Soli Deo Gloria
May 1998

Alvin Plantinga: A Short Chronology

1932	Born in Ann Arbor, Michigan, to Cornelius and Lettie Plantinga
1953	Graduated with Bachelor of Arts from Calvin College
1955	Graduated with Master of Arts from the University of Michigan
1957	Began teaching at Wayne State University
1958	Graduated with Doctor of Philosophy from Yale University
1963	Moved from Wayne State to Calvin College
1981-82	Served as President of the American Philosophical Asociation Central Division
1982	Moved from Calvin College to the University of Notre Dame
1983-86	Served as President of the Society of Christian Philosophers
1986	Received Calvin College Distinguished Alumni Award
1987	Presented Gifford Lectures, Aberdeen University
1995	Received Honorary Doctorate Degree from the Free University of Amsterdam

INTRODUCTION

The Analytic Theist: An Appreciation

I first met Alvin Plantinga while I was a graduate student at the University of Nebraska. My close friend Roger Ebertz and I drove from Lincoln to Wheaton, Illinois, to hear Plantinga present the 1986 Wheaton College Lectureship on Christianity and Philosophy. The lectures he presented there evolved over the next few months into his 1987 Gifford Lectures (I remember Arthur Holmes quipping that it was quite gracious of Aberdeen to accept Wheaton's hand-me-downs) and over the next few years into his important and impressive two-volume work on epistemic warrant (Bibliography #28 and #29). As a second-year graduate student, I had no grasp of the momentous nature of those ideas. Over the past decade they have helped shape the very domain of discourse for analytic epistemology and philosophy of religion.

But something else was happening at that Wheaton conference that was just as momentous, that was just as much Plantinga's doing, and about which I was just as ignorant. I did not realize how amazing it was, given recent history, that over 100 professional philosophers — many of them among the most important names in philosophy today — should be gathered together on the basis of their common profession of Christian faith and their common interest in issues at the intersection of Christianity and philosophy. Little did I know that such a scene would have been unheard of just one generation previous or that the difference between that generation and this was due in large part to the efforts, both theoretical and practical, of the man we had all come to hear.

In the spring of 1980, *Time* magazine reported, "In a quiet revolution in thought and arguments that hardly anyone could have foreseen only two decades ago, God is making a comeback. Most intriguingly, this is happening not among theologians or ordinary believers . . . but in the crisp, intellectual circles of academic philosophers, where the consensus had long banished the Almighty

xi

from fruitful discourse."[1] Kelly James Clark names Plantinga as the leader of this revolution,[2] and *Time* called him "America's leading orthodox Protestant philosopher of God" (p. 66). Without doubt, Plantinga's successes as a world-class philosopher have contributed greatly to this renewal of Christian philosophy. It is a purpose of this volume to demonstrate and celebrate those successes. However, what many may not realize is how instrumental Plantinga has been on a practical, hands-on level in promoting and encouraging the development of theistic philosophy in general and Christian philosophy in particular.

Clark lists two catalytic events in the resurgence of Christian philosophy, and Plantinga is at the center of both of them. First is the formation of the Society of Christian Philosophers in 1978, when Plantinga joined together with William Alston, Robert and Marilyn Adams, Arthur Holmes, and George Mavrodes to begin what has become "the largest single interest group among American philosophers" (Clark, pp. 9f.). The society boasts over 1100 members at the time of this writing. Plantinga later served as the third president of the Society, after William Alston and Robert Adams.

The second event Clark discusses is "the presentation, publication and subsequent discussion of Plantinga's 'Advice to Christian Philosophers,' " his 1983 inaugural address as John A. O'Brien Professor of Philosophy at the University of Notre Dame. (This lecture is reprinted as chapter 11 in the current volume.) In this address Plantinga issued a call for those who would become "the philosophers of the Christian community" — not satisfied simply with forensic, reactionary philosophical sparring with the unbelieving academic majority, but determined to explore the rich and profound philosophical implications of a wide range of Christian claims and practices. I cannot hope to improve on Clark's commentary on this bold move:

> This radical call to independence suggests that Christians can carry out their own agenda and not have it set by philosophers with fundamentally different presuppositions. The Christian's calling is primarily to be faithful to the believing community and not to the problematic set by the programs of the secular university. . . . The Christian has as much right to start from Christian assumptions as secular thinkers have to start from the assumption of naturalism. The Christian need not always be on the defensive, and may start with Christian beliefs and theorize on the basis of them. (p. 10)

Just as the calls from Dwight L. Moody and other great nineteenth-century evangelists motivated many Christian young people into crosscultural

1. "Modernizing the Case for God," *Time* 115, no. 14 (April 7, 1980): 65-68.
2. "Introduction: The Literature of Confession," in Kelly James Clark, editor, *Philosophers Who Believe: The Spiritual Journeys of 11 Leading Thinkers* (Downers Grove, Ill.: InterVarsity Press, 1993), p. 8.

missionary careers, Plantinga's challenge has drawn many young Christian scholars into the study of philosophy and the pursuit of "faith seeking understanding." I myself can report that, upon reading "Advice to Christian Philosophers" for the first time, the sensation was that of scales falling from my eyes, and I simultaneously rejoiced in the liberation and wondered at the implications of Plantinga's challenge. And I know from countless conversations with colleagues and students that my experience is a common one.

It is important to realize, however, that a big reason Christian philosophers have been able to take up the challenge of Plantinga's inaugural address within the confines of academic philosophy is because Plantinga himself has done so much to pave the way. He has done a great deal to shatter the facade of invulnerability that atheistic philosophy had through the first six decades of this century and to demonstrate as never before in the contemporary period that theistic claims can be rationally held and systematically defended. His rational parity argument in *God and Other Minds* (chapter 1 of the current volume), his transworld depravity version of the Free Will Defense (chapter 2), his modal ontological argument (chapter 3), and his argument for the direct justification of theistic belief (chapters 5 and 6) all fell like bombshells on the analytic landscape. Christian philosophy wasn't supposed to be that good. But it is, and Plantinga has been too important to be ignored. And in the wake of his strafing runs have come hundreds of Christian foot soldiers, ready to take their place in the once-occupied land of analytic philosophy.

One of Plantinga's most prominent qualities — and one which, no doubt, proves most frustrating to his interlocutors — is the steadfastness with which he holds to theistic, Christian, and evangelical convictions. He is never allured by the attractiveness of dominant academic or cultural views, and never assumes that his position bears some disproportionate share of the burden of proof. As will become evident in the reading of this volume, Plantinga refuses to let dominant views dissuade him just on the strength of their position as dominant views. He is doggedly persistent in asking, "Why should I think *that* is so?" and "Why should *that* count as a reason?" He stands undaunted against the intellectual tide and insists the proponents of atheism make *their* case to *his* satisfaction. He often sets the dialectical agenda with one powerful question: "If orthodox Christianity is true, then what you say is false. Why should I reject the former in favor of the latter rather than vice-versa?"

Today Christian philosophers enjoy a *prima facie* credibility that we did not have just a generation ago. In many secular universities and colleges it is now possible to conduct research projects that answer Plantinga's call in "Advice to Christian Philosophers," to gain tenure and promotion doing Christian philosophy, and to teach courses that treat philosophical issues, at least in part, from a Christian perspective. (The current work is the result of just such a project at a state university.) It is no longer the unspoken discipline-wide assumption that theism in general and Christianity in particular are intellectually indefensible and out of place in the academic arena. Those who hold such a naive conviction betray themselves as out of touch with the most current sentiments in the profession at large. It is once again respectable, in many places at least, for a Christian philosopher to do his or her philosophy as a Christian. And this incredible turn of events is due in very large part to the career of Alvin Plantinga.[3]

Plantinga's impact on the resurgence of Christian philosophy in these ways cannot be overestimated. However, I want to mention another way in which he has been vital to the revival — one that is not as public nor as discretely measurable, but is nonetheless as important. I speak of the personal interest that he has taken in young and developing philosophers for more than 35 years, many of whom were not even his students. Again I employ personal testimony. During the years that I wrote my dissertation on Plantinga's theistic philosophy project, he made himself available to me in many ways. He always made time to speak with me extensively at meetings of the Society of Christian Philosophers and the American Philosophical Association, as well as during a special visit to Notre Dame. Several times he read many pages of draft material that I sent him, and composed thoughtful, penetrating response and criticism. (I will never forget the time he wrote to congratulate me on finally getting his transworld depravity doctrine right.) And through it all this gracious man of God took every effort to help me believe I could succeed — even when that success entailed constructing criticisms of his work.

Recently Plantinga penned these words:

> [I]t is . . . hard to think of any task more important, for a Christian philosopher, than doing what one can to train and equip the next generation of Christian philosophers. This means seeing younger philosophers, fledgling philosophers and graduate students as of immense value. Their well-being and development as members of the community of Christian philosophers is a source of real concern: it requires our best efforts and any encouragement and help we can give. (#21, p. 81)

It is my testimony here that Plantinga is a man of his word. These sentiments are not hollow rhetoric, but an accurate description of the attitude and concern he took for this fledgling philosopher.

---

3. I do not mean to suggest, of course, that Plantinga has accomplished all of this single-handedly. He himself is the first to give credit to other giants of contemporary Christian philosophy such as Robert and Marilyn Adams, William Alston, Richard Swinburne, Nicholas Wolterstorff, and others. And Christian philosophers owe every one of them an unspeakable debt of gratitude. However, each of these would in turn be the first to point back to Plantinga as the one who primarily embodies the Christian resurgence in philosophy and who has done the most to establish its current respectability.

And once again, my story is not unique. The philosophy departments of America today house many Christian philosophers who owe a significant portion of their skill and confidence to personal investments of time, thought, and energy from the O'Brien Professor. Many other Christian philosophers who have not had the privilege to be personally acquainted with Plantinga can nonetheless point to him as a source of encouragement in and influence on their development. Those who have studied his writings carefully and have taken advantage of opportunities to observe him in public presentation or informal philosophical interchange cannot help but be inspired and challenged by his confident and uncompromising theistic stand. It is one thing to hear the challenge of "Advice to Christian Philosophers" or understand the rational parity that should be afforded theism as argued in *God and Other Minds* (chapter 1 of the current volume). It is quite another to find the courage one needs to excel as a Christian philosopher in a professional discipline still rife with unbelief and unjustified prejudice toward academics who are also people of faith. Careful study of Plantinga as a philosopher supplies not only the intellectual ingredients to meet the challenge, but the emotional and motivational ones as well.

One side note is appropriate here. Throughout my long study of Plantinga's work, I have been ceaselessly impressed by the care and precision he demonstrates in his analytical method. A few years ago I noted this dimension of Plantinga's work thus:

> Plantinga is among the most careful and precise philosophers working today. He takes great pains to avoid ambiguity and achieve clarity. Even when his work reaches great levels of technicality, as it often does, careful study reveals that the waters are deep, not muddy. It is clear from the responding literature that Plantinga's penchant for accuracy is having a healthy influence on the writings of many philosophers.[4]

It is also apparent from examining the literature being produced by Christian philosophers in recent years that the level of rigor is very high and rising all the time. One need only peruse a recent issue of *Faith and Philosophy* (the journal of the Society of Christian Philosophers) to see the care with which difficult and complex philosophical issues are addressed by many members of this burgeoning community. There can be no doubt that a significant influence on this development is the pervasive presence and centrality of Plantinga's work. Such precision and care can only increase the effectiveness of the Christian philosophical project.

One may wonder, after all of this concentration on Plantinga's role in

---

4. James F. Sennett, *Modality, Probability, and Rationality: A Critical Examination of Alvin Plantinga's Philosophy* (New York: Peter Lang Publishing, 1992), pp. v-vi.

the resurgence of Christian philosophy, why I have titled this collection *The Analytic Theist*, rather than *The Analytic Christian*. Without a doubt, Plantinga has helped restore Christian philosophy to a place of dignity and respect in the academic philosophical world. However, it is important to realize that the first, and perhaps more amazing, step in this restoration is the resurrection of theism from the ashes of positivism, ordinary language philosophy, and the general predominance of atheism in the academic world. (C. S. Lewis noted that he had to be converted to theism first before he could even consider Christianity.) Much of Plantinga's work, particularly early on, was aimed at this initial step of arguing that *any* form of theism was rationally feasible. In "Advice to Christian Philosophers," Plantinga notes, "Although my advice is directed specifically to Christian philosophers, it is relevant to all philosophers who believe in God, whether Christian, Jewish or Moslem." So also with the gamut of his corpus. In this age of renewed interest in interfaith dialog, it is especially critical that the commonalities among theists be accentuated. Though Plantinga himself is unashamedly and enthusiastically Christian, he recognizes and relishes the fact that his philosophy of religion is good news for all theism. I acknowledge and applaud this sentiment in the title of this collection.

* * *

In *Modality, Probability, and Rationality* I examined Plantinga's work in philosophy of religion in light of a "scarlet thread" I saw running through much of his work. That thread was a claim regarding the epistemology of theistic belief that I called "The Plantinga Thesis":

> PT: There is no plausible epistemological theory that rules out theistic belief as a category of epistemologically appropriate belief. (p. 1)

In other words, Plantinga maintains that any epistemological theory entailing that theistic belief *qua* theistic belief is irrational, unjustified, or in some other sense an epistemic ne'er-do-well is a theory that will show itself to be defective and unacceptable. From *God and Other Minds* to the closing chapters of the *Warrant* volumes Plantinga addresses over and over again the theme that any adequate account of human epistemic capacities and norms will allow for, perhaps even suggest or require, the epistemic appropriateness of theistic belief.

Of course, a career as rich, deep, and variegated as Plantinga's cannot be adequately summed up in a single thesis. However, I believe that the Plantinga Thesis is a driving motivational force in much of Plantinga's philosophy of religion, and I believe that using it as a compass can greatly aid in getting a handle on the profundity and importance of his work. In *Modality,*

Probability, and Rationality I attempted to exegete Plantinga's work as a defense of the Plantinga Thesis. In the current collection I let the master speak for himself. The selections here go well beyond the Plantinga Thesis in many regards, but I believe they all touch on it in important ways.

I have divided the collection into four sections, reflecting four major areas in which Plantinga has been quite influential. The first two are well-known to anyone familiar with contemporary analytic philosophy of religion. Section I is titled "Natural Theology and Atheology," and includes much of the early work that helped build and solidify Plantinga's reputation in the 1960s and early 1970s. The subjects have already been referred to: his rational parity argument in *God and Other Minds* and his ingenious renditions of the free will defense and the ontological argument. These works cemented Plantinga's place among the most influential philosophers of his time.[5] Included with these classic discussions is a fairly new piece, representing Plantinga's latest foray into natural theology and apologetics — an attack on the cohesiveness and rationality of metaphysical naturalism.

Section II likewise presents classic pieces together with a new endeavor. This section, titled "Reformed Epistemology," contains the two foundational documents of this famous project — "Reason and Belief in God," which presented in mature form the notion of the proper basicality of theistic belief,[6] and "Justification and Theism," which couched Reformed Epistemology claims in the externalist "proper function" motif to which Plantinga moved through the middle 1980s. This section is rounded out with "A Defense of Religious Exclusivism," which presents an intriguing application of Reformed Epistemology to a couple of very hot topics in contemporary theology and religious studies — religious pluralism and interfaith dialogue.

Section III, "Divine Nature and Attributes," presents some lesser-known but very important explorations by Plantinga of some more traditional areas of philosophical theology. The three selections here all deal with the nature of God, the third being a masterful study of that venerated theological conun-

---

5. They also served to earn him two entries in that unofficial Hall of Fame of philosophy, Daniel Dennett's *The Philosophical Lexicon* (7th edition, © 1987). Dennett defines the verb *alvinize* thus: "To stimulate protracted discussion by making a bizarre claim. 'His contention that natural evil is due to Satanic agency alvinized his listeners' " (p. 5). He also gives us *planting,* a verb meaning "To use twentieth-century fertilizer to encourage new shoots from eleventh-century ideas which everyone thought had gone to seed; hence, *plantinger* [obviously intended to be read with a Tufts/MIT accent], n., one who plantings" (p. 15).

6. This piece was not Plantinga's first presentation of the Reformed Epistemology thesis. He began toying with the notion near the end of his paper "The Probabilistic Argument from Evil," Bibliography #82) and addressed it directly in "Is Belief in God Properly Basic?" (#74) and a couple of articles in *The Reformed Journal* during 1982 (#71 and #72). It is "Reason and Belief in God," however, that gives the doctrine its fullest expression and defense, and it is this piece that has received the most attention in the literature and has come to be recognized as the cornerstone piece in the Reformed Epistemology project.

drum, the problem of free will and divine foreknowledge. These essays have not been as frequently addressed by the philosophical community as those in sections I and II, and their oversight is a regrettable error. A big part of my motive in putting them here is to help jump-start the productive discussion Plantinga's insights should engender.

Finally, section IV gives examples of Plantinga's writings bearing specifically on the issue of Christian philosophy itself. His already heralded O'Brien Inaugural Address is included here, as well as two papers recommended for inclusion by Plantinga himself — a review of Thomas Sheehan's *The First Coming: How the Kingdom of God Became Christianity* and a recent paper with the intriguing title, "Christian Philosophy at the End of the Twentieth Century."

* * *

In "A Christian Life Partly Lived," Plantinga contrasts the Christian philosophical situation at the beginning of his career and today. "When I left graduate school in 1957," he observes, "there were few Christian philosophers in the United States, and even fewer Christian philosophers willing to identify themselves as such." The contrast to today, as we have noted, is startling. "Now, some 35 years later, things look different indeed. There are hundreds of young Christian philosophers in the United States, many of them people of great philosophical power; much first-rate work is going on in Christian or theistic philosophy and allied topics. . . ." In typical humility, Plantinga never assumes any credit for this drastic change of affairs, but chooses simply to relish it. "[I]t looks as if Christian philosophy, for the next generation or two, will be in good hands indeed. For me personally this is a source of amazement, delight, and gratitude" (pp. 81-82).

On behalf of those "hundreds of young Christian philosophers," I present this volume as our tribute to one who has made a unique and irreplaceable contribution to this glad situation.

Thanks, Al. We're having a great time, and we owe it all to you.

James F. Sennett
McNeese State University

SECTION I

Natural Theology and Atheology

Introduction

In the opening sentence of the preface of his first monograph, *God and Other Minds* (Bibliography #106), Plantinga states, "In this study I set out to investigate the rational justification of belief in the existence of God as He is conceived in the Hebrew Christian tradition." In many ways this statement could also serve as the theme for Plantinga's career in the philosophy of religion. Always an epistemologist at heart, Plantinga has concerned himself for almost forty years with the question of the rationality of theistic beliefs. While his concern for and defense of such beliefs has been articulate, impressive, and persuasive to many, it has never been predictable or formulaic. And nowhere is his innovative approach to theistic philosophy more evident than in *God and Other Minds*.

The initial project of the book is a surprising one: a theist writing over one hundred pages showing that the three most venerable theistic arguments — the cosmological, ontological, and teleological — all fail in their attempts to demonstrate conclusively that God exists. These verdicts are somewhat provisional, but they are nonetheless startling ones. And when in the second part of the book Plantinga delivers the same verdict for the most common defenses of atheism, so that both natural theology and natural atheology fail, one begins to wonder if religious skepticism isn't the unavoidable conclusion. It is here that Plantinga prepares to shoot an epistemological shot heard 'round the philosophy-of-religion world.

In the third section of *God and Other Minds,* Plantinga turns to that perennial philosophical chestnut, the "problem of other minds." Plantinga then examines the most common — and, he argues, most promising — argument for the rationality of belief in other minds, the so-called "argument from

1

analogy." Plantinga shows that this argument suffers the same fate as the natural theological and atheological arguments examined earlier — it fails to compel rational consent to its conclusion. But all is not lost. The failure of the argument from analogy has a familiar ring to it. In fact, Plantinga shows, it suffers from the exact same logical problem that caused the failure of the teleological argument. This fact leads Plantinga to a startling and intriguing examination of the nature of rational belief and its relation to philosophical argument. This examination is the subject of chapter 10 of the book, and is reprinted as chapter 1 of this collection.

The reader should be warned that this chapter is unique in this collection in that its main subject matter is not theism at all, but philosophy of mind. However, I include it in its entirety because, apart from the fact of its intrinsically interesting argument, it illustrates one of Plantinga's most significant contributions to theistic philosophy. Plantinga has helped remove the double standard that has so long been applied to philosophy of religion and argued vehemently that religious claims need not be judged any more rigorously than other claims with philosophical import. Criteria that count for acceptability in epistemology, metaphysics, and ethics must also count as such in religion. In chapter 1 Plantinga reveals clearly the standard of rationality to which belief in other minds is held, and argues in the closing paragraphs that such a standard is also applicable to theistic beliefs.

In *God and Other Minds* Plantinga constructed an elaborate and sophisticated version of the classical response to the problem of evil known as the "Free Will Defense." Over the next several years Plantinga reworked and sharpened up his free will defense, using the tools and concepts of contemporary modal logic and modal metaphysics. In chapter 9 of his 1974 study of modality *The Nature of Necessity* (#44 and #95), Plantinga presented his mature version of the defense, based in a concept he called "transworld depravity." While this argument is steeped in complex logical and metaphysical concepts, Plantinga offers a more accessible version of it in his popular study *God, Freedom, and Evil* (#94) — a version that does not require the modal background presented in the first eight chapters of *The Nature of Necessity.* I present this version of the argument as chapter 2 in this collection.

Plantinga's dismissal of the ontological argument — that remarkable philosophical effort by St. Anselm to prove God's existence based simply on the concept of *God* itself — was tentative at best in *God and Other Minds.* There he cautioned, "I shall not argue that no version of the ontological argument can possibly succeed, but only that none of the more obvious ways of stating it do in fact succeed" (p. 64). And after his arguments he offered the following reservations: "I can scarcely claim to have refuted the argument *überhaupt.* But until other interpretations are suggested, the verdict must be that the ontological argument is unsuccessful" (pp. 81-82).

It is ironic, though not at all surprising, that the most famous and controversial interpretation of the argument to be offered since Plantinga penned those words comes from that selfsame pen. On the heels of his modal free will defense, Plantinga offers in chapter 10 of *The Nature of Necessity* a modal ontological argument which he argues is valid and contains premises that theists can rationally accept. He claims that, while the argument "cannot, perhaps, be said to *prove* or *establish*" theism, it nonetheless shows "that it is rational to *accept* that conclusion. And perhaps that is all that can be expected of any such argument" (p. 221). Plantinga likewise presents a less technical, more popularly accessible version of his ontological argument in *God, Freedom, and Evil.* That version is included here as chapter 3.

As I mentioned above, Plantinga argues in *God and Other Minds* that natural atheology does not succeed in its efforts to prove the nonexistence of God. Over twenty years after the publication of that book Plantinga developed a more telling argument against atheism, or at least against its most prevalent contemporary expression in evolutionary naturalism. This argument is part of a larger program Plantinga has developed in recent years confronting the dominant naturalistic worldview and its presumed ownership of the scientific enterprise.[1] Grounded in his epistemological notion of "proper function" (see chapter 6 of the current volume), this argument reasons from the nature of human cognitive capacities to the conclusion that "evolutionary naturalism . . . is self-defeating and can't rationally be believed or accepted." This thesis is defended in his essay "An Evolutionary Argument Against Naturalism," presented at a conference on religious epistemology at Santa Clara University in 1991 and published in a collection of papers from that conference (#24 and #37). Plantinga revised the argument and included it as chapter 12 of his second *Warrant* volume (#28). This revision is reprinted here as chapter 4, and is juxtaposed with the older material of chapters 1-3 as a representation of Plantinga's ongoing and maturing thought regarding natural theology and atheology.

---

1. See, e.g., "When Faith and Reason Clash: Science and the Bible" (#40), "Methodological Naturalism" (#12), and the last two chapters of *Warrant and Proper Function* (#28).

CHAPTER ONE

God and Analogy

In the last two chapters I defended the analogical position against several objections and argued that it was more successful than any current alternative to it.[1] We should note, furthermore, that the analogical argument for other minds strongly resembles the teleological argument for the existence of God. They answer similar questions and both are inductive or analogical arguments; each is perhaps the most successful answer to the question it addresses. In this chapter I shall argue that the analogical position finally falls prey to the very objection that, in Chapter Four, I urged against the teleological argument.

I

Perhaps we may begin by considering A. J. Ayer's statement of the analogical position: "On the basis of my own experience I form a general hypothesis to the effect that certain physical phenomena are accompanied by certain feelings. When I observe that some other person is in the appropriate physical state, I am thereby enabled to infer that he is having these feelings; feelings which are similar to those that in similar circumstances I have myself."[2] Noting that this formulation seems open to the "one case alone" objection, Ayer suggests that

> the objections that one is generalizing from a single instance can perhaps be countered by maintaining that it is not a matter of extending to all other

1. Of course I did not consider every alternative that has been proposed. See below, pp. 19-20.
2. *The Problem of Knowledge* (Edinburgh, 1956), p. 249.

4

persons a conclusion which has been found to hold for only one, but rather of proceeding from the fact that certain properties have been found to be conjoined in various circumstances. . . . So the question that I put is not: Am I justified in assuming that what I have found to be true only of myself is also true of others? but: Having found that in various circumstances the possession of certain properties is united with the possession of a certain feeling, does this union continue to obtain when the circumstances are still further varied? The basis of the argument is broadened by absorbing the difference of persons into the difference of the situations in which the psycho-physical connections are supposed to hold.[3]

This version of the analogical argument may bear fuller statement. Initially it is pointed out that while a person can observe another's behavior and circumstances, he cannot perceive another's mental states. Hence we cannot come to know that another is in pain, for example, by perceiving his pain. And, on the other hand, although some propositions ascribing pain to a person are incorrigible for *him,* no proposition ascribing pain to him is incorrigible for anyone else. We might put these things technically by saying that no one can *determine by observation* that another is in pain.

According to the analogical position, I nevertheless have or can easily acquire evidence for such propositions as that some other person is in pain and that some person is feeling pain in a bodily area in which I feel nothing. Let us say that S's *total evidence* is a set of propositions such that p is a member of it if and only if (1) p is either necessarily true or solely about[4] S's mental states or solely about physical objects, or a consequence of such propositions, and (2) S knows p to be true. According to the analogical position, my total evidence yields an argument for each of the above conclusions. For

(1) Every case of pain-behavior such that I have determined by observation whether or not it was accompanied by pain in the body displaying it, *was* accompanied by pain in that body.[5]

Applying the so-called straight rule of induction, I conclude that

(2) Probably every case of pain-behavior is accompanied by pain in the body displaying it.

---

3. Ibid., pp. 250-51.

4. Where a necessary (but not sufficient) condition of a proposition's being solely about my own mind or physical objects is that it not entail the existence of mental states that are not mine.

5. Where, of course, I determine by observation that pain-behavior on the part of a given body is accompanied by pain in that body only if I feel pain in it; and where the term "pain-behavior" is simply a label for a recognizable pattern of behavior (and hence from the fact that a man displays pain-behavior it does not follow that he is in pain).

But then on a certain occasion I observe that

(3) B over there (a body other than my own) is displaying pain-behavior.

From (2) it follows that B is pained; since I do not feel a pain there, I conclude that

(4) Some other sentient creature has a pain.

And so I am not the only sentient creature.

But here an objection arises. Consider how I establish (4): I observe that B is displaying pain-behavior. But no matter how intensely I concentrate, no matter how carefully I canvass my feelings, my attempt to feel a pain in B is futile. I feel no pain there. Doesn't this state of affairs provide me with a *disconfirming instance* of (2)? Should I not reject the suggestion that B contains a pain in favor of the conclusion that (2) is false? Consider the following analogy. Justice Douglas is walking through Racehorse Canyon, idly inspecting his surroundings. It occurs to him suddenly that every maple in the Canyon of which he has determined by observation whether it has leaves, does indeed have leaves. (Peculiar things occur to Justice Douglas.) So, he concludes, probably all maples in Racehorse Canyon have leaves. Walking a bit farther, he encounters another maple. Carefully inspecting this one, he fails to see any sign of leaves. He concludes that the maple has invisible leaves.

This procedure on Justice Douglas' part is surely perverse and absurd. What he should have concluded is not that there are leaves that cannot be seen, but that some of the maples in Racehorse Canyon lack leaves. And, by analogy, should I not take my failure to observe pain in B to provide me with a counterinstance to the generalization that every case of pain-behavior is accompanied by pain in the body displaying it?

One who accepts the analogical position, of course, will be quick to reject this suggestion. And perhaps his answer could proceed along the following lines. There is a difference, in general, between failing to observe the presence of A's and observing the absence of A's (observing that no A's are present).[6] A man may fail to see the mountain goats on a distant crag without thereby seeing that no mountain goats are there. But just as there are circumstances in which killing someone constitutes murdering him, so there are circumstances in which failing to perceive a thing constitutes observing its absence. Suppose, for example, that a person with good eyesight is looking at a maple ten feet away to see if it has leaves; the light is ample, his view of the tree is unobstructed, etc. If he sees no leaves, then in failing to see

6. I owe this way of putting the distinction to Robert C. Sleigh, Jr.

leaves he sees that the tree has no leaves. We might call any set of conditions in which failing to observe leaves on a tree constitutes observing that it has no leaves, an *optimal* set of conditions for observing the presence or absence of leaves. And though it may be difficult, perhaps, to specify the members of such an optimal set, there is no doubt that we are sometimes in circumstances of just that sort. Now if a man justifiably believes that he is in an optimal set of conditions for observing whether or not a tree has leaves, and fails to observe that it does, then he can justifiably believe that he is observing the absence of leaves there; perhaps, indeed, he is *rationally obliged,* in these circumstances, to take it that there are no leaves on the tree.

On the other hand, of course, if he knew that he was *not* in a position to observe whether leaves were present or absent, then his failure to observe leaves would scarcely oblige him to believe that he has a counterinstance to the generalization that all maples have leaves. More generally, under what conditions is a man obliged to take his observing an A and failing to observe that it is[7] B as providing him with a counterinstance to all A's are B? Consider the following three conditions:

(5) There are no possible circumstances in which failing to observe that an A is B constitutes observing that it is not B.

(6) No one can ever be in a position to observe that an A is not B.

(7) It is not possible to observe that an A is not B.

These three conditions hold with respect to observing whether or not a given bodily area is pained. There are no circumstances in which failing to feel pain in a body other than my own, for example, constitutes observing that that body is free from pain; I cannot observe the absence of pain in a body other than mine. But of course the same really holds for my own body as well; as Wittgenstein says, it is logically possible that someone else feel a pain in my body;[8] I can never tell by observation that my body is free from pain (although of course I can tell that I do not feel a pain there). And surely a man who *knows* that one cannot tell by observation that a given bodily area contains no pain is not obliged to conclude that he has a counterinstance to (2). Hence we may assert

(8) A person S is obliged to take his observing that something is A and failing to observe that it is B as providing him with a counterinstance to *All A's are B* only if (a) he does not know that it is impossible to observe that an A is not B, and (b) he does not know that there are

---

7. Since *"B"* is presumably a variable whose substituends are singular referring expressions, the verb here, strictly speaking, should be "has." For stylistic reasons I shall continue to use "is" except where genuine ambiguity results.

8. *Philosophical Investigations,* par. 302.

no circumstances in which failing to observe that an A is B constitutes observing that it is not B, and (c) he does not know that he cannot be in a position to observe that an A is not B.

Since, of course, I might very well know any or all of these things, I am not obliged, in discovering that (4) is true, to take it that I have a counterinstance to (2); and hence this objection to the analogical position fails.

The fact that one cannot observe the absence of pain delivers the analogical position from the above objection; that fact, nevertheless, is the rock upon which it founders. To see this we must characterize more fully the sort of argument which, on the analogical position, is available to each of us. Let us say that *a simple inductive argument for S* is an argument of the following form:

Every A such that S has determined by observation whether or not A is B is such that S has determined by observation that A is B.[9] Therefore, probably every A is a B.

And let us say that *a direct inductive argument for S* is an ordered pair of arguments of which the first member is a simple inductive argument a for S, and the second a valid deductive argument one premise of which is the conclusion of a, the other premises being drawn from S's total evidence.

The contention of the analogical position, then, is that for any person S (or at least for most persons) there is a direct inductive argument for S, for such conclusions as that at a given time t someone other than S is in pain. But this is not all that the analogical position holds. For it is of course possible that there be for a person S a direct argument for p although p is improbable on S's total evidence. What the analogical position must hold here is that for any person S there are direct arguments for the propositions in question and no comparable evidence against them; they must be *more probable than not* on his total evidence.

Finally, according to the analogical position, the bulk of my commonsense beliefs[10] about minds and mental states must be more probable than not on my total evidence. It is not sufficient that my total evidence confirm the proposition that there are other sentient beings; it must also confirm, in one way or another, the whole range of commonsense beliefs about the behavioral accompaniments or aspects of anger, joy, depression, and pain, as well as beliefs about the connections between body and mind generally. It need be

9. This account would be complicated but not essentially modified if it were so generalized as to take account of the sort of argument where, of his sample of A's, S determines by observation that m/n of them are B and concludes that probably m/n A's are B.

10. The term "belief" is here so used that "Jones believes p" is not inconsistent with (and indeed is entailed by) "Jones knows p."

no part of the analogical position to maintain that for *each* of these propositions there is, for me, a direct argument. For some of them, perhaps, my only evidence is the fact that they are probable with respect to *other* propositions for which I do have direct arguments. But each (or most) of us must have a basic set K of such propositions for each member of which he has a direct argument; and perhaps the remainder of his relevant commonsense beliefs can be shown to be confirmed by the conjunction of the members of K. Furthermore, then, not only must each member of K be more probable than not on my total evidence; their *conjunction* must be. This, of course, is a much stronger claim; it is possible that $p_1 \ldots p_n$ are individually more probable than not on q while their conjunction is not.[11] And among the members of K we should certainly find such propositions as the following:

(a) I am not the only being that feels pain.
(b) There are some pains that I do not feel.
(c) Sometimes certain areas of my body are free from pain.
(d) There are some pains that are not in my body.
(e) There are some cases of pain that are not accompanied by pain-behavior on the part of my body.
(f) I am the only person who feels pain in my body.
(g) Sometimes someone feels pain when I do not.

Propositions (a)-(g), of course, are stated for *me:* but there is for any person an analogue, in an obvious sense, of each of those propositions. Now, perhaps, we can summarily restate the analogical position as follows:

(9) For any (or almost any) person S there is a set of propositions K such that the appropriate analogues of (a)-(g) are members of K; and S's total evidence *directly supports* each member of K (i.e., for any member m of K there is a direct argument for S supporting m but no direct argument for S against m); and the conjunction of the members of K is more probable than not on S's total evidence.

So stated, this position is dubious at best. The conjunction of (a)-(g) is not more probable than not on the sort of evidence to which the analogical position directs our attention; nor (with one exception) does the analogical position give us any reason for supposing that (a)-(g) are individually more probable than not on that evidence.

---

11. Let q be *a fair die is about to be thrown;* let p_1 through p_5 be, respectively, *face one will not come up, face two will not come up, face three will not come up, face four will not come up,* and *face five will not come up.* Each of p_1 through p_5 is then more probable than not on q; but their conjunction is not.

II

Suppose we begin with propositions (a) and (b). Recall that my argument of (a) involves a simple inductive argument from

(1) Every case of pain-behavior such that I have determined by observation whether or not it was accompanied by pain in the body displaying it, *was* accompanied by pain in that body

to

(2) Probably every case of pain-behavior is accompanied by pain in the body displaying it.

But

(3) B over there (a body other than mine) is displaying pain-behavior,

hence

(10) Probably B contains a pain.

And since I feel no pain, in B, I conclude that

(b) I do not feel every pain.

Of course if B contains a pain, then some sentient creature or other is feeling a pain in B; hence

(a) I am not the only being that feels pain.

Such is my evidence, on the analogical position, for (a) and (b). There is a peculiarity about the inference of (2) from (1), however, that ought not to pass unmentioned. As we have noted, I determine by observation that a given body or bodily area contains a pain just in case I feel a pain there. Further, I cannot determine by observation that a bodily area does *not* contain a pain — not even if the area in question is part of my own body. The best I can do along these lines is to determine that I do not feel a pain there; but of course it does not follow that *no one* does. So, for any bodily area, I determine by observation whether or not that area is pained *only if* what I determine is that it *is* pained. And consequently no counterinstance to (2) (the argument's conclusion) can possibly turn up in my sample. There are other arguments of this same sort and most of them deserve to be regarded with the gravest suspicion. Consider, for example, the inductive argument for epistemological idealism:

(11) Every physical object of which it has been determined whether or not it has ever been conceived (i.e., perceived or thought of) *has* been conceived.

Therefore,

> (12) Probably every physical object is conceived; so there are no un-conceived physical objects.

Now it might be said that an alleged inductive argument of this sort clearly proves nothing at all. For if there were any counterinstances to the conclusion, it would be logically impossible for one of them ever to turn up in the sample; and hence we know, in any instance of this sort, that there is no reason to suppose that our sample is a random or fair one. Suppose we are drawing colored marbles from an inexhaustible urn and know that Descartes' evil genius is so guiding our hands that we draw only red ones. Ought we then to take the fact that all the marbles we have so far drawn have been red as evidence for the view that all the marbles in the urn are red? If it is impossible for a counterinstance to the conclusion of a simple inductive argument to turn up in its sample (where the conclusion is not itself necessarily true), then the argument is unacceptable. Perhaps we do well, therefore, to accept some such principle as the following:

> (A) A simple inductive argument is acceptable only if it is logically possible that its sample class contain a counterinstance to its conclusion.

Now (A) appears to be inadequate[12] on the grounds that it fails to eliminate certain arguments that such a principle ought to eliminate. Consider, for example, the following argument for the conclusion that I am not the only human person. Let us say that x is *crowman* just in case x is either a crow or a human body and that a thing is *minded* if it is the (human) body of a human person. Then

> (13) Every crowman such that I have determined by observation whether or not it was either black or minded, *was* either black or minded.

So probably

> (14) Every crowman is either black or minded.

But

> (15) *B* over there (a human body other than my own) is a crowman and is not black.

Hence *B* is probably minded; hence there is at least one other human person. This argument will not meet with instant approval. And yet its premise

12. As I was reminded by Lawrence Powers.

will be true for any of us. For any crow in my sample will have the sample property (i.e., the property of being black or minded); my own body will be in my sample and will have the sample property; and of no human body will I be able to determine that it lacks the sample property. Furthermore, the inference of (14) from (13) does not violate (A); clearly it is *possible* (though it will not happen) that my sample class contain a counterinstance (a white crow, for example) to (14).

Perhaps, therefore, we can restate (A). Let us suppose for the moment that we know what it is for a property to have a disjunct or conjunct: the property *being black or minded,* for example, has as one disjunct the property *being black.* And let us say that a property P is a part of a property P' just in case P is the same property as P' or P is a disjunct, conjunct, antecedent, or consequent of P' or of a part of P'. Then

(A$'$) Where α, β, is a simple inductive argument for S, β is of the form, *All A's have B,* and where C is any part of B α, β is acceptable for S only if the propositions S *has examined an A and determined by observation that it lacks C* and S *has examined an A and determined by observation that it has C* are both logically possible.

I am by no means certain that (A$'$) rules out all of the sorts of arguments it is designed to rule out. With sufficient patience and ingenuity we could perhaps construct an argument that does not violate (A$'$) but is nonetheless preposterous in pretty much the same way as the above argument. But at any rate (A$'$) seems to be *true.* And if it is, the argument from (1) to (2) must be rejected, so that we are left without a direct argument for (a) or (b).

The following (merely suggestive) argument indicates that *any* direct argument for (a) will run afoul of (A$'$). To get a direct argument for (a) we must first, presumably, get a direct argument for (b) (there are some pains I do not feel). Presumably (b) will follow from some proposition of the form

(24) Every case of ϕ is accompanied by pain meeting condition ψ*

together with a premise asserting that I have observed a case of ϕ but feel no pain meeting condition ψ. The proposition (call it (24$'$) of the form exhibited by (24) will not, of course, be necessarily true; it will require inductive support. But any simple inductive argument for (24$'$) will run afoul of (A$'$), since its premise will be of the form

(25) Every case of ϕ such that I have determined by observation whether or not it was accompanied by pain meeting condition ψ was so accompanied.

*Editor's Note: Propositions (16)-(23) appeared in a tangential section that was omitted from this reprint.

Of course, (24′) need not be the conclusion of a simple inductive argument; perhaps it follows from propositions of the forms

(26) Every case of ϕ is a case of β

and

(27) Every case of β is accompanied by pain meeting condition ψ.

But then obviously the same problem will arise with the proposition of the form depicted in (27), which is of course the same form as depicted in (13). It looks as if any direct argument from my total evidence for (a) will involve a simple inductive argument for a proposition like (24′); but in that case we will find that no such direct argument for (a) is palatable if we accept (A′). The fact that one cannot observe the absence of pain appeared earlier to deliver the analogical position from disaster; here it returns to wreak destruction upon it.

But perhaps we should ask at this juncture whether the argument I gave above for (A′) is conclusive. (It *does* seem a bit harsh to insist that my observing that *some* cases of pain-behavior are accompanied by pain gives me no reason at all for supposing that all such cases are so accompanied.) I think the argument is indeed conclusive; but on the other side it might be urged that we never have good reason to suppose that the sample of an inductive argument is a fair sample. This last is a large and complex question. Fortunately we need not enter it at present. For we cannot succor the analogical position by rejecting (A′); if we reject (A′) (and adopt no similar principle) we then open the gates to direct argument from my total evidence *against* (a) and (b):

(28) Every pain which is such that I have determined by observation whether or not it was felt by me, was felt by me.

So probably

(29) Every pain is felt by me,

which is the denial of (b), and of an essential premise in our argument for (a). This, no doubt, is a preposterous argument. And yet its peculiarity consists just in the fact that it violates (A′); if we reject (A′) we must accept this argument as of equal weight with the argument *for* (b). But then so far as direct arguments are concerned, the *denials* of (a) and (b) are as probable on my total evidence as (a) and (b) themselves, in which case my total evidence does not directly support the latter. Whether or not (A′) is to be accepted, therefore, my total evidence does not support (a) and (b).

III

Next, let us consider

(c) Sometimes certain areas of my body are free from pain.

Each of us takes a proposition like (c) to be evidently and obviously true. What sort of evidence, according to the analogical position, do I have for (c)? I cannot, of course, *observe* the absence of pain in my body any more than I can observe its absence in some other body; it is logically possible that when I feel no pain in my arm, someone else does.

However, it does not follow from this (contrary to what one might be tempted to suppose) that I can never, on the analogical position, get evidence for the proposition that a certain area of my body is at a certain time free from pain. For evidence of the following sort is available to me:

(30) Every pain which is such that I have determined by observation whether or not it was accompanied by pain-behavior on the part of the body in which it was located, has been so accompanied.

So probably

(31) Every pain is accompanied by pain-behavior on the part of the body in which it is located.

(And of course this inference does not violate (A').) But

(32) At present my body is not displaying pain-behavior.

Hence probably

(33) No area of my body is presently pained.

From which, of course, (c) follows. Accordingly my total evidence provides me with a direct argument for (c). We might be tempted to think that it also provides me with a direct argument against (c). Consider those ordered pairs *(a, t)* whose first members are areas of my body and whose second members are times:

(34) Every ordered pair *(a, t)* which is such that I have determined by observation whether or not *a* was pained at *t*, has been such that *a was* pained at *t*.

So probably

(35) Every ordered pair *(a, t)* is such that *a* is pained at *t*.

But then

(36) Probably every area of my body always contains a pain.

But the inference of (35) from (34) runs afoul of (A′), along with, apparently, any other direct argument from my total evidence against (c). If we accept (A′), therefore, we get a direct argument for (c) but none against it; hence on (A′) the analogical position with respect to (c) appears to be vindicated.

We might note parenthetically that if (A′) is to be rejected, my total evidence provides me with direct argument for propositions even more preposterous than (36); if we let 'a' range over human bodies generally, the analogue of (34) will remain true and we get the conclusion that probably every area of every human body is always pained. If we let 'a' range over areas of physical objects generally the analogue of (34) still remains true and we get the outrageous result that probably every area of every physical object is always pained. Leibniz and Whitehead apparently overlooked this fertile source of evidence for certain of their conclusions.

IV

The propositions

(d) There are some pains that are not in my body

and

(e) There are some cases of pain that are not accompanied by pain-behavior on the part of my body

may be considered together. What presents itself as the direct argument for (d) is the following:

(1) Every case of pain-behavior such that I have determined by observation whether or not it was accompanied by pain in the body displaying it, *was* accompanied by pain in that body.

Then

(2) Probably every case of pain-behavior is accompanied by pain in the body displaying it.

But

(3) *B* over there (a body other than mine) is displaying pain-behavior,

hence

(10) Probably *B* has a pain.

Hence

   (d) There are some pains that are not in my body.

The argument for (e) shares steps (1), (2), (3), and (10) with the above argument. If, in addition,

   (37) My body is not now displaying pain-behavior

is part of my total evidence, (e) follows.

The inference from (1) to (2), again, is ruled out by (A′). And, as in the case of (a) and (b), if we accept (A′) we appear to have no direct argument at all for either (d) or (c). On the other hand, my total evidence appears to provide me with direct arguments *against* both (d) and (e):

   (38) Every pain which is such that I have determined by observation
        whether or not it was in my body, *was* in my body.

Hence probably,

   (39) All pains are in my body.

This argument does not violate (A′). But is it an acceptable inductive argument? It might be objected that it is causally *impossible* for a person to feel pain anywhere but in his own body, and that, where it is impossible to observe an A which is B (although possibly some A's are B), it is illegitimate to conclude that no A's are B from premise reporting that no observed A's are B. If a man *knows* that it is impossible to observe an A which is B, then indeed he cannot reasonably conclude that no A's are B from the fact that every A which is such that he has determined by observation whether or not it is B, has turned out not to be B. But things are quite different if he does not know this. A newcomer to the mountains, for example, might not know that mountain goats can't be seen on a glacier at 800 yards, and after watching a particular glacier from this distance for several weeks might conclude that mountain goats never go near the thing. Of course, as an analogical arguer I do not initially know that one can feel pain only in his own body; it is just this sort of belief that the analogical argument is supposed to ground and justify. This argument, therefore, is apparently successful.

   A similar direct argument holds against (e). Every case of pain which is such that I have determined by observation whether or not it was accompanied by pain-behavior on the part of my body *was* so accompanied; probably, therefore, every case of pain is accompanied by pain-behavior on the part of my body, in which case (e) is false.

   If we accept (A′), therefore, we get direct arguments against (d) and (e) but no direct arguments for them. If we reject (A′), of course, we get direct arguments both for and against them; hence in neither case does my total evidence directly support either (d) or (e).

V

This brings us to

(f) I am the only person who feels pain in my body

and

(g) Sometimes someone feels pain when I do not.

Does my total evidence provide me with a direct argument for (f)? Apparently not.

(40) Every pain in my body which is such that I have determined by observation whether or not it is felt by me, has been felt by me

presents itself as the relevant premise; but of course the argument from (40) to (f) flatly conflicts with (A'). Nor, on the other hand, does my total evidence seem to provide me with a direct argument against (f). To get such an argument we should need a direct argument for

(41) Sometimes my body contains a pain I do not feel.

And in order to do that we should need to employ some such premise as

(34) Every ordered pair (a, t) such that I have determined by observation whether a was pained at t is such that a *was* pained at t.

But as we have already seen, any simple argument with (34) as its premise will violate (A').

Now suppose (as seems to be the case) that my total evidence yields no direct argument for (f) but does yield a direct argument for p and for q, where p and q are logically independent of each other, of (f), and of my total evidence; and where the conjunction of p with q entails (f). (In such a case, let us say that my total evidence provides an *indirect* argument for (f).) Would it then follow that my total evidence supports (f)? No. It is of course true that if p is more probable than not on q, and p entails r, then r is more probable than not on q. But from the fact that p is more probable than not on q, and r is more probable than not on q, it does not follow that p *and* r is more probable than not on q. And of course where p, q, and r are logically independent and q supports p and q supports r, q supports the conjunction of p with r to a lesser degree than it supports either p or r. So even if my total evidence yielded an indirect argument for (f), it would not follow that my total evidence supports (f). But the fact is that we seem to be unable to find even an indirect argument from my total evidence. That evidence, as we have seen, yields a direct argument for

(42) Whenever my body is pained it displays pain-behavior,

and for

(43) Whenever my body displays pain-behavior, I feel pain.

But (42) and (43) do not entail that I feel every pain in my body or that I alone feel pain in my body; they entail only that whenever *anyone* feels pain there, I do. We seem, therefore, to be able to find neither a direct nor an indirect argument for (f) if we accept (A′); if we reject (A′), of course, we will find direct arguments both for and against (f).

(g) Sometimes someone feels pain when I do not

resembles (f) in that there seems to be no direct argument from my total evidence either for or against it. It differs from (f) in that there seems to be an indirect argument *against* it. My total evidence directly supports

(44) Every case of pain is accompanied by pain-behavior on the part of my body.

It also yields an argument for

(45) Whenever my body displays pain-behavior, I feel pain.

But (44) and (45) entail

(46) Whenever any sentient being feels pain, I feel pain,

which is the denial of (g). The upshot of the above is clear. If we reject (A′), we find that a person's total evidence provides direct arguments both for and against each of those commonsense beliefs which, on the analogical position, it is alleged to support. But if we accept (A′) (as I believe we should) we still find that the total evidence does not support the conjunction of those commonsense beliefs. It does not even support the conjunction of the members of K. Indeed, it does not so much as support the members of K individually; (c) alone appears more probable than not on my total evidence while (d), (e), and perhaps (f) appear to be improbable on it. What the analogical arguer should conclude is that every pain occurs in his own body and is accompanied by pain-behavior on the part of his body (and so, perhaps, he could perform a splendid humanitarian service by *destroying* that wretched body).[13]

---

13. But what about the following version of the analogical argument:

Every human body of which I have determined by observation whether or not it has a human mind connected with it (in a certain complicated way) *has* had a mind connected with it (in that way). Therefore probably every human body has a human mind connected with it in that way.

This formulation is explicitly open to the charge that its sample class consists in just one member — my own body. Hence the argument is a hasty generalization. Furthermore, a little reflection reveals that it suffers from the very same defect as the version considered above.

The objection to which the analogical position falls victim is clearly an analogue of the objection urged in Chapter Four against the teleological argument for the existence of God. For according to each of these, a certain set of propositions is supported by evidence of a certain kind. The objection, in each case, is that the evidence to which our attention is called supports only *some* of these propositions; but then, of course, the conjunction of these propositions is not, in either case, more probable than not on that evidence.

VI

I began this study by asking whether belief in the existence of God is rational. The natural theologian's answer, it turned out, is of dubious worth at best. The teleological argument is perhaps his most powerful weapon; and yet it suffers from a crucial and crippling deficiency. But if the answer of the natural theologian does not carry conviction, that of the natural atheologian is even less satisfactory. I then proposed to explore an analogous question in the philosophy of mind: the question how I know — and what my reasons are for believing — that I am not the only creature that thinks and feels, reasons and believes. Here I argued that while the analogical position is as good an answer as we have to this question, it nonetheless shares the crippling defect of the teleological argument. And my final query is this: exactly what bearing do these conclusions have on the initial question — whether it is rational to accept theistic belief?

The answer is not easy, and what I have to say is merely tentative. I think it must be conceded that the theist has no very good answer to the request that he explain his reasons for believing in the existence of God; at any rate he has no answer that need convince the skeptic. But must he have or must there be an answer to this question if his belief in God is reasonable, rationally justifiable: must there be, for any proposition p that I rationally believe (and that is, let us say, contingent and corrigible), a good answer to the "epistemological question": "How do you know that p: what are your reasons for supposing that p is true?" Presumably not. If I am right, the analogical position is the best answer I have to the relevant epistemological question; but even if it is unsatisfactory my belief in (a)-(g) is by no means irrational. Of course there may be other answers; it is sometimes said that propositions (a)-(g) constitute, for each of us, parts of a well-confirmed scientific hypothesis.[14] But this is really a case of *obscuram per obscuras:* the relationship between a scientific theory and the grounds for accepting it is still a black and boundless

14. Cf. Paul Ziff, "The Simplicity of Other Minds," *Journal of Philosophy* LXII (Oct. 1965): 575-85. See also an abstract of my reply to Ziff's paper (ibid.: 585-87).

mystery. Does each of us have grounds for accepting the proposition that he is not the only being that thinks and reasons, senses and feels, *as a scientific theory?* The question can hardly be considered until we have a clearer understanding of the nature of scientific theories and how they are confirmed; its answer is pretty much anyone's guess. Our understanding of scientific theory is too meager to make it more than a shot in the dark. Still, if it is on target with respect to propositions (a)-(g) of this chapter there seems no reason why it should be wide of the mark for (a)-(f) of Chapter Four.*

But let us suppose, as seems to me to be true, that there are no viable alternatives to the analogical position. Then we must conclude, I believe, that a man may rationally hold a contingent, corrigible belief even if there is no answer to the relevant epistemological question. Of course it follows only that *some* such beliefs may be held rationally under the indicated conditions; it does not follow that a man can hold *just any* such belief without a reason or evidence. And, it might be held, although rational belief in other minds does not require an answer to the epistemological question, rational belief in God does. In this connection it is important and relevant that the body of evidence with respect to which we considered (a)-(f) of Chapter Four (the "teleological hypothesis")* is different from the relevant evidence in the case of the analogical argument (above, p. 5). I referred to this latter as a man's "total evidence"; let us refer to the former body of evidence as the "teleological evidence." Now the fact is, these bodies of evidence do not coincide. For in scrutinizing the teleological argument we take it for granted that we know a great many facts about minds — for example, that there are *several* of them — that are not to be found in the analogical evidence. The teleological evidence obviously contains the analogical evidence and a great deal more. And hence what has been shown is that (a)-(f) of Chapter Four is as probable, relative to *one* body of evidence, as (a)-(g) of the present chapter is to *another;* and this goes no way at all, it might be said, toward showing that the two are on a par.

*Editor's Note: Plantinga considers "Propositions (a)-(f) of Chapter Four" as essential to theism and relevant to the Teleological Argument. They are:

(a) The universe is designed.
(b) The universe is designed by exactly one person.
(c) The universe was created *ex nihilo*.
(d) The universe was created by the person who designed it.
(e) The creator of the universe is omniscient, omnipotent, and perfectly good.
(f) The creator of the universe is an eternal spirit, without body, and in no way dependent upon physical objects.

In regards to these propositions, Plantinga states, "The teleological arguer may have some evidence (not very strong, perhaps, but not completely negligible) for (a); but with respect to (b)-(f) our evidence is altogether ambiguous. In the case of propositions (b)-(f) our total evidence affords in each case an argument *against* it as strong as any it yields *for* it (*God and Other Minds,* p. 109).

That the two bodies of evidence differ in the way suggested must, of course, be conceded. Nonetheless, it is true, I think, that if propositions (a)-(f) of Chapter Four are as probable on the first evidence as (a)-(g) of the present chapter on the second, then there is nothing to choose from between them so far as evidence or reasons go; the teleological evidence is the evidence appropriate to the teleological argument. I shall not argue this here, however; instead, let me point out, first, that the conjunction of (a)-(f) of Chapter Four is about as probable on the analogical evidence as it is on the teleological. Recall, of (a)-(f), that

(b) The universe was designed by exactly one person

was not confirmed by the relevant evidence in that we knew of many cases where things exhibiting the degree of unity characterizing the universe may have been the work of *several* persons. But of course if my evidence is limited to the analogical evidence, this objection falls by the wayside; my analogical evidence contains no such cases. On the other side, (a), which was supported by the teleological evidence, is not apparently confirmed by the analogical evidence; the latter seems to yield no direct argument for it that does not violate (A′). So (a)-(f) of Chapter Four is about as probable on the analogical evidence as it is on the teleological. But then it follows that (a)-(f) of Chapter Four is as probable on the analogical evidence as is (a)-(g) of the present chapter. For if (a)-(f) is as probable on the teleological evidence as (a)-(g) is on the analogical evidence, and (a)-(f) is as probable on the analogical evidence as on the teleological evidence, then (a)-(f) is as probable on the analogical evidence as (a)-(g).

Of course there may be other reasons for supposing that although rational belief in other minds does not require an answer to the epistemological question, rational belief in the existence of God does. But it is certainly hard to see what these reasons might be. Hence my tentative conclusion: if my belief in other minds is rational, so is my belief in God. But obviously the former is rational; so, therefore, is the latter.

CHAPTER TWO

The Free Will Defense

Although many atheologians claim that the theist is involved in contradiction when he asserts both

(1) God is omniscient, omnipotent, and wholly good

and

(2) There is evil

this set, obviously, is neither *explicitly* nor *formally* contradictory. The claim, presumably, must be that it is *implicitly* contradictory. To make good this claim the atheologian must find some necessarily true proposition p (it could be a conjunction of several propositions) such that the addition of p to set A yields a set that is formally contradictory.* No atheologian has produced even a plausible candidate for this role, and it certainly is not easy to see what such a proposition might be. Now we might think we should simply declare set A implicitly consistent on the principle that a proposition (or set) is to be presumed consistent or possible until proven otherwise. This course, however, leads to trouble. The same principle would impel us to declare the atheologian's claim — that set A is *in*consistent — possible or consistent. But the claim that a given set of propositions is implicitly contradictory, is itself either necessarily true or necessarily false; so if such a claim is *possible,* it is not necessarily false and is, therefore, true (in fact, necessarily true). If we followed the suggested principle, therefore, we should be obliged to declare set A implicitly consistent (since it hasn't been shown to be otherwise); but we should have to say the same thing about the atheologian's claim, since we haven't shown *that* claim to be inconsistent or impossible. The atheologian's

*Editor's note: Set A is (1) and (2) above.

22

claim, furthermore, is necessarily true if it is possible. Accordingly, if we accept the above principle, we shall have to declare set A both implicitly consistent and implicitly inconsistent. So all we can say at this point is that set A has not been shown to be implicitly inconsistent.

Can we go any further? One way to go on would be to try to *show* that set A is implicitly consistent or possible in the broadly logical sense.* But what is involved in showing such a thing? Although there are various ways to approach this matter, they all resemble one another in an important respect. They all amount to this: to show that a set S is consistent you think of a *possible state of affairs* (it needn't actually obtain) which is such that if it were actual, then all of the members of S would be true. This procedure is sometimes called *giving a model of S.* For example, you might construct an axiom set and then show that it is consistent by giving a model of it; this is how it was shown that the denial of Euclid's parallel postulate is formally consistent with the rest of his postulates.

There are various special cases of this procedure to fit special circumstances. Suppose, for example, you have a pair of propositions p and q and wish to show them consistent. And suppose we say that a proposition p_1 *entails* a proposition p_2 if it is impossible that p_1 be true and p_2 false — if the conjunctive proposition p_1 *and not* p_2 is necessarily false. Then one way to show that p is consistent with q is to find some proposition r whose conjunction with p is both possible, in the broadly logical sense, and entails q. A rude and unlettered behaviorist, for example, might hold that thinking is really nothing but movements of the larynx; he might go on to hold that

P Jones did not move his larynx after April 30

is inconsistent (in the broadly logical sense) with

Q Jones did some thinking during May.

By way of rebuttal, we might point out that P appears to be consistent with

R While convalescing from an April 30 laryngotomy, Jones whiled away the idle hours by writing (in May) a splendid paper on Kant's *Critique of Pure Reason.*

So the conjunction of P and R appears to be consistent; but obviously it also entails Q (you can't write even a passable paper on Kant's *Critique of Pure Reason* without doing some thinking); so P and Q are consistent.

---

*Editor's Note: A proposition is possible in the broadly logical sense just in case its denial is not a necessary truth. Plantinga adopts the notion of broadly logical modality to allow for the necessity of propositions that are neither truths of logic nor mathematics, nor the denials of the truths of logic or mathematics. See *God, Freedom, and Evil* (#94), pp. 13-15.

We can see that this is a special case of the procedure I mentioned above. The proposition R is consistent with $P;$ so the proposition P and R is possible; it describes a possible state of affairs. But P and R entails $Q;$ hence if P and R were true, Q would also be true, and hence both P and Q would be true. So this is really a case of producing a possible state of affairs such that, if it were actual, all the members of the set in question (in this case the pair set of P and Q) would be true. The problem, then, is to show that (1) and (2) (evil exists) are consistent. This could be done by finding a proposition r that is consistent with (1) and such that (1) and *(r)* together entail (2). One proposition that might do the trick is

> (3) God creates a world containing evil and has a good reason for doing so.

If (3) is consistent with (1), then it follows that (1) and (2) (and hence set A) are consistent. Accordingly, one thing some theists have tried is to show that (3) and (1) are consistent.

One can attempt this in at least two ways. On the one hand, we could try to apply the same method again. Conceive of a possible state of affairs such that, if it obtained, an omnipotent, omniscient, and wholly good God would have a good reason for permitting evil. On the other, someone might try to specify *what God's reason is* for permitting evil and try to show, if it is not obvious, that it is a good reason. St. Augustine, for example, one of the greatest and most influential philosopher-theologians of the Christian Church, writes as follows:

> . . . some people see with perfect truth that a creature is better if, while possessing free will, it remains always fixed upon God and never sins; then, reflecting on men's sins, they are grieved, not because they continue to sin, but because they were created. They say: He should have made us such that we never willed to sin, but always to enjoy the unchangeable truth.
>
> They should not lament or be angry. God has not compelled men to sin just because He created them and gave them the power to choose between sinning and not sinning. There are angels who have never sinned and never will sin.
>
> Such is the generosity of God's goodness that He has not refrained from creating even that creature which He foreknew would not only sin, but remain in the will to sin. As a runaway horse is better than a stone which does not run away because it lacks self-movement and sense perception, so the creature is more excellent which sins by free will than that which does not sin because it has no free will.[1]

---

1. *The Problem of Free Choice*, vol. 22 of *Ancient Christian Writers* (Westminster, Md.: The Newman Press, 1955), bk. 2, pp. 14-15.

In broadest terms Augustine claims that God could create a better, more perfect universe by permitting evil than He could by refusing to do so:

> Neither the sins nor the misery are necessary to the perfection of the universe, but souls as such are necessary, which have the power to sin if they so will, and become miserable if they sin. If misery persisted after their sins had been abolished, or if there were misery before there were sins, then it might be right to say that the order and government of the universe were at fault. Again, if there were sins but no consequent misery, that order is equally dishonored by lack of equity.[2]

Augustine tries to tell us *what God's reason is* for permitting evil. At bottom, he says, it's that God can create a more perfect universe by permitting evil. A really top-notch universe requires the existence of free, rational, and moral agents; and some of the free creatures He created went wrong. But the universe with the free creatures it contains and the evil they commit is better than it would have been had it contained neither the free creatures nor this evil. Such an attempt to specify God's reason for permitting evil is what I earlier called a *theodicy;* in the words of John Milton it is an attempt to "justify the ways of God to man," to show that God is just in permitting evil. Augustine's kind of theodicy might be called a Free Will Theodicy, since the idea of rational creatures with free will plays such a prominent role in it.

A theodicist, then, attempts to tell us why God permits evil. Quite distinct from a Free Will Theodicy is what I shall call a Free Will Defense. Here the aim is not to say what God's reason *is,* but at most what God's reason *might possibly be.* We could put the difference like this. The Free Will Theodicist and Free Will Defender are both trying to show that (1) is consistent with (3). The Free Will Theodicist tries to do this by finding some proposition r which in conjunction with (1) entails (3); he claims, furthermore, that this proposition is *true,* not just consistent with (1). He tries to tell us what God's reason for permitting evil *really is.* The Free Will Defender, on the other hand, though he also tries to find a proposition r that is consistent with (1) and in conjunction with it entails (3), does *not* claim to know or even believe that r is true. And here, of course, he is perfectly within his rights. His aim is to show that (1) is consistent with (3); all he need do then is find an r that is consistent with (1) and such that (1) and *(r)* entail (3); whether r is *true* is quite beside the point.

So there is a significant difference between a Free Will Theodicy and a Free Will Defense. The latter is sufficient (if successful) to show that Set A is consistent; in a way a Free Will Theodicy goes beyond what is required.

---

2. *The Problem of Free Choice,* bk. 3, p. 9.

On the other hand, a theodicy would be much more satisfying, if possible to achieve. No doubt the theist would rather know what God's reason *is* for permitting evil than simply that it's possible He has a good one. But in the present context the latter is all that's needed. Neither a defense nor a theodicy, of course, gives any hint as to what God's reason for some *specific* evil — the death or suffering of someone close to you, for example — might be. And there is still another function — a sort of pastoral function[3] — in the neighborhood that neither serves. Confronted with evil in his own life or suddenly coming to realize more clearly than before the *extent* and *magnitude* of evil, a believer in God may undergo a crisis of faith. He may be tempted to follow the advice of Job's "friends"; he may be tempted to "curse God and die." Neither a Free Will Defense nor a Free Will Theodicy is designed to be of much help or comfort to one suffering from such a storm in the soul (although in a specific case, of course, one or the other could prove useful). Neither is to be thought of first of all as a means of pastoral counseling. Probably neither will enable someone to find peace with himself and with God in the face of the evil the world contains. But then, of course, neither is intended for that purpose.

I. The Free Will Defense

In what follows I shall focus attention on the Free Will Defense. I shall examine it more closely, state it more exactly, and consider objections to it; and I shall argue that in the end it is successful. Earlier we saw that among good states of affairs there are some that not even God can bring about without bringing about evil: those goods, namely, that *entail* or *include* evil states of affairs. The Free Will Defense can be looked upon as an effort to show that there may be a very different kind of good that God can't bring about without permitting evil. These are good states of affairs that don't include evil; they do not entail the existence of any evil whatever; nonetheless God Himself can't bring them about without permitting evil.

So how does the Free Will Defense work? And what does the Free Will Defender mean when he says that people are or may be free? What is relevant to the Free Will Defense is the idea of *being free with respect to an action.* If a person is free with respect to a given action, then he is free to perform that action and free to refrain from performing it; no antecedent conditions and/or causal laws determine that he will perform the action, or that he won't.

---

3. I am indebted to Henry Schuurman (in conversation) for helpful discussion of the difference between this pastoral function and those served by a theodicy or a defense.

It is within his power, at the time in question, to take or perform the action and within his power to refrain from it. Freedom so conceived is not to be confused with unpredictability. You might be able to predict what you will do in a given situation even if you are free, in that situation, to do something else. If I know you well, I may be able to predict what action you will take in response to a certain set of conditions; it does not follow that you are not free with respect to that action. Secondly, I shall say that an action is *morally significant*, for a given person, if it would be wrong for him to perform the action but right to refrain or *vice versa*. Keeping a promise, for example, would ordinarily be morally significant for a person, as would refusing induction into the army. On the other hand, having Cheerios for breakfast (instead of Wheaties) would not normally be morally significant. Further, suppose we say that a person is *significantly free,* on a given occasion, if he is then free with respect to a morally significant action. And finally we must distinguish between *moral evil* and *natural evil.* The former is evil that results from free human activity; natural evil is any other kind of evil.[4]

Given these definitions and distinctions, we can make a preliminary statement of the Free Will Defense as follows. A world containing creatures who are significantly free (and freely perform more good than evil actions) is more valuable, all else being equal, than a world containing no free creatures at all. Now God can create free creatures, but He can't *cause* or *determine* them to do only what is right. For if He does so, then they aren't significantly free after all; they do not do what is right *freely.* To create creatures capable of *moral good,* therefore, He must create creatures capable of moral evil; and at the same time prevent them from doing so. As it turned out, sadly enough, some of the free creatures God created went wrong in the exercise of their freedom; this is the source of moral evil. The fact that free creatures sometimes go wrong, however, counts neither against God's omnipotence nor against His goodness; for He could have forestalled the occurrence of moral evil only by removing the possibility of moral good.

I said earlier that the Free Will Defender tries to find a proposition that is consistent with (1) and together with (1) entails that there is evil. According to the Free Will Defense, we must find this proposition somewhere in the above story. The heart of the Free Will Defense is the claim that it is *possible* that God could not have created a universe containing moral good (or as much moral good as this world contains) without creating one that also contained moral evil. And if so, then it is possible that God has a good reason for creating a world containing evil.

Now this defense has met with several kinds of objections. For example,

---

4. This distinction is not very precise (how, exactly, are we to construe "results from"?); but perhaps it will serve our present purposes.

some philosophers say that *causal determinism* and *freedom,* contrary to what we might have thought, are not really incompatible.[5] But if so, then God could have created free creatures who were free, and free to do what is wrong, but nevertheless were causally determined to do only what is right. Thus He could have created creatures who were free to do what was wrong, while nevertheless preventing them from ever performing any wrong actions — simply by seeing to it that they were causally determined to do only what is right. Of course this contradicts the Free Will Defense, according to which there is incon- sistency in supposing that God determines free creatures to do only what is right. But is it really possible that all of a person's actions are causally determined while some of them are free? How could that be so? According to one version of the doctrine in question, to say that George acts freely on a given occasion is to say only this: *if George had chosen to do otherwise, he would have done otherwise.* Now George's action A is causally determined if some event E — some event beyond his control — has already occurred, where the state of affairs consisting in E's occurrence conjoined with George's *refraining* from performing A, is a causally impossible state of affairs. Then one can consistently hold both that all of a man's actions are causally deter- mined and that some of them are free in the above sense. For suppose that all of a man's actions are causally determined and that he *couldn't,* on any occasion, have made any choice or performed any action different from the ones he did make and perform. It could still be true that if he *had* chosen to do otherwise, he would have done otherwise. Granted, he couldn't have chosen to do otherwise; but this is consistent with saying that *if* he had, things would have gone differently.

This objection to the Free Will Defense seems utterly implausible. One might as well claim that being in jail doesn't limit a man's freedom on the grounds that if he were *not* in jail, he'd be free to come and go as he pleased. So I shall say no more about this objection here.[6]

A second objection is more formidable. In essence it goes like this. Surely it is possible to do only what is right, even if one is free to do wrong. It is *possible,* in that broadly logical sense, that there be a world containing free creatures who always do what is right. There is certainly no *contradiction* or *inconsistency* in this idea. But God is omnipotent; his power has no non- logical limitations. So if it's possible that there be a world containing creatures who are free to do what is wrong but never in fact do so, then it follows that an omnipotent God could create such a world. If so, however, the Free Will Defense must be mistaken in its insistence upon the possibility that God is

5. See, for example, A. Flew, "Divine Omnipotence and Human Freedom," in *New Essays in Philosophical Theology,* eds. A. Flew and A. MacIntyre (London: SCM, 1955), pp. 150-53.
6. For further discussion of it see Plantinga, *God and Other Minds,* pp. 132-35.

omnipotent but unable to create a world containing moral good without permitting moral evil. J. L. Mackie states this objection:

> If God has made men such that in their free choices they sometimes prefer what is good and sometimes what is evil, why could he not have made men such that they always freely choose the good? If there is no logical impossibility in a man's freely choosing the good on one, or on several occasions, there cannot be a logical impossibility in his freely choosing the good on every occasion. God was not, then, faced with a choice between making innocent automata and making beings who, in acting freely, would sometimes go wrong; there was open to him the obviously better possibility of making beings who would act freely but always go right. Clearly, his failure to avail himself of this possibility is inconsistent with his being both omnipotent and wholly good.[7]

Now what, exactly, is Mackie's point here? This. According to the Free Will Defense, it is possible both that God is omnipotent and that He was unable to create a world containing moral good without creating one containing moral evil. But, replies Mackie, this limitation on His power to create is inconsistent with God's omnipotence. For surely it's *possible* that there be a world containing perfectly virtuous persons — persons who are significantly free but always do what is right. Surely there are *possible worlds* that contain moral good but no moral evil. But God, if He is omnipotent, can create any possible world He chooses. So it is *not* possible, contrary to the Free Will Defense, both that God is omnipotent and that He could create a world containing moral good only by creating one containing moral evil. If He is omnipotent, the only limitations of His power are *logical* limitations; in which case there are no possible worlds He could not have created.

This is a subtle and important point. According to the great German philosopher G. W. Leibniz, *this* world, the actual world, must be the best of all possible worlds. His reasoning goes as follows. Before God created anything at all, He was confronted with an enormous range of choices; He could create or bring into actuality any of the myriads of different possible worlds. Being perfectly good, He must have chosen to create the best world He could; being omnipotent, He was able to create any possible world He pleased. He must, therefore, have chosen the best of all possible worlds; and hence *this* world, the one He did create, must be the best possible. Now Mackie, of course, agrees with Leibniz that God, if omnipotent, could have created any world He pleased and would have created the best world he could. But while Leibniz draws the conclusion that this world, despite appearances, must be

---

7. Mackie, in *The Philosophy of Religion,* ed. Basil Mitchell (London: Oxford University Press, 1971) pp. 100-101.

the best possible, Mackie concludes instead that there is no omnipotent, wholly good God. For, he says, it is obvious enough that this present world is not the best of all possible worlds.

The Free Will Defender disagrees with both Leibniz and Mackie. In the first place, he might say, what is the reason for supposing that *there is* such a thing as the best of all possible worlds? No matter how marvelous a world is — containing no matter how many persons enjoying unalloyed bliss — isn't it possible that there be an even better world containing even more persons enjoying even more unalloyed bliss? But what is really characteristic and central to the Free Will Defense is the claim that God, though omnipotent, could not have actualized just any possible world He pleased.

II. Was It within God's Power to Create Any Possible World He Pleased?

This is indeed the crucial question for the Free Will Defense. If we wish to discuss it with insight and authority, we shall have to look into the idea of *possible worlds.* And a sensible first question is this: what sort of thing is a possible world? The basic idea is that a possible world is a *way things could have been;* it is a *state of affairs* of some kind. What sort of thing is a state of affairs? The following would be examples:

> Nixon's having won the 1972 election
> 7 + 5's being equal to 12
> All men's being mortal

and

> Gary, Indiana's, having a really nasty pollution problem.

These are *actual* states of affairs: states of affairs that do in fact *obtain.* And corresponding to each such actual state of affairs there is a true proposition — in the above cases, the corresponding propositions would be *Nixon won the 1972 presidential election, 7 + 5 is equal to 12, all men are mortal,* and *Gary, Indiana, has a really nasty pollution problem.* A proposition p corresponds to a state of affairs s, in this sense, if it is impossible that p be true and s fail to obtain and impossible that s obtain and p fail to be true.

But just as there are false propositions, so there are states of affairs that do *not* obtain or are *not* actual. *Kissinger's having swum the Atlantic* and *Hubert Horatio Humphrey's having run a mile in four minutes* would be examples. Some states of affairs that do not obtain are *impossible:* e.g.,

Hubert's having drawn a square circle, 7 + 5's being equal to 75, and *Agnew's having a brother who was an only child.* The propositions corresponding to these states of affairs, of course, are necessarily false. So there are states of affairs that *obtain* or *are actual* and also states of affairs that don't obtain. Among the latter some are *impossible* and others are possible. And a possible world is a possible state of affairs. Of course not every possible state of affairs is a possible world; *Hubert's having run a mile in four minutes* is a possible state of affairs but not a possible world. No doubt it is an *element* of many possible worlds, but it isn't itself inclusive enough to be one. To be a possible world, a state of affairs must be very large — so large as to be *complete* or *maximal.*

To get at this idea of completeness we need a couple of definitions. A state of affairs A *includes* a state of affairs B if it is not possible that A obtain and B not obtain or if the conjunctive state of affairs A *but not* B — the state of affairs that obtains if and only if A obtains and B does not — is not possible. For example, *Jim Whittaker's being the first American to climb Mt. Everest* includes *Jim Whittaker's being an American.* It also includes *Mt. Everest's being climbed, something's being climbed, no American's having climbed Everest before Whittaker did,* and the like. *Inclusion* among states of affairs is like *entailment* among propositions; and where a state of affairs A includes a state of affairs B, the proposition corresponding to A entails the one corresponding to B. Accordingly, *Jim Whittaker is the first American to climb Everest* entails *Mt. Everest has been climbed, something has been climbed,* and *no American climbed Everest before Whittaker did.* Now suppose we say further that a state of affairs A *precludes* a state of affairs B if it is not possible that *both* obtain, or if the conjunctive state of affairs A *and* B is impossible. Thus *Whittaker's being the first American to climb Mt. Everest* precludes *Luther Jerstad's being the first American to climb Everest,* as well as *Whittaker's never having climbed any mountains.* If A precludes B, then A's corresponding proposition entails the denial of the one corresponding to B. Still further, let's say that the *complement* of a state of affairs is the state of affairs that obtains just in case A does not obtain. [Or we might say that the complement (call it $\overline{A}$) of A is the state of affairs corresponding to the *denial* or *negation* of the proposition corresponding to A.] Given these definitions, we can say what it is for a state of affairs to be *complete:* A is a complete state of affairs if and only if for every state of affairs B, either A *includes* B or A *precludes* B. (We could express the same thing by saying that if A is a complete state of affairs, then for every state of affairs B, either A includes B or A includes $\overline{B}$, the complement of B.) And now we are able to say what a possible world is: a possible world is any possible state of affairs that is complete. If A is a possible world, then it says something about everything; every state of affairs S is either included in or precluded by it.

Corresponding to each possible world W, furthermore, there is a set of propositions that I'll call *the book on W*. A proposition is in the book on W just in case the state of affairs to which it corresponds is included in W. Or we might express it like this. Suppose we say that a proposition P is *true in a world W* if and only if P *would have been true if W had been actual* — if and only if, that is, it is not possible that W be actual and P be false. Then the book on W is the set of propositions true in W. Like possible worlds, books are *complete;* if B is a book, then for any proposition P, either P or the denial of P will be a member of B. A book is a *maximal consistent set* of propositions; it is so large that the addition of another proposition to it always yields an explicitly inconsistent set.

Of course, for each possible world there is exactly one book corresponding to it (that is, for a given world W there is just one book B such that each member of B is true in W); and for each book there is just one world to which it corresponds. So every world has its book.

It should be obvious that exactly one possible world is actual. At *least* one must be, since the set of true propositions is a maximal consistent set and hence a book. But then it corresponds to a possible world, and the possible world corresponding to this set of propositions (since it's the set of *true* propositions) will be actual. On the other hand there is at *most* one actual world. For suppose there were two: W and W'. These worlds cannot include all the very same states of affairs; if they did, they would be the very same world. So there must be at least one state of affairs S such that W includes S and W' does not. But a possible world is maximal; W', therefore, includes the complement $\bar{S}$ of S. So if both W and W' were actual, as we have supposed, then both S and $\bar{S}$ would be actual — which is impossible. So there can't be more than one possible world that is actual.

Leibniz pointed out that a proposition p is necessary if it is true in every possible world. We may add that p is possible if it is true in one world and impossible if true in none. Furthermore, p *entails* q if there is no possible world in which p is true and q is false; and p *is consistent with* q if there is at least one world in which both p and q are true.

A further feature of possible worlds is that people (and other things) *exist* in them. Each of us exists in the actual world, obviously; but a person also exists in many worlds distinct from the actual world. It would be a mistake, of course, to think of all of these worlds as somehow "going on" at the same time, with the same person reduplicated through these worlds and actually existing in a lot of different ways. This is not what is meant by saying that the same person exists in different possible worlds. What is meant, instead, is this: a person Paul exists in each of those possible worlds W which is such that, if W *had been actual,* Paul would have existed — actually existed. Suppose Paul had been an inch taller than he is, or a better tennis player. Then the world that does in fact obtain would not have been actual; some other world — W', let's say — would have obtained instead. If W' had been actual, Paul would have existed; so Paul exists in W'. (Of course there are still other possible worlds in which Paul does not exist — worlds, for example, in which there are no people at all.) Accordingly, when we say that Paul exists in a world W, what we mean is that Paul *would have* existed had W been actual. Or we could put it like this: Paul exists in each world W that includes the state of affairs consisting in Paul's existence. We can put this still more simply by saying that Paul exists in those worlds whose books contain the proposition *Paul exists.*

But isn't there a problem here? *Many* people are named "Paul": Paul the apostle, Paul J. Zwier, John Paul Jones, and many other famous Pauls. So who goes with "Paul exists"? Which Paul? The answer has to do with the fact that books contain *propositions* — not sentences. They contain the sort of thing sentences are used to express and assert. And the same sentence — "Aristotle is wise," for example — can be used to express many different propositions. When Plato used it, he asserted a proposition predicating wisdom of his famous pupil; when Jackie Onassis uses it, she asserts a proposition predicating wisdom of her wealthy husband. These are distinct propositions (we might even think they differ in truth value); but they are expressed by the same sentence. Normally (but not always) we don't have much trouble determining which of the several propositions expressed by a given sentence is relevant in the context at hand. So in this case a given person, Paul, exists in a world W if and only if W's book contains the proposition that says that *he* — that particular person — exists. The fact that the sentence we use to express this proposition can also be used to express *other* propositions is not relevant.

After this excursion into the nature of books and worlds we can return to our question. Could God have created just any world He chose? Before addressing the question, however, we must note that God does not, strictly speaking, *create* any possible worlds or states of affairs at all. What He creates are the heavens and the earth and all that they contain. But He has not created states of affairs. There are, for example, the state of affairs consisting in God's existence and the state of affairs consisting in His nonexistence. That is, there is such a thing as the state of affairs consisting in the existence of God, and there is also such a thing as the state of affairs consisting in the nonexistence of God, just as there are the two propositions *God exists* and *God does not exist.* The theist believes that the first state of affairs is actual and the first proposition true; the atheist believes that the second state of affairs is actual and the second proposition true. But, of course, both propositions *exist,* even though just one is true. Similarly, there are two states of affairs here, just one of which is actual. So both states of affairs *exist,* but only one *obtains.* And

God has not created either one of them since there never was a time at which either did not exist. Nor has He created the state of affairs consisting in the earth's existence; there was a time when *the earth* did not exist, but none when the state of affairs consisting in the earth's existence didn't exist. Indeed, God did not bring into existence any states of affairs at all. What He did was to perform actions of a certain sort — creating the heavens and the earth, for example — which resulted in the *actuality* of certain states of affairs. God *actualizes* states of affairs. He actualizes the possible world that does in fact obtain; He does not create it. And while He has created Socrates, He did not create the state of affairs consisting in Socrates' existence.[8]

Bearing this in mind, let's finally return to our question. Is the atheologian right in holding that if God is omnipotent, then he could have actualized or created any possible world He pleased? Not obviously. First, we must ask ourselves whether God is a *necessary* or a *contingent* being. A *necessary* being is one that exists in every possible world — one that would have existed no matter which possible world had been actual; a contingent being exists only in some possible worlds. Now if God is not a necessary being (and many, perhaps most, theists think that He is not), then clearly enough there will be many possible worlds He could not have actualized — all those, for example, in which He does not exist. Clearly, God could not have created a world in which He doesn't even exist.

So, if God is a contingent being then there are many possible worlds beyond His power to create. But this is really irrelevant to our present concerns. For perhaps the atheologian can maintain his case if he revises his claim to avoid this difficulty; perhaps he will say something like this: if God is omnipotent, then He could have actualized any of those possible worlds *in which He exists.* So if He exists and is omnipotent, He could have actualized (contrary to the Free Will Defense) any of those possible worlds in which He exists and in which there exist free creatures who do no wrong. He could have actualized worlds containing moral good but no moral evil. Is this correct?

Let's begin with a trivial example. You and Paul have just returned from an Australian hunting expedition: your quarry was the elusive double-wattled cassowary. Paul captured an aardvark, mistaking it for a cassowary. The creature's disarming ways have won it a place in Paul's heart; he is deeply attached to it. Upon your return to the States you offer Paul $500 for his aardvark, only to be rudely turned down. Later you ask yourself, "What would he have done if I'd offered him $700?" Now what is it, exactly, that you are

---

8. Strict accuracy demands, therefore, that we speak of God as *actualizing* rather than creating possible worlds. I shall continue to use both locutions, thus sacrificing accuracy to familiarity. For more about possible worlds see my book *The Nature of Necessity* (Oxford: Clarendon Press, 1974), chapters 4-8.

asking? What you're really asking in a way is whether, under a *specific set of conditions,* Paul would have sold it. These conditions include your having offered him $700 rather than $500 for the aardvark, everything else being as much as possible like the conditions that did in fact obtain. Let S' be this set of conditions or state of affairs. S' includes the state of affairs consisting in your offering Paul $700 (instead of the $500 you did offer him); of course it does not include his *accepting* your offer, and it does not include his *rejecting* it; for the rest, the conditions it includes are just like the ones that did obtain in the actual world. So, for example, S' includes Paul's being free to accept the offer and free to refrain; and if in fact the going rate for an aardvark was $650, then S' includes the state of affairs consisting in the going rate's being $650. So we might put your question by asking which of the following conditionals is true:

(4) If the state of affairs S' had obtained, Paul would have accepted the offer.

(5) If the state of affairs S' had obtained, Paul would not have accepted the offer.

It seems clear that at least one of these conditionals is true, but naturally they can't both be; so exactly one is.

Now since S' includes neither Paul's accepting the offer nor his rejecting it, the antecedent of (4) and (5) does not entail the consequent of either. That is,

(6) S' obtains

does not entail either

(7) Paul accepts the offer

or

(8) Paul does not accept the offer.

So there are possible worlds in which both (6) and (7) are true, and other possible worlds in which both (6) and (8) are true.

We are now in a position to grasp an important fact. Either (4) or (5) is in fact true; and either way there are possible worlds God could not have actualized. Suppose, first of all, that (4) is true. Then it was beyond the power of God to create a world in which (1) Paul is free to sell his aardvark and free to refrain, and in which the other states of affairs included in S' obtain, and (2) Paul does not sell. That is, it was beyond His power to create a world in which (6) and (8) are both true. There is at least one possible world like this, but God, despite His omnipotence, could not have brought about its actuality. For let W be such a world. To actualize W, God must bring it about that Paul is free with respect to this action, and that the other states of affairs included in S' obtain. But (4), as we are supposing, is true; so if God had actualized S' and left Paul *free* with respect to this action, he would have sold: in which case W would not have been actual. If, on the other hand, God had *brought it about* that Paul didn't sell or had *caused him* to refrain from selling, then Paul would not have been free with respect to this action; then S' would not have been actual (since S' includes Paul's being free with respect to it), and W would not have been actual since W includes S'.

Of course, if it is (5) rather than (4) that is true, then another class of worlds was beyond God's power to actualize — those, namely, in which S' obtains and Paul *sells* his aardvark. These are the worlds in which both (6) and (7) are true. But either (4) or (5) is true. Therefore, these are possible worlds God could not have actualized. If we consider whether or not God could have created a world in which, let's say, both (6) and (7) are true, we see that the answer depends upon a peculiar kind of fact; it depends upon what Paul would have freely chosen to do in a certain situation. So there are any number of possible worlds such that it is partly up to Paul whether God can create them.[9]

That was a past tense example. Perhaps it would be useful to consider a future tense case, since this might seem to correspond more closely to God's situation in choosing a possible world to actualize. At some time t in the near future Maurice will be free with respect to some insignificant action — having freeze-dried oatmeal for breakfast, let's say. That is, at time t Maurice will be free to have oatmeal but also free to take something else — shredded wheat, perhaps. Next, suppose we consider S', a state of affairs that is included in the actual world and includes Maurice's being free with respect to taking oatmeal at time t. That is, S' includes Maurice's being free at time t to take oatmeal and free to reject it. S' does not include Maurice's taking oatmeal, however; nor does it include his rejecting it. For the rest S' is as much as possible like the actual world. In particular there are many conditions that do in fact hold at time t and are *relevant* to his choice — such conditions, for example, as the fact that he hasn't had oatmeal lately, that his wife will be annoyed if he rejects it, and the like; and S' includes each of these conditions. Now God no doubt knows what Maurice will do at time t, if S' obtains; He knows which action Maurice would freely perform if S' were to be actual. That is, God knows that one of the following conditionals is true:

(9) If S' were to obtain, Maurice will freely take the oatmeal

or

---

9. For a fuller statement of this argument see Plantinga, *The Nature of Necessity,* chapter 9, secs. 4-6.

(10) If S' were to obtain, Maurice will freely reject it.

We may not know which of these is true, and Maurice himself may not know; but presumably God does.

So either God knows that (9) is true, or else He knows that (10) is. Let's suppose it is (9). Then there is a possible world that God, though omnipotent, cannot create. For consider a possible world W' that shares S' with the actual world (which for ease of reference I'll name 'Kronos') and in which Maurice does *not* take oatmeal. (We know there *is* such a world, since S' does not include Maurice's taking the oatmeal.) S' obtains in W' just as it does in Kronos. Indeed, everything in W' is just as it is in Kronos up to time t. But whereas in Kronos Maurice takes oatmeal at time t, in W' he does not. Now W' is a perfectly possible world; but it is not within God's power to create it or bring about its actuality. For to do so He must actualize S'. But (9) is in fact true. So if God actualizes S' (as He must to create W') and leaves Maurice free with respect to the action in question, then he will take the oatmeal; and then, of course, W' will not be actual. If, on the other hand, God causes Maurice to *refrain* from taking the oatmeal, then he is not *free* to take it. That means, once again, that W' is not actual; for in W' Maurice is free to take the oatmeal (even if he doesn't do so). So if (9) is true, then this world W' is one that God can't actualize; it is not within His power to actualize it even though He is omnipotent and it is a possible world.

Of course, if it is (10) that is true, we get a similar result; then too there are possible worlds that God can't actualize. These would be worlds which share S' with Kronos and in which Maurice *does* take oatmeal. But either (9) or (10) *is* true; so either way there is a possible world that God can't create. If we consider a world in which S' obtains and in which Maurice freely chooses oatmeal at time t, we see that whether or not it is within God's power to actualize it depends upon what Maurice would do if he were free in a certain situation. Accordingly, there are any number of possible worlds such that it is partly up to Maurice whether or not God can actualize them. It is, of course, up to God whether or not to create Maurice and also up to God whether or not to make him free with respect to the action of taking oatmeal at time t. (God could, if He chose, cause him to succumb to the dreaded *equine obsession*, a condition shared by some people and most horses, whose victims find it *psychologically impossible* to refuse oats or oat products.) But if He creates Maurice and creates him free with respect to this action, then whether or not he actually performs the action is up to Maurice — not God.[10]

Now we can return to the Free Will Defense and the problem of evil. The Free Will Defender, you recall, insists on the possibility that it is not

10. For a more complete and more exact statement of this argument see Plantinga, *The Nature of Necessity*, chapter 9, secs. 4-6.

within God's power to create a world containing moral good without creating one containing moral evil. His atheological opponent — Mackie, for example — agrees with Leibniz in insisting that *if* (as the theist holds) God is omnipotent, then it *follows* that He could have created any possible world He pleased. We now see that this contention — call it 'Leibniz's Lapse' — is a mistake. The atheologian is right in holding that there are many possible worlds containing moral good but no moral evil; his mistake lies in endorsing Leibniz's Lapse. So one of his premises — that God, if omnipotent, could have actualized just any world He pleased — is false.

III. Could God Have Created a World Containing Moral Good but No Moral Evil?

Now suppose we recapitulate the logic of the situation. The Free Will Defender claims that the following is possible.

(11) God is omnipotent, and it was not within His power to create a world containing moral good but no moral evil.

By way of retort the atheologian insists that there are possible worlds containing moral good but no moral evil. He adds that an omnipotent being could have actualized any possible world he chose. So if God is omnipotent, it follows that He could have actualized a world containing moral good but no moral evil; hence (11), contrary to the Free Will Defender's claim, is not possible. What we have seen so far is that his second premise — Leibniz's Lapse — is false.

Of course, this does not settle the issue in the Free Will Defender's favor. Leibniz's Lapse (appropriately enough for a lapse) is false; but this doesn't show that (11) is possible. To show this latter we must demonstrate the possibility that among the worlds God could not have actualized are all the worlds containing moral good but no moral evil. How can we approach this question?

Instead of choosing oatmeal for breakfast or selling an aardvark, suppose we think about a morally significant action such as taking a bribe. Curley Smith, the mayor of Boston, is opposed to the proposed freeway route; it would require destruction of the Old North Church along with some other antiquated and structurally sound buildings. L. B. Smedes, the director of highways, asks him whether he'd drop his opposition for $1 million. "Of course," he replies. "Would you do it for $2?" asks Smedes. "What do you take me for?" comes the indignant reply. "That's already been established," smirks Smedes; "all that remains is to nail down your price." Smedes then offers him a bribe of $35,000; unwilling to break with the fine old traditions of Bay State politics, Curley accepts. Smedes then spends a sleepless night wondering whether he could have bought Curley for $20,000.

Now suppose we assume that Curley was free with respect to the action of taking the bribe — free to take it and free to refuse. And suppose, furthermore, that he would have taken it. That is, let us suppose that

(12) If Smedes had offered Curley a bribe of $20,000, he would have accepted it.

If (12) is true, then there is a state of affairs S' that (1) includes Curley's being offered a bribe of $20,000; (2) does not include either his accepting the bribe or his rejecting it; and (3) is otherwise as much as possible like the actual world. Just to make sure S' includes every relevant circumstance, let us suppose that it is a *maximal world segment.* That is, add to S' any state of affairs compatible with but not included in it, and the result will be an entire possible world. We could think of it roughly like this: S' is included in at least one world W' in which he rejects it. If S' is a maximal world segment, then S' is what remains of W' when *Curley's taking the bribe* is deleted; it is also what remains of W' when *Curley's rejecting the bribe* is deleted. More exactly, if S' is a maximal world segment, then every possible state of affairs that includes S', but isn't included by S', is a possible world. So if (12) is true, then there is a maximal world segment S' that (1) includes Curley's being offered a bribe of $20,000; (2) does not include either his accepting the bribe or his rejecting it; (3) is otherwise as much as possible like the actual world — in particular, it includes Curley's being free with respect to the bribe; and (4) is such that if it were actual then Curley would have taken the bribe. That is,

(13) If S' were actual, Curley would have accepted the bribe

is true.

Now, of course, there is at least one possible world W' in which S' is actual and Curley does not take the bribe. But God could not have created W'; to do so, He would have been obliged to actualize S', leaving Curley free with respect to the action of taking the bribe. But under these conditions Curley, as (13) assures us, would have accepted the bribe, so that the world thus created would not have been S'.

Curley, as we see, is not above a bit of Watergating. But there may be worse to come. Of course, there are possible worlds in which he is significantly free (i.e., free with respect to a morally significant action) and never does what is wrong. But the sad truth about Curley may be this. Consider W', any of these worlds: in W' Curley is significantly free, so in W' there are some actions that are morally significant for him and with respect to which he is free. But at least one of these actions — call it A — has the following peculiar property. There is a maximal world segment S' that obtains in W' and is such that (1) S' includes Curley's being free re A but neither his performing A nor his refraining from A; (2) S' is otherwise as much as possible like W'; and (3) if S' had been actual, Curley would have gone wrong with respect to A.[11] (Notice that this third condition holds in fact, in the actual world; it does not hold in that world W'.)

This means, of course, that God could not have actualized W'. For to do so He'd have been obliged to bring it about that S' is actual; but then Curley would go wrong with respect to A. Since in W' he always does what is right, the world thus actualized would not be W'. On the other hand, if God *causes* Curley to go right with respect to A or *brings it about that* he does so, then Curley isn't free with respect to A; and so once more it isn't W' that is actual. Accordingly God cannot create W'. But W' was just any of the worlds in which Curley is significantly free but always does only what is right. It therefore follows that it was not within God's power to create a world in which Curley produces moral good but no moral evil. Every world God can actualize is such that if Curley is significantly free in it, he takes at least one wrong action.

Obviously Curley is in serious trouble. I shall call the malady from which he suffers *transworld depravity*. (I leave as homework the problem of comparing transworld depravity with what Calvinists call 'total depravity.') By way of explicit definition:

(14) A person P *suffers from transworld depravity* if and only if the following holds: for every world W such that P is significantly free in W and P does only what is right in W, there is an action A and a maximal world segment S' such that

(1) S' includes A's being morally significant for P
(2) S' includes P's being free with respect to A
(3) S' is included in W and includes neither P's performing A nor P's refraining from performing A

and

(4) If S' were actual, P would go wrong with respect to A.

(In thinking about this definition, remember that (4) is to be true in fact, in the actual world — not in that world W.)

What is important about the idea of transworld depravity is that if a person suffers from it, then it wasn't within God's power to actualize any

---

11. A person goes wrong with respect to an action if he either wrongfully performs it or wrongfully fails to perform it.

world in which that person is significantly free but does no wrong — that is, a world in which he produces moral good but no moral evil.

We have been considering a crucial contention of the Free Will Defender: the contention, namely, that

(11) God is omnipotent, and it was not within His power to create a world containing moral good but no moral evil.

How is transworld depravity relevant to this? As follows. Obviously it is possible that there be persons who suffer from transworld depravity. More generally, it is possible that *everybody* suffers from it. And if this possibility were actual, then God, though omnipotent, could not have created any of the possible worlds containing just the persons who do in fact exist, and containing moral good but no moral evil. For to do so He'd have to create persons who were significantly free (otherwise there would be no moral good) but suffered from transworld depravity. Such persons go wrong with respect to at least one action in any world God could have actualized and in which they are free with respect to morally significant actions; so the price for creating a world in which they produce moral good is creating one in which they also produce moral evil.

IV. Transworld Depravity and Essence

Now we might think this settles the question in favor of the Free Will Defender. But the fact is it doesn't. For suppose all the people that exist in Kronos, the actual world, suffer from transworld depravity; it doesn't follow that God could not have created a world containing moral good without creating one containing moral evil. God could have created *other people*. Instead of creating us, i.e., the people that exist in Kronos, He could have created a world containing people, but not containing any of us — or perhaps a world containing some of us along with some others who do not exist in Kronos. And perhaps if He'd done that, He could have created a world containing moral good but no moral evil.

Perhaps. But then again, perhaps not. Suppose we look into the matter a little further. Let W be a world distinct from Kronos that contains a significantly free person x who does not exist in Kronos. Let us suppose that this person x does only what is right. I can see no reason to doubt that there *are* such worlds; but what reason do we have for supposing that God would have created any of them? How do we know that He can? To investigate this question, we must look into the idea of an *individual nature* or *essence*. I said earlier that the same individual — Socrates, for example — exists in many different possible worlds. In some of these he has properties quite different from those he has in Kronos, the actual world. But some of his properties are ones he has in every world in which he exists; these are his *essential* properties.[12] Among them would be some that are *trivially* essential — such properties as *being unmarried if a bachelor, being either six feet tall or else not six feet tall, being self-identical,* and the like. Another and more interesting kind of essential property can be explained as follows. Socrates has the property of being snubnosed. This property, presumably, is not essential to him; he could have had some other kind of nose. So there are possible worlds in which he is not snubnosed. Let W' be any such world. If W' had been actual, Socrates would not have been snubnosed; that is to say, Socrates has the property *being nonsnubnosed in* W'. For to say that an object x has a property of this sort — the property of having P in W, where P is a property and W is a possible world — is to say simply that x *would have had P if W had been actual.* Properties of this sort are *world-indexed* properties.[13] Socrates has the world-indexed property *being nonsnubnosed in* W'. He has this property in Kronos, the actual world. On the other hand, in W' Socrates has the property *being snubnosed in Kronos.* For suppose W' had been actual: then, while Socrates would not have been snubnosed, it would have been true that if *Kronos* had been actual, Socrates would have been snubnosed.

It is evident, I take it, that if indeed Socrates *is* snubnosed in Kronos, the actual world, then it is true in every world that Socrates is *snubnosed in Kronos.*[14] So he has the property *being snubnosed in Kronos* in every world in which he exists. This property, therefore, is essential to him; there is no world in which he exists and lacks it. Indeed, it is easy to see, I think, that every world-indexed property he has will be essential to him; and every world-indexed property he *lacks* will be such that its complement is essential to him.

But how many world-indexed properties does he have? Quite a few. We should note that for any world W and property P, there is the world-indexed property *has P in W;* and for any such world-indexed property, either Socrates has it or he has its complement — the property of *not* having P in W. For any world W and property P, either Socrates would have had P, had W been actual, or it's false that Socrates would have had P under that condition. So each world-indexed property P is such that either Socrates has P essentially, or else its complement $\bar{P}$ is essential to him.

12. For a discussion of essential properties see Plantinga, *The Nature of Necessity,* chapters 2-4.

13. For more about world-indexed properties see Plantinga, *The Nature of Necessity,* chapter 4, sec. 11.

14. For argument see Alvin Plantinga, "World and Essence," *Philosophical Review* 79 (October 1970): 487 and *The Nature of Necessity,* chapter 4, sec. 11.

Now suppose we define Socrates' *essence* as the set of properties essential to him. His essence is a set of properties, each of which is essential to him; and this set contains all his world-indexed properties, together with some others. But furthermore, it is evident, I think, that no *other* person has all of these properties in this set. Another person might have *some* of the same world-indexed properties as Socrates: he might be *snubnosed in Kronos* for example. But he couldn't have *all* of Socrates' world-indexed properties for then he would just *be* Socrates. So there is no person who shares Socrates' essence with him. But we can say something even stronger: there *couldn't* be any such person. For such a person would just be Socrates and hence not *another* person. The essence of Socrates, therefore, is a set of properties each of which he has essentially. Furthermore, there neither is nor could be another person distinct from Socrates that has all of the properties in this set. And finally, Socrate's essence contains a *complete* set of world-indexed properties — that is, if P is world-indexed, then either P is a member of Socrates' essence or else $\overline{P}$ is.[15]

Returning to Curley, we recall that he suffers from transworld depravity. This fact implies something interesting about Curleyhood, Curley's essence. Take those worlds W such that *is significantly free in W* and *never does what is wrong in W* are contained in Curley's essence. Each of these worlds has an important property if Curley suffers from transworld depravity; each is such that God could not have created or actualized it. We can see this as follows. Suppose W' is some world such that Curley's essence contains the property *is significantly free in W' but never does what is wrong in W'*. That is, W' is a world in which Curley is significantly free but always does what is right. But, of course, Curley suffers from transworld depravity. This means that there is an action A and a maximal world segment S' such that

(1) S' includes A's being morally significant for Curley
(2) S' includes Curley's being free with respect to A
(3) S' is included in W' but includes neither Curley's performing A nor his refraining from A

and

(4) If S' had been actual, Curley would have gone wrong with respect to A.

But then (by the argument of pp. 39-40) God could not have created or instantiated W'. For to do so He would have had to bring it about that S' obtain; and then Curley would have gone wrong with respect to A. Since in W' he always does what is right, W' would not have been actual. So if Curley

15. For more discussion of essences see Plantinga, *The Nature of Necessity,* chapter 5.

suffers from transworld depravity, then Curley's essence has this property: God could not have created any world W such that Curleyhood contains the properties *is significantly free in W* and *always does what is right in W*.

We can use this connection between Curley's transworld depravity and his essence as the basis for a definition of transworld depravity as applied to essences rather than persons. We should note first that if E is a person's essence, then that person is the *instantiation* of E; he is the thing that has (or exemplifies) every property in E. To instantiate an essence, God creates a person who has that essence; and in creating a person He instantiates an essence. Now we can say that

(15) An essence E *suffers from transworld depravity* if and only if for every world W such that E contains the properties *is significantly free in W* and *always does what is right in W,* there is an action A and a maximal world segment S' such that

(1) S' includes E' being instantiated and *E's instantiation's being free with respect to A* and *A's being morally significant for E's instantiation,*

(2) S' is included in W but includes neither *E's instantiation's performing A* nor *E's instantiation's refraining from A*

and

(3) if S' were actual, then the instantiation of E would have gone wrong with respect to A.

By now it is evident, I take it, that if an essence E suffers from transworld depravity, then it was not within God's power to actualize a possible world W such that E contains the properties *is significantly free in W* and *always does what is right in W.* Hence it was not within God's power to create a world in which E is instantiated and in which its instantiation is significantly free but always does what is right.

And the interesting fact here is this: it is possible that every creaturely essence — every essence including the property of being created by God — suffers from transworld depravity. But now suppose this is true. Now God can create a world containing moral good only by creating significantly free persons. And, since every person is the instantiation of an essence, He can create significantly free persons only by instantiating some essences. But if every essence suffers from transworld depravity then no matter which essences God instantiates, the resulting persons, if free with respect to morally significant actions, would always perform at least some wrong actions. If every essence suffers from transworld depravity, then it was beyond the power of God Himself to create a world containing moral good but no moral evil. He might have been able to create worlds in which moral evil is very considerably outweighed by moral good; but it was not within His power to create worlds containing moral good but no moral evil — and this despite the fact that He is omnipotent. Under these conditions God could have created a world containing no moral evil only by creating one without significantly free persons. But it is possible that every essence suffers from transworld depravity; so it's possible that God could not have created a world containing moral good but no moral evil.

V. The Free Will Defense Vindicated

Put formally, you remember, the Free Will Defender's project was to show that

(1) God is omniscient, omnipotent, and wholly good

is consistent with

(3) There is evil.

What we have just seen is that

(16) It was not within God's power to create a world containing moral good but no moral evil

is possible and consistent with God's omnipotence and omniscience. But then it is clearly consistent with (1). So we can use it to show that (1) is consistent with (3). For consider

(1) God is omnipotent, omniscient, and wholly good

(16) It was not within God's power to create a world containing moral good without creating one containing moral evil

and

(17) God created a world containing moral good.

These propositions are evidently consistent — i.e., their conjunction is a possible proposition. But taken together they entail

(3) There is evil.

For (17) says that God created a world containing moral good; this together with (16) entails that He created one containing moral evil. But if it contains moral evil, then it contains evil. So (1), (16), and (17) are jointly consistent and entail (3); hence (1) is consistent with (3); hence set A is consistent. Remember: to serve in this argument (16) and (17) need not be known to be true, or likely on our evidence, or anything of the sort; they need only be consistent with (1). Since they are, there is no contradiction in set A; so the Free Will Defense appears to be successful.

VI. Is God's Existence Compatible with the Amount of Moral Evil the World Contains?

The world, after all, contains a *great deal* of moral evil; and what we've seen so far is only that God's existence is compatible with *some* moral evil. Perhaps the atheologian can regroup; perhaps he can argue that at any rate God's existence is not consistent with the vast *amount* and *variety* of moral evil the universe actually contains. Of course, there doesn't seem to be any way to measure moral evil — that is, we don't have units like volts or pounds or kilowatts so that we could say "this situation contains exactly 35 turps of moral evil." Still, we can compare situations in terms of evil, and we can often see that one state of affairs contains more moral evil than another. Now perhaps the atheologian could maintain that at any rate God could have created a world containing *less* moral evil than the actual world contains.

But is this really obvious? It is obvious, but, considered by itself it is also irrelevant. God could have created a world with *no* moral evil just by creating no significantly free creatures. A more relevant question is this: was it within God's power to create a world that contained a better mixture of moral good and evil than Kronos — one, let's say, that contained as much moral good but less moral evil? And here the answer is not obvious at all. Possibly this was *not* within God's power, which is all the Free Will Defender needs. We can see this as follows. Of course, there are many possible worlds containing as much moral good as Kronos, but less moral evil. Let W' be any such world. If W' had been actual, there would have been as much moral good (past, present, and future) as in fact there was, is, and will be; and there would have been less moral evil in all. Now in W' a certain set S of essences is instantiated (that is, there is a set S of essences such that if W' had been actual, then each member of S would have been instantiated.) So to create W' God would have had to create persons who were the instantiations of these essences. The following, however, is possible. There is an action A, a maximal world segment S' and a member E of S such that

(a) E contains the properties: *is significantly free with respect to A in W'* and *goes right with respect to A in W'*.

(b) S' is included in W' and includes *E's being instantiated*, but includes neither *E's instantiation's performing A* nor *E's instantiation's refraining from A*

and

> (c) if S' had been actual, E's instantiation would have gone wrong with respect to A.

If this possibility is actual, then God could not have actualized W'. For to do so He'd have had to instantiate E, cause E's instantiation to be free with respect to A, and bring it about that S' was actual. But then the instantiation of E would have gone wrong with respect to A, so that the world thus created would not have been W'; for in W' E's instantiation goes *right* with respect to A.

More generally, it's possible that every world containing as much moral good as the actual world, but less moral evil, resembles W' in that God could not have created it. For it is possible that

> (18) For every world W containing as much moral good as Kronos, but less moral evil, there is at least one essence E, an action A, and a maximal world segment S' such that
>
> (1) E contains the properties: *is free with respect to A* in W and *goes right with respect to A* in W
>
> (2) S' is included in W and includes E's being instantiated but includes neither *E's instantiation's performing A* nor *E's instantiation's refraining from A*

and

> (3) if S' were actual, E's instantiation would have gone wrong with respect to A.

(18) is possible; if it is *true*, then it wasn't within the power of God to create a world containing as much moral good as this one but less moral evil. So it's possible that this was not within God's power; but if so, then (1) is compatible with the proposition that there is as much moral evil as Kronos does in fact contain. And, of course, what the Free Will Defender claims is not that (18) is *true*; he claims only that it is compatible with the existence of a wholly good, omnipotent God.

The Free Will Defense, then, successfully shows that set A is consistent. It can also be used to show that

> (1) God is omnipotent, omniscient, and morally perfect

is consistent with

> (19) There is as much moral evil as Kronos contains.

For clearly enough (1), (18), and

(20) God has created a world containing as much moral good as Kronos contains

are jointly consistent. But (18) tells us that God could not have created a world containing more moral good but less moral evil than Kronos; so these three propositions entail (19). It follows that (1) and (19) are consistent.

VII. Is God's Existence Compatible with *Natural* Evil?

Perhaps the atheologian can regroup once more. What about *natural* evil? Evil that can't be ascribed to the free actions of human beings? Suffering due to earthquakes, disease, and the like? Is the existence of evil of *this sort* compatible with (1)? Here two lines of thought present themselves. On the one hand, it is conceivable that some natural evils and some persons are so related that the persons would have produced *less* moral good if the evils had been absent. Some people deal creatively with certain kinds of hardship or suffering, acting in such a way that on balance the whole state of affairs is valuable. And perhaps the response would have been less impressive and the total situation less valuable if the evil had not taken place. But a more traditional line of thought is indicated by St. Augustine, who attributes much of the evil we find to *Satan* or to Satan and his cohorts. Satan, so the traditional doctrine goes, is a mighty nonhuman spirit who, along with many other angels, was created long before God created man. Unlike most of his colleagues, Satan rebelled against God and has since been wreaking whatever havoc he can. The result is natural evil. So the natural evil we find is due to free actions of nonhuman spirits.

Augustine is presenting what I earlier called a *theodicy,* as opposed to a *defense.* He believes that *in fact* natural evil (except for what can be attributed to God's punishment) is to be ascribed to the activity of beings that are free and rational but nonhuman. The Free Will Defender, of course, does not assert that this is *true;* he says only that it is *possible* [(and consistent with (1)]. He points to the possibility that natural evil is due to the actions of significantly free but nonhuman persons. We have noted that there is no inconsistency in the idea that God could not have created a world with a better balance of moral good over moral evil than this one displays. Something similar holds here; possibly natural evil is due to the free activity of nonhuman persons; and possibly it wasn't within God's power to create a set of such persons whose free actions produced a greater balance of good over evil. That is to say, it is possible that

(21) Natural evil is due to the free actions of nonhuman persons; there is a balance of good over evil with respect to the actions of these

nonhuman persons; and it was not within the power of God to create a world that contains a more favorable balance of good over evil with respect to the actions of the nonhuman persons it contains.

Again, it must be emphasized that (21) is not required to be *true* for the success of the Free Will Defense; it need only be compatible with (1). And it certainly looks as if it is. If (21) *is* true, furthermore, then *natural* evil significantly resembles *moral* evil in that, like the latter, it is the result of the activity of significantly free persons. In fact both moral and natural evil would then be special cases of what we might call *broadly moral evil* — evil resulting from the free actions of personal beings, whether human or not. Given this idea, we can combine (18) and (21) into one compendious statement:

(22) All the evil in Kronos is broadly moral evil, and it was not within the power of God to create a world containing a better balance of broadly moral good and evil.

(22) appears to be consistent with (1) and

(23) God creates a world containing as much broadly moral good as Kronos contains.

But (1), (22), and (23) together entail that there is as much evil as Kronos contains. So (1) is consistent with the proposition that there is as much evil as Kronos contains. I therefore conclude that the Free Will Defense successfully rebuts the charge of inconsistency brought against the theist.

CHAPTER THREE

The Ontological Argument

In this chapter I wish to discuss the famous "ontological argument" first formulated by Anselm of Canterbury in the eleventh century. This argument for the existence of God has fascinated philosophers ever since Anselm first stated it. Few people, I should think, have been brought to belief in God by means of this argument; nor has it played much of a role in strengthening and confirming religious faith. At first sight Anselm's argument is remarkably unconvincing if not downright irritating; it looks too much like a parlor puzzle or word magic. And yet nearly every major philosopher from the time of Anselm to the present has had something to say about it; this argument has a long and illustrious line of defenders extending to the present. Indeed, the last few years have seen a remarkable flurry of interest in it among philosophers. What accounts for its fascination? Not, I think, its religious significance, although that can be underrated. Perhaps there are two reasons for it. First, many of the most knotty and difficult problems in philosophy meet in this argument. Is existence a property? Are existential propositions — propositions of the form x *exists* — ever necessarily true? Are existential propositions about what they seem to be about? Are there, in any respectable sense of "are," some objects that do not exist? If so, do they have any properties? Can they be compared with things that do exist? These issues and a hundred others arise in connection with Anslem's argument. And second. Although the argument certainly looks at first sight as if it ought to be unsound, it is profoundly difficult to say what, exactly, is wrong with it. Indeed, I do not believe that any philosopher has ever given a cogent and conclusive refutation of the ontological argument in its various forms.

Anselm states his argument as follows:

And so, Lord, do thou, who dost give understanding to faith, give me, so far as thou knowest it to be profitable, to understand that thou art as we believe; and that thou art that which we believe. And indeed, we believe that thou are a being than which nothing greater can be conceived. Or is there no such nature, since the fool hath said in his heart, there is no God? . . . But, at any rate, this very fool when he hears of this being of which I speak — a being than which nothing greater can be conceived — understands what he hears, and what he understands is in his understanding, although he does not understand it to exist.

For, it is one thing for any object to be in the understanding, and another to understand that the object exists. When a painter first conceives of what he will afterwards perform, he has it in his understanding, but he does not yet understand it to be, because he has not yet performed it. But after he has made the painting, he both has it in his understanding, and he understands that it exists, because he has made it.

Hence, even the fool is convinced that something exists in the understanding, at least, than which nothing greater can be conceived. For when he hears of this, he understands it. And whatever is understood, exists in the understanding. And assuredly that, than which nothing greater can be conceived, cannot exist in the understanding alone. For, suppose it exists in the understanding alone; then it can be conceived to exist in reality; which is greater.

Therefore, if that, than which nothing greater can be conceived, exists in the understanding alone, the very being, than which nothing greater can be conceived, is one, than which a greater can be conceived. But obviously this is impossible. Hence, there is no doubt that there exists a being, than which nothing greater can be conceived, and it exists both in the understanding and in reality.[1]

At first sight, this argument smacks of trumpery and deceit; but suppose we look at it a bit more closely. Its essentials are contained in these words:

And assuredly that, than which nothing greater can be conceived, cannot exist in the understanding alone. For suppose it exists in the understanding alone; then it can be conceived to exist in reality; which is greater.

Therefore, if that, than which nothing greater can be conceived, exists in the understanding alone, the very being, than which nothing greater can be conceived, is one, than which a greater can be conceived. But obviously this is impossible. Hence there is no doubt that there exists a being, than which nothing greater can be conceived, and it exists both in the understanding and in reality.[2]

1. St. Anselm, *Proslogium,* chapter 2, in *The Ontological Argument,* ed. A. Plantinga (New York: Doubleday Anchor, 1965), pp. 3-4.

2. Ibid., p. 4.

How can we outline this argument? It is best construed, I think, as a *reductio ad absurdum* argument. In a *reductio* you prove a given proposition p by showing that its denial, *not-p,* leads to (or more strictly, entails) a contradiction or some other kind of absurdity. Anselm's argument can be seen as an attempt to deduce an absurdity from the proposition that there is no God. If we use the term 'God' as an abbreviation for Anselm's phrase "the being than which nothing greater can be conceived," then the argument seems to be approximately as follows: Suppose

(1) God exists in the understanding but not in reality.

(2) Existence in reality is greater than existence in the understanding alone. (premise)

(3) God's existence in reality is conceivable. (premise)

(4) If God did exist in reality, then He would be greater than He is. [from (1) and (2)]

(5) It is conceivable that there is a being greater than God is. [(3) and (4)]

(6) It is conceivable that there be a being greater than the being than which nothing greater can be conceived. [(5) by the definition of 'God']

But surely (6) is absurd and self-contradictory; how could we conceive of a being greater than the being than which none greater can be conceived? So we may conclude that

(7) It is false that God exists in the understanding but not in reality.

It follows that if God exists in the understanding, He also exists in reality; but clearly enough He *does* exist in the understanding, as even the fool will testify; therefore, He exists in reality as well.

Now when Anselm says that a being *exists in the understanding,* we may take him, I think, as saying that someone has *thought of* or thought about that being. When he says that something *exists in reality,* on the other hand, he means to say simply that the thing in question really does exist. And when he says that a certain state of affairs is *conceivable,* he means to say, I believe, that this state of affairs is possible in our broadly logical sense;* there is a possible world in which it obtains. This means that step (3) above may be put more perspicuously as

(3′) It is possible that God exists

and step (6) as

(6′) It is possible that there be a being greater than the being than which it is not possible that there be a greater.

*See editor's note, p. 23 above.

An interesting feature of this argument is that all of its premises are *necessarily* true if true at all. (1) is the assumption from which Anselm means to deduce a contradiction. (2) is a premise, and presumably necessarily true in Anselm's view; and (3) is the only remaining premise (the other items are consequences of preceding steps); it says of some *other* proposition *(God exists)* that it is possible. Propositions which thus ascribe a modality — possibility, necessity, contingency — to another proposition are themselves either necessarily true or necessarily false. So all the premises of the argument are, if true at all, necessarily true. And hence if the premises of this argument are true, then [provided that (6) is really inconsistent] a contradiction can be deduced from (1) together with necessary propositions; this means that (1) entails a contradiction and is, therefore, necessarily false.

I. Gaunilo's Objection

Gaunilo, a contemporary of Anselm's, wrote a reply which he entitled *On Behalf of the Fool.* Here is the essence of his objection.

> For example: it is said that somewhere in the ocean is an island, which, because of the difficulty, or rather the impossibility, of discovering what does not exist, is called the lost island. And they say that this island has an inestimable wealth of all manner of riches and delicacies in greater abundance than is told of the Islands of the Blest; and that having no owner or inhabitant, it is more excellent than all other countries, which are inhabited by mankind, in the abundance with which it is stored.
>
> Now if some one should tell me that there is such an island, I should easily understand his words, in which there is no difficulty. But suppose that he went on to say, as if by a logical inference: "You can no longer doubt that this island which is more excellent than all lands exists somewhere, since you have no doubt that it is in your understanding. And since it is more excellent not to be in the understanding alone, but to exist both in the understanding and in reality, for this reason it must exist. For if it does not exist, any land which really exists will be more excellent than it; and so the island already understood by you to be more excellent will not be more excellent."
>
> If a man should try to prove to me by such reasoning that this island truly exists, and that its existence should no longer be doubted, either I should believe that he was jesting, or I know not which I ought to regard as the greater fool: myself, supposing that I should allow this proof; or him, if he should suppose that he had established with any certainty the existence of this island.[3]

3. Plantinga, *The Ontological Argument,* p. 11.

Gaunilo was the first of many to try to discredit the ontological argument by showing that one can find similar arguments to prove the existence of all sorts of absurd things — a greatest possible island, a highest possible mountain, a greatest possible middle linebacker, a meanest possible man, and the like. But Anselm was not without a reply.[4]

He points out, first, that Gaunilo misquotes him. What is under consideration is not a being that is *in fact* greater than any other, but one such that a greater *cannot be conceived;* a being than which it's *not possible* that there be a greater. Guanilo seems to overlook this. And thus his famous lost island argument isn't strictly parallel to Anselm's argument; his conclusion should be only that there is an island such that no other island is greater than it — which, if there are any islands at all, is a fairly innocuous conclusion.

But obviously Gaunilo's argument can be revised. Instead of speaking, as he did, of an island that is more excellent than all others, let's speak instead of an island than which a greater or more excellent cannot be conceived — an island, that is, than which it's not possible that there be a greater. Couldn't we use an argument like Anselm's to "establish" the existence of such an island, and if we could, wouldn't that show that Anselm's argument is fallacious?

II. Anselm's Reply

Not obviously. Anselm's proper reply, it seems to me, is that it's impossible that there be such an island. The idea of an island than which it's not possible that there be a greater is like the idea of a natural number than which it's not possible that there be a greater, or the idea of a line than which none more crooked is possible. There neither is nor could be a greatest possible natural number; indeed, there isn't a greatest *actual* number, let alone a greatest possible. And the same goes for islands. No matter how great an island is, no matter how many Nubian maidens and dancing girls adorn it, there could always be a greater — one with twice as many, for example. The qualities that make for greatness in islands — number of palm trees, amount and quality of coconuts, for example — most of these qualities have no *intrinsic maximum.* That is, there is no degree of productivity or number of palm trees (or of dancing girls) such that it is impossible that an island display more of that quality. So the idea of a greatest possible island is an inconsistent or incoherent idea; it's not possible that there be such a thing. And hence the analogue of step (3) of Anselm's argument (it is possible that God exists) is not true for the perfect island argument; so that argument fails.

4. Ibid., pp. 13-27.

But doesn't Anselm's argument itself founder upon the same rock? If the idea of a greatest possible island is inconsistent, won't the same hold for the idea of a greatest possible being? Perhaps not. For what are the properties in virtue of which one being is greater, just as a being, than another? Anselm clearly has in mind such properties as wisdom, knowledge, power, and moral excellence or moral perfection. And certainly knowledge, for example, does have an intrinsic maximum: if for every proposition p, a being B knows whether or not p is true, then B has a degree of knowledge that is utterly unsurpassable. So a greatest possible being would have to have this kind of knowledge: it would have to be *omniscient*. Similarly for *power;* omnipotence is a degree of power that can't possibly be excelled. Moral perfection or moral excellence is perhaps not quite so clear; still a being could perhaps always do what is morally right, so that it would not be possible for it to be exceeded along those lines. But what about a quality like *love?* Wouldn't that be a property that makes for greatness? God, according to Christian theism, loves His children and demonstrated His love in the redemptive events of the life and death of Jesus Christ. And what about the relevant qualities here — love, or acting out of love: do they have intrinsic maxima? The answer isn't very clear either way. Rather than pause to discuss this question, let's note simply that there may be a weak point here in Anselm's argument and move on.

III. Kant's Objection

The most famous and important objection to the ontological argument is contained in Immanuel Kant's *Critique of Pure Reason*.[5] Kant begins his criticism as follows:

> If, in an identical proposition, I reject the predicate while retaining the subject, contradiction results; and I therefore say that the former belongs necessarily to the latter. But if we reject the subject and predicate alike, there is no contradiction; for nothing is then left that can be contradicted. To posit a triangle, and yet to reject its three angles, is self-contradictory; but there is no contradiction in rejecting the triangle together with its three angles. The same holds true of the concept of an absolutely necessary being. If its existence is rejected, we reject the thing itself with all its predicates; and no question of contradiction can than arise. There is nothing outside it that would then be contradicted, since the necessity of the thing is not

5. Immanuel Kant, *Critique of Pure Reason,* ed. Norman Kemp Smith (New York: Macmillan Co., 1929). Some relevant passages are reprinted in Plantinga, *The Ontological Argument,* pp. 57-64.

supposed to be derived from anything external; nor is there anything internal that would be contradicted, since in rejecting the thing itself we have at the same time rejected all its internal properties. "God is omnipotent" is a necessary judgment. The omnipotence cannot be rejected if we posit a Deity, that is, an infinite being; for the two concepts are identical. But if we say "There is no God," neither the omnipotence nor any other of its predicates is given; they are one and all rejected together with the subject, and there is therefore not the least contradiction in such a judgment. . . .

For I cannot form the least concept of a thing which, should it be rejected with all its predicates, leaves behind a contradiction.[6]

One characteristic feature of Anselm's argument, as we have seen, is that if successful, it establishes that *God exists* is a *necessary* proposition. Here Kant is apparently arguing that no *existential* proposition — one that asserts the existence of something — is necessarily true; the reason, he says, is that no *contra-existential* (the denial of an existential) is contradictory or inconsistent. But in which of our several senses of inconsistent? What he means to say, I believe, is that no existential proposition is necessary in the broadly logical sense. And this claim has been popular with philosophers ever since. But why, exactly, does Kant think it's true? What is the argument? When we take a careful look at the purported reasoning, it looks pretty unimpressive; it's hard to make out an argument at all. The conclusion would apparently be this: if we deny the existence of something or other, we can't be contradicting ourselves; no existential proposition is necessary and no contra-existential is impossible. Why not? Well, if we say, for example, that God does not exist, then says Kant, "There is nothing outside it (i.e., God) that would then be contradicted, since the necessity of the thing is not supposed to be derived from anything external; nor is there anything internal that would be contradicted, since in rejecting the thing itself we have at the same time rejected all its internal properties."

But how is this even *relevant?* The claim is that *God does not exist* can't be necessarily false. What could be meant, in this context, by saying that there's nothing "outside of" God that would be contradicted if we denied His existence? What would contradict a proposition like *God does not exist* is some other proposition — *God does exist,* for example. Kant seems to think that if the proposition in question *were* necessarily false, it would have to contradict, not a proposition, but some *object* external to God — or else contradict some internal part or aspect or property of God. But this certainly looks like confusion; it is *propositions* that contradict each other; they aren't contradicted by objects or parts, aspects or properties of objects. Does he

6. Plantinga, *The Ontological Argument,* p. 59.

mean instead to be speaking of *propositions* about things external to God, or about his aspects or parts or properties? But clearly many such propositions do contradict *God does not exist;* an example would be *the world was created by God.* Does he mean to say that no *true* proposition contradicts *God does not exist?* No, for that would be to affirm the *nonexistence* of God, an affirmation Kant is by no means prepared to make.

So this passage is an enigma. Either Kant was confused or else he expressed himself very badly indeed. And either way we don't have any argument for the claim that contra-existential propositions can't be inconsistent. This passage seems to be no more than an elaborate and confused way of *asserting* this claim.

The heart of Kant's objection to the ontological argument, however, is contained in the following passage:

'Being' is obviously not a real predicate; that is, it is not a concept of something which could be added to the concept of a thing. It is merely the positing of a thing, or of certain determinations, as existing in themselves. Logically, it is merely the copula of a judgment. The proposition 'God is omnipotent' contains two concepts, each of which has its object — God and omnipotence. The small word 'is' adds no new predicate, but only serves to posit the predicate in its relation to the subject. If, now, we take the subject (God) with all its predicates (among which is omnipotence), and say 'God is,' or 'There is a God,' we attach no new predicate to the concept of God, but only posit it as an object that stands in relation to my concept. The content of both must be one and the same; nothing can have been added to the concept, which expresses merely what is possible, by my thinking its object (through the expression 'it is') as given absolutely. Otherwise stated, the real contains no more than the merely possible. A hundred real thalers do not contain the least coin more than a hundred possible thalers. For as the latter signify the concept and the former the object and the positing of the concept, should the former contain more than the latter, my concept would not, in that case, express the whole object, and would not therefore be an adequate concept of it. My financial position, however, is affected very differently by a hundred real thalers than it is by the mere concept of them (that is, of the possibility). For the object, as it actually exists, is not analytically contained in my concept, but is added to my concept (which is a determination of my state) synthetically; and yet the conceived hundred thalers are not themselves in the least increased through thus acquiring existence outside my concept.

By whatever and by however many predicates we may think a thing — even if we completely determine it — we do not make the least addition to the thing when we further declare that this thing is. Otherwise it would not be exactly the same thing that exists, but something more than we had thought in the concept: and we could not, therefore, say that the object of my concept exists. If we think in a thing every feature of reality except one, the missing reality is not added by my saying that this defective thing exists.[7]

Now how, exactly is all this relevant to Anselm's argument? Perhaps Kant means to make a point that we could put by saying that it's not possible to *define things into existence*. (People sometimes suggest that the ontological argument is just such an attempt to define *God* into existence.) And this claim is somehow connected with Kant's famous but perplexing *dictum* that *being* (or existence) is not a real predicate or property. But how shall we understand Kant here? What does it mean to say that existence isn't (or is) a real property?

Apparently Kant thinks this is equivalent to or follows from what he puts variously as "the real *contains* no more than the merely possible"; "the *content* of both (i.e., concept and object) must be one and the same"; "being is not the concept of something that could be *added to* the concept of a thing," and so on. But what does all this mean? And how does it bear on the ontological argument? Perhaps Kant is thinking along the following lines. In defining a concept — *bachelor,* let's say, or *prime number* — one lists a number of properties that are *severally necessary* and *jointly sufficient* for the concept's applying to something. That is, the concept applies to a given thing only if that thing has each of the listed properties, and if a thing does have them all, then the concept in question applies to it. So, for example, to define the concept *bachelor* we list such properties as *being unmarried, being male, being over the age of twenty-five,* and the like. Take any one of these properties: a thing is a bachelor only if it has it, and if a thing has all of them, then it follows that it is a bachelor.

Now suppose you have a concept C that has application *contingently* if at all. That is to say, it is not necessarily true that there are things to which this concept applies. The concept *bachelor* would be an example; the proposition *there are bachelors,* while *true,* is obviously not necessarily true. And suppose $P_1, P_2 \ldots, P_n$ are the properties jointly sufficient and severally necessary for something's falling under C. Then C can be defined as follows:

A thing x is an instance of C (i.e., C applies to x) if and only if x has P_1, $P_2 \ldots, P_n$.

Perhaps Kant's point is this. There is a certain kind of mistake here we may be tempted to make. Suppose $P_1 \ldots, P_n$ are the defining properties for the concept *bachelor.* We might try to define a new concept *superbachelor* by adding *existence* to $P_1 \ldots, P_n$. That is, we might say

7. *The Ontological Argument,* pp. 61-62.

x is a superbachelor if and only if x has $P_1, P_2 \ldots, P_n$, and x exists.

Then (as we might mistakenly suppose) just as it is a necessary truth that bachelors are unmarried, so it is a necessary truth that superbachelors exist. And in this way it looks as if we've defined superbachelors into existence.

But of course this is a mistake, and perhaps that is Kant's point. For while indeed it is a necessary truth that bachelors are unmarried, what this means is that the proposition

(8) Everything that is a bachelor is unmarried

is necessarily true. Similarly, then,

(9) Everything that is a superbachelor exists

will be necessarily true. But obviously it doesn't follow that there *are* any superbachelors. All that follows is that

(10) All the superbachelors there are *exist*

which is not really very startling. If it is a contingent truth, furthermore, that there are bachelors, it will be equally contingent that there are superbachelors. We can see this by noting that the defining properties of the concept *bachelor* are included among those of *superbachelor;* it is a necessary truth, therefore, that every superbachelor is a bachelor. This means that

(11) There are some superbachelors

entails

(12) There are some bachelors.

But then if (12) is contingent, so is (11). Indeed, the concepts *bachelor* and *superbachelor* are equivalent in the following sense: it is impossible that there exists an object to which one but not the other of these two concepts applies. We've just seen that every superbachelor must be a bachelor. Conversely, however, every bachelor is a superbachelor. Now perhaps we can put Kant's point more exactly. Suppose we say that a property or predicate P is *real* only if there is some list of properties P_1 to P_n such that the result of adding P to the list does not define a concept equivalent (in the above sense) to that defined by the list. It then follows, of course, that existence is not a real property or predicate. Kant's point, then, is that one cannot *define things into existence* because *existence* is not a real property or predicate in the explained sense.[8]

---

8. For a more detailed and extensive discussion of this argument, see Plantinga, *God and Other Minds,* pp. 29-38, and A. Plantinga, "Kant's Objection to the Ontological Argument," *Journal of Philosophy* 63 (1966): 537.

IV. The Irrelevance of Kant's Objection

If this is what he means, he's certainly right. But is it relevant to the ontological argument? Couldn't Anselm thank Kant for this interesting point and proceed merrily on his way? Where did he try to define God into being by adding existence to a list of properties that defined some concept? According to the great German philosopher and pessimist Arthur Schopenhauer, the ontological argument arises when "someone excogitates a conception, composed out of all sorts of predicates, among which, however, he takes care to include the predicate actuality or existence, either openly or wrapped up for decency's sake in some other predicate, such as perfection, immensity, or something of the kind." If this were Anselm's procedure — if he had simply added existence to a concept that has application contingently if at all — then indeed his argument would be subject to the Kantian criticism. But he didn't, and it isn't.

The usual criticisms of Anselm's argument, then, leave much to be desired. Of course, this doesn't mean that the argument is successful, but it does mean that we shall have to take an independent look at it. What about Anselm's argument? Is it a good one? The first thing to recognize is that the ontological argument comes in an enormous variety of versions, some of which may be much more promising than others. Instead of speaking of *the* ontological argument, we must recognize that what we have here is a whole family of related arguments. (Having said this I shall violate my own directive and continue to speak of *the* ontological argument.)

V. The Argument Restated

Let's look once again at our initial schematization of the argument. I think perhaps it is step (2)

> (2) Existence in reality is greater than existence in the understanding alone

that is most puzzling here. Earlier we spoke of the properties in virtue of which one being is greater, just as a being, than another. Suppose we call them *great-making properties*. Apparently Anselm means to suggest that *existence* is a great-making property. He seems to suggest that a nonexistent being would be greater than in fact it is, if it did exist. But how can we make sense of that? How could there be a nonexistent being anyway? Does that so much as make sense?

Perhaps we can put this perspicuously in terms of possible worlds. You recall that an object may exist in some possible worlds and not others. There are possible worlds in which you and I do not exist; these worlds are impoverished, no doubt, but are not on that account impossible. Furthermore, you recall that an object can have different properties in different worlds. In the actual world Paul J. Zwier is not a good tennis player; but surely there are worlds in which he wins the Wimbledon Open. Now if a person can have different properties in different worlds, then he can have different degrees of greatness in different worlds. In the actual world Raquel Welch has impressive assets; but there is a world RW_f in which she is fifty pounds overweight and mousy. Indeed, there are worlds in which she does not so much as exist. What Anselm means to be suggesting, I think, is that Raquel Welch enjoys very little greatness in those worlds in which she does not exist. But of course this condition is not restricted to Miss Welch. What Anselm means to say, more generally, is that for any being x and worlds W and W', if x exists in W but not in W', then x's greatness in W exceeds x's greatness in W'. Or, more modestly, perhaps he means to say that if a being x does not exist in a world W (and there is a world in which x does exist), then *there is at least one world* in which the greatness of x exceeds the greatness of x in W. Suppose Raquel Welch does not exist in some world W. Anselm means to say that there is at least one possible world in which she has a degree of greatness that exceeds the degree of greatness she has in that world W. (It is plausible, indeed, to go much further and hold that she has *no greatness at all* in worlds in which she does not exist.)

But now perhaps we can restate the whole argument in a way that gives us more insight into its real structure. Once more, use the term 'God' to abbreviate the phrase "the being than which it is not possible that there be a greater." Now suppose

(13) God does not exist in the actual world.

Add the new version of premise (2):

(14) For any being x and world W, if x does not exist in W, then there is a world W' such that the greatness of x in W' exceeds the greatness of x in W.

Restate premise (3) in terms of possible worlds:

(15) There is a possible world in which God exists.

And continue on:

(16) If God does not exist in the actual world, then there is a world W' such that the greatness of God in W' exceeds the greatness of God in the actual world. [from (14)]

(17) So there is a world W' such that the greatness of God in W' exceeds the greatness of God in the actual worlds. [(13) and (16)]

(18) So there is a possible being x and a world W' such that the greatness of x in W' exceeds the greatness of God in actuality. [(17)]

(19) Hence it's possible that there be a being greater than God is. [(18)]

(20) So it's possible that there be a being greater than the being than which it's not possible that there be a greater. [(19), replacing 'God' by what it abbreviates.]

But surely

(21) It's not possible that there be a being greater than the being than which it's not possible that there be a greater.

So (13) [with the help of premises (14) and (15)] appears to imply (20), which, according to (21), is necessarily false. Accordingly, (13) is false. So the actual world contains a being than which it's not possible that there be a greater — that is, God exists.

Now where, if anywhere, can we fault this argument? Step (13) is the hypothesis for *reductio,* the assumption to be reduced to absurdity, and is thus entirely above reproach. Steps (16) through (20) certainly look as if they follow from the items they are said to follow from. So that leaves only (14), (15), and (21). Step (15) says only that it is possible that God exists. Step (14) also certainly seems plausible: if a being doesn't even *exist* in a given world, it can't have much by way of greatness in that world. At the very least it can't have its *maximum* degree of greatness — a degree of greatness that it does not excel in any other world — in a world where it doesn't exist. And consider (21): surely it has the ring of truth. How could there be a being greater than the being than which it's not possible that there be a greater? Initially, the argument seems pretty formidable.

VI. Its Fatal Flaw

But there is something puzzling about it. We can see this if we ask what sorts of things (14) is supposed to be *about.* It starts off boldly: "For any being x and world $W, \ldots$" So (14) is talking about worlds and beings. It says something about each world-being pair. And (16) follows from it, because (16) asserts of *God* and *the actual world* something that according to (14) holds of every being and world. But then if (16) follows from (14), God must be a *being.* That is, (16) follows from (14) only with the help of the additional premise that God is a being. And doesn't this statement — that God is a being — imply that *there is* or *exists* a being than which it's not possible that there be a greater? But if so, the argument flagrantly begs the question; for then we can accept the inference from (14) to (16) only if we already know that the conclusion is true.

We can approach this same matter by a slightly different route. I asked earlier what sorts of things (14) was *about;* the answer was: beings and worlds. We can ask the same or nearly the same question by asking about the *range* of the *quantifiers* — 'for any being,' 'for any world' — in (14). What do these quantifiers range over? If we reply that they range over possible worlds and beings — *actually existing* beings — then the inference to (16) requires the additional premise that God is an actually existing being, that there *really is* a being than which it is not possible that there be a greater. Since this is supposed to be our conclusion, we can't very gracefully add it as a *premise.* So perhaps the quantifiers don't range just over actually existing beings. But what else is there? Step (18) speaks of a *possible being* — a thing that may not in fact exist, but *could* exist. Or we could put it like this. A possible being is a thing that exists in some possible world or other; a thing x for which there is a world W, such that if W had been actual, x would have existed. So (18) is really about worlds and *possible beings.* And what it says is this: take any possible being x and any possible world W. If x does not exist in W, then there is a possible world W' where x has a degree of greatness that surpasses the greatness that it has in W. And hence to make the argument complete perhaps we should add the affirmation that God is a *possible being.*

But *are* there any possible beings — that is, *merely* possible beings, beings that don't in fact exist? If so, what sorts of things are they? Do they have properties? How are we to think of them? What is their status? And what reasons are there for supposing that there are any such peculiar items at all?

These are knotty problems. Must we settle them in order even to consider this argument? No. For instead of speaking of *possible beings* and the worlds in which they do or don't exist, we can speak of *properties* and the worlds in which they do or don't *have instances,* are or are not *instantiated* or *exemplified.* Instead of speaking of a possible being named by the phrase, "the being than which it's not possible that there be a greater," we may speak of the property *having an unsurpassable degree of greatness* — that is, *having a degree of greatness such that it's not possible that there exist a being having more.* And then we can ask whether this property is instantiated in this or other possible worlds. Later on I shall show how to restate the argument this way. For the moment please take my word for the fact that we can speak as freely as we wish about possible objects; for we can always translate ostensible talk about such things into talk about properties and the worlds in which they are or are not instantiated.

The argument speaks, therefore, of an unsurpassably great being — of a being whose greatness is not excelled by any being in any world. This being has a degree of greatness so impressive that no other being in any world has more. But here we hit the question crucial for this version of the argument. *Where* does this being have that degree of greatness? I said above that the same being may have different degrees of greatness in different worlds; in which world does the possible being in question have the degree of greatness in question? All we are really told, in being told that God is a possible being, is this: among the possible beings there is one that in some world or other has a degree of greatness that is nowhere excelled.

And this fact is fatal to this version of the argument. I said earlier that (21) has the ring of truth; a closer look (listen?) reveals that it's more of a dull thud. For it is ambiguous as between

> (21') It's not possible that there be a being whose greatness surpasses that enjoyed by the unsurpassably great being *in the worlds where its greatness is at a maximum*

and

> (21") It's not possible that there be a being whose greatness surpasses that enjoyed by the unsurpassably great being *in the actual world.*

There is an important difference between these two. The greatest possible being may have different degrees of greatness in different worlds. Step (21') points to the worlds in which this being has its maximal greatness; and it says, quite properly, that the degree of greatness this being has in those worlds is nowhere excelled. Clearly this is so. The greatest possible being is a possible being who in some world or other has unsurpassable greatness. Unfortunately for the argument, however, (21') does not contradict (20). Or to put it another way, what follows from (13) [together with (14) and (15)] is not the denial of (21'). If that *did* follow, then the *reductio* would be complete and the argument successful. But what (20) says is not that there is a possible being whose greatness exceeds that enjoyed by the greatest possible being *in a world where the latter's greatness is at a maximum;* it says only that there is a possible being whose greatness exceeds that enjoyed by the greatest possible being *in the actual world* — where, for all we know, its greatness is *not* at a maximum. So if we read (21) as (21'), the *reductio* argument falls apart.

Suppose instead we read it as (21"). Then what it says is that there couldn't be a being whose greatness surpasses that enjoyed by the greatest possible being in Kronos, the actual world. So read, (21) does contradict (20). Unfortunately, however, we have no reason, so far, for thinking that (21") is true at all, let alone necessarily true. If, among the possible beings, there is one whose greatness *in some world or other* is absolutely maximal — such that no being in any world has a degree of greatness surpassing it — then indeed there couldn't be a being that was greater than *that.* But it doesn't follow that this being has that degree of greatness in the *actual* world. It has it *in some world or other* but not necessarily in Kronos, the actual world. And so the argument fails. If we take (21) as (21'), then it follows from the assertion that God is a possible being; but it is of no use to the argument. If we take it as (21″), on the other hand, then indeed it is useful in the argument, but we have no reason whatever to think it true. So this version of the argument fails.[9]

VII. A Modal Version of the Argument

But of course there are many other versions; one of the argument's chief features is its many-sided diversity. The fact that *this* version is unsatisfactory does not show that *every* version is or must be. Professors Charles Hartshorne[10] and Norman Malcolm[11] claim to detect two quite different versions of the argument in Anselm's work. In the first of these versions *existence* is held to be a perfection or a great-making property; in the second it is *necessary existence*. But what could *that* amount to? Perhaps something like this. Consider a pair of beings A and B that both do in fact exist. And suppose that A exists in every other possible world as well — that is, if any other possible world had been actual, A would have existed. On the other hand, B exists in only some possible worlds; there are worlds W such that had any of *them* been actual, B would not have existed. Now according to the doctrine under consideration, A is so far greater than B. Of course, *on balance* it may be that A is not greater than $B;$ I believe that the number seven, unlike Spiro Agnew, exists in every possible world; yet I should be hesitant to affirm on that account that the number seven is greater than Agnew. Necessary existence is just one of several great-making properties, and no doubt Agnew has more of some of these others than does the number seven. Still, all this is compatible with saying that necessary existence is a great-making property. And given this notion, we can restate the argument as follows:

(22) It is possible that there is a greatest possible being.

(23) Therefore, there is a possible being that in some world W' or other has a maximum degree of greatness — a degree of greatness that is nowhere exceeded.

(24) A being B has the maximum degree of greatness in a given possible world W only if B *exists in every possible world.*

---

9. This criticism of this version of the argument essentially follows David Lewis, "Anselm and Actuality," *Nous* 4 (1970): 175-88. See also Plantinga, *The Nature of Necessity,* pp. 202-5.

10. Charles Hartshorne, *Man's Vision of God* (New York: Harper and Row, 1941). Portions reprinted in Plantinga, *The Ontological Argument,* pp. 123-35.

11. Norman Malcolm, "Anselm's Ontological Arguments," *Philosophical Review* 69 (1960); reprinted in Plantinga, *The Ontological Argument,* pp. 136-59.

(22) and (24) are the premises of this argument; and what follows is that if W' had been actual, B would have existed in every possible world. That is, if W' had been actual, B's nonexistence would have been impossible. But logical possibilities and impossibilities do not vary from world to world. That is to say, if a given proposition or state of affairs is impossible in at least one possible world, then it is impossible in every possible world. There are no propositions that in fact are possible but could have been impossible; there are none that are in fact impossible but could have been possible.[12] Accordingly, B's nonexistence is impossible in every possible world; hence it is impossible in *this* world; hence B exists and exists necessarily.

VIII. A Flaw in the Ointment

This is an interesting argument, but it suffers from at least one annoying defect. What it shows is that if it is possible that there be a greatest possible being (if the idea of a greatest possible being is coherent) and if that idea includes necessary existence, then in fact there is a being that exists in every world and in *some* world has a degree of greatness that is nowhere excelled. Unfortunately it doesn't follow that the being in question has the degree of greatness in question in Kronos, the actual world. For all the argument shows, this being might *exist* in the actual world but be pretty insignificant here. In some world or other it has maximal greatness; how does this show that it has such greatness in Kronos?

But perhaps we can repair the argument. J. N. Findlay once offered what can only be called an ontological *disproof* of the existence of God.[13] Findlay begins by pointing out that God, if He exists, is an "adequate object of religious worship." But such a being, he says, would have to be a *necessary* being; and, he adds, this idea is incredible "for all who share a contemporary outlook." "Those who believe in necessary truths which aren't merely tautological think that such truths merely connect the *possible* instances of various characteristics with each other; they don't expect such truths to tell them whether there *will* be instances of any characteristics. This is the outcome of the whole medieval and Kantian criticism of the ontological proof."[14] I've argued above that "the whole medieval and Kantian criticism" of Anselm's

---

12. See Plantinga, "World and Essence," *Philosophical Review* 79 (October 1970): 475; and Plantinga, *The Nature of Necessity,* chapter 4, sec. 6.

13. J. N. Findlay, "Can God's Existence Be Disproved?" *Mind* 57 (1948): 176-83. Reprinted in Plantinga (ed.), *The Ontological Argument,* pp. 111-22.

14. J. N. Findlay, "Can God's Existence Be Disproved?" p. 119. Mr. Findlay no longer endorses this sentiment. See the preface to his *Ascent to the Absolute* (1970).

argument may be taken with a grain or two of salt. And certainly most philosophers who believe that there are necessary truths, believe that *some* of them *do* tell us whether there will be instances of certain characteristics; the proposition *there are no married bachelors* is necessarily true, and it tells us that there will be no instances whatever of the characteristic *married bachelor.* Be that as it may, what is presently relevant in Findlay's piece is this passage:

> Not only is it contrary to the demands and claims inherent in religious attitudes that their object should *exist* "accidentally"; it is also contrary to these demands that it should *possess its various excellences* in some merely adventitious manner. It could be quite unsatisfactory from the religious stand point, if an object merely *happened* to be wise, good, powerful, and so forth, even to a superlative degree. . . . And so we are led on irresistibly, by the demands inherent in religious reverence, to hold that an adequate object of our worship must possess its various excellences *in some necessary manner.*[15]

I think there is truth in these remarks. We could put the point as follows. In determining the greatness of a being B in a world W, what counts is not merely the qualities and properties possessed by B *in* W; what B is like in *other* worlds is also relevant. Most of us who believe in God think of Him as a being than whom it's not possible that there be a greater. But we don't think of Him as a being who, had things been different, would have been powerless or uninformed or of dubious moral character. God doesn't *just happen* to be a greatest possible being; He couldn't have been otherwise.

Perhaps we should make a distinction here between *greatness* and *excellence*. A being's excellence in a given world W, let us say, depends only upon the properties it has in W; its *greatness* in W depends upon these properties but also upon what it is like in other worlds. Those who are fond of the calculus might put it by saying that there is a function assigning to each being in each world a degree of excellence; and a being's *greatness* is to be computed (by someone unusually well informed) by integrating its excellence over all possible worlds. Then it is plausible to suppose that the maximal degree of greatness entails *maximal excellence in every world*. A being, then, has the maximal degree of *greatness* in a given world W only if it has *maximal excellence in every possible world*. But *maximal excellence* entails *omniscience, omnipotence,* and *moral perfection*. That is to say, a being B has maximal excellence in a world W only if B would have been omniscient, omnipotent, and morally perfect if W had been actual.

---

15. J. N. Findlay, "Can God's Existence Be Disproved?" p. 117.

IX. The Argument Restated

Given these ideas, we can restate the present version of the argument in the following more explicit way.

(25) It is possible that there be a being that has maximal greatness.

(26) So there is a possible being that in some world W has maximal greatness.

(27) A being has maximal greatness in a given world only if it has maximal excellence in every world.

(28) A being has maximal excellence in a given world only if it has omniscience, omnipotence, and moral perfection in that world.

And now we no longer need the supposition that necessary existence is a perfection; for obviously a being can't be omnipotent (or for that matter omniscient or morally perfect) in a given world unless it *exists* in the world. From (25), (27), and (28) it follows that there actually exists a being that is omnipotent, omniscient, and morally perfect; this being, furthermore, exists and has these qualities in every other world as well. For (26), which follows from (25), tells us that there is a possible world W', let's say, in which there exists a being with maximal greatness. That is, had W' been actual, there would have been a being with maximal greatness. But then according to (27) this being has maximal excellence in every world. What this means, according to (28), is that in W' this being has omniscience, omnipotence, and moral perfection in *every world*. That is to say, if W' had been actual, there would have existed a being who was omniscient and omnipotent and morally perfect and who would have had these properties in every possible world. So if W' had been actual, it would have been *impossible* that there be no omnipotent, omniscient, and morally perfect being. But while *contingent* truths vary from world to world, what is logically impossible does not. Therefore, in every possible world W it is impossible that there be no such being; each possible world W is such that if it had been actual, it would have been impossible that there be no such being. And hence it is impossible in the *actual* world (which is one of the possible worlds) that there be no omniscient, omnipotent, and morally perfect being. Hence there really does exist a being who is omniscient, omnipotent, and morally perfect and who exists and has these properties in every possible world. Accordingly these premises, (25), (27), and (28), entail that God, so thought of, exists. Indeed, if we regard (27) and (28) as consequences of a *definition* — a definition of maximal greatness — then the only premise of the argument is (25).

But now for a last objection suggested earlier. What about (26)? It says that there is a *possible being* having such and such characteristics. But what *are* possible beings? We know what *actual* beings are — the Taj Mahal,

Socrates, you and I, the Grand Teton — these are among the more impressive examples of actually existing beings. But what is a *possible* being? Is there a possible mountain just like Mt. Rainier two miles directly south of the Grand Teton? If so, it is located at the same place as the Middle Teton. Does that matter? Is there another such possible mountain three miles east of the Grand Teton, where Jenny Lake is? Are there possible mountains like this all over the world? Are there also possible oceans at all the places where there are possible mountains? For any place you mention, of course, it is *possible* that there be a mountain there; does it follow that in fact *there is* a possible mountain there?

These are some questions that arise when we ask ourselves whether there are merely possible beings that don't in fact exist. And the version of the ontological argument we've been considering seems to make sense only on the assumption that there are such things. The earlier versions also depended on that assumption; consider, for example, this step of the first version we considered:

(18) So there is a possible being x and a world W' such that the greatness of x in W' exceeds the greatness of God in actuality.

This possible being, you recall, was God Himself, supposed not to exist in the actual world. We can make sense of (18), therefore, only if we are prepared to grant that there are possible beings who don't in fact exist. Such beings exist in other worlds, of course; had things been appropriately different, they would have existed. But in fact they don't exist, although nonetheless there *are* such things.

I am inclined to think the supposition that there are such things — things that are possible but don't in fact exist — is either unintelligible or necessarily false. But this doesn't mean that the present version of the ontological argument must be rejected. For we can restate the argument in a way that does not commit us to this questionable idea. Instead of speaking of *possible beings* that do or do not exist in various possible worlds, we may speak of *properties* and the worlds in which they are or are not *instantiated*. Instead of speaking of the possible fat man in the corner, noting that he doesn't exist, we may speak of the property *being a fat man in the corner,* noting that it isn't instantiated (although it could have been). Of course, the *property* in question, like the property *being a unicorn,* exists. It is a perfectly good property which exists with as much equanimity as the property of equininity, the property of being a horse. But it doesn't happen to apply to anything. That is, in *this* world it doesn't apply to anything; in other possible worlds it does.

X. The Argument Triumphant

Using this idea we can restate this last version of the ontological argument in such a way that it no longer matters whether there are any merely possible beings that do not exist. Instead of speaking of the possible being that has, in some world or other, a maximal degree of greatness, we may speak of *the property of being maximally great* or *maximal greatness*. The premise corresponding to (25) then says simply that maximal greatness is possibly instantiated, i.e., that

> (29) There is a possible world in which maximal greatness is instantiated.

And the analogues of (27) and (28) spell out what is involved in maximal greatness:

> (30) Necessarily, a being is maximally great only if it has maximal excellence in every world

and

> (31) Necessarily, a being has maximal excellence in every world only if it has omniscience, omnipotence, and moral perfection in every world.

Notice that (30) and (31) do not imply that there are possible but nonexistent beings — any more than does, for example,

> (32) Necessarily, a thing is a unicorn only if it has one horn.

But if (29) is true, then there is a possible world W such that if it had been actual, then there would have existed a being that was omnipotent, omniscient, and morally perfect; this being, furthermore, would have had these qualities in every possible world. So it follows that if W had been actual, it would have been *impossible* that there be no such being. That is, if W had been actual,

> (33) There is no omnipotent, omniscient, and morally perfect being

would have been an impossible proposition. But if a proposition is impossible in at least one possible world, then it is impossible in every possible world; what is impossible does not vary from world to world. Accordingly (33) is impossible in the *actual* world, i.e., impossible *simpliciter.* But if it is impossible that there be no such being, then there actually exists a being that is omnipotent, omniscient, and morally perfect; this being, furthermore, has these qualities essentially and exists in every possible world.

What shall we say of this argument? It is certainly valid; given its premise, the conclusion follows. The only question of interest, it seems to me, is whether its main premise — that maximal greatness *is* possibly instantiated — is *true*. I think it *is* true; hence I think this version of the ontological argument is sound.

But here we must be careful; we must ask whether this argument is a successful piece of natural theology, whether it *proves* the existence of God. And the answer must be, I think, that it does not. An argument for God's existence may be *sound,* after all, without in any useful sense proving God's existence.[16] Since I believe in God, I think the following argument is sound:

Either God exists or $7 + 5 = 14$
It is false that $7 + 5 = 14$
Therefore God exists.

But obviously this isn't a *proof;* no one who didn't already accept the conclusion, would accept the first premise. The ontological argument we've been examining isn't just like this one, of course, but it must be conceded that not everyone who understands and reflects on its central premise — that the existence of a maximally great being is *possible* — will accept it. Still, it is evident, I think, that there is nothing *contrary to reason* or *irrational* in accepting this premise.[17] What I claim for this argument, therefore, is that it establishes, not the *truth* of theism, but its rational acceptability. And hence it accomplishes at least one of the aims of the tradition of natural theology.

16. See George Mavrodes, *Belief in God* (New York: Macmillan Co., 1970), pp. 22ff.
17. For more on this see Plantinga, *The Nature of Necessity,* chapter 10, sec. 8.

CHAPTER FOUR

Is Naturalism Irrational?

I. The Problem

Suppose you believe that there really is such a thing as proper function for our cognitive faculties* (or for any natural organs or systems), and suppose you also believe that there is no naturalistic account, reduction, or analysis of the notion of proper function: then you have the materials for a powerful argument against metaphysical naturalism. This is an argument for the *falsehood* of naturalism: if your premises are true, naturalism is false. In this chapter I propose to develop two epistemological arguments against metaphysical naturalism: the main one, however, is not for the falsehood of naturalism, but for the conclusion that it is irrational to accept it. The difference between them is like the difference between arguing, by way of the argument from evil, that theism is *false,* versus arguing, by way of the evidentialist objection to theistic belief, that whether or not theism is true, at any rate it can't be rationally accepted.[1]

Most of us think (or would think on reflection) that at least *a* function or purpose of our cognitive faculties is to provide us with true beliefs. Moreover, we go on to think that when they function properly, in accord with our design plan, then for the most part they do precisely that. Qualifications are necessary, of course. There are various exceptions and special cases: visual illusions, mechanisms like forgetting the pain of childbirth, optimism about recovery not warranted by the relevant statistics, unintended conceptual by-products, and so on. There are also those areas of cognitive endeavor marked

---

*Editor's Note: See chapter 6 below on the notion of proper function. See also *Warrant and Proper Function* (Bibliography #28), from which the current chapter is taken.

1. See my "Reason and Belief in God," chapter 5 below, pp. 103ff.

72

by enormous disagreement, wildly varying opinion: philosophy and Scripture scholarship come to mind. Here the sheer volume of disagreement and the great variety and contrariety of options proposed suggest that either not all of us are such that our cognitive faculties *do* function according to the design plan, in these areas, or that it is not the case that the relevant modules of the design plan are aimed at truth, or that the design plan for those areas is defective.

Nevertheless over a vast area of cognitive terrain we take it both that the purpose (function) of our cognitive faculties is to provide us with true or verisimilitudinous beliefs, and that, for the most part, that is just what they do. We suppose, for example, that most of the deliverances of memory are at least approximately correct. True, if you ask five witnesses how the accident happened, you may get five different stories. Still, they will agree that there was indeed an *accident,* and that it was an *automobile* accident (as opposed, say, to a naval disaster or a volcanic eruption); there will usually be agreement as to the number of vehicles involved (particularly if it is a small number), as well as the rough location of the accident (Aberdeen, Scotland, as opposed to Aberdeen, South Dakota), and so on. And all this is against the background of massive and much deeper agreement: that there are automobiles; that they do not disappear when no one is looking; that if released from a helicopter they fall down rather than up, that they are driven by people who use them to go places, that they are seldom driven by three-year-olds, that their drivers have purposes, hold beliefs, and often act on those purposes and beliefs, that few of them (or their drivers) have been more than a few miles from the surface of the earth, that the world has existed for a good long time — much longer than ten minutes, say — and a million more such Moorean truisms. (Of course, there is the occasional dissenter — in the grip, perhaps, of cognitive malfunction or a cognitively crippling philosophical theory.)

We think our faculties much better adapted to reach the truth in some areas than others; we are good at elementary arithmetic and logic, and the perception of middle-sized objects under ordinary conditions. We are also good at remembering certain sorts of things: I can easily remember what I had for breakfast this morning, where my office was located yesterday, and whether there was a large explosion in my house last night. Things get more difficult, however, when it comes to an accurate reconstruction of what it was like to be, say, a fifth-century B.C. Greek (not to mention a bat), or whether the axiom of choice or the continuum hypothesis is true; things are even more difficult, perhaps, when it comes to figuring out how quantum mechanics is to be understood, and what the subnuclear realm of quark and gluon is really like, if indeed there really is a subnuclear realm of quark and gluon. Still, there remains a vast portion of our cognitive terrain where we think that our cognitive faculties do furnish us with truth.

But isn't there a problem, here, for the naturalist? At any rate for the naturalist who thinks that we and our cognitive capacities arrived upon the scene after some billions of years of evolution (by way of natural selection, genetic drift, and other blind processes working on such sources of genetic variation as random genetic mutation)? Richard Dawkins (according to Peter Medawar, "one of the most brilliant of the rising generation of biologists") once leaned over and remarked to A. J. Ayer at one of those elegant, candle-lit, bibulous Oxford college dinners that he couldn't imagine being an atheist before 1859 (the year Darwin's *Origin of Species* was published); "although atheism might have been logically tenable before Darwin," said he, "Darwin made it possible to be an intellectually fulfilled atheist."[2]

Now Dawkins thinks Darwin made it possible to be an intellectually fulfilled atheist. But perhaps Dawkins is dead wrong here. Perhaps the truth lies in the opposite direction. If our cognitive faculties have originated as Dawkins thinks, then their ultimate purpose or function (if they *have* a purpose or function) will be something like *survival* (of individual, species, gene, or genotype); but then it seems initially doubtful that among their functions — ultimate, proximate, or otherwise — would be the production of true beliefs. Taking up this theme, Patricia Churchland declares that the most important thing about the human brain is that it has evolved; hence, she says, its principal function is to enable the organism to *move* appropriately:

> Boiled down to essentials, a nervous system enables the organism to succeed in the four F's: feeding, fleeing, fighting and reproducing. The principal chore of nervous systems is to get the body parts where they should be in order that the organism may survive. . . . Improvements in sensorimotor control confer an evolutionary advantage: a fancier style of representing is advantageous *so long as it is geared to the organism's way of life and enhances the organism's chances of survival* [Churchland's emphasis]. Truth, whatever that is, definitely takes the hindmost.[3]

Her point, I think, is that (from a naturalistic perspective) what evolution guarantees is (at most) that we *behave* in certain ways — in such ways as to promote survival, or survival through childbearing age. The principal function or purpose, then, (the "chore" says Churchland) of our cognitive faculties is not that of producing true or verisimilitudinous beliefs, but instead that of contributing to survival by getting the body parts in the right place. What evolution underwrites is only (at most) that our *behavior* be reasonably adaptive to the circumstances in which our ancestors found themselves; hence (so far forth) it does not guarantee mostly true or verisimilitudinous beliefs. Of

2. *The Blind Watchmaker* (New York: Norton, 1986), pp. 6, 7.
3. *Journal of Philosophy* 84 (October 1987), p. 548.

course our beliefs *might* be mostly true or verisimilitudinous (hereafter I'll omit the "verisimilitudinous"); but there is no particular reason to think they *would* be: natural selection is interested not in truth, but in appropriate behavior. What Churchland says suggests, therefore, that naturalistic evolution — that is, the conjunction of metaphysical naturalism with the view that we and our cognitive faculties have arisen by way of the mechanisms and processes proposed by contemporary evolutionary theory — gives us reason to doubt two things: (a) that a *purpose* of our cognitive systems is that of serving us with true beliefs, and (b) that they *do,* in fact, furnish us with mostly true beliefs.

W. V. O. Quine and Karl Popper, however, apparently demur. Popper argues that since we have evolved and survived, we may be pretty sure that our hypotheses and guesses as to what the world is like are mostly correct.[4] And Quine says he finds encouragement in Darwin:

> What does make clear sense is this other part of the problem of induction: why does our innate subjective spacing of qualities accord so well with the functionally relevant groupings in nature as to make our inductions tend to come out right? Why should our subjective spacing of qualities have a special purchase on nature and a lien on the future?
>
> There is some encouragement in Darwin. If people's innate spacing of qualities is a gene-linked trait, then the spacing that has made for the most successful inductions will have tended to predominate through natural selection. Creatures inveterately wrong in their inductions have a pathetic but praiseworthy tendency to die before reproducing their kind.[5]

Indeed, Quine finds a great deal more encouragement in Darwin than Darwin did: "With me," says Darwin,

> the horrid doubt always arises whether the convictions of man's mind, which has been developed from the mind of the lower animals, are of any value or at all trustworthy. Would any one trust in the convictions of a monkey's mind, if there are any convictions in such a mind?[6]

So here we appear to have Quine and Popper on one side and Darwin and Churchland on the other. Who is right? But a prior question: what, precisely, is the issue? Darwin and Churchland seem to believe that (natural-

---

4. *Objective Knowledge: An Evolutionary Approach* (Oxford: Clarendon Press, 1972), p. 261.

5. "Natural Kinds," in *Ontological Relativity and Other Essays* (New York: Columbia University Press, 1969), p. 126.

6. Letter to William Graham Down, July 3, 1881, in *The Life and Letters of Charles Darwin Including an Autobiographical Chapter,* ed. Francis Darwin (London: John Murray, Albermarle Street, 1887), 1: 315-16.

istic) evolution gives one a reason to doubt that human cognitive faculties produce for the most part true beliefs: call this "Darwin's Doubt." Quine and Popper, on the other hand, apparently hold that evolution gives us reason to believe the opposite: that human cognitive faculties *do* produce for the most part true beliefs. How shall we understand this opposition?

II. Darwin's Doubt

One possibility: perhaps Darwin and Churchland mean to propose that a certain objective conditional probability is relatively low: the probability of human cognitive faculties' being reliable (producing mostly true beliefs), given that human beings *have* cognitive faculties (of the sort we have) and given that these faculties have been produced by evolution (Darwin's blind evolution, unguided by the hand of God or any other person). If metaphysical naturalism and this evolutionary account are both true, then our cognitive faculties will have resulted from blind mechanisms like natural selection, working on such sources of genetic variation as random genetic mutation. Evolution is interested, not in true belief, but in survival or fitness. It is therefore unlikely that our cognitive faculties have the production of true belief as a proximate or any other function, and the probability of our faculties' being reliable (given naturalistic evolution) would be fairly low. Popper and Quine, on the other side, judge that probability fairly high.

The issue, then, is the value of a certain conditional probability: $P(R/(N\&E\&C))$.[7] Here N is metaphysical naturalism. It isn't easy to say precisely what naturalism *is,* but perhaps that isn't necessary in this context; prominent examples would be the views of (say) David Armstrong, the later Darwin, Quine, and Bertrand Russell. (Crucial to metaphysical naturalism, of course, is the view that there is no such person as the God of traditional theism.) E is the proposition that human cognitive faculties arose by way of the mechanisms to which contemporary evolutionary thought directs our attention; and C is a complex proposition whose precise formulation is both difficult and unnecessary, but which states what cognitive faculties we have — memory, perception, reason, Reid's sympathy — and what sorts of beliefs they produce. R, on the other hand, is the claim that our cognitive faculties are reliable (on the whole, and with the qualifications mentioned), in the sense

---

7. We could think of this probability in two ways: as a conditional *epistemic* probability, or as a conditional *objective* probability. Either will serve for my argument, but I should think the better way to think of it would be as an objective probability; for in this sort of context epistemic probability, presumably, should follow known (or conjectured) objective probability.

that they produce mostly true beliefs in the sorts of environments that are normal for them. And the question is: what is the probability of R on N&E&C? (Alternatively, perhaps the interest of *that* question lies in its bearing on *this* question: what is the probability that a belief produced by human cognitive faculties is *true,* given N&E&C?) And if we construe the dispute in this way, then what Darwin and Churchland propose is that this probability is relatively low, whereas Quine and Popper think it fairly high.

A. Stich versus Pangloss

Well, what sorts of considerations would be relevant to this question? Consider the sort of argument implicit in the passage from Quine: "Creatures inveterately wrong in their inductions have a pathetic but praiseworthy tendency to die before reproducing their kind," he says; humankind, happily enough, has not died before reproducing its kind; so probably we human beings are not inveterately wrong in our inductions. This claim is specified to inductions, of course; but presumably the same would go for some or all of our other characteristic beliefs. (According to J. Fodor, "Darwinian selection guarantees that organisms either know the elements of logic or become posthumous."[8]) The claim seems to be that the selection processes involved in evolution are likely to produce cognitive faculties that are reliable, given that they produce cognitive faculties at all.

Stephen Stich attempts to set out the argument implicit in Quine's and Popper's brief and cryptic remarks. (He notes that versions of this argument circulate widely in the oral tradition, but are seldom if ever developed in any detail.) As he sees it, this argument essentially involves two premises: (a) that "evolution produces organisms with good approximations to optimally well-designed characteristics or systems,"[9] and (b) that "an optimally well-designed cognitive system is a rational cognitive system," where (on one of the two understandings of 'rational' he considers) a *rational* cognitive system, in turn, is a *reliable* cognitive system, one that produces a preponderance of true beliefs. Stich proposes "to make it clear that there are major problems to be overcome by those who think that evolutionary considerations impose interesting limits on irrationality";[10] what he shows, I think, is that the denials of (a) and (b) are wholly compatible with contemporary evolutionary theory, and not implausible with respect to it.

8. "Three Cheers for Propositional Attitudes," in *Representations* (Cambridge, Mass.: MIT Press, 1981), p. 121.

9. Here I assume that (a) is to be understood as "evolution *always* or *nearly always* produces organisms with good approximations."

10. *The Fragmentation of Reason* (Cambridge, Mass.: MIT Press, 1990), p. 56.

By way of attack on (a) he points out that natural selection is not the only process at work in evolution; there is also (among others) random genetic drift, which "can lead to the elimination of a more fit gene and the fixation of a less fit one." For example, a genetically based and adaptively favorable trait might arise within a population of sea gulls; perhaps six members of the flock enjoy it. Being birds of a feather, they flock together — sadly enough, at the site of a natural disaster, so that all are killed in a tidal wave or volcanic eruption or by a large meteorite. The more fit gene thus gets eliminated from the population. (There is also the way in which a gene can be fixed, in a small population, by way of random walk.) He points out further, with respect to (a), that there is no reason to think it inevitable that natural selection will have the *opportunity* to select for optimal design. For example, an adaptively positive trait might be linked with an adaptively negative trait by pleiotropy (where one gene codes for more than one trait or system); then it could happen that the gene gets selected and perpetuated by virtue of its link with the positive trait, and the negative trait gets perpetuated by way of its link with the gene. A truly optimal system — one with the positive trait but without the negative — may never show up, or may show up too late to fit in with the current development of the organism.[11]

With respect to (b), the claim that an optimally designed cognitive system is rational (that is, reliable), Stich observes, first, that optimal design, presumably, is to be understood in terms of fitness: "From the point of view of natural selection, it is plausible to say that one system is better designed than a second if an organism having the first would be more fit — that is, more likely to survive and reproduce successfully — than a conspecific having the second. A system is optimally well designed if it enhances biological fitness more than any alternative" (p. 57). He then argues that reliable cognitive systems are not necessarily more fitness-enhancing than unreliable ones; it is not the case, he argues, that for any two cognitive systems S_1 and S_2, if S_1 is more reliable than S_2, than S_1 is more fitness-enhancing than S_2. S_1, for example, might cost too much by way of energy or memory capacity; alternatively, the less reliable S_2 might produce more by way of false beliefs but nonetheless contribute more to survival.[12]

---

11. *The Fragmentation of Reason,* p. 64. He also makes more fanciful suggestions as to how it is that natural selection may never get to select for truly optimal systems: "Modern technology builds prosthetic limbs out of space-age alloys and communications systems that transmit messages with the speed of light. It seems very likely indeed that certain organisms would have a real competitive edge if they were born with such limbs, or with nerves that conduct impulses at the speed of light. The fact that there are no such creatures surely does not indicate that the imagined changes would not enhance fitness. Rather, we can be pretty confident natural selection never had the chance to evaluate organisms that utilize such materials" (p. 65).

12. "A very cautious, risk-aversive inferential strategy — one that leaps to the conclusion that danger is present on very slight evidence — will typically lead to false beliefs more often,

So Stich's point is this: as far as contemporary evolutionary theory is concerned, there is little reason to endorse either (a) or (b). But has he correctly identified the conclusions (or the premises) of those he sets out to refute?[13] "We now have a pair of arguments," he says, "for the claim that evolution and natural selection *guarantee* at least a close approximation to full rationality in normal organisms, ourselves included" (p. 59, my emphasis) and "An essential component in both arguments, aimed at showing that evolution will *insure* rationality, is . . ." (p. 63, my emphasis). If his aim is to cast doubt on these arguments, taken as arguments for the claim that evolution and natural selection *guarantee* or *insure* rationality, then he has certainly fulfilled his aim. But perhaps Quine and Popper and their allies do not mean to argue anything quite so strong. Perhaps what they mean to argue is only that it is fairly or highly *probable,* given that we and our cognitive faculties have evolved according to the processes endorsed by contemporary evolutionary theory, that those faculties are reliable; perhaps they mean to argue only that $P(R/(N\&E\&C))$ is fairly high. What Stich shows is that it is perfectly possible both that we and our cognitive faculties have evolved in the ways approved by current evolutionary theory, and that those cognitive faculties are not reliable. But that does not address Quine's argument taken as an implicit argument for the claim that $P(R/(N\&E\&C))$ is fairly high, and *a fortiori* it does not serve as an argument for Darwin's Doubt, that is, for the claim that $P(R/(N\&E\&C))$ is fairly low.

B. The Doubt Developed

Can we assemble an argument for Darwin's Doubt from (among other things) the materials Stich presents? In order to avoid irrelevant distractions, suppose we think, first, not about ourselves and our ancestors, but about a hypothetical population of creatures a lot like ourselves on a planet similar to Earth. (Darwin proposed that we think about another species, such as monkeys.) Suppose these

---

and true ones less often, than a less hair-trigger one that waits for more evidence before rendering a judgment. Nonetheless, the unreliable, error-prone, risk-aversive strategy may well be favored by natural selection. For natural selection does not care about truth; it cares only about reproductive success" (p. 62). The point seems correct, but its relevance is not wholly obvious. The claim he proposes to refute is that an optimally fit system would also be reliable (and maybe even optimally reliable); but this claim is compatible with the existence of a pair of systems one of which is both more fitness-enhancing but less reliable than the other. By way of analogy, consider the ontological argument: maximal greatness, no doubt, would require, say, maximal excellence with respect to knowledge; but it does not follow that if x is greater than y, then x is more excellent with respect to knowledge than y.

13. Of course, it would be easy to misunderstand the arguments of those he tries to refute, given their authors' reluctance to state them explicitly.

creatures have cognitive faculties, hold beliefs, change beliefs, make inferences, and so on; and suppose these creatures have arisen by way of the selection processes endorsed by contemporary evolutionary thought. What is the probability that their faculties are reliable? What is $P(R/(N\&E\&C))$, specified not to us, but to them? According to Quine and Popper, the probability in question would be rather high: belief is connected with action in such a way that extensive false belief would lead to maladaptive behavior, in which case it is likely that the ancestors of those creatures would have displayed that pathetic but praiseworthy tendency Quine mentions.

But now for the contrary argument. First, perhaps it is likely that their *behavior* is adaptive; but nothing follows about their *beliefs*. We aren't given, after all, that their beliefs are so much as causally connected with their behavior; for we aren't given that their beliefs are more than mere epiphenomena, not causally involved with behavior at all. Perhaps their beliefs neither figure into the causes of their behavior, nor are caused by that behavior. (No doubt beliefs would be caused by *something* in or about these creatures, but it need not be by their behavior.) You may object that as *you* use 'belief,' beliefs just *are* among the processes (neural structures, perhaps) that (together with desire, fear, and the like) *are* causally efficacious. Fair enough (you have a right to use that word as you please); but then my point can be put as follows: in *that* use of 'belief' it may be that things with propositional contents are not beliefs, that is, do not have causal efficacy. It can't be a matter of definition that there are neural structures or processes displaying both propositional content and causal efficacy with respect to behavior; and perhaps the things that display causal efficacy do not display the sort of relation to content (to a proposition) that a belief of the proposition p must display toward p. You say that in that case the things, if any, that stand in that relation to a proposition would not be beliefs (because, as you see it, beliefs must have causal efficacy). Well, there is no sense in arguing about words: I'll give you the term 'belief' and put my case using other terms. What I say is possible is that the things (mental acts, perhaps) that stand in that relation to content (to propositions) do not also enjoy causal efficacy. Call those things whatever you like: *they* are the things that are true or false, and it is about the likelihood of *their* truth or falsehood that we are asking. If these things, whatever we call them, are not causally connected with behavior, then they would be, so to speak, *invisible* to evolution; and then the fact that they arose during the evolutionary history of these beings would confer no probability on the idea that they are mostly true, or mostly nearly true, rather than wildly false. Indeed, the probability of their being for the most part true would have to be estimated as fairly low.

A second possibility is that the beliefs of these creatures are not among the *causes* of their behavior, but are *effects* of that behavior, or effects of proximate causes that also cause behavior. Their beliefs might be like a sort of decoration that isn't involved in the causal chain leading to action. Their waking beliefs might be no more causally efficacious, with respect to their behavior, than our dream beliefs are with respect to ours. This could go by way of pleiotropy: genes that code for traits important to survival also code for consciousness and belief; but the latter don't figure into the etiology of action. Under these conditions, of course, their beliefs could be wildly false. It *could* be that one of these creatures believes that he is at that elegant, bibulous Oxford dinner, when in fact he is slogging his way through some primeval swamp, desperately fighting off hungry crocodiles. Under this possibility as under the first, the probability that their cognitive faculties are reliable, is low.

A third possibility is that beliefs do indeed have causal efficacy with respect to behavior, but not by virtue of their *content;* to put it in currently fashionable jargon, this would be the suggestion that while beliefs are causally efficacious, it is only by virtue of their *syntax,* not by virtue of their *semantics.* Indeed just this thesis is part of a popular contemporary view: the computational theory of mind.[14] I read a poem very loudly, so loudly as to break a glass;[15] the sounds I utter have meaning, but their meaning is causally irrelevant to the breaking of the glass. In the same way it might be that these creatures' beliefs have causal efficacy, but not by way of the content of those beliefs. A substantial share of probability must be reserved for this option; and under this option, as under the preceding two, the likelihood that the beliefs of these creatures would be for the most part true would be low.

A fourth possibility: it could be that belief is causally efficacious — 'semantically' as well as 'syntactically' — with respect to behavior, but *maladaptive.* As Stich points out, it is quite possible (and quite in accord with current evolutionary theory) that a system or trait that is in fact maladaptive — at any rate less adaptive than available alternatives — should nonetheless become fixed and survive. Perhaps the belief systems of these creatures are like the albinism found in many arctic animals, or like sickle-cell anemia:

14. See, for example, J. Fodor's "Methodological Solipsism Considered as a Research Strategy in Cognitive Psychology," *Behavioral and Brain Sciences* (1980), p. 68; see Stephen Stich's *From Folk Psychology to Cognitive Science* (Cambridge: MIT Press, 1983), chapter 8 and elsewhere. See also P. Churchland, "Eliminative Materialism and Propositional Attitudes," *Journal of Philosophy* 78 (1981); Fred Dretske, *Knowledge and the Flow of Information* (Cambridge: MIT Press, 1981); J. Fodor, *Psychosemantics* (Cambridge: MIT Press, 1987); B. Loar, *Mind and Meaning* (Cambridge: Cambridge University Press, 1981); and Z. Pylyshyn, *Computation and Cognition* (Cambridge: MIT Press, 1984). Robert Cummins goes so far as to call this view — the view that representations have causal efficacy only with respect to their syntax, not with respect to their semantics or content — the 'received view,' in *Meaning and Mental Representation* (Cambridge: MIT Press, 1989), p. 130. In *Explaining Behavior* (Cambridge: MIT Press, 1988), Fred Dretske takes as his main project that of explaining how it could be that beliefs (and other representations) play a causal role by virtue of their contents.

15. The example is Dretske's.

maladaptive, but connected with genes coding for behavior or traits conducive to survival. They could be maladaptive in two ways. First, perhaps their beliefs are a sort of energy-expensive distraction, causing these creatures to engage in survival-enhancing behavior, all right, but in a way less efficient and economic than if the causal connections by-passed belief altogether. Second, it could be that beliefs in fact produce maladaptive behavior. Perhaps a mildly maladaptive belief-behavior structure is coded for by the same genetic structure that produces some adaptive behavior. Suppose these creatures' beliefs do not for the most part produce adaptive behavior: the mechanisms that produce them might nonetheless survive. Perhaps on balance their behavior is sufficiently adaptive, even if not every segment of it is. Some probability, then, must be reserved for the possibility that these creatures have cognitive faculties that are maladaptive, but nonetheless survive; and on this possibility, once more, the probability that their beliefs would be for the most part true is fairly low.

A fifth (and final) possibility is that the beliefs of our hypothetical creatures are indeed both causally connected with their behavior and also adaptive. Assume, then, that our creatures have belief systems, and that these systems are adaptive: they produce adaptive behavior, and at not too great a cost in terms of resources. What is the probability (on this assumption together with N&E&C) that their cognitive faculties are reliable; and what is the probability that a belief produced by those faculties will be true?

Not as high as you might think. For, of course, beliefs don't causally produce behavior *by themselves;* it is beliefs, desires, and other things that do so together. Suppose we oversimplify a bit and say that my behavior is a causal product just of my beliefs and desires. Then the problem is that clearly there will be any number of *different* patterns of belief and desire that would issue in the same action; and among those there will be many in which the beliefs are wildly false. Paul is a prehistoric hominid; the exigencies of survival call for him to display tiger-avoidance behavior. There will be many behaviors that are appropriate: fleeing, for example, or climbing a steep rock face, or crawling into a hole too small to admit the tiger, or leaping into a handy lake. Pick any such appropriate specific behavior B. Paul engages in B, we think, because, sensible fellow that he is, he has an aversion to being eaten and believes that B is a good means of thwarting the tiger's intentions.

But clearly this avoidance behavior could be a result of a thousand other belief-desire combinations: indefinitely many other belief-desire systems fit B equally well. (Here let me ignore the complication arising from the fact that belief comes in degrees.) Perhaps Paul very much *likes* the idea of being eaten, but whenever he sees a tiger, always runs off looking for a better prospect because he thinks it unlikely that the tiger he sees will eat him. This will get his body parts in the right place so far as survival is concerned, without involving much by way of true belief. (Of course we must postulate other changes in Paul's ways of reasoning, including how he changes belief in response to experience, to maintain coherence.) Or perhaps he thinks the tiger is a large, friendly, cuddly pussycat and wants to pet it; but he also believes that the best way to pet it is to run away from it. Or perhaps he confuses running *toward* it with running *away* from it, believing of the action that is really running away from it, that it is running toward it; or perhaps he thinks the tiger is a regularly recurring illusion, and, hoping to keep his weight down, has formed the resolution to run a mile at top speed whenever presented with such an illusion; or perhaps he thinks he is about to take part in a sixteen-hundred-meter race, wants to win, and believes the appearance of the tiger is the starting signal; or perhaps. . . . Clearly there are any number or belief-cum-desire systems that equally fit a given bit of behavior where the beliefs are mostly false. Indeed, even if we fix desire, there will still be any number of systems of belief that will produce a given bit of behavior: perhaps Paul does not want to be eaten, but (a) thinks the best way to avoid being eaten is to run toward the tiger, and (b) mistakenly believes that he is running toward it when in fact he is running away.

But these possibilities are wholly preposterous, you say. Following Richard Grandy, you point out that when we ascribe systems of belief and desire to persons, we make use of "principles of humanity," whereby we see others as resembling what we take ourselves to be.[16] You go on to endorse David Lewis's suggestion that a theory of content requires these "principles of humanity" in order to rule out as "deeply irrational" those nonstandard belief-desire systems; the contents involved are "unthinkable," and are hence disqualified as candidates for someone's belief-desire structure.[17] Surely you (and Grandy and Lewis) are right: in ascribing beliefs to others, we *do* think of them as like what we think we are. (This involves, among other things, thinking that the purpose or function of their cognitive systems, like that of ours, is the production of true beliefs.) And a theory of content ascription does indeed require more than just the claim that the content of my beliefs must fit my behavior and desires: that leaves entirely too much latitude as to what that content, on a given occasion, might in fact be. These principles of humanity will exclude vast hordes of logically possible belief-desire systems as systems (given human limitations) no human being *could* have; thus such principles will exclude my attributing logical omniscience (or probabilistic coherence) to Paul, or even a system involving the *de re* belief, with respect to each real number in the (open) unit interval, that it is indeed

16. "Reference, Meaning and Belief," *Journal of Philosophy* 70 (1973): 443ff.
17. *On the Plurality of Worlds* (Oxford: Basil Blackwell, 1986), pp. 38ff., 107-8.

greater than 0. These principles will also exclude some systems as systems we think no properly functioning human being *would* have: accordingly, I will not attribute to Paul the view that emeralds are blue, or the belief that it would be good to have a nice saucer of mud for lunch (Elizabeth Anscombe, *Intention,* sec. 38).

These points are quite correct; but they do not bear on the present question. It is true that a decent theory of content ascription must require more than that the belief fit the behavior; for a decent theory of content ascription must also respect or take for granted what we ordinarily think about our desires, beliefs, and circumstances, and the relations between these items. But in the case of our hypothetical population, these "principles of humanity" are not relevant. For we are not given that its members are human; more important, we are not given that those principles of humanity, those commonsense beliefs about how their behavior, belief, and desire are related, are true of them. We can't assume that their beliefs, for given circumstances, would be similar to what we take it *we* would believe in those circumstances. We must ask what sorts of belief-desire systems are *possible* for these creatures, given only that they have evolved according to the principles of contemporary evolutionary theory; clearly these gerrymanders are perfectly possible. So perhaps their behavior has been adaptive, and their systems of belief and desire such as to fit that adaptive behavior; those beliefs could nonetheless be wildly wrong. There are indefinitely many belief-desire systems that fit adaptive behavior, but where the beliefs involved are not for the most part true. A share of probability has to be reserved for these possibilities as well.

Our question was this: given our hypothetical population along with N&E&C, what is the probability that the cognitive systems of beliefs these creatures display are reliable? Suppose we briefly review. First, on the condition in question, there is some probability that their beliefs are not causally connected with behavior at all. It would be reasonable to suppose, on that condition, that the probability of a given belief's being true would not be far from $\frac{1}{2}$, and hence reasonable to suppose that the probability that their cognitive faculties are reliable (produce a substantial preponderance of verisimilitudinous beliefs) is very low. Second, there is some probability that their beliefs are causally connected with behavior, but only as epiphenomenal effect of causes that also cause behavior; in that case too it would be reasonable to suppose that the probability of their cognitive systems' being reliable is very low. Third, there is the possibility that belief is only 'syntactically,' not 'semantically,' connected with behavior; on this possibility, too, there would be a low probability that their cognitive faculties are reliable. Fourth, there is the possibility that their beliefs are causally connected ('semantically' as well as 'syntactically') with their behavior, but maladaptive; again, in this case it would be reasonable to suppose that the probability of R is low. Fifth, there is also some probability that their beliefs are causally connected with their behavior, and are adaptive; as we saw, however, there are indefinitely many belief-desire systems that would yield adaptive behavior, but are unreliable. Here one does not quite know what to say about the probability that their cognitive systems would produce mainly true beliefs, but perhaps it would be reasonable to estimate it as somewhat more than $1/2$.[18] These possibilities are mutually exclusive and jointly exhaustive; if we had definite probabilities for each of the five cases and definite probabilities for R on each of them, then the probability of R would be the weighted average of the probabilities for R on each of those possibilities — weighted by the probabilities of those possibilities. (Of course we don't have definite probabilities here, but only vague estimates; it imparts a spurious appearance of precision to so much as mention the relevant formula.)

Trying to combine these probabilities in an appropriate way, then, it would be reasonable to suppose that the probability of R, of these creatures' cognitive systems being reliable, is relatively low, somewhat less than $1/2$. More exactly, a reasonable posture would be to think it very unlikely that the statistical probability of their belief-producing mechanisms' being reliable, given that they have been produced in the suggested way, is very high; and rather likely that (on N&E&C) R is less probable than its denial.

Now return to Darwin's Doubt. The reasoning that applies to these hypothetical creatures, of course, also applies to *us;* so if we think the probability of R with respect to *them* is relatively low on N&E&C, we should think the same thing about the probability of R with respect to *us.* Something like this reasoning, perhaps, is what underlay Darwin's doubt — although Darwin did not have the benefit of pleiotropy, random genetic drift, gene fixation by random walk, and the other bells and whistles that adorn current evolutionary theory. So taken, his claim is that $P(R/(N\&E\&C))$ (specified to us) is rather low, perhaps somewhat less than $1/2$. Arguments of this sort are less than coercive; but it would be perfectly sensible to estimate these probabilities in this way.

---

18. Of course it might be, with respect to this fifth case, that the relevant probabilities differ with respect to different cognitive faculties. Perhaps the probabilities are highest with respect to, say, perception and other sources of belief coming into play in situations crucial to survival; perhaps the probabilities are considerably lower with respect to the sorts of intellectual pursuits favored by people past their reproductive prime: such pursuits as philosophy, literary criticism, set theory, and evolutionary biology. See pp. 90ff.

III. A Preliminary Argument against Naturalism

Suppose you do estimate these probabilities in roughly this way: suppose you concur in Darwin's Doubt, taking $P(R/(N\&E\&C))$ to be fairly low. But suppose you also think, as most of us do, that in fact our cognitive faculties *are* reliable (with the qualifications and nuances introduced previously). Then you have a straightforward probabilistic argument against naturalism — and for traditional theism, if you think these two the significant alternatives. According to Bayes's Theorem,

$$P((N\&E\&C)/R) = \frac{(P(N\&E\&C) \times P(R/(N\&E\&C))}{P(R)}$$

where $P(N\&E\&C)$ is your estimate of the probability for $N\&E\&C$ independent of the consideration of R. You believe R, so you assign it a probability near 1 and you take $P(R/(N\&E\&C))$ to be no more than $\frac{1}{2}$. Then $P((N\&E\&C)/R)$ will be no greater than $\frac{1}{2}$ times $P(N\&E\&C)$, and will thus be fairly low. You believe C (the proposition specifying the sorts of cognitive faculties we have); so you assign it a very high probability; accordingly $P((N\&E)/R)$ will also be low. No doubt you will also assign a very high probability to the conditional *if naturalism is true, then our faculties have arisen by way of evolution;* then you will judge that $P(N/R)$ is also low. But you do think R is true; you therefore have evidence against N. So your belief that our cognitive faculties are reliable gives you a reason for rejecting naturalism and accepting its denial.

The same argument will not hold, of course, for traditional theism; on that view the probability that our cognitive faculties are reliable will be much higher than $\frac{1}{2}$; for, according to traditional (Jewish, Christian, Moslem) theism, God created us in his image, a part of which involves our having knowledge over a wide range of topics and areas.[19] So (provided that for you the prior probabilities of traditional theism and naturalism are comparable) P(traditional theism/R) will be considerably greater than P(N/R).

---

19. Thus, for example, Thomas Aquinas:

Since human beings are said to be in the image of God in virtue of their having a nature that includes an intellect, such a nature is most in the image of God in virtue of being most able to imitate God. (*Summa Theologiae,* Ia, q. 93, a. 4)

Only in rational creatures is there found a likeness of God which counts as an image. . . . As far as a likeness of the divine nature is concerned, rational creatures seem somehow to attain a representation of [that] type in virtue of imitating God not only in this, that he is and lives, but especially in this, that he understands. (*Summa Theologiae,* Ia, q. 93 a. 6)

IV. The Main Argument against Naturalism

A. *The Doubt Developed Again*

Still, the argument for a low estimate of $P(R/(N\&E\&C))$ is by no means irresistible. In particular, our estimates of the various probabilities involved in estimating $P(R/(N\&E\&C))$ with respect to that hypothetical population were (of necessity) both extremely imprecise and also poorly grounded. You might reasonably hold, therefore, that the right course here is simple agnosticism: one just does not know (and has no good way of finding out) *what* $(P/R(N\&E\&C))$ might be. It could be very low; on the other hand it could be rather high. With our limited cognitive resources, you say, the proper course is to hold no view about what that probability might be; the proper course is agnosticism. This also seems sensible; accordingly, let's suppose, for the moment, that the proper course *is* agnosticism about that probability. What would then be the appropriate attitude toward R (specified to that hypothetical population)? Someone who accepts N&E and also believes that the proper attitude toward $P(R/(N\&E\&C))$ is one of agnosticism clearly enough has good reason for being agnostic about R as well. She has no other source of information about R (for that population); but the source of information she does have gives her no reason to believe R and no reason to disbelieve it. The proposition in question is the sort of which one needs evidence if one is to believe it reasonably; since there is no evidence the reasonable course is to withhold belief.

But now suppose we again apply the same sort of reasoning to ourselves and our condition. Suppose we think N&E is true: we ourselves have evolved according to the mechanisms suggested by contemporary evolutionary theory, unguided and unorchestrated by God or anyone else. Suppose we think, furthermore, that there is no way to determine $P(R/(N\&E\&C))$ (specified to us). What would be the right attitude to take to R? Well, if we have no further information, then wouldn't the right attitude here, just as with respect to that hypothetical population, be agnosticism, withholding belief?

Compare the case of a believer in God, who, perhaps through an injudicious reading of Freud, comes to think that religious belief generally and theistic belief in particular is almost always produced by wish fulfillment. Such beliefs, she now thinks, are not produced by cognitive faculties functioning properly in a congenial environment according to a design plan successfully aimed at truth; instead they are produced by wish fulfillment, which, while indeed it has a function, does not have the function of producing true beliefs. Suppose she considers the objective probability that wish fulfillment, as a belief-producing mechanism, is reliable. She might quite properly estimate this probability as relatively low; alternatively, however, she might think the right course, here, is agnosticism; and she might also be equally agnostic about the probability that a belief should be true, given that it is produced by wish fulfillment. But then in either case she has a defeater for any belief she takes to be produced by the mechanism in question. Consider the first case: she thinks the probability that wish fulfillment is reliable is low, and the probability that a belief should be true, given that it is produced by wish fulfillment, not far from $\frac{1}{2}$. Then she has a straightforward defeater for any of her beliefs she takes to be produced by wish fulfillment. Her situation is like that of the person who comes into a factory, sees an assembly line carrying apparently red widgets, and is then told by the shop superintendent that these widgets are being irradiated by a variety of red light, which makes it possible to detect otherwise undetectable hairline cracks. She should take it that the probability that a widget is red, given that it looks red, is fairly low; and she then has a reason, with respect to any particular widget coming down the line, to doubt that it is red, despite the fact that it looks red. To use John Pollock's terminology (and since I am already filching his example, why not?), she has an *undercutting* defeater (rather than a *rebutting* defeater). It isn't that she has acquired some evidence for that widget's being nonred, thus rebutting the belief that it is red; it is rather that her grounds for thinking it red have been undercut. And, indeed, upon hearing (and believing) that the widgets are being thus irradiated, she will probably no longer believe that the widget in question is red.

Consider, on the other hand, a second kind of case: here she does not come to believe that the probability of a widget's being red, given that it looks red, is low; instead, she is agnostic about that probability. As before, the shop superintendent tells her that those widgets are being irradiated by red light; but then a vice-president comes along and tells her that the shop superintendent suffers from a highly resilient but fortunately specific hallucination, so that he is reliable on other topics even if totally unreliable on red lights and widgets. Still, the vice president *himself* doesn't look wholly reliable: there is a certain shiftiness about the eyes. . . .

Then she doesn't know *what* to believe about those alleged red lights. What will she properly think about the color of the widgets? She will presumably be agnostic about the probability of a widget's being red, given that it looks red; she won't know what that probability might be; for all she knows it could be very low, but also, for all she knows, it could be high. The rational course for her, therefore, is to be agnostic about the deliverances of her visual perception (so far as color detection is concerned) in this situation. But then she also has a good reason for being equally agnostic about the proposition *a is red,* where *a* is any of those red-appearing widgets coming down the assembly line. She has an undercutting defeater for the proposition *a is red;*

this defeater gives her a reason to be agnostic with respect to that proposition. If she has no defeater for that defeater, and no further evidence for the proposition, then on balance the right attitude for her to take toward it would be agnosticism.

By parity of reason, the same goes, I should think, for the believer in God of a couple of paragraphs back. She too has an undercutting defeater for belief in God; if that defeater remains itself undefeated and if she has no other source of evidence, then the rational course would be to reject belief in God. That is not to say, of course, that she would in fact be *able* to do so; but it remains the rational course.

But now suppose we return to the person convinced of N&E who is agnostic about P(R/(N&E&C)): something similar goes for him. He is in the same position with respect to any belief B of his, as is that believer in God. He is in the same condition, with respect to B, as the widget observer who didn't know what or who to believe about those red lights. So he too has a defeater for B, and a good reason for being agnostic with respect to it. If he has no defeater for that defeater, and no other source of evidence, the right attitude toward B would be agnosticism. That is not to say that he would in fact be able to reject B. Due to that animal faith noted by Hume, Reid, and Santayana (but so-called only by the last-named), chances are he would not; still, agnosticism is what reason requires. Here, then, we have another way of developing Darwin's Doubt, a way that does not depend upon estimating P(R/(N&E&C)) as low, but requires instead only agnosticism about that probability.

B. The Argument

By way of brief review: Darwin's Doubt can be taken as the claim that the probability of R on N&E&C is fairly low; as I argued, that is plausible. But Darwin's Doubt can also be taken as the claim that the rational attitude to take, here, is agnosticism about that probability; that is more plausible. Still more plausible is the disjunction of these two claims: either the rational attitude to take toward this probability is the judgment that it is low, or the rational attitude is agnosticism with respect to it. But then the devotee of N&E has a defeater for any belief B he holds. Now the next thing to note is that B *might be N&E itself;* our devotee of N&E has an undercutting defeater for N&E, a reason to doubt it, a reason to be agnostic with respect to it. (This also holds if he isn't agnostic about P(R/(N&E&C)) but thinks it low, as in the preliminary argument; he has a defeater either way.) If he has no defeater for this defeater and not independent evidence — if his reason for doubting N&E remains defeated — then the rational course would be to reject belief in N&E.

And here we must note something special about N&E. So far, we have been lumping together all of our cognitive faculties, all of our sources of belief, and all the sorts of beliefs they produce. But perhaps these different sorts of faculties should be treated differentially; clearly the argument can be narrowed down to specific faculties or powers or belief-producing mechanisms, with possibly different results for different cases. And surely the argument does apply more plausibly to some cognitive powers than to others. If there are such differences among those faculties or powers, presumably *perception* and *memory* would be at an advantage as compared with the cognitive mechanisms whereby we come to such beliefs as, say, that arithmetic is incomplete and the continuum hypothesis is independent of ordinary set theory. For even if we evaluated the probabilities differently from the way I suggested, even if we thought it likely, on balance, that evolution would select for reliable cognitive faculties, this would be so only for cognitive mechanisms producing beliefs relevant to survival and reproduction. It would not hold, for example, for the mechanisms producing the beliefs involved in a logic or mathematics or set theory course. According to Fodor (as we saw), "Darwinian selection guarantees that organisms either know the elements of logic or become posthumous"; but this would hold at most[20] for the most elementary bits of logic. It is only the occasional assistant professor of logic who needs to know even that first-order logic is complete in order to survive and reproduce.

Indeed, the same would go generally for the more theoretical parts of science.[21]

Evolution suggests a status for the distinctions we naturally make, that removes them far from the role of fundamental categories in scientific description. Classification by colour, or currently stable animal-mating groups is crucial to our survival amidst the dangers of poison and fang. This story suggests that the ability to track directly certain classes and divisions

20. "At most" because, as I argued, if Darwinian selection guarantees anything, it is only that the organism's *behavior* is adaptive: there isn't anything in particular it needs to *believe* (or, *a fortiori,* to know).

21. This hasn't been lost on those who have thought about the matter. According to Erwin Schrödinger, the fact that we human beings can discover the laws of nature is "a miracle that may well be beyond human understanding" (*What is Life?* [Cambridge: Cambridge University Press, 1945], p. 31). According to Eugene Wigner, "The enormous usefulness of mathematics in the natural sciences is something bordering on the mysterious, and there is no rational explanation for it" ("The Unreasonable Effectiveness of Mathematics in the Natural Sciences," in *Communications on Pure and Applied Mathematics* [13, p. 2]); and "It is difficult to avoid the impression that a miracle confronts us here, quite comparable in its striking nature to the miracle that the human mind can string a thousand arguments together without getting itself into contradictions, or to the two miracles of the existence of laws of nature and of the human mind's capacity to divine them" (p. 7). And Albert Einstein thought the intelligibility of the world a "miracle or an eternal mystery" (*Lettres à Maurice Solovine* [Paris: Gauthier-Villars, 1956], p. 115).

in the world is not a factor that guides scientists in theory choice. For there is no such close connection between the jungle and the blackboard. The evolutionary story clearly entails that such abilities of discrimination were 'selected for', by a filtering process that has nothing to do with successful theory choice in general. Indeed, no faculty of spontaneous discrimination can plausibly be attributed a different status within the scientific account of our evolution. Even if successful theory choice will in the future aid survival of the human race, it cannot be a trait 'selected for' already in our biological history.[22]

So even if you think Darwinian selection would make it probable that certain belief-producing mechanisms — those involved in the production of beliefs relevant to survival — are reliable, that would not hold for the mechanisms involved in the production of the theoretical claims of science, such beliefs, for example, as E, the evolutionary story itself. And of course the same would go for N.

What we have seen so far, therefore, is that the devotee of N&E has a defeater for any belief he holds, and a stronger defeater for N&E itself. If he has no defeater for this defeater, and no independent evidence, then the rational attitude toward N&E would be one of agnosticism.

But perhaps he will claim to have independent evidence. "True," he says, "if N&E were all I had to go on, then the right cognitive stance would be agnosticism about R and in fact about any proposition produced by my belief-producing faculties, including N&E itself. But why can't I reason inductively as follows? My cognitive faculties must indeed be reliable. For consider A_1, any of my beliefs. Naturally enough, I believe A_1; that is, I believe that A_1 is true. So A_1 is one of my beliefs and A_1 is true; A_2 is one of my beliefs and A_2 is true; A_3 is one of my beliefs and A_3 is true; and so on. So, by induction, I argue that all or nearly all of my beliefs are true; I therefore conclude that my faculties are probably reliable (or at any rate probably reliable *now*) because as a matter of fact it is probable that each of the beliefs they have presently produced is true."

This argument ought to meet with less than universal acclaim. The friend of N&E does no better, arguing this way, than the theist who argues that wish fulfillment must be a reliable belief-producing mechanism by running a similar argument with respect to the beliefs he holds that he thinks are produced by wish fulfillment. He does no better than the widget observer who, by virtue of a similar argument, continues to believe that those widgets are red, even after having been told by the building superintendent that they are irradiated by red light. Clearly this is not the method of true philosophy.

22. Bas van Fraassen, *Laws and Symmetry* (Oxford: Clarendon Press, 1989), pp. 52-53.

Accordingly, the friend of N&E can't argue in this way that he has independent evidence for R. Of course, he isn't likely to argue in *that* way; he is more likely to suggest that we consult the scientific result on the matter: what does science tell us about the likelihood that our cognitive faculties are reliable? But this can't work either. For consider any argument from science (or anywhere else) he might produce. This argument will have premises; and these premises, he claims, give him good reason to believe R (or N&E). But note that he has the very same defeater for each of those premises that he has for R and for N&E; and he has the same defeater for his belief that those premises constitute a good reason for R (or N&E). For that belief, and for each of the premises, he has a reason for doubting it, a reason for being agnostic with respect to it. This reason, obviously, cannot be defeated by an ultimately undefeated defeater. For every defeater of this reason he might have, he knows that he has a defeater-defeater: the very undercutting defeater that attached itself to R and to N&E in the first place.

We could also put it like this: any argument he offers, for R, is in this context delicately circular or question-begging. It is not *formally* circular; its conclusion does not appear among its premises. It is instead (we might say) *pragmatically* circular in that it purports to give a reason for trusting our cognitive faculties, but is itself trustworthy only if those faculties (at least the ones involved in its production) are indeed trustworthy. In following this procedure and giving this argument, therefore, he subtly assumes the very proposition he proposes to argue for. Once I come to doubt the reliability of my cognitive faculties, I can't properly try to allay that doubt by producing an *argument;* for in so doing I rely on the very faculties I am doubting. The conjunction of evolution with naturalism gives its adherents a reason for doubting that our beliefs are mostly true; perhaps they are mostly wildly mistaken. But then it won't help to *argue* that they can't be wildly mistaken; for the very reason for mistrusting our cognitive faculties generally will be a reason for mistrusting the faculties generating the beliefs involved in the argument.

But (someone might say) isn't there a problem with this argument for pragmatic circularity? The devotee of N&E begins (naturally enough) by accepting N&E; upon being apprised for the previous argument (so I say), he comes to see that he has an undefeated undercutting defeater for R and hence an undefeated reason for doubting N&E; hence (so I say) it is irrational for him to accept N&E, unless he has other evidence; but any purported other evidence will be subject to the same defeater as N&R. But now comes the rejoinder: as soon as our devotee of N&E comes to doubt R, he should also come to doubt his *defeater* for R; for that defeater, after all, depends upon his beliefs, which are a product of his cognitive faculties. So his defeater for R (and N&E) is also a defeater for that defeater, that is, for *itself.* But then when he notes *that,* and *doubts* his defeater for R, he no longer *has* a defeater (undefeated or otherwise) for N&E; so how is it irrational for him to accept N&E?

What we really have is one of those nasty dialectical loops to which Hume calls our attention:

> The skeptical reasonings, were it possible for them to exist, and were they not destroy'd by their subtlety, wou'd be successively both strong and weak, according to the successive dispositions of the mind. Reason first appears in possession of the throne, prescribing laws, and imposing maxims, with an absolute sway and authority. Her enemy, therefore, is oblig'd to take shelter under her protection, and by making use of rational arguments to prove the fallaciousness and imbecility of reason, produces in a matter, a patent under her hand and seal. This patent has at first an authority, proportioned to the present and immediate authority of reason, from which it is deriv'd. But as it is suppos'd to be contradictory to reason, it gradually diminishes the force of that governing power, and its own at the same time; till at last they both vanish away into nothing by a regular and just diminution. . . . 'Tis happy, therefore, that nature breaks the force of all skeptical arguments in time, and keeps them from having any considerable influence on the understanding.[23]

When the devotee of N&E notes that he has a defeater for R, then at that stage he also notes (if apprised of the present argument) that he has a defeater for N&E; indeed, he notes that he has a defeater for anything he believes. Since, however, his having a defeater for N&E depends upon some of his beliefs, what he now notes is that he has a defeater for his defeater of R and N&E; so now he no longer *has* that defeater for R and N&E. So then his original condition of believing R and assuming N&E reasserts itself: at which point he again has a defeater for R and N&E. But then he notes that *that* defeater is also a defeater for the defeater of R and N&E; hence . . . So goes the paralyzing dialectic. After a few trips around this loop, we may be excused for throwing up our hands in despair, or disgust, and joining Hume in a game of backgammon. The point remains, therefore: one who accepts N&E (and is apprised of the present argument) has a defeater for N&E, a defeater that cannot be defeated by an ultimately undefeated defeater. And isn't it irrational to accept a belief for which you know you have an ultimately undefeated defeater?

Hence the devotee of N&E has a defeater D for N&E — a defeater, furthermore, that can't be ultimately defeated; for obviously D attaches to any

---

23. *A Treatise of Human Nature,* with an analytical index, ed. L. A. Selby-Bigge (Oxford: Clarendon Press, 1888), I, IV, i, p. 187.

consideration one might bring forward by way of attempting to defeat it. If you accept N&E, you have an ultimately undefeated reason for rejecting N&E: but then the rational thing to do is to reject N&E. If, furthermore, one also accepts the conditional *if N is true, then so is E,* one has an ultimately undefeated defeater for N. One who contemplates accepting N, and is torn, let's say, between N and theism, should reason as follows: if I were to accept N, I would have good and ultimately undefeated reason to be agnostic about N; so I should not accept it. Unlike the preliminary argument, this is not an argument for the *falsehood* of naturalism and thus (given that naturalism and theism are the live options) for the truth of theism; for all this argument shows, naturalism might still be true. It is instead an argument for the conclusion that (for one who is aware of the present argument) accepting naturalism is irrational. It is like the self-referential argument against classical foundationalism: classical foundationalism is either false or such that I would be unjustified in accepting it; so (given that I am aware of this fact) I can't justifiably accept it.[24] But of course it does not follow that classical foundationalism is not *true;* for all this argument shows, it could be true, though not rationally acceptable. Similarly here; the argument is not for the falsehood of naturalism, but for the irrationality of accepting it. The conclusion to be drawn, therefore, is that the conjunction of naturalism with evolutionary theory is self-defeating: it provides for itself an undefeated defeater. Evolution, therefore, presents naturalism with an undefeated defeater. But if naturalism is true, then, surely, so is evolution. Naturalism, therefore, is unacceptable.

The traditional theist, on the other hand, isn't forced into the appalling loop. On this point his set of beliefs is stable. He has no corresponding reason for doubting that it is a purpose of our cognitive systems to produce true beliefs, nor any reason for thinking that $P(R/(N\&E\&C))$ is low, nor any reason for thinking the probability of a belief's being true, given that it is a product of his cognitive faculties, is no better than in the neighborhood of $1/2$. He may indeed endorse some form of evolution; but if he does, it will be a form of evolution guided and orchestrated by God. And *qua* traditional theist — *qua* Jewish, Moslem, or Christian theist[25] — he believes that God is the premier knower and has created us human beings in his image, an important part of which involves his endowing them with a reflection of his powers as a knower.[26]

---

24. See my "Reason and Belief in God," chapter 5 below, pp. 135ff.

25. Things may stand differently with a *bare* theist — one who holds only that there is an omnipotent, omniscient, and wholly good creator, but does not add that God has created humankind in his own image.

26. Of course, God's knowledge is significantly different from human knowledge: God has not been designed and does not have a design plan (in the sense of that term in which it applies to human beings). When applied to both God and human beings, such terms as 'design

Of course he can't sensibly *argue* that in fact our beliefs are mostly true, from the premise that we have been created by God in his image. More precisely, he can't sensibly follow Descartes, who started from a condition of general doubt about whether our cognitive nature is reliable, and then used his theistic belief as a premise in an argument designed to resolve that doubt. Here Thomas Reid is surely right:

> Descartes certainly made a false step in this matter, for having suggested this doubt among others — that whatever evidence he might have from his consciousness, his senses, his memory, or his reason, yet possibly some malignant being had given him those faculties on purpose to impose upon him; and therefore, that they are not to be trusted without a proper voucher. To remove this doubt, he endeavours to prove the being of a Deity who is no deceiver; whence he concludes, that the faculties he had given him are true and worthy to be trusted.
>
> It is strange that so acute a reasoner did not perceive that in this reasoning there is evidently a begging of the question.
>
> For, if our faculties be fallacious, why may they not deceive us in this reasoning as well as in others?[27]

Suppose, therefore, you find yourself with the doubt that our cognitive faculties produce truth: you can't quell that doubt by producing an argument about God and his veracity, or indeed, any argument at all; for the argument, of course, will be under as much suspicion as its source. Here no argument will help you; here salvation will have to be by grace, not by works. But the theist has nothing impelling him in the direction of such skepticism in the first place;

---

plan,' 'proper function,' and 'knowledge,' as Aquinas pointed out, apply *analogously* rather than univocally. What precisely is the analogy in this case? Multifarious (for example, divine knowledge as well as human knowledge requires both belief and truth); but perhaps the central analogy lies in the following direction. God has not been designed; still, there is a way in which (if I may say so) his cognitive or epistemic faculties work. This way is given by his being essentially omniscient and necessarily existent: God is essentially omniscient, but also a necessary being, so that it is a necessary truth that God believes a proposition A if and only if A is true. Call that way of working 'W.' W is something like an *ideal* for cognitive beings — beings capable of holding beliefs, seeing connections between propositions, and holding true beliefs. It is an ideal in the following sense. Say that a cognitive design plan P is *more excellent than* a design plan P^* just if a being designed according to P would be epistemically or cognitively more excellent than one designed according to P^*. (There will be environmental relativity here; furthermore, one thing that will figure into the comparison between a pair of design plans will be stability of its reliability under change of environment.) Add W to the set to be ordered. Then perhaps the resulting ordering will not be connected; there may be elements that are incomparable. But there will be a *maximal* element under the ordering: W. W, therefore, is an ideal for cognitive design plans, and it is (partly) in virtue of that relation that the term 'knowledge' is analogically extended to apply to God.

27. *Essays on the Intellectual Powers of the Human Mind,* in *Inquiries and Essays,* ed. R. Beanblossom and Keith Lehrer (Indianapolis: Hackett, 1983), V, 7, p. 276.

no element of his noetic system points in this direction; there are no propositions he already accepts just by way of being a theist, which together with forms of reason (the defeater system, for example) lead to the rejection of the belief that our cognitive faculties have the apprehension of truth as their purpose and for the most part fulfill that purpose.

Once again, therefore, we see that naturalist epistemology flourishes best in the garden of supernaturalistic metaphysics. Naturalistic epistemology conjoined with naturalistic metaphysics leads *via* evolution to skepticism or to violations of canons of rationality; conjoined with theism it does not. The naturalistic epistemologist should therefore prefer theism to metaphysical naturalism.[28]

28. Victor Reppert reminds me that the argument of this chapter bears a good bit of similarity to arguments to be found in chapters III and XIII of C. S. Lewis's *Miracles;* the argument also resembles Richard Taylor's argument in chapter X of his *Metaphysics.*

SECTION II

Reformed Epistemology

Introduction

Plantinga's religious parity argument at the close of *God and Other Minds* (chapter 1 above) drove home an important point about theistic belief — it need not be grounded in *compelling* argument in order to be rational. That is, one can be rational in her theistic belief even though her reasons are not such that they would elicit assent from all reasonable people. After all, much of what we seem to believe rationally and even know — that there are other minds, for example — seems to have no compelling argument in its favor. So if these beliefs are rational, then apparently rational belief is possible without compelling argument. In light of this conclusion, continued insistence that *theistic* belief does have such a rationality requirement would be the height of double standards and *ad hoc* attack.

But a more drastic and more surprising thesis is hinted at in the closing pages of *God and Other Minds*. At one point Plantinga says:

> I think it must be conceded that the theist has no very good answer to the request that he explain his reasons for believing in the existence of God; at any rate he has no answer that need convince the skeptic. But must he have or must there be an answer to this question if his theistic belief in God is reasonable, rationally justifiable: must there be, for any proposition p that I rationally believe . . . a good answer to the "epistemological question": "How do you know that p; what are your reasons for supposing that p is true?" Presumably not. (P. 19 above)

Here Plantinga seems to be suggesting that theistic belief could be rational without appeal to argument *at all*. Those familar with the theology and religious epistemology of John Calvin, as well as with Plantinga's Reformed

97

background, would not be surprised at such a suggestion. But to the philosophical world at large such a suggestion might appear to be the height of epistemological nonsense.[1]

It was not until quite a few years later that Plantinga's attention turned fully to this intriguing hypothesis. At the close of his paper "The Probabilistic Argument from Evil" (Bibliography #82) he muses:

> Suppose we say that the *foundation* of S's noetic structure is the set of propositions S accepts but does not accept on the basis of other propositions; the foundation of my noetic structue is the set of propositions I start with, we might say; and I properly judge the acceptability of other propositions by their relation to those in this set. And now the central question is this: why shouldn't the existence of God be in the foundations of my noetic structure? Why can't I properly take G [the proposition *God exists and is omniscient, omnipotent, and wholly good*] to be a member of this set . . . ? What propositions can properly go into the foundations of a noetic structure? (p. 51)

In a series of articles throughout the 1980s Plantinga developed and defended a view of theistic belief he calls "Reformed Epistemology": that theistic belief is perfectly rational, perfectly justified, epistemically above board, and a legitimate candidate for knowledge without recourse to argument — even if the one holding the beliefs is unable to defend them to someone else's satisfaction. The flagship article of this thesis is "Reason and Belief in God" (#68), a very large and detailed study that explores everything from medieval science to contemporary philosophy of mind. The article is excerpted as chapter 5 in this volume.[2]

It is important to keep Plantinga's Reformed epistemology thesis distinct

---

1. From Plantinga's own comments on his work it is unclear the extent to which he was thinking along these lines as he closed out *God and Other Minds*. Reflecting on the thesis of the book he says merely:

> In *God and Other Minds,* I assumed that the proper way to approach the question of the rationality of theistic belief is in terms of argument for and against the existence of God. Once it was clear that this approach is inconclusive — because there aren't any really cogent arguments either for or against the existence of God — I began to consider explicitly the evidentialist objection to theistic belief: the objection that theistic belief is irrational just because there is no evidence or at any rate insufficient evidence for it.

"Self Profile" (Bibliography #60), p. 56

2. The editing of this mammoth paper (78 pages in its original publication) was a simple task. The original was published with the text in two different type sizes. Plantinga explained the two sizes thus: "The main lines of the argument are to be found in the large print, where technicalities and side issues will be kept to a minimum. The sections in small print will amplify, qualify, and add detail" (p. 17). Chapter 5 omits only this smaller type, and contains all the material Plantinga saw to be essential to his thesis.

from two related but importantly different issues in philosophical theology. First, Reformed epistemology is not fideism. Fideism is the view that the canons of reason are inappropriate and inadequate to judge the propriety of theistic belief. According to fideism, the question "Is theistic belief rational?" is as inappropriate as the question "Is the number 7 green?" Plantinga sees the question "Is theistic belief rational?" to be quite appropriate. His challenge is to those who claim that the only way theistic belief *can* be rational is by appeal to propositional evidence or argument. He argues that there are other, more basic or foundational, ways for beliefs to be rational, and theistic beliefs can be rational according to these criteria.

Second, it is important to note that Plantinga does not claim to be providing an argument from religious experience in the classic natural theology sense. The argument from religious experience is an attempt to prove that God exists (in the traditional sense of "proof" utilized in natural theology) by appeal to the existence, pervasiveness, and characteristics of religious experience. The general strategy is usually to argue that the truth of theism provides the best explanation for these experiences. Granted, Plantinga does look to the experiences of believers for the non-evidential rational grounding of theistic belief. However, there are at least two important ways in which his project differs from the argument from religious experience. First, Plantinga concentrates on common, everyday experiences of faith, rather than on the extraordinary, miraculous, or so-called "mystical" experiences that are usually the locus of arguments from experience. Second, Plantinga does not appeal to these experiences as theistic proofs in the natural theology sense. He is not claiming that these experiences can serve as the basis for arguments that God exists. He is not even claiming that these experiences can ever legitimately serve to ground belief for anyone other than the subject of the experiences. Plantinga's claim is that such experiences can and do rationally ground theistic belief for the subject, even if they cannot provide rational grounds for theistic belief for anyone else.

This paper and the project it embodies may well be the most famous and most controversial of Plantinga's career. While his response to most criticisms has been rebuttal or clarification, Plantinga did respond to calls — primarily from Calvin College's Stephen Wykstra and Northwestern's Jay van Hook[3] — that he "refocus" the question. These critics charged that, even if theistic belief is rational in some weak sense, Plantinga had not yet shown that it could ever count as knowledge, even if theism is true. In other words,

---

3. Wykstra, "Toward a Sensible Evidentialism: On the Notion of 'Needing Evidence,' " in William Rowe and William Wainwright, editors, *Philosophy of Religion: Selected Readings,* 2nd edition (San Diego: Harcourt, Brace, Jovanovich, 1989), pp. 426-37 (3rd ed., 1998, pp. 481-91). Van Hook, "Knowledge, Belief and Reformed Epistemology," *Reformed Journal* 32 (July 1982): 3-5, and " 'Knowledge' in Quotes," *Reformed Journal* 32 (April 1982): 8-9.

for all Plantinga had said in "Reason and Belief in God" and related papers, it may still be that one could still never *know* that God exists without argument.

Plantinga's response to this critique was to raise the question of what must be added to true belief to convert it into knowledge — a question that has bothered analytic epistemologists since the advent of the so-called "Gettier Problem" in 1963.[4] Dubbing this mystery property "warrant," he set out on a quest for the proper analysis of warrant that resulted in his recent two-volume work (#28 and #29) on epistemology, which has been the subject of much discussion and debate in the American philosophical world.[5] Along the way he developed stinging critiques of traditional Cartesian "internalist" epistemology, as well as all of the more popular contemporary attempts to provide internalist and externalist alternatives to Cartesianism. The result of his study is an analysis of warrant of which Plantinga makes two claims: first, it is the proper analysis, avoiding all the pitfalls that doom its rivals; and second, it provides a sophisticated epistemological framework within which theistic belief can count as knowledge if true, even though the belief is not grounded in argument or propositional evidence.[6]

Several years before the publication of the warrant volumes, Plantinga published two papers that argued for these two claims. "Positive Epistemic Status and Proper Function" (#49) outlined his critique of other approaches to epistemology and his own analysis of warrant. "Justification and Theism" (#50) demonstrated the applicability of this analysis to the Reformed epistemology project. This latter article is included below as chapter 6. (One important note: both of these articles were written before Plantinga adopted the term "warrant" to refer to that property that converts true belief into knowledge. At this early

4. Edmund Gettier, "Is Justified True Belief Knowledge?" *Analysis* 23 (1963): 121-23. In this paper Gettier challenges the once sacrosanct analysis of knowledge as justified true belief with two counterexamples startling for their simplicity and their profundity. Much of analytic epistemological research in the last 30+ years has been occupied with the question of exactly what problem in the analysis Gettier's counterexamples reveal, and how that problem is to be solved. For an excellent overview of the kinds of responses these questions have elicited, see Robert K. Shope, *The Analysis of Knowing: A Decade of Research* (Princeton: Princeton University Press, 1983).

5. See, for example, the symposium on the books published in *Philosophy and Phenomenological Research* 55 (1995): 393-464. The symposium contains critical articles from William Alston, Carl Ginet, Matthias Steup, Richard Swinburne, and James Taylor, as well as a *Précis* and reply by Plantinga (#16 and #17). Also Jonathan Kvanvig has edited a volume of new essays on the books entitled *Warrant in Contemporary Epistemology: Essays in Honor of Alvin Plantinga's Theory of Knowledge* (Savage, Md.: Rowman & Littlefield, 1996).

6. Actually the two warrant volumes only hint at this second claim, and do not give it full treatment. The projected third volume in this study, in preparation at the time of this writing and tentatively titled *Warranted Christian Belief,* will be a full examination of the applicability of Plantinga's analysis of warrant to the questions of Reformed epistemology, natural theology, and other issues of religious epistemology.

stage he was using the term "positive epistemic status," borrowed from Roderick Chisholm, to denote the conversion property.)

The third chapter in this section is a fairly recent paper by Plantinga in which he explores the implications of Reformed epistemology for one of the most popular and controversial topics in contemporary religious studies: religious pluralism. In "A Defense of Religious Exclusivism" Plantinga argues that the standard objections to religious exclusivism — that it is both morally objectionable and epistemically indefensible — are unpersuasive. In his defense of exclusivism against various forms of these charges, Plantinga makes much use of the kinds of experiences that he understands to give rise to rational theistic belief, as well as many of the particulars about the nature of knowledge and warrant that he develops in his books on the subject. Besides the straightforward argumentation and vintage Plantinga-esque reasoning it offers, the essay serves as an excellent example of how the implications of Reformed epistemology can be used to bring new insights to traditional and current debates in philosophy and religion.

CHAPTER FIVE

Reason and Belief in God

Belief in God is the heart and center of the Christian religion — as it is of Judaism and Islam. Of course Christians may disagree, at least in emphasis, as to how to think of God; for example, some may emphasize his hatred of sin; others, his love of his creatures. Furthermore, one may find, even among professedly Christian theologians, supersophisticates who proclaim the liberation of Christianity from belief in God, seeking to replace it by trust in "Being itself" or "Ground of Being" or some such thing. It remains true, however, that belief in God is the foundation of Christianity.

In this essay I want to discuss a connected constellation of questions: Does the believer-in-God accept the existence of God by *faith?* Is belief in God contrary to reason, unreasonable, irrational? Must one have *evidence* to be rational or reasonable in believing in God? Suppose belief in God is *not* rational; does that matter? And what about proofs of God's existence? Many Reformed or Calvinist thinkers and theologians have taken a jaundiced view of natural theology, thought of as the attempt to give proofs or arguments for the existence of God; are they right? What underlies this hostility to an undertaking that, on the surface, at least, looks perfectly harmless and possibly useful? These are some of the questions I propose to discuss. They fall under the general rubric *faith and reason,* if a general rubric is required. I believe Reformed or Calvinist thinkers have had important things to say on these topics and that their fundamental insights here are correct. What they say, however, has been for the most part unclear, ill-focused, and unduly inexplicit. I shall try to remedy these ills; I shall try to state and clearly develop their insight; and I shall try to connect these insights with more general epistemological considerations.

Like the Missouri River, what I have to say is best seen as the confluence of three streams — streams of clear and limpid thought, I hasten to

102

add, rather than turbid, muddy water. These three streams of thought are first, reflection on the evidentialist objection to theistic belief, according to which belief in God is unreasonable or irrational because there is insufficient evidence for it; second, reflection on the Thomistic conception of faith and reason; and third, reflection on the Reformed objection to natural theology. In Part I I shall explore the evidentialist objection, trying to see more clearly just what it involves and what it presupposes. Part II will begin with a brief look at Thomas Aquinas's views on faith and knowledge; I shall argue that the evidentialist objection and the Thomistic conception of faith and knowledge can be traced back to a common root in *classical foundationalism* — a pervasive and widely accepted picture or total way of looking at faith, knowledge, belief, rationality, and allied topics. I shall try to characterize this picture in a revealing way and then go on to argue that classical foundationalism is both false and self-referentially incoherent; it should therefore be summarily rejected. In Part III I shall explore the Reformed rejection of natural theology; I will argue that it is best understood as an implicit rejection of classical foundationalism in favor of the view that belief in God is properly basic. What the Reformers meant to hold is that it is entirely right, rational, reasonable, and proper to believe in God without any evidence or argument at all; in this respect belief in God resembles belief in the past, in the existence of other persons, and in the existence of material objects. I shall try to state and clearly articulate this claim and in Part IV to defend it against objections.

I. The Evidentialist Objection to Belief in God

My first topic, then, is the evidentialist objection to theistic belief. Many philosophers — W. K Clifford,[1] Brand Blanshard,[2] Bertrand Russell,[3] Michael Scriven,[4] and Anthony Flew,[5] to name a few — have argued that belief in God is irrational or unreasonable or not rationally acceptable or intellectually irresponsible or somehow noetically below par because, as they say, there is *insufficient evidence* for it. Bertrand Russell was once asked what he would say if, after dying, he were brought into the presence of God and asked why

1. W. K. Clifford, "The Ethics of Belief," in *Lectures and Essays* (London: Macmillan, 1879), pp. 345f.
2. Brand Blanshard, *Reason and Belief* (London: Allen & Unwin, 1974), pp. 400f.
3. Bertrand Russell, "Why I Am Not a Christian," in *Why I Am Not a Christian* (New York: Simon & Schuster, 1957), pp. 3ff.
4. Michael Scriven, *Primary Philosophy* (New York: McGraw-Hill, 1966), pp. 87ff.
5. Anthony Flew, *The Presumption of Atheism* (London: Pemberton, 1976), pp. 22ff.

he had not been a believer. Russell's reply: "I'd say 'Not enough evidence God! Not enough evidence!' "[6] We may have our doubts as to just how that sort of response would be received; but Russell, like many others, held that theistic belief is unreasonable because there is insufficient evidence for it.

A. How Shall We Construe "Theistic Belief"?

But how shall we construe "theistic belief" here? I have been speaking of "belief in God"; but this is not entirely accurate. For the subject under discussion is not really the rational acceptability of belief *in* God, but the rationality of belief that God exists — that there *is* such a person as God. And belief in God is not at all the same thing as belief that there is such a person as God. To believe that God exists is simply to accept as true a certain proposition: perhaps the proposition that there is a personal being who has created the world, who has no beginning, and who is perfect in wisdom, justice, knowledge, and power. According to the book of James, the devils do that, and they tremble. The devils do not believe *in* God, however; for belief in God is quite another matter. One who repeats the words of the Apostles' Creed "I believe in God the Father Almighty, . . ." and means what he says is not simply announcing the fact that he accepts a certain proposition as true; much more is involved than that. Belief in God means *trusting* God, accepting God, accepting his purposes, committing one's life to him and living in his presence. To the believer the entire world speaks of God. Great mountains, surging ocean, verdant forests, blue sky and bright sunshine, friends and family, love in its many forms and various manifestations — the believer sees these things and many more as gifts from God. The universe thus takes on a personal cast for him; the fundamental truth about reality is truth about a *person.* So believing in God is indeed more than accepting the proposition that God exists. But if it is more than that, it is also at least that. One cannot sensibly believe in God and thank him for the mountains without believing that there *is* such a person to be thanked and that he is in some way responsible for the mountains. Nor can one trust in God and commit oneself to him without believing that he exists; as the author of Hebrews says, "He who would come to God must believe that he is and that he is a rewarder of those who seek him" (Heb. 11:6).

So belief in God must be distinguished from the belief that God exists. Having made this distinction, however, I shall ignore it for the most part, using "belief in God" as a synonym for "belief that there is such a person

6. Wesley Salmon, "Religion & Science: A New Look at Hume's Dialogues," *Philosophical Studies* 33 (1978): 176.

as God." The question I want to address, therefore, is the question whether belief in God — belief in the existence of God — is rationally acceptable. But what is it to believe or assert that God exists? Just which belief is it into the rational acceptability of which I propose to inquire? Which God do I mean to speak of? The answer, in brief, is: the God of Abraham, Isaac, and Jacob; the God of Jewish and Christian revelation: the God of the Bible.

To believe that God exists, therefore, is first of all to hold a *belief* of a certain sort — an existential belief. To assert that God exists is to make an *assertion* of a certain sort — an existential assertion. It is to answer at the most basic level the ontological question "What is there?" This may seem excessively obvious. I would not so much as mention it, were it not for the fact that some philosophers and theologians seem to disagree. Oddly enough, they seem to use the phrase "belief in God" and even "belief that God exists" in such a way that to believe in God is not to hold any such existential beliefs at all. Much of what Rudolph Bultmann says, for example, seems to suggest that to believe in God is not at all to believe that there exists a being of a certain sort. Instead, it is to adopt a certain attitude or policy, or to make a kind of resolve: the resolve, perhaps, to accept and embrace one's finitude, giving up the futile attempt to build hedges and walls against guilt, failure, and death. And according to the philosopher Richard Braithwaite, a religious assertion is "the assertion of an intention to carry out a certain behavioral policy, subsumable under a sufficiently general principle to be a moral one, together with the implicit statement, but not necessarily the assertion, of certain stories."[7] But then it looks as if according to Braithwaite when the Christian asserts "I believe in God the Father Almighty" he is not, contrary to appearances, asserting that he believes that there exists a *being* of a certain kind; instead he is asserting that he intends to carry out a certain behavioral policy. As *I* use the phrase "belief in God," however, that phrase denotes a *belief,* not a resolve or the adoption of a policy. And the assertion that God exists is not an *existential* assertion, not the assertion of an intention to carry out a certain policy, behavioral or otherwise. To believe or assert that God exists is to believe or assert that there exists a being of a certain very special sort.

What sort? Some contemporary theologians, under the baneful influence of Kant, apparently hold that the name 'God,' as used by Christians and others, denotes an *idea,* or a *concept,* or a *mental construct* of some kind. The American theologian Gordon Kaufman, for example, claims that the word 'God' "raises special problems of meaning because it is a noun which by definition refers to a reality transcendent of and thus not locatable within

7. Richard Braithwaite, *An Empiricist's View of the Nature of Religious Belief* (Cambridge: Cambridge University Press, 1955), p. 32.

experience."[8] In a striking echo of one of Kant's famous distinctions, Kaufman distinguishes what he calls the "real referent" of the term 'God' from what he calls "the available referent":

> The real referent for 'God' is never accessible to us or in any way open to our observation or experience. It must remain always an unknown X, a mere limiting idea with no content.[9]
>
> For all practical purposes, it is the *available referent* — a particular imaginative construct — that bears significantly on human life and thought. It is the "available God" whom we have in mind when we worship or pray; . . . It is the available God in terms of which we speak and think whenever we use the word 'God.' In this sense 'God' denotes for all practical purposes what is essentially a mental or imaginative construct.[10]

Professor John Hick makes a similar suggestion; in his inaugural address at the Claremont School of Theology he suggested that when Christians speak of God, they are speaking of a certain *image,* or *mental construction,* or *imaginative creation* of some sort.

Now these are puzzling suggestions. If it is Kaufman's "available referent" "in terms of which we speak whenever we use the word 'God'," and if the available referent is a mental or imaginative construct, then presumably when we say "there is a God" or "God exists" we are affirming the existence of a certain kind of mental or imaginative construct. But surely we are not. And when Christians say that God has created the world, for example, are they really claiming that an image or imaginative construct, whatever precisely that may be, has created the world? That seems at best preposterous. In any event, the belief I mean to identify and discuss is not the belief that there exists some sort of imaginative construct or mental construction or anything of the sort. It is instead the belief, first, that there exists a *person* of a certain sort — a being who acts, holds beliefs, and has aims and purposes. This person, secondly, is immaterial, exists *a se,* is perfect in goodness, knowledge, and power, and is such that the world depends on him for its existence.

B. Objections to Theistic Belief

Now many objections have been put forward to belief in God. First, there is the claim that as a matter of fact there is no such thing as belief in God, because the

8. Gordon Kaufman, *God the Problem* (Cambridge, Mass.: Harvard University Press, 1972), p. 8.
9. Ibid., p. 85.
10. Ibid., p. 86.

sentence "God exists" is, strictly speaking, nonsense.[11] This is the positivists' contention that such sentences as "God exists" are unverifiable and hence "cognitively meaningless" (to use their charming phrase), in which case they altogether fail to express propositions. On this view those who claim to believe in God are in the pitiable position of claiming to believe a proposition that as a matter of fact does not so much as exist. This objection, fortunately, has retreated into the obscurity it so richly deserves, and I shall say no more about it.[12]

Second, there is the claim that belief in God is *internally inconsistent* in that it is impossible, in the broadly logical sense, that there be any such person as theists say God is. For example, theists say that God is a person who has no body but nonetheless acts in the world; some philosophers have retorted that the idea of a bodiless person is impossible and the idea of a bodiless person *acting* is *obviously* impossible. Some versions of some of these objections are of great interest, but I do not propose to discuss them here. Let me just record my opinion that none of them is at all compelling; so far as I can see, the concept of God is perfectly coherent. Third, some critics have urged that the existence of God is incompatible with other beliefs that are plainly true and typically accepted by theists. The most widely urged objection to theistic belief, the deductive argument from evil, falls into this category. According to this objection the existence of an omnipotent, omniscient, and wholly good God is *logically incompatible* with the presence of evil in the world — a presence conceded and indeed insisted upon by theists.[13] For their part, theists have argued that there is no inconsistency here;[14] and I think the present consensus, even among those who urge some form of the argument from evil, is that the deductive form of the argument from evil is unsuccessful.

More recently, philosophers have claimed that the existence of God, while perhaps not inconsistent with the existence of the amount and kinds of evil we actually find, is at any rate *unlikely* or *improbable* with respect to it; that is, the probability of God's existence with respect to evil is less than that of its denial with respect to evil. Hence the existence of God is improbable with respect to what we know. But if theistic belief *is* improbable with respect

11. A. J. Ayer, *Language, Truth and Logic,* 2nd ed. (London: Gollantz, Ltd., 1946), pp. 114-20.

12. For further discussion of positivism and its dreaded verifiability criterion of meaning, see Alvin Plantinga, *God and Other Minds* (Ithaca: Cornell University Press, 1967), pp. 156-68.

13. This claim has been made by Epicurus, perhaps by David Hume, by some of the French Encyclopedists, by F. H. Bradley, J. McTaggart, and many others. For an influential contemporary statement of the claim, see J. Mackie, "Evil and Omnipotence," *Mind* 64 (1955): 200ff.

14. C. S. Lewis, *The Problem of Pain* (New York: Macmillan, 1943); and see Plantinga, *God and Other Minds,* 115-55; idem, *The Nature of Necessity* (Oxford: Clarendon Press, 1974), chapter 9. A more accessible form of the argument can be found in Alvin Plantinga, *God, Freedom and Evil* (1974; reprint ed., Grand Rapids: Eerdmans, 1978), pp. 1-50. [See chapter 3 above.]

to what we know, then, so goes the claim, it is irrational or intellectually improper to accept it. Although this objection — the probabilistic argument from evil — is not of central concern here, it bears an interesting relation to one of my main topics — the question whether belief in God is properly basic. So suppose we briefly examine it. The objector claims that

(1) God is the omnipotent, omniscient, wholly good creator of the world

is improbable or unlikely with respect to the amounts and varieties of evil we find in the world. Perhaps *some* of the evil is necessary to achieve certain good states of affairs, but there is so *much* evil, much of which seems, on the face of things, utterly gratuitous. The objector claims, therefore, that (1) is improbable or unlikely, given

(2) There are 10^{13} turps of evil

where the turp is the basic unit of evil — equal, as you may have guessed, to $\frac{1}{10}^{13}$ (the evil in the actual world).

Suppose we stipulate for purposes of argument that (1) is in fact improbable on (2). Let us agree that it is unlikely, given the existence of 10^{13} turps of evil, that the world has been created by a God who is perfect in power, knowledge, and goodness. What is supposed to follow from that? How is this to be construed as an objection to theistic belief? How does the argument go from there? It does not follow, of course, that theism is false. Nor does it follow that one who accepts both (1) and (2) (and, let us add, recognizes that (1) is improbable with respect to (2)) has an irrational system of beliefs or is in any way guilty of noetic impropriety. For it *could* be, obviously enough, that (1) is improbable with respect to (2) but probable with respect to something else we know. I might know, for example, both that

(3) Feike is a Frisian, and 9 out of 10 Frisians cannot swim,

and

(4) Feike is a Frisian lifeguard, and 99 out of 100 Frisian lifeguards *can* swim;

it is plausible to hold that

(5) Feike can swim

is probable with respect to (4) but improbable with respect to (3). If, furthermore, (3) and (4) are all we know about Feike's swimming ability, then the view that he can swim is epistemically more acceptable for us than the view that he cannot — even though we know something with respect to which the former is improbable.

Indeed, we might very well *know* both (3) and (5); we might very well know a pair of propositions A and B such that A is improbable on B. So even if it were a fact that (2) is evidence against (1) or that (1) is improbable on (2), that fact would not be of much consequence. But then how can this objection be developed? How can the objector proceed?

Presumably what he means to hold is that (1) is improbable, not just on (2) but on some appropriate body of *total evidence* — perhaps all the evidence the theist has, or perhaps the body of evidence he is rationally obliged to have. The objector must be supposing that there is a relevant body of total evidence here, a body of evidence that includes (2); and his claim is that (1) is improbable with respect to this relevant body of total evidence.

Suppose we step back a moment and reconsider the overall structure of the probabilistic argument. The objector's claim is that the theist is irrational in accepting belief in God because it is improbable with respect to (2), the proposition that there are 10^{13} turps of evil — a proposition whose truth the theist acknowledges. As we have seen, however, even if the existence of God is improbable with respect to (2), that fact is utterly insufficient for demonstrating irrationality in the theist's structure of beliefs; there may be many propositions A and B such that even though A is improbable on B, we can nonetheless accept both in perfect propriety. What the objector must be supposing, then, is something like this. For any theist T you pick, there is a set of propositions T_s that constitute his *total evidence;* and now for any proposition A the theist accepts, he is rational in accepting A only if A is not improbable with respect to T_s. And the objector's claim is that the existence of God *is* improbable with respect to T_s for any (or nearly any) theist.

Suppose we say that T_s is the theist's *evidential set.* This is the set of propositions to which, as we might put it, his beliefs are responsible. A belief is rationally acceptable for him only if it is not improbable with respect to T_s. Now so far we have not been told what sorts of propositions are to be found in T_s. Perhaps these are the propositions the theist *knows* to be true, or perhaps the largest subset of his beliefs that he can rationally accept without evidence from other propositions, or perhaps the set of propositions he knows *immediately* — knows, but does not know on the basis of other propositions. However exactly we characterize this set T_s, the presently pressing question is this: Why cannot belief in God be itself a member of T_s? Perhaps for the theist — for some theists, at any rate — belief in God is a member of T_s, in which case it obviously will not be improbable with respect to T_s. Perhaps the theist is entirely within his epistemic rights in *starting from* belief in God, taking that proposition to be one of the ones probability with respect to which determines the rational propriety of *other* beliefs he holds. If so, the fact, if it is a fact, that theistic belief is improbable with respect to the existence of evil does not even begin to show that the theist is irrational in accepting it. The high-road reply to the probabilistic argument from evil, therefore, leads directly to one of the questions I am fundamentally concerned with: What sorts of beliefs, if any, is it rational or reasonable to *start from?* Which beliefs are such that one may properly accept them without evidence, that is, without the evidential support of other beliefs? One who offers the probabilistic argument from evil simply *assumes* that belief in God does not have that status; put perhaps he is mistaken.

C. The Evidentialist Objection Stated

Now suppose we turn explicit attention to the evidentialist objection. Many philosophers have endorsed the idea that the strength of one's belief ought always to be proportional to the strength of the evidence for that belief. Thus, according to John Locke a mark of the rational person is "the not entertaining any proposition with greater assurance than the proofs it is built upon will warrant." According to David Hume "A wise man . . . proportions his belief to the evidence." In the nineteenth century we have W. K. Clifford, that "delicious *enfant terrible*" as William James calls him, insisting that it is wicked, immoral, monstrous, and maybe even impolite to accept a belief for which you do not have sufficient evidence:

> Whoso would deserve well of his fellows in this matter will guard the purity of his belief with a very fanaticism of jealous care, lest at any time it should rest on an unworthy object, and catch a stain which can never be wiped away.[15]

He adds that if

> belief has been accepted on insufficient evidence, the pleasure is a stolen one. Not only does it deceive ourselves by giving us a sense of power which we do not really possess, but it is sinful, because it is stolen in defiance of our duty to mankind. That duty is to guard ourselves from such beliefs as from a pestilence, which may shortly master our body and spread to the rest of the town. (184)

And finally:

> To sum up: it is wrong always, everywhere, and for anyone to believe anything upon insufficient evidence. (186)

15. W. K. Clifford, "The Ethics of Belief," p. 183.

It is not hard to detect, in these quotations, the "tone of robustious pathos" with which James credits him. Clifford, of course, held that one who accepts belief in God *does* accept that belief on insufficient evidence and has therefore defied his duty to mankind. More recently, Bertrand Russell has endorsed the same idea: "Give to any hypothesis which is worth your while to consider," he says, "just that degree of credence which the evidence warrants"; and in his view the evidence warrants no credence in the existence of God.

1. A. Flew: The Presumption of Atheism

Still more recently Anthony Flew has commended what he calls Clifford's "luminous and compulsive essay" (perhaps "compulsive" here is to be understood as "compelling"); and Flew goes on to claim that there is, in his words, a "presumption of atheism." What is a presumption of atheism, and why should we think there is one? Flew puts it as follows:

> What I want to examine is the contention that the debate about the existence of God should properly begin from the presumption of atheism, that the onus of proof must lie upon the theist.
>
> The word 'atheism,' however, has in this contention to be construed unusually. Whereas nowadays the usual meaning of 'atheist' in English is 'someone who asserts there is no such being as God,' I want the word to be understood not positively but negatively. I want the original Greek preface 'a' to be read in the same way in 'atheist' as it is customarily read in such other Greco-English words as 'amoral,' 'atypical,' and 'asymmetrical.' In this interpretation an atheist becomes: not someone who positively asserts the non-existence of God; but someone who is simply not a theist.[16]
>
> What the protagonist of my presumption of atheism wants to show is that the debate about the existence of God ought to be conducted in a particular way, and that the issue should be seen in a certain perspective. His thesis about the onus of proof involves that it is up to the theist: first to introduce and to defend his proposed concept of God; and second, to provide sufficient reason for believing that this concept of his does in fact have an application. (14-15)

How shall we understand this? What does it mean, for example, to say that the debate "should properly begin from the presumption of atheism"? What sorts of things do debates begin from, and what is it for one to begin from such a thing? Perhaps Flew means something like this: to speak of

16. Flew, *The Presumption of Atheism,* p. 14.

where a debate should begin is to speak of the sorts of premises to which the affirmative and negative sides can properly appeal in arguing their cases. Suppose you and I are debating the question whether, say, the United States has a right to seize Mideast oilfields if the OPEC countries refuse to sell us oil at what we think is a fair price. I take the affirmative and produce for my conclusion an argument one of whose promises is the proposition that the United States has indeed a right to seize these oilfields under those conditions. Doubtless that maneuver would earn me few points. Similarly, a debate about the existence of God cannot sensibly start from the assumption that God does indeed exist. That is to say, the affirmative cannot properly appeal, in its arguments, to such premises as that there is such a person as God; if she could, she would have much too easy a time of it. So in this sense of "start" Flew is quite right: the debate cannot start from the assumption that God exists.

Of course, it is also true that the debate cannot start from the assumption that God does *not* exist; using "atheism" in its ordinary sense, there is equally a presumption of aatheism. So it looks as if there is in Flew's sense a presumption of atheism, all right, but in that same sense an equal presumption of aatheism. If this is what Flew means, then what he says is entirely correct, if something of a truism.

In other passages, however, Flew seems to understand the presumption of atheism in quite a different fashion:

> It is by reference to this inescapable demand for grounds that the presumption of atheism is justified. If it is to be established that there is a God, then we have to have good grounds for believing that this is indeed so. Until or unless some such grounds are produced we have literally no reason at all for believing; and in that situation the only reasonable posture must be that of either the negative atheist or the agnostic. (22)

Here we have a claim much more contentious than the mere suggestion that a debate about the existence of God ought not to start from the assumption that indeed there is such a person as God; here Flew is claiming that it is irrational or unreasonable to accept theistic belief in the absence of arguments or evidence for the existence of God. That is, Flew claims that if we know of no propositions that serve as evidence for God's existence, then we cannot rationally believe in God. And of course Flew, along with Russell, Clifford, and many others, holds that in fact there are not sufficient grounds or evidence for belief in God. Flew, therefore, seems to endorse the following two principles:

> (6) It is irrational or unreasonable to accept theistic belief in the absence of sufficient evidence or reasons

and

(7) We have no evidence or at any rate not sufficient evidence for the proposition that God exists.

2. M. Scriven: Atheism Is Obligatory in the Absence of Evidence.

According to Michael Scriven, if the arguments for God's existence fail, then the only rational posture is not merely not believing in God; it is atheism, the belief that there is no God. Speaking of the theistic proofs, he says, "It will now be shown that if they fail, there is no alternative to atheism."[17] He goes on to say: "we need not have a proof that God does not exist in order to justify atheism. Atheism is obligatory in the absence of any evidence for God's existence. . . . The proper alternative, where there is no evidence, is not mere suspension of belief, e.g., about Santa Claus; it is *disbelief*" (103). But Scriven's claim seems totally arbitrary. He holds that if the arguments *for* God's existence fail and the arguments *against* God's existence *also* fail, then atheism is rationally obligatory. If you have no evidence *for* the existence of God, then you are rationally obliged to believe there is no God — whether or not you have any evidence *against* the existence of God. The first thing to note, then, is that Scriven is not treating

(8) God exists

and

(9) God does not exist

in the same way. He claims that if there is no evidence for (8), then the only rational course is to believe its denial, namely (9). But of course he does not propose the same treatment for (9); he does not suggest that if there is no evidence for (9), then we are rationally obliged to believe *its* denial, namely (8). (If he *did* propose that (9) should be treated like (8), then he would be committed to supposing that if we had no evidence either way, the rational thing to do would be to believe the denial of (8) namely (9), and *also* the denial of (9), namely (8).) Why then does he propose this lack of parity between (8) and (9)? What is the justification for treating these propositions so differently? Could not the theist just as sensibly say, "If the arguments for *atheism* fail and there is no evidence for (9), then theism is rationally obligatory"? Scriven's claim, initially at any rate, looks like a piece of merely arbitrary intellectual imperialism.

17. Michael Scriven, *Primary Philosophy,* pp. 102-3.

Scriven's extravagant claim, then, does not look at all promising. Let us therefore return to the more moderate evidentialist position encapsulated by

(6) It is irrational or unreasonable to accept theistic belief in the absence of sufficient evidence or reasons

and

(7) There is no evidence or at any rate no sufficient evidence for the proposition that God exists.

3. The Evidentialist Objection and Intellectual Obligation

Now (7) is a strong claim. What about the various arguments that have been proposed for the existence of God — the traditional cosmological and teleological arguments for example? What about the versions of the *moral* argument as developed, for example, by A. E. Taylor and more recently by Robert Adams? What about the broadly inductive or probabilistic arguments developed by F. R. Tennant, C. S. Lewis, E. L. Mascall, Basil Mitchell, Richard Swinburne, and others? What about the ontological argument in its contemporary versions?[18] Do none of these provide evidence? Notice: the question is not whether these arguments, taken singly or in combinations, constitute *proofs* of God's existence; no doubt they do not. The question is only whether someone might be rationally justified in believing in the existence of God on the basis of the alleged evidence offered by them; and that is a radically different question.

At present, however, I am interested in the objector's other premise — the claim that it is irrational or unreasonable to accept theistic belief in the absence of evidence or reasons. Why suppose *that* is true? Why should we think a theist must have evidence, or reason to think there *is* evidence, if he is not to be irrational? Why not suppose, instead, that he is entirely within his epistemic rights in believing in God's existence even if he has no argument or evidence at all? This is what I want to investigate. Suppose we begin by asking what the objector means by describing a belief as *irrational.* What is the force of his claim that theistic belief is irrational, and how is it to be understood? The first thing to see is that this objection is rooted in a *normative* view. It lays down conditions that must be met by anyone whose system of beliefs is *rational,* and here "rational" is to be taken as a normative or evaluative term. According to the objector there is a right way and a wrong

---

18. See, for example, Plantinga, *The Nature of Necessity,* chapter 10. [Ed. note: See also chapter 3 above.]

way with respect to belief. People have responsibilities, duties, and obligations with respect to their believings just as with respect to their actions, or if we think believings are a kind of action, their *other* actions. Professor Brand Blanshard puts this clearly:

> Everywhere and always belief has an ethical aspect. There is such a thing as a general ethics of the intellect. The main principle of that ethic I hold to be the same inside and outside religion. This principle is simple and sweeping: Equate your assent to the evidence.[19]

And according to Michael Scriven:

> Now even belief in something for which there is no evidence, i.e., a belief which goes beyond the evidence, although a lesser sin than belief in something which is contrary to well-established laws, is plainly irrational in that it simply amounts to attaching belief where it is not justified. So the proper alternative, when there is no evidence, is not mere suspension of belief, e.g., about Santa Claus; it is disbelief. It most certainly is not faith.[20]

Perhaps this sort of obligation is really just a special case of a more general moral obligation; perhaps, on the other hand, it is unique and *sui generis*. In any event, says the objector, there are such obligations: to conform to them is to be rational and to go against them is to be irrational.

Now what the objector says seems plausible here; there do seem to be duties and obligations with respect to belief, or at any rate in the general *neighborhood* of belief. One's own welfare and that of others sometimes depends on what one believes. If we are descending the Grand Teton and I am setting the anchor for the 120-foot rappel into the Upper Saddle, I have an obligation to form such beliefs as *this anchor point is solid* only after careful scrutiny and testing. One commissioned to gather intelligence — the spies Joshua sent into Canaan, for example — has an obligation to get it right. I have an obligation with respect to the belief that Justin Martyr was a Greek apologist — an obligation arising from the fact that I teach medieval philosophy, must make a declaration on this issue, and am obliged not to mislead my students here. The precise nature of these obligations may be hard to specify: What exactly *is* my obligation here? Am I obliged to believe that Justin Martyr was a Greek apologist if and only if Justin Martyr *was* a Greek apologist? Or to form a belief on this topic only after the appropriate amount of checking and investigating? Or maybe just to tell the students the truth about it, whatever I myself believe in the privacy of my own study? Or to tell

---

19. Blanshard, *Reason and Belief,* p. 401.
20. Scriven, *Primary Philosophy,* p. 103.

them what is generally thought by those who should know? In the rappel case, did I have a duty to believe that the anchor point is solid if and only if it is? Or just to check carefully before forming the belief? Or perhaps there is no obligation to *believe* at all, but instead an obligation to *act on* a certain belief only after appropriate investigation. In any event, it seems plausible to hold that there are obligations and norms with respect to belief, and I do not intend to contest this assumption.

Now perhaps the evidentialist objector thinks there are intellectual obligations of the following sorts. With respect to certain kinds of propositions perhaps I have a duty not to believe them unless I have evidence for them. Perhaps I have a duty not to accept the denial of an apparently self-evident proposition unless I can see that it conflicts with other propositions that seem self-evident. Perhaps I have a duty to accept such a proposition as *I see a tree* under certain conditions that are hard to spell out in detail but include at least my entertaining that proposition and my having a certain characteristic sort of visual experience along with no reason to think my perceptual apparatus is malfunctioning.

Of course these obligations would be *prima facie* obligations; in special sorts of circumstances they could be overridden by other obligations. I have an obligation not to take bread from the grocery store without permission and another to tell the truth. Both sorts of obligation can be overridden, in specific circumstances, by other obligations — in the first case, perhaps, an obligation to feed my starving children and in the second (when the Nazis are pounding on the door) an obligation to protect a human life. So we must distinguish *prima facie* duties or obligations from *all-things-considered* or *on-balance (ultima facie?)* obligations. I have a *prima facie* obligation to tell the truth; in a given situation, however, that obligation may be overridden by others, so that my duty, all things considered, is to tell a lie. This is the grain of truth contained in situation ethics and the ill-named "new morality."

And *prima facie* intellectual obligations, like obligations of other sorts, can conflict. Perhaps I have a *prima facie* obligation to believe what seems to me self-evident, and what seems to me to follow self-evidently from what seems to me self-evident. But what if, as in the Russell paradoxes, something that seems self-evidently false apparently follows, self-evidently, from what seems self-evidently true? Here *prima facie* intellectual obligations conflict, and no matter what I do, I will violate a *prima facie* obligation. Another example: in reporting the Grand Teton rappel I neglected to mention the violent electrical storm coming in from the southwest; to escape it we must get off in a hurry, so that I have a *prima facie* obligation to inspect the anchor point carefully, but another to set up the rappel rapidly, which means I cannot spend a lot of time inspecting the anchor point.

Thus lightly armed, suppose we return to the evidentialist objector. Does he mean to hold that the theist without evidence is violating some intellectual obligation? If so, which one? Does he claim, for example, that the theist is violating his all-things-considered intellectual obligation in thus believing? Perhaps he thinks anyone who believes in God without evidence is violating his all-things-considered intellectual duty. This, however, seems unduly harsh. What about the 14-year-old theist brought up to believe in God in a community where everyone believes? This 14-year-old theist, we may suppose, does not believe in God on the basis of evidence. He has never heard of the cosmological, teleological, or ontological arguments; in fact no one has ever presented him with any evidence at all. And although he has often been told about God, he does not take that testimony as evidence; he does not reason thus: everyone around here says God loves us and cares for us; most of what everyone around here says is true; so probably *that* is true. Instead, he simply believes what he is taught. Is he violating an all-things-considered intellectual duty? Surely not. And what about the mature theist — Thomas Aquinas, let us say — who thinks he *does* have adequate evidence? Let us suppose he is wrong; let us suppose all of his arguments are failures. Nevertheless he has reflected long, hard, and conscientiously on the matter and thinks he *does* have adequate evidence. Shall we suppose he is violating an all-things-considered intellectual duty here? I should think not. So construed, the objector's contention is totally implausible.

Perhaps, then, the objector is to be understood as claiming that there is a *prima facie* intellectual duty not to believe in God without evidence. This duty can be overridden by circumstances, of course, but there is a *prima facie* obligation to believe propositions of this sort only on the basis of evidence. The theist without evidence, he adds, is flouting this obligation and is therefore not living up to his intellectual obligations. But here too there are problems. The suggestion is that I now have the *prima facie* duty to comply with the following command: either have evidence or do not believe. But this may be a command I cannot obey. I may not know of any way to acquire evidence for this proposition; and of course if the objector is right, there is no adequate evidence for it. But it is also not within my power to refrain from believing this proposition. My beliefs are not for the most part directly within my control. If you order me now, for example, to cease believing that the earth is very old, there is no way I can comply with your order. But in the same way it is not now within my power to cease believing in God now. So this alleged *prima facie* duty is one such that it is not within my power to comply with it. But how can I have a duty, *prima facie* or otherwise, to do what it is not within my power to do?

4. Can I Have Intellectual Obligations If My Beliefs Are Not within My Control?

This is a difficult and vexing question. The suggestion here is that I cannot now have a *prima facie* obligation to comply with a command which it is not now within my power to obey. Since what I believe is not normally within my power, I cannot have an obligation to believe a certain proposition or to refrain from believing it; but then, *contra* the objector, I do not have an obligation to refrain from believing in God if I have no evidence. This response to the objector is, I think, inadequate. In the first place the response is unbecoming from the theist, since many of those who believe in God follow St. Paul (for example, Romans 1) in holding that under certain circumstances failure to believe in God is culpable. And there are cases where most of us — theist and nontheist alike — do in fact believe that a person is culpable or condemnable for holding a given belief, as well as cases where we hold a person responsible for *not* accepting certain beliefs. Consider the following. Suppose someone comes to believe that Jews are inferior, in some important way, to Gentiles. Suppose he goes on to conclude that Jews should not be permitted to share public facilities such as restaurants and hotels with the rest of us. Further reflection leads him to the view that they should not be provided with the protection of law and that the rest of us have a right to expropriate their property if that is convenient. Finally, he concludes that they ought to be eliminated in order to preserve the purity of the alleged Aryan race. After soul-searching inquiry he apparently believes in all honesty that it is his duty to do what he can to see that this view is put into practice. A convincing sort, he gets the rest of us to see things his way: we join him in his pogroms, and his policy succeeds.

Now many of us will agree that such a person is culpable and guilty. But wherein does his guilt consist? Not, presumably, in doing what he believes he ought to do, in trying to carry out his duty as he sees it. Suppose, to vary the example, he tries to encourage and institute these abhorrent policies at considerable cost to himself: he loses his job; his friends turn their backs on him; he is finally arrested and thrown into prison. Nonetheless he valiantly persists. Does he not deserve moral *credit* for doing what he sees as his duty? His guilt, surely, does not consist solely in his taking the *actions* he takes; at least part of the guilt lies in accepting those abhorrent views. If he *had not* acted on his beliefs — out of fear of the consequences, perhaps — would he not have been guilty nonetheless? He would not have caused as much trouble, but would he not have been guilty? I should think so. We do in fact sometimes think that a person is guilty — has violated norms or obligations — by virtue of the beliefs he holds.

The theist, accordingly, should not reply to the evidentialist objector by claiming that since our beliefs are not within our control, we cannot have a *prima facie* duty to refrain from believing certain propositions. But there is a second reason why this response to the evidentialist is inadequate. I have been using the terms 'accept' and 'believe' interchangeably, but in fact there is an important distinction they can nicely be used to mark. This distinction is extremely hard to make clear but nonetheless, I think, important. Perhaps we can make an initial stab at it as follows. Consider a Christian beset by doubts. He has a hard time believing certain crucial Christian claims — perhaps the teaching that God was in Christ, reconciling the world to himself. Upon calling that belief to mind, he finds it cold, lifeless, without warmth or attractiveness. Nonetheless he is committed to this belief; it is his position; if you ask him what he thinks about it, he will unhesitatingly endorse it. He has, so to speak, thrown in his lot with it. Let us say that he *accepts* this proposition, even though when he is assailed by doubt, he may fail to *believe* it — at any rate explicitly — to any appreciable degree. His commitment to this proposition may be much stronger than his explicit and occurrent belief in it; so these two — that is, acceptance and belief — must be distinguished.

Take another example. A person may accept the proposition that alleged moral distinctions are unreal, and our tendency to make them is a confused and superstitious remnant of the infancy of our race — while nonetheless sometimes finding himself compelled to believe, for example, that gross injustice is wicked. Such a person adopts as his position the proposition that moral distinctions are unreal, and he accepts that proposition; but (at certain times and in certain conditions) he cannot help believing, *malgré lui,* that such distinctions are not unreal. In the same way, someone with solipsistic inclination — acquired, perhaps, by an incautious reading of Hume — could *accept* the proposition that, say, there really is no external world — no houses, horses, trucks, or trees — but could find himself, under certain conditions, regularly believing that there *are* such things.

Now I am quite aware that I have not been able to make this distinction between acceptance and belief wholly clear. I think there is such a distinction in the neighborhood, however, and I believe it is important. It is furthermore one the objector may be able to make use of; for while it is plausible to hold that what I believe is not within my direct control, it is also plausible to suppose that what I *accept* is or can be at least in part a matter of deliberate decision, a matter of voluntarily taking up a certain position. But then the objector can perhaps restate his objection in terms of *acceptance.* Perhaps (because of an unfortunate upbringing, let us say) I cannot refrain from believing in God. Nevertheless it is within my power, says the evidentialist objector, to refuse to *accept* that proposition. And now his claim that there are duties with respect to our beliefs may be reconstrued as the claim that we have *prima facie* duties with respect to our acceptances, one of these duties being not to accept such a proposition as *there is such a person as God* in the absence of evidence.

Finally, while we may perhaps agree that what I believe is not *directly* within my control, some of my beliefs are indirectly within my control, at least in part. First, what I accept has a long-term influence on what I believe. If I refuse to accept belief in God, and if I try to ignore or suppress my tendency to believe, then perhaps eventually I will no longer believe. And as Pascal pointed out, there are other ways to influence one's beliefs. Presumably, then, the evidentialist objector could hold that it is my *prima facie* duty not to accept belief in God without evidence, and to do what I can to bring it about that I no longer believe. Although it is not within my power now to cease believing now, there may be a series of actions, such that I can now take the first and, after taking the first, will be able to take the second, and so on; and after taking the whole series of actions I will no longer believe in God. Perhaps I should read a lot of Voltaire and Bertrand Russell and Thomas Paine, eschewing St. Augustine and C. S. Lewis and, of course, the Bible. Even if I cannot now stop believing without evidence, perhaps there are other actions I can take, such that if I were to take them, then at some time in the future I will not be in this deplorable condition.

So far, then, we have been construing the evidentialist objector as holding that the theist without sufficient evidence — evidence in the sense of other propositions that prove or make probable or support the existence of God — is violating a *prima facie* intellectual obligation of some sort. As we have seen, the fact that belief is not within direct control may give him pause; he is not, however, without plausible replies. But the fact is, there is a quite different way of construing the evidentialist objection; the objector need not hold that the theist without evidence is violating or has violated some duty, *prima facie, ultima facie,* or otherwise. Consider someone who believes that Venus is smaller than Mercury, not because he has evidence, but because he read it in a comic book and always believes everything he reads — or consider someone who holds this belief on the basis of an outrageously bad argument. Perhaps there is no obligation he has failed to meet; nevertheless his intellectual condition is defective in some way; or perhaps alternatively there is a commonly achieved excellence he fails to display. Perhaps he is like someone who is easily gulled, or has a serious astigmatism, or is unduly clumsy. And perhaps the evidentialist objection is to be understood, not as the claim that the theist without evidence has failed to meet some obligation, but that he suffers from a certain sort of intellectual deficiency. If this is the objector's view then his proper attitude toward the theist would be one of sympathy rather than censure.

But of course the crucial question here is this: Why does the objector think these things? Why does he think there *is* a *prima facie* obligation to try not to believe in God without evidence? Or why does he think that to do so is to be in a deplorable condition? Why is it not permissible and quite satisfactory to believe in God without any evidence — proof or argument — at all? Presumably the objector does not mean to suggest that *no* propositions can be believed or accepted without evidence, for if you have evidence for *every* proposition you believe, then (granted certain plausible assumptions about the formal properties of the evidence relation) you will believe infinitely many propositions; and no one has time, these busy days, for that. So presumably *some* propositions can properly be believed and accepted without evidence. Well, why not belief in God? Why is it not entirely acceptable, desirable, right, proper, and rational to accept belief in God without any argument or evidence whatever?

II. Aquinas and Foundationalism

In this section I shall give what I take to be the evidentialist objector's answer to these questions; I shall argue that his answer is not in the least compelling and that the prospects for his project are not bright. But it is not only evidentialist objectors that have thought theists need evidence if their belief is to be rational; many Christians have thought so too. In particular, many Christian thinkers in the tradition of natural theology have thought so. Thomas Aquinas, of course, is the natural theologian *par excellence*. Thomist thought is also, as it seems to me, the natural starting point for philosophical reflection on these topics, Protestant as well as Catholic. No doubt there are mountains between Rome and Geneva; nevertheless Protestants should in these matters be what Ralph McInerny calls "peeping Thomists" — at any rate they should *begin* as peeping Thomists. We must therefore look at some of Aquinas's views on these matters.

A. Aquinas and Evidentialism

1. Aquinas on Knowledge

According to Aquinas it is possible for us to have scientific knowledge — *scientia* — of the existence and immateriality, unity, simplicity, and perfection of God. As Aquinas sees it, *scientia* is knowledge that is inferred from what is *seen* to be true:

> Any science is possessed by virtue of principles known immediately and therefore seen. Whatever, then, is an object of science is in some sense seen.[21]

21. Aquinas, *Summa Theologiae* (hereafter "ST"), IIa, IIae, I, 5.

Aristotle suggests that the principles of a science must be *self-evident;* and Aquinas sometimes seems to follow him in holding that *scientia,* properly speaking, consists in a body of propositions deduced syllogistically from self-evident first principles — or perhaps *scientia* consists not just in those syllogistic conclusions but in the syllogisms themselves as well. Logic and mathematics seem to be the best examples of science so thought of. Consider, for example, propositional logic: here one can start from self-evident axioms and proceed to deduce theorems by argument forms — *modus ponens,* for example — that are themselves self-evidently valid in an obvious sense.[22] Other good examples of science, so thought of, would be first order logic and arithmetic.[23] And here it would be the *theorems,* not the axioms, of these systems that would constitute science. *Scientia* is *mediate* knowledge, so that one does not have *scientia* of what is self-evident. Strictly speaking, then, only those arithmetical truths that are not self-evident would constitute science. The proposition $3 + 1 = 4$ is unlikely to appear as an axiom in a formulation of arithmetic; since it is self-evident, however, it does not constitute *scientia,* even if it appears as a theorem in some axiomatization of arithmetic.

Of course the "first principles" of a science — the axioms as opposed to the theorems, so to say — are also *known.* They are known *immediately* rather than mediately, and are known by "understanding."

Now a truth can come into the mind in two ways, namely, as known in itself, and as known through another. What is known in itself is like a principle, and is perceived immediately by the mind. And so the habit which perfects the intellect in considering such a truth is called 'understanding'; it is a firm and easy quality of mind which sees into principles. A truth, however, which is known through another is understood by the intellect not immediately, but through an inquiry of reason of which it is the terminus.[24]

22. In fact, these argument forms are self-evidently valid in two senses: (a) it is self-evident that for any instance of the form in question, if the premises are true, then so is the conclusion, and (b) the corresponding conditional of the argument form is itself self-evident.

23. Although the quantification rule presents a bit of a problem in some formulations, in that it does not have the sheer see-through ability demanded by self-evidence. The fact, incidentally, that propositional and first-order logic are not *uniquely* axiomatizable is no obstacle to seeing them as sciences in this Aristotelian sense; nor does the incompleteness of arithmetic show that arithmetic is not a science in this sense.

24. Verum autem est dupliciter considerabile: uno modo, sicut per se notum; alio modo, sicut per aliud notum. Quod autem est per se notum se habet ut principium, et percipitur statim ab intellectu. Et ideo habitus perficiens intellectum ad hujusmodi veri considerationem vocatur *intellectus,* qui est habitus principiorum. Verum autem quod est per aliud notum, non statim percipitur ab intellectu, sed per inquisitionem rationis, et se habet in ratione termini. (Aquinas, *Summa Theologiae,* Ia, q. 84, a.2; my italics)

Like many of Aquinas's distinctions, this one comes from Aristotle:

> Now of the thinking states by which we grasp truth, some are unfailingly true; others admit of error — opinion, for example, and calculation, whereas scientific knowledge and intuition are always true; further, no other kind of thought except intuition is more accurate than scientific knowledge, whereas primary premises are more knowable than demonstrations, and all scientific knowledge is discursive. From these considerations it follows that there will be no scientific knowledge of the primary premises, and since, except intuition, nothing can be truer than scientific knowledge, it will be intuition that apprehends the primary premises. (*Posterior Analytics,* II,19)

Following Aristotle, then, Aquinas distinguishes what is self-evident, or known through itself *(per se nota),* from what is known through another *(per aliud nota);* the former are "principles" and are apprehended by understanding, while the latter constitute science. Aquinas's central point here is that self-evident propositions are known *immediately.* Consider a proposition like

(1) $2 + 1 = 3$

and contrast it with one like

(2) $281 \times 29 = 8,149$

We know the first but not the second *immediately:* we know it, and we do not know it by way of inference from other propositions or on the basis of our knowledge of other propositions. Instead, we can simply see that it is true. Elsewhere Aquinas says that a proposition that is self-evident to us *(per se notam quod nos)* is such that we cannot grasp or apprehend it without believing, indeed, knowing it. (2), on the other hand, does not have this status for us; few of us can simply see that it is true. Instead we must resort to calculation; we go through a chain of inferences, the ultimate premises of which are self-evident.

Of course self-evident propositions are *known,* even though they do not constitute *scientia* in the strict sense. Indeed, their epistemic status, according to Aquinas, is higher than that of propositions known by demonstration. More exactly, *our* epistemic condition, in grasping a truth of this sort, is superior to the condition we are in with respect to a proposition of which we have knowledge by demonstration. The emerging picture of scientific knowledge, then, is the one to be found in Aristotle's *Posterior Analytics:* we know what is self-evident and what follows from what is self-evident by self-evident argument forms. Knowledge consists of *scientia* and *intellectus,* or understanding. By understanding we grasp first principles, self-evident truths; from these we infer or deduce further truths. What we know consists in what we find self-evident together with what we can infer from it by logical means.

And if we take this picture seriously, it looks as if knowledge is restricted to what is necessarily true in the broadly logical sense.[25] Presumably a proposition is *per se nota* only if it is necessarily true, and any proposition that follows from necessary truths by self-evident argument forms will itself be necessarily true. As Aristotle puts it, "Since the object of pure scientific knowledge cannot be other than it is, the truth obtained by demonstrative knowledge [Aquinas's *scientia*] will be necessary" (*Posterior Analytics,* I, 3).

As a picture of Aquinas's view of science, however, this is at best incomplete; for Aquinas obviously believes we have knowledge, scientific knowledge, of much that is not logically necessary. He thinks there is such a thing as natural science *(scientia naturalis),* whose subject matter is changeable material objects:

> On the other hand there is the fact that demonstrative knowledge *(scientia)* is found in the intellect. Had the intellect no knowledge of material things, it could not have demonstrative knowledge *(scientia)* of them. Thus there would be no natural science *(scientia naturalis)* dealing with changeable material beings. (ST, Ia, 84, 1)

Aquinas means to say, furthermore, not merely that in natural science we know some necessary truths about contingent and changeable objects (as we do in knowing, for example, that whatever is moved is moved by another); he means that among the truths we know are such contingent propositions as that there is a tree outside the window and that its branches are moving in the wind.

According to Aquinas, therefore, we have *scientia* of what changes, and presumably some of this *scientia* involves contingent propositions. Indeed Aquinas elsewhere holds that the kind of knowledge most characteristic of human beings and most proper to them is knowledge of material objects:

> Cognitive faculties are proportioned to their objects. For instance, an angel's intellect, which is totally separate from corporeal reality, has as its proper object intelligible substances separate from corporeal reality, and it is by means of these intelligible objects that it knows material realities. The proper object of the human intellect, on the other hand, since it is joined to a body, is a nature or whatness *(quidditas)* found in corporeal matter — the intellect, in fact, rises to the limited knowledge it has of invisible things by way of the nature of visible things. (ST, Ia, 84, 8 Resp.)

> We know incorporeal realities . . . by analogy with sensible bodies, which do have images, just as we understand truth in the abstract by a consideration of things in which we see truth. (ST, Ia, 84, 8, ad 3)

25. See editor's note on p. 23 above.

There are two sorts of propositions whose truth we simply *see*. First, there are those that are self-evident, or *per se nota;* these are the object of *intellectus* or understanding, and we see their truth in the way in which we see that 2 + 1 = 3. Second, there are propositions "evident to the senses," as he puts it: "That some things move is evident to the senses" (ST, Ia, 2, 3), as is the proposition that the sun moves.[26] His examples of propositions evident to the senses are for the most part propositions whose truth we determine by *sight.* Although of course Aquinas did not think of vision as the only sense yielding knowledge, he did give it pride of place; because it is immaterial, he says, it is "more a knower" than the other senses. It is not easy to see just what Aquinas means by "evident to the senses," but perhaps the following is fairly close: a proposition is evident to the senses if we human beings have the power to determine its truth by looking at, listening to, tasting, touching, or smelling some physical object. Thus

(3) There is a tree outside my window,

(4) The cat on the mat is fuscous,

and

(5) This wall is yellow

are propositions evident to the senses.

In the first place, then, there are those propositions we simply see to be true; in the second place there are those propositions we see to follow from those in the first group. These propositions can be deduced from those in the first group by arguments we see to be valid.[27] So the basic picture of knowledge is this: we know what we see to be true together with what we can infer from what we see to be true by arguments we can see to be valid.

2. Aquinas on Knowledge of God

Now Aquinas believes that human beings (even in our earthly condition here below) can have knowledge, *scientific* knowledge, of God's existence, as well as knowledge that he has such attributes as simplicity, eternity, immateriality, immutability, and the like. In *Summa Theologiae* Aquinas sets out his famous "Five Ways," or five proofs of God's existence: in *Summa Contra Gentiles* he sets out the proof from motion in much greater detail; and in each case he follows these alleged demonstrations with alleged demonstrations that God possesses the attributes just mentioned. So natural knowledge of God is

26. Aquinas, *Summa Contra Gentiles* (hereafter "SCG"), I, 13, 3.
27. That is, by arguments whose corresponding conditionals are self-evident to us.

possible. But the vast majority of those who believe in God, he thinks, do not have knowledge of God's existence but must instead take it on faith. Only a few of us have the time, inclination, and ability to follow the theistic proofs; the rest of us take this truth on faith. And even though God's existence is demonstrable — even though we are capable of *knowing* it — nevertheless it is appropriately proposed to human beings as an object of faith. The reason, in brief, is that our welfare demands that we believe the proposition in question, but *knowledge* of it is exceedingly hard to come by:

> For the rational truth about God would have appeared to only a few, and even so after a long time and mixed with many errors; whereas on knowing this depends our whole welfare, which is in God. (ST, Ia, I,1)

> From all this it is clear that, if it were necessary to use a strict demonstration as the only way to reach a knowledge of the things we must know about God, very few could ever construct such a demonstration and even these could do it only after a long time. From this it is evident that the provision of the way of faith, which gives all easy access to salvation at any time, is beneficial to man.[28]

So most of those who believe in God do so on faith. Fundamentally, for Aquinas, to accept a proposition on faith is to accept it on God's authority; faith is a matter of "believing God" (ST, IIa, IIae, ii, 2): "for that which is above reason we believe only because God has revealed it" (SCG, I, 9). Now what about those who believe in God on faith even though they do not know that God exists? How can that be a rational procedure? So far as I know, Aquinas does not explicitly address this question. He does discuss a closely related question, however: the question whether those who believe (take on faith) what is "above reason" are irrational or foolish, or in his terms, "believe with undue levity":

> [1] Those who place their faith in this truth, however, "for which the human reason offers no experimental evidence," do not believe foolishly, as though "following artificial fables" (2 Pet. 1:16). For these "secrets of divine Wisdom" (Job 11:6) the divine Wisdom itself, which knows all things to the full, has deigned to reveal to men. It reveals its own presence, as well as the truth of its teaching and inspiration, by fitting arguments; and in order to confirm those truths that exceed natural knowledge, it gives visible manifestation to works that surpass the ability of all nature. Thus, there are the wonderful cures of illnesses, there is the raising of the dead, and the wonderful immutation in the heavenly bodies; and what is more wonderful, there is the inspiration given to human minds, so that simple and untutored persons, filled with the gift of the Holy Spirit, come to possess instan-

28. Aquinas, *De Veritate*, question 14, article 10.

taneously the highest wisdom and the readiest eloquence. When these arguments were examined, through the efficacy of the above-mentioned proof, and not the violent assault of arms or the promise of pleasures, and (what is most wonderful of all) in the midst of the tyranny of the persecutors, an innumerable throng of people, both simple and most learned, flocked to the Christian faith. In this faith there are truths preached that surpass every human intellect; the pleasures of the flesh are curbed; it is taught that the things of the world should be spurned. Now, for the minds of mortal men to assent to these things is the greatest of miracles just as it is a manifest work of divine inspiration that, spurning visible things, men should seek only what is invisible. Now, that this has happened neither without preparation nor by chance, but as a result of the disposition of God, is clear from the fact that through many pronouncements of the ancient prophets God had foretold that He would do this. The books of these prophets are held in veneration among us Christians, since they give witness to our faith. (SCG, I, 6)

Here the point, I think, is the following. It is of course totally proper and entirely sensible to take a belief on God's say-so, to accept it on his authority. Clearly I am not foolish or irrational in believing something on the authority of my favorite mathematician, even if I cannot work it out for myself. I may thus come to believe, for example, that the four-color problem has been solved. But then a fortiori I would not be foolish or irrational in accepting a belief on the basis of *God*'s authority. If I know that God proposes p to me for belief, then, clearly enough, it is eminently sensible to believe p. The question is not whether it is foolish to believe something on God's authority, but whether it is foolish to believe that God has in fact proposed a given item for my belief. Obviously, if he *has,* then I should believe it; but what is my reason or motive for supposing that in fact it is *God* who has proposed for our belief, for example, the teaching of the Trinity?

This is the question Aquinas addresses in the above passage; he means to argue that it is not foolish or irrational to take it that God has proposed for our belief just those items Christians suppose that he has — the articles of faith. What he means to say, I think, is that to believe in the mysteries of the faith is not to be foolish or to believe with undue levity, because we have *evidence for* the conclusion that God has proposed them for our belief. This evidence consists in the fulfillment of prophecy and in the signs and wonders accompanying the proclamation of these mysteries. Aquinas refers here to "works that surpass the ability of all nature," such as "wonderful cures of illness," "the raising of the dead," and the like. The greatest miracle of all, he says, is the marvelous rapidity with which the Christian faith has spread, despite the best efforts of tyrants and despite the fact that "In this faith there are truths preached that surpass every human intellect;

the pleasures of the flesh are curbed; it is taught that the things of the world should be spurned.''

I think he means to suggest, furthermore, that if we did *not* have this evidence, or some other evidence, we would be foolish or irrational in accepting the mysteries of the faith. It is just because we have evidence for these things that we are not irrational in accepting them. Here by way of contrast he cites the followers of Mohammed, who, he says, do not have evidence: "It is thus clear that those who place any faith in his words believe foolishly" (SCG, I, 6).

What is important to see here is the following. Aquinas clearly believes that there are some propositions we are rationally justified in accepting, even though we do not have evidence for them, or reason to them from other propositions, or accept them on the basis of other propositions. Let us say that a proposition is *basic* for me if I believe it and do not believe it on the basis of other propositions. This relationship is familiar but hard to characterize in a revealing and nontrivial fashion. I believe that the word 'umbrageous' is spelled u-m-b-r-a-g-e-o-u-s: this belief is based on another belief of mine, the belief that that is how the dictionary says it is spelled. I believe that $72 \times 71 = 5,112$. This belief is based upon several other beliefs I hold: that $1 \times 72 = 72$; $7 \times 2 = 14$; $7 \times 7 = 49$; $49 + 1 = 50$; and others. Some of my beliefs, however, I accept but do not accept on the basis of any other beliefs. Call these beliefs *basic*. I believe that $2 + 1 = 3$, for example, and do not believe it on the basis of other propositions. I also believe that I am seated at my desk, and that there is a mild pain in my right knee. These too are basic for me; I do not believe them on the basis of others. Now the propositions we are rationally justified in accepting as basic, thinks Aquinas, are the ones we see to be true: those that are self-evident or evident to the senses. As for the rest of the propositions we believe, we are rational in accepting them only if they stand in a certain relationship to those that are properly basic. Among the nonbasic propositions we rationally accept, some we see to follow from those that *are* basic; these are the propositions we know. Others are not known to us, do not follow from basic propositions, but are nonetheless rationally acceptable because they are *probable* or likely with respect to them. I believe Aquinas means to hold, more generally, that a proposition is rationally acceptable for us only if it is at least probable with respect to beliefs that are properly basic for us — that is, with respect to beliefs that are self-evident or evident to the senses. And hence on his view, as on the evidentialist objector's, belief in God is rational for us only if we have evidence for it.

B. *Foundationalism*

Aquinas and the evidentialist objector concur, then, in holding that belief in God is rationally acceptable only if there is evidence for it — only if, that is, it is probable with respect to some body of propositions that constitutes the evidence. And here we can get a better understanding of Aquinas and the evidentialist objector if we see them as accepting some version of *classical foundationalism.* This is a *picture* or total way of looking at faith, knowledge, justified belief, rationality, and allied topics. This picture has been enormously popular in Western thought; and despite a substantial opposing groundswell, I think it remains the dominant way of thinking about these topics. According to the foundationalist some propositions are properly basic and some are not; those that are not are rationally accepted only on the basis of *evidence,* where the evidence must trace back, ultimately, to what *is* properly basic. The existence of God, furthermore, is not among the propositions that are properly basic; hence a person is rational in accepting theistic belief only if he has evidence for it. The vast majority of those in the Western world who have thought about our topic have accepted some form of classical foundationalism. The evidentialist objection to belief in God, furthermore, is obviously rooted in this way of looking at things. So suppose we try to achieve a deeper understanding of it.

Earlier I said the first thing to see about the evidentialist objection is that it is a *normative* contention or claim. The same thing must be said about foundationalism: this thesis is a normative thesis, a thesis about how a system of beliefs *ought* to be structured, a thesis about the properties of a correct, or acceptable, or rightly structured system of beliefs. According to the foundationalist there are norms, or duties, or obligations with respect to belief just as there are with respect to actions. To conform to these duties and obligations is to be rational; to fail to measure up to them is to be irrational. To be rational, then, is to exercise one's epistemic powers *properly* — exercise them in such a way as to go contrary to none of the norms for such exercise.

I think we can understand foundationalism more fully if we introduce the idea of a *noetic structure.* A person's noetic structure is the set of propositions he believes, together with certain epistemic relations that hold among him and these propositions. As we have seen, some of my beliefs may be based upon others; it may be that there are a pair of propositions A and B such that I believe $B,$ and believe A *on the basis of* B. An account of a person's noetic structure, then, would specify which of his beliefs are basic and which nonbasic. Of course it is abstractly possible that *none* of his beliefs is basic; perhaps he holds just three beliefs, $A, B,$ and $C,$ and believes each of them on the basis of the other two. We might think this improper or irrational, but that is not to say it could not be done. And it is also possible that *all* of his beliefs are basic; perhaps he believes a lot of propositions but does not believe any of them on the basis of any others. In the typical case, however, a noetic structure will include both basic and nonbasic beliefs. It may be useful to give some examples of beliefs that are often basic for a person. Suppose I seem to see a tree; I have that characteristic sort of experience that goes with perceiving a tree. I may then believe the proposition that I see a tree. It is *possible* that I believe that proposition *on the basis of* the proposition that I seem to see a tree; in the typical case, however, I will not believe the former on the basis of the latter because in the typical case I will not believe the latter at all. I will not be paying any attention to my experience but will be concentrating on the tree. Of course I *can* turn my attention to my experience, notice how things look to me, and acquire the belief that I seem to see something that looks like *that;* and if you challenge my claim that I see a tree, perhaps I *will* thus turn my attention to my experience. But in the typical case I will not believe that I see a tree on the basis of a proposition about my experience; for I believe *A* on the basis of *B* only if I believe *B,* and in the typical case where I perceive a tree I do not believe (or entertain) any propositions about my experience. Typically I take such a proposition as basic. Similarly, I believe I had breakfast this morning; this too is basic for me. I do not believe this proposition on the basis of some proposition about my experience — for example, that I seem to remember having had breakfast. In the typical case I will not have even considered *that* question — the question whether I *seem* to remember having had breakfast; instead I simply believe that I had breakfast; I take it as basic.

Second, an account of a noetic structure will include what we might call an index of *degree* of belief. I hold some of my beliefs much more firmly than others. I believe both that $2 + 1 = 3$ and that London, England, is latitudinally north of Saskatoon, Saskatchewan; but I believe the former more resolutely than the latter. Some beliefs I hold with maximum firmness; others I do in fact accept, but in a much more tentative way.

Third, a somewhat vaguer notion: an account of a person's noetic structure would include something like an index of *depth of ingression.* Some of my beliefs are, we might say, on the periphery of my noetic structure. I accept them, and may even accept them firmly, but I could give them up without much change elsewhere in my noetic structure. I believe there are some large boulders on the top of the Grand Teton. If I come to give up this belief (say by climbing it and not finding any), that change need not have extensive reverberations throughout the rest of my noetic structure; it could be accommodated with minimal alteration elsewhere. So its depth of ingression into my noetic structure is not great. On the other hand, if I were to come to believe that there simply is no such thing as the Grand Teton, or no mountains at all, or no such thing as the state of Wyoming, that would have much greater reverberations. And suppose I were to come to think there had not been much of a past (that the world was created just five minutes ago, complete with all its apparent memories and traces of the past) or that there were not any other persons: these changes would have even greater reverberations; these beliefs of mine have great depth of ingression into my noetic structure.

Now foundationalism is best construed, I think, as a thesis about *rational* noetic structures. A noetic structure is rational if it could be the noetic structure of a person who was completely rational. To be completely rational, as I am here using the term, is not to believe only what is true, or to believe all the logical consequences of what one believes, or to believe all necessary truths with equal firmness, or to be uninfluenced by emotion in forming belief; it is, instead, to do the right thing with respect to one's believings. It is to violate no epistemic duties. From this point of view, a rational person is one whose believings meet the appropriate standards; to criticize a person as irrational is to criticize her for failing to fulfill these duties or responsibilities, for failing to conform to the relevant norms or standards. To draw the ethical analogy, the irrational is the impermissible; the rational is the permissible.

We may think of the foundationalist as beginning with the observation that some of our beliefs are based upon others. According to the foundationalist a rational noetic structure will *have a foundation* — a set of beliefs not accepted on the basis of others; in a rational noetic structure some beliefs will be basic. Nonbasic beliefs, of course, will be accepted on the basis of other beliefs, which may be accepted on the basis of still other beliefs, and so on until the foundations are reached. In a rational noetic structure, therefore, every nonbasic belief is ultimately accepted on the basis of basic beliefs.

But a belief cannot properly be accepted on the basis of just *any* other belief; in a rational noetic structure, A will be accepted on the basis of B only if B *supports* A or is a member of a set of beliefs that together support A. It is not clear just what this relation — call it the 'supports' relation — is; and different foundationalists propose different candidates. Presumably, however, it lies in the neighborhood of *evidence;* if A supports B, then A is evidence for B, or makes B evident; or perhaps B is likely or probable with respect to A. This relation admits degrees. My belief that Feike can swim is supported by my knowledge that nine out of ten Frisians can swim and Feike is a Frisian; it is supported more strongly by my knowledge that the evening paper contains a picture of Feike triumphantly finishing first in the 1500-meter freestyle in the 1980 summer Olympics. And the foundationalist holds, sensibly enough, that in a rational noetic structure the strength of a nonbasic belief will depend on the degree of support from foundational beliefs.

By way of summary, then, let us say that according to foundationalism:

(1) in a rational noetic structure the believed-on-the-basis-of relation is asymmetric and irreflexive, (2) a rational noetic structure has a foundation, and (3) in a rational noetic structure nonbasic belief is proportional in strength to support from the foundations.

C. Conditions of Proper Basicality

Next we note a further and fundamental feature of classic varieties of foundationalism: they all lay down certain conditions of proper basicality. From the foundationalist point of view not just any kind of belief can be found in the foundations of a rational noetic structure; a belief to be properly basic (that is, basic in a rational noetic structure) must meet certain conditions. It must be capable of functioning foundationally, capable of bearing its share of the weight of the whole noetic structure. Thus Thomas Aquinas, as we have seen, holds that a proposition is properly basic for a person only if it is self-evident to him or "evident to the senses."

Suppose we take a brief look at self-evidence. Under what conditions does a proposition have it? What kinds of propositions are self-evident? Examples would include very simple arithmetical truths such as

(6) $2 + 1 = 3$;

simple truths of logic such as

(7) No man is both married and unmarried;

perhaps the generalizations of simple truths of logic, such as

(8) For any proposition p the conjunction of p with its denial is false;

and certain propositions expressing identity and diversity; for example,

(9) Redness is distinct from greenness,
(10) The property of being prime is distinct from the property of being composite,

and

(11) The proposition *all men are mortal* is distinct from the proposition *all mortals are men.*

There are others; Aquinas gives as examples:

(12) The whole is greater than the part,

where, presumably, he means by "part" what we mean by "proper part," and, more dubiously,

(13) Man is an animal.

Still other candidates — candidates which may be less than entirely uncontroversial — come from many other areas; for example,

(14) If p is necessarily true and p entails q, then q is necessarily true,
(15) If e^1 occurs before e^2 and e^2 occurs before e^3, then e^1 occurs before e^3,

and

(16) It is wrong to cause unnecessary (and unwanted) pain just for the fun of it.

What is it that characterizes these propositions? According to the tradition the outstanding characteristic of a self-evident proposition is that one simply sees it to be true upon grasping or understanding it. Understanding a self-evident proposition is sufficient for apprehending its truth. Of course this notion must be relativized to *persons;* what is self-evident to you might not be to me. Very simple arithmetical truths will be self-evident to nearly all of us, but a truth like $17 + 18 = 35$ may be self-evident only to some. And of course a proposition is self-evident to a person only if he does in fact grasp it, so a proposition will not be self-evident to those who do not apprehend the concepts it involves. As Aquinas says, some propositions are self-evident only to the learned; his example is the truth that immaterial substances do not occupy space. Among those propositions whose concepts not everyone grasps, some are such that anyone who *did* grasp them would see their truth; for example,

(17) A model of a first-order theory T assigns truth to the axioms of T.

Others — $17 + 13 = 30$, for example — may be such that some but not all of those who apprehend them also see that they are true.

But how shall we understand this "seeing that they are true"? Those who speak of self-evidence explicitly turn to this visual metaphor and expressly explain self-evidence by reference to vision. There are two important aspects to the metaphor and two corresponding components to the idea of self-evidence. First, there is the *epistemic* component: a proposition p is self-evident to a person S only if S has *immediate* knowledge of p — that is, knows p, and does not know p on the basis of his knowledge of other propositions. Consider a simple arithmetic truth such as $2 + 1 = 3$ and compare it with one like $24 \times 24 = 576$. I know each of these propositions, and I know the second but not the first on the basis of computation, which is a kind of inference. So I have immediate knowledge of the first but not the second.

But there is also a phenomenological component. Consider again our two propositions; the first but not the second has about it a kind of luminous aura or glow when you bring it to mind or consider it. Locke speaks, in this connection, of an "evident luster"; a self-evident proposition, he says, displays a kind of "clarity and brightness to the attentive mind." Descartes speaks instead of "clarity and distinctness"; each, I think, is referring to the same phenomenological feature. And this feature is connected with another: upon understanding a proposition of this sort one feels a strong inclination to accept it; this luminous obviousness seems to compel or at least impel assent. Aquinas and Locke, indeed, held that a person, or at any rate a normal, well-formed human being, finds it impossible to withhold assent when considering a self-evident proposition. The phenomenological component of the idea of self-evidence, then, seems to have a double aspect: there is the luminous aura that $2 + 1 = 3$ displays, and there is also an experienced tendency to accept or believe it. Perhaps, indeed, the luminous aura *just is* the experienced impulsion toward acceptance; perhaps they are the very same thing. In this case the phenomenological component would not have the double aspect that I suggested; in either case, however, we must recognize this phenomenological aspect of self-evidence.

Aquinas therefore holds that self-evident propositions are properly basic. I think he means to add that propositions "evident to the senses" are also properly basic. By this latter term I think he means to refer to *perceptual* propositions — propositions whose truth or falsehood we can determine by looking or employing some other sense. He has in mind, I think, such propositions as

(18) There is a tree before me,
(19) I am wearing shoes,

and

(20) That tree's leaves are yellow.

So Aquinas holds that a proposition is properly basic if and only if it is either self-evident or evident to the senses. Other foundationalists have insisted that propositions basic in a rational noetic structure must be *certain* in some important sense. Thus it is plausible to see Descartes as holding that the foundations of a rational noetic structure include, not such propositions as (18)-(20) but more cautious claims — claims about one's own mental life; for example,

(21) It seems to me that I see a tree,
(22) I seem to see something green,

or, as Professor Chisholm puts it,

(23) I am appeared greenly to.

Propositions of this latter sort seem to enjoy a kind of immunity from error not enjoyed by those of the former. I could be mistaken in thinking I see a pink rat; perhaps I am hallucinating or the victim of an illusion. But it is at the least very much harder to see that I could be mistaken in believing that I *seem* to see a pink rat, in believing that I am appeared pinkly (or pink ratly) to. Suppose we say that a proposition with respect to which I enjoy this sort of immunity from error is incorrigible for me; then perhaps Descartes means to hold that a proposition is properly basic for S only if it is either self-evident or incorrigible for S.

By way of explicit definition:

(24) p is incorrigible for S if and only if (a) it is not possible that S believe p and p be false, and (b) it is not possible that S believe $\sim p$ and p be true.

Here we have a further characteristic of foundationalism: the claim that not just any proposition is properly basic. Ancient and medieval foundationalists tended to hold that a proposition is properly basic for a person only if it is either self-evident or evident to the senses: modern foundationalists — Descartes, Locke, Leibniz, and the like — tended to hold that a proposition is properly basic for S only if either self-evident or incorrigible for S. Of course this is a historical generalization and is thus perilous; but perhaps it is worth the risk. And now let us say that a *classical foundationalist* is anyone who is either an ancient and medieval or a modern foundationalist.

D. The Collapse of Foundationalism

Now suppose we return to the main question: Why should not belief in God be among the foundations of my noetic structure? The answer, on the part of the classical foundationalist, was that even if this belief is *true,* it does not have the characteristics a proposition must have to deserve a place in the foundations. There is no room in the foundations for a proposition that can be rationally accepted only on the basis of other propositions. The only properly basic propositions are those that are self-evident or incorrigible or evident to the senses. Since the proposition that God exists is none of the above, it is not properly basic for anyone; that is, no well-formed, rational noetic structure contains this proposition in its foundations. But now we must take a closer look at this fundamental principle of classical foundationalism:

(25) A proposition p is properly basic for a person S if and only if p is either self-evident for S or incorrigible for S or evident to the senses for S.

(25) contains two claims: first, a proposition is properly basic *if* it is self-evident, incorrigible, or evident to the senses, and, second, a proposition is properly basic *only if* it meets this condition. The first seems true enough; suppose we concede it. But what is to be said for the second? Is there any reason to accept it? Why does the foundationalist accept it? Why does he think the theist ought to?

We should note first that if this thesis, and the correlative foundationalist thesis that a proposition is rationally acceptable only if it follows from or is probable with respect to what is properly basic — if these claims are true, then enormous quantities of what we all in fact believe are irrational. One crucial lesson to be learned from the development of modern philosophy — Descartes through Hume, roughly — is just this: relative to propositions that are self-evident and incorrigible, most of the beliefs that form the stock in trade of ordinary everyday life are not probable — at any rate there is no reason to think they are probable. Consider all those propositions that entail, say, that there are enduring physical objects, or that there are persons distinct from myself, or that the world has existed for more than five minutes: none of these propositions, I think, is more probable than not with respect to what is self-evident or incorrigible for me; at any rate no one has given good reason to think any of them is. And now suppose we add to the foundations propositions that are evident to the senses, thereby moving from modern to ancient and medieval foundationalism. Then propositions entailing the existence of material objects will of course be probable with respect to the foundations, because included therein. But the same cannot be said either for propositions about the past or for propositions entailing the existence of persons distinct from myself; as before, they will not be probable with respect to what is properly basic.

And does not this show that the thesis in question is false? The contention is that

(26) A is properly basic for me only if A is self-evident or incorrigible or evident to the senses for me.

But many propositions that do not meet these conditions *are* properly basic for me. I believe, for example, that I had lunch this noon. I do not believe this proposition on the basis of other propositions; I take it as basic; it is in the foundations of my noetic structure. Furthermore, I am entirely rational in so taking it, even though this proposition is neither self-evident nor evident to the senses nor incorrigible for me. Of course this may not convince the foundationalist; he may think that in fact I do *not* take that proposition as basic, or perhaps he will bite the bullet and maintain that if I really *do* take it as basic, then the fact is I *am,* so far forth, irrational.

Perhaps the following will be more convincing. According to the classical foundationalist (call him F) a person S is rational in accepting (26) only if either (26) is properly basic (self-evident or incorrigible or evident to the senses) for him, or he believes (26) on the basis of propositions that are properly basic for him and support (26). Now presumably if F knows of some support for (26) from propositions that are self-evident or evident to the senses or incorrigible, he will be able to provide a good argument — deductive, inductive, probabilistic, or whatever — whose premises are self-evident or evident to the senses or incorrigible and whose conclusion is (26). So far as I know, no foundationalist has provided such an argument. It therefore appears that the foundationalist does not know of any support for (26) from propositions that are (on his account) properly basic. So if he is to be rational in accepting (26), he must (on his own account) accept it as basic. But according to (26) itself, (26) is properly basic for F only if (26) is self-evident or incorrigible or evident to the senses for him. Clearly (26) meets none of these conditions. Hence it is not properly basic for F. But then F is self-referentially inconsistent in accepting (26); he accepts (26) as basic, despite the fact that (26) does not meet the condition for proper basicality that (26) itself lays down.

Furthermore, (26) is either false or such that in accepting it the foundationalist is violating his epistemic responsibilities. For F does not know of any argument or evidence for (26). Hence if it is true, he will be violating his epistemic responsibilities in accepting it. So (26) is either false or such that F cannot rationally accept it. Still further, if the theist were to accept (26) at the foundationalist's urging but without argument, he would be adding to his noetic structure a proposition that is either false or such that in accepting it he violates his noetic responsibilities. But if there is such a thing as the ethics of belief, surely it will proscribe believing a proposition one knows to be either false or such that one ought not to believe it. Accordingly, I ought not to accept (26) in the absence of argument from premises that meet the condition it lays down. The same goes for the foundationalist: if he cannot find such an argument for (26), he ought to give it up. Furthermore, he ought not to urge and I ought not to accept any objection to theistic belief that crucially depends upon a proposition that is true only if I ought not believe it.

We might try amending (26) in various ways. Nearly everyone accepts as basic some propositions entailing the existence of other persons and some propositions about the past; not nearly everyone accepts the existence of God as basic. Struck by this fact, we might propose:

(27) p is properly basic for S if and only if p is self-evident or incor-
    rigible or evident to the senses for S, or is accepted as basic by
    nearly everyone.

There are problems with (27). It is meant to legitimize my taking as basic
such deliverances of memory as that I had lunch this noon; but not nearly
everyone takes that proposition as basic. Most of you, I daresay, have not so
much as given it a thought; you are much too busy thinking about your own
lunch to think about mine. So (27) will not do the job as it stands. That is of
no real consequence, however; for even if we had an appropriate statement
of (27), it would suffer from the same sort of malady as does (26). Not nearly
everyone takes (27) as basic; I do not, for example. Nor is it self-evident,
incorrigible, or evident to the senses. So unless we can find an argument for
it from propositions that meet the conditions it lays down, we shall, if we
believe it, be believing a proposition that is probably either false or such that
we ought not believe it. Therefore we ought not believe it, at least until
someone produces such an argument for it.

Now we could continue to canvass other revisions of (26), and in Part
III I shall look into the proper procedure for discovering and justifying such
criteria for proper basicality. It is evident, however, that classical foundationalism is bankrupt and insofar as the evidentialist objection is rooted in classical
foundationalism, it is poorly rooted indeed.

Of course the evidentialist objection *need* not presuppose classical foundationalism; someone who accepted quite a different version of foundationalism could no doubt urge this objection. But in order to evaluate it, we should
have to see what criterion of proper basicality was being invoked. In the
absence of such specification the objection remains at best a promissory note.
So far as the present discussion goes, then, the next move is up to the
evidentialist objector. He must specify a criterion for proper basicality that is
free from self-referential difficulties, rules out belief in God as properly basic,
and is such that there is some reason to think it is true.

III. The Reformed Objection to Natural Theology

Suppose we think of natural theology as the attempt to prove or demonstrate
the existence of God. This enterprise has a long and impressive history —
a history stretching back to the dawn of Christendom and boasting among
its adherents many of the truly great thinkers of the Western world. One
thinks, for example, of Anselm, Aquinas, Scotus, and Ockham, of Descartes,
Spinoza, and Leibniz. Recently — since the time of Kant, perhaps — the

tradition of natural theology has not been as overwhelming as it once was; yet it continues to have able defenders both within and without officially Catholic philosophy.

Many Christians, however, have been less than totally impressed. In particular Reformed or Calvinist theologians have for the most part taken a dim view of this enterprise. A few Reformed thinkers — B. B. Warfield, for example — endorse the theistic proofs, but for the most part the Reformed attitude has ranged from tepid endorsement, through indifference, to suspicion, hostility, and outright accusations of blasphemy. And this stance is initially puzzling. It looks a little like the attitude some Christians adopt toward faith healing: it can't be done, but even if it could it shouldn't be. What exactly, or even approximately, do these sons and daughters of the Reformation have against proving the existence of God? What *could* they have against it? What could be less objectionable to any but the most obdurate atheist?

A. *The Objection Initially Stated*

By way of answering this question, I want to consider three representative Reformed thinkers. Let us begin with the nineteenth-century Dutch theologian Herman Bavinck:

> A distinct natural theology, obtained apart from any revelation, merely through observation and study of the universe in which man lives, does not exist. . . .
>
> Scripture urges us to behold heaven and earth, birds and ants, flowers and lilies, in order that we may see and recognize God in them. "Lift up your eyes on high, and see who hath created these." Isaiah 40:26. Scripture does not reason in the abstract. It does not make God the conclusion of a syllogism, leaving it to us whether we think the argument holds or not. But it speaks with authority. Both theologically and religiously it proceeds from God as the starting point.
>
> We receive the impression that belief in the existence of God is based entirely upon these proofs. But indeed that would be "a wretched faith, which, before it invokes God, must first prove his existence." The contrary, however, is the truth. There is not a single object the existence of which we hesitate to accept until definite proofs are furnished. Of the existence of self, of the world round about us, of logical and moral law, etc., we are so deeply convinced because of the indelible impressions which all these things make upon our consciousness that we need no arguments or demonstration. Spontaneously, altogether involuntarily: without any constraint or coercion, we accept that existence. Now the same is true in regard to the

existence of God. The so-called proofs are by no means the final grounds of our most certain conviction that God exists. This certainty is established only by faith; that is, by the spontaneous testimony which forces itself upon us from every side.[29]

According to Bavinck, then, belief in the existence of God is not based upon proofs or arguments. By "argument" here I think he means arguments in the style of natural theology — the sort given by Aquinas and Scotus and later by Descartes, Leibniz, Clarke, and others. And what he means to say, I think, is that Christians do not *need* such arguments. Do not need them for what?

Here I think Bavinck means to hold two things. First, arguments or proofs are not, in general, the source of the believer's confidence in God. Typically the believer does not believe in God on the basis of arguments; nor does he believe such truths as that God has created the world on the basis of arguments. Second, argument is not needed for *rational justification;* the believer is entirely within his epistemic right in believing, for example, that God has created the world, even if he has no argument at all for that conclusion. The believer does not need natural theology in order to achieve rationality or epistemic propriety in believing; his belief in God can be perfectly rational even if he knows of no cogent argument, deductive or inductive, for the existence of God — indeed, even if there is no such argument.

Bavinck has three further points. First he means to add, I think, that we cannot come to knowledge of God on the basis of argument; the arguments of natural theology just do not work. (And he follows this passage with a more or less traditional attempt to refute the theistic proofs, including an endorsement of some of Kant's fashionable confusions about the ontological argument.) Second, Scripture "proceeds from God as the starting point," and so should the believer. There is nothing by way of proofs or arguments for God's existence in the Bible; that is simply presupposed. The same should be true of the Christian believer then; he should *start* from belief in God rather than from the premises of some argument whose conclusion is that God exists. What is it that makes those premises a better starting point anyway? And third, Bavinck points out that belief in God relevantly resembles belief in the existence of the self and the external world — and, we might add, belief in other minds and the past. In none of these areas do we typically *have* proof or arguments, or *need* proofs or arguments.

Suppose we turn next to John Calvin, who is as good a Calvinist as any. According to Calvin God has implanted in us all an innate tendency, or nisus, or disposition to believe in him:

29. Herman Bavinck, *The Doctrine of God,* tr. William Hendriksen (Grand Rapids: Eerdmans, 1951), pp. 78-79. *The Doctrine of God* is the translation of the second volume of Bavinck's *Gereformeerde Dogmatiek,* published 1895-99.

'There is within the human mind, and indeed by natural instinct, an awareness of divinity.' This we take to be beyond controversy. To prevent anyone from taking refuge in the pretense of ignorance, God himself has implanted in all men a certain understanding of his divine majesty. Ever renewing its memory, he repeatedly sheds fresh drops. Since, therefore, men one and all perceive that there is a God and that he is their Maker, they are condemned by their own testimony because they have failed to honor him and to consecrate their lives to his will. If ignorance of God is to be looked for anywhere, surely one is most likely to find an example of it among the more backward folk and those more remote from civilization. Yet there is, as the eminent pagan says, no nation so barbarous, no people so savage, that they have not a deep-seated conviction that there is a God. So deeply does the common conception occupy the minds of all, so tenaciously does it inhere in the hearts of all! Therefore, since from the beginning of the world there has been no region, no city, in short, no household, that could do without religion, there lies in this a tacit confession of a sense of deity inscribed in the hearts of all.

Indeed, the perversity of the impious, who though they struggle furiously are unable to extricate themselves from the fear of God, is abundant testimony that this conviction, namely, that *there is some God,* is naturally inborn in all, and is fixed deep within, as it were in the very marrow. . . . From this we conclude *that it is not a doctrine that must first be learned in school,* but one of which each of us is master from his mother's womb and which nature itself permits no one to forget.[30]

Calvin's claim, then, is that God has created us in such a way that we have a strong tendency or inclination toward belief in him. This tendency has been in part overlaid or suppressed by sin. Were it not for the existence of sin in the world, human beings would believe in God to the same degree and with the same natural spontaneity that we believe in the existence of other persons, an external world, or the past. This is the natural human condition; it is because of our presently unnatural sinful condition that many of us find belief in God difficult or absurd. The fact is, Calvin thinks, one who does not believe in God is in an epistemically substandard position — rather like a man who does not believe that his wife exists, or thinks she is like a cleverly constructed robot and has no thought, feelings, or consciousness.

Although this disposition to believe in God is partially suppressed, it is nonetheless universally present. And it is triggered or actuated by a widely realized condition:

30. John Calvin, *Institutes of the Christian Religion,* tr. Ford Lewis Battles (Philadelphia: Westminster Press, 1960), book 1, chapter 3, pp. 43-44.

> Lest anyone, then, be excluded from access to happiness, he not only sowed in men's minds that seed of religion of which we have spoken, but revealed himself and daily discloses himself in the whole workmanship of the universe. As a consequence, men cannot open their eyes without being compelled to see him. (51)

Like Kant, Calvin is especially impressed in this connection, by the marvelous compages of the starry heavens above:

> Even the common folk and the most untutored, who have been taught only by the aid of the eyes, cannot be unaware of the excellence of divine art, for it reveals itself in this innumerable and yet distinct and well-ordered variety of the heavenly host. (50)

And Calvin's claim is that one who accedes to this tendency and in these circumstances accepts the belief that God has created the world — perhaps upon beholding the starry heavens, or the splendid majesty of the mountains, or the intricate, articulate beauty of a tiny flower — is entirely within his epistemic rights in so doing. It is not that such a person is justified or rational in so believing by virtue of having an implicit argument — some version of the teleological argument, say. No; he does not need any argument for justification or rationality. His belief need not be based on any other propositions at all; under these conditions he is perfectly rational in accepting belief in God in the utter absence of any argument, deductive or inductive. Indeed, a person in these conditions, says Calvin, *knows* that God exists.

Elsewhere Calvin speaks of "arguments from reason" or rational arguments:

> The prophets and apostles do not boast either of their keenness or of anything that obtains credit for them as they speak; nor do they dwell upon rational proofs. Rather, they bring forward God's holy name, that by it the whole world may be brought into obedience to him. Now we ought to see how apparent it is not only by plausible opinion but by clear truth that they do not call upon God's name heedlessly or falsely. If we desire to provide in the best way for our consciences — that they may not be perpetually beset by the instability of doubt or vacillation, and that they may not also boggle at the smallest quibbles — we ought to seek our conviction in a higher place than human reasons, judgments, or conjectures, that is, in the secret testimony of the Spirit. (book 1, chapter 7, p. 78)

Here the subject for discussion is not belief in the existence of God, but belief that God is the author of the Scriptures; I think it is clear, however, that Calvin would say the same thing about belief in God's existence. The Christian does not *need* natural theology, either as the source of his confidence or to justify his belief. Furthermore, the Christian *ought* not to believe on the basis of argument; if he does, his faith is likely to be "unstable and wavering," the "subject of perpetual doubt." If my belief in God is based on argument, then if I am to be properly rational, epistemically responsible, I shall have to keep checking the philosophical journals to see whether, say, Anthony Flew has finally come up with a good objection to my favorite argument. This could be bothersome and time-consuming; and what do I do if someone *does* find a flaw in my argument? Stop going to church? From Calvin's point of view believing in the existence of God on the basis of rational argument is like believing in the existence of your spouse on the basis of the analogical argument for other minds — whimsical at best and unlikely to delight the person concerned.

B. The Barthian Dilemma

The twentieth-century theologian Karl Barth is particularly scathing in his disapproval of natural theology. *That* he disapproves is overwhelmingly clear. His *reasons* for thus disapproving, however, are much less clear; his utterances on this topic, as on others, are fascinating but Delphic in everything but length. Sometimes, indeed, he is outrageous, as when he suggests that the mere act of believing or accepting the Christian message is a manifestation of human pride, self-will, contumacy, and sin. Elsewhere, however, he is both more moderate and thoroughly intriguing:

> Now suppose the partner in the conversation [that is, natural theology] discovers that faith is trying to use the well-known artifice of dialectic in relation to him. We are not taking him seriously because we withhold from him what we really want to say and represent. It is only in appearance that we devote ourselves to him, and therefore what we say to him is only an apparent and unreal statement. What will happen then? Well, not without justice — although misconstruing the friendly intention which perhaps motivates us — he will see himself despised and deceived. He will shut himself up and harden himself against the faith which does not speak out frankly, which deserts its own standpoint for the standpoint of unbelief. What use to unbelief is a faith which obviously knows different? And how shocking for unbelief is a faith which only pretends to take up with unbelief a common position. . . . This dilemma betrays the inner contradiction in every form of a "Christian" natural theology. It must really represent and affirm the standpoint of faith. Its true objective to which it really wants to lead unbelief is the knowability of the real God through Himself in His revelation. But as a "natural" theology, its initial aim is to disguise this and therefore to pretend to share in the life-endeavor of natural man. It therefore thinks that

it should appear to engage in the dialectic of unbelief in the expectation that here at least a preliminary decision in regard to faith can and must be reached. Therefore, as a natural theology it speaks and acts improperly. . . . We cannot experiment with unbelief, even if we think we know and possess all sorts of interesting and very promising possibilities and recipes for it. We must treat unbelief seriously. Only one thing can be treated more seriously than unbelief; and that is faith itself — or rather, the real God in whom faith believes. But faith itself — or rather, the real God in whom faith believes — must be taken so seriously that there is no place at all for even an apparent transposition to the standpoint of unbelief, for the pedagogic and playful self-lowering into the sphere of its possibilities.[31]

We must try to penetrate a bit deeper into these objections to natural theology, and suppose we start with Barth. Precisely what is the objection to which he is pointing? That somehow it is improper or un-Christian or dishonest or impious to try to prove God's existence; but *how* exactly? Barth speaks here of a *dilemma* that confronts the natural theologian. Dilemmas have horns; what are the horns of this one? The following, I think. In presenting a piece of natural theology, either the believer must adopt what Barth calls "the standpoint of unbelief" or he must pretend to his unbelieving interlocutor to do so. If he does the former, he deserts his Christian standpoint; but if he does the latter, he is dishonest, in bad faith, professing to believe what in fact he does not believe. But what *is* the standpoint of unbelief and what is it to adopt it? And how could one fall into this standpoint just by working at natural theology, just by making a serious attempt to prove the existence of God?

Perhaps Barth is thinking along the following lines. In *arguing* about the existence of God, in attempting to prove it, one implicitly adopts a certain stance. In adopting this stance one presupposes that it is not yet known whether there is a God; that remains to be seen; that is what is up for discussion. In adopting this stance, furthermore, the natural theologian implicitly concedes that what one ought to believe here depends on the result of the inquiry; if there are good arguments *for* the existence of God, then we — that is, we believers and unbelievers who together are engaged in this inquiry — ought to accept God's existence; if there are good arguments *against* the existence of God, we ought to accept its denial; and if the arguments on both sides are equally strong (and equally weak) then perhaps the right thing to do is to remain agnostic.

In adopting this stance one concedes that the rightness or propriety of belief and unbelief depends upon the outcome of a certain inquiry. Belief in God is right and proper only if there is on balance better reason to believe

31. Karl Barth, *Church Dogmatics,* tr. G. T. Thompson and Harold Knight (Edinburgh: T&T Clark, 1956), volume 1, part I, pp. 93-95.

than not to believe — only if, that is, the arguments for the existence of God are stronger than those against it. But of course an inquiry has a starting point, and arguments have premises. In supposing the issue thus dependent upon the outcome of argument, one supposes the appropriate premises are available. What about these premises? In adopting this stance the natural theologian implicitly commits himself to the view that there is a certain set of propositions from which the premises of theistic and antitheistic arguments are to be drawn — a set of propositions such that belief in God is rational or proper only if it stands in the right relation to that set. He concurs with his unbelieving interlocutor that there is a set of propositions both can appeal to, a set of propositions accepted by all or nearly all rational persons; and the propriety or rightness of belief in God depends on its relation to these propositions.

What are these propositions and where do they come from? We shall have to enter that question more deeply later; for the moment let us call them "the deliverances of reason." Then to *prove* or *demonstrate* that God exists is to exhibit a deductive argument whose conclusion is that God exists, whose premises are drawn from the deliverances of reason, and each of whose steps is by way of an argument whose corresponding conditional is among the deliverances of reason. Aquinas's first three ways would be attempts to demonstrate the existence of God in just this sense. A demonstration that God does not exist, of course, would be structurally isomorphic; it would meet the second and third condition just mentioned but have as conclusion the proposition that there is no such person as God. An alleged example would be the deductive argument from evil — the claim that the existence of evil is among the deliverances of reason and is inconsistent with the existence of God.

Of course it might be that the existence of God does not thus follow from the deliverances of reason but is nonetheless *probable* or *likely* with respect to them. One could then give a probabilistic or inductive argument for the existence of God, thus showing that theistic belief is rational, or epistemically proper, in that it is more likely than not with respect to the deliverances of reason. Perhaps Aquinas's Fifth Way and Paley's argument from design can be seen as falling into this category, and perhaps the probabilistic argument from evil — the claim that it is unlikely that God exists, given all the evil there is — can then be seen as a structurally similar argument for the conclusion that unbelief is the proper attitude.

According to Barth, then, the natural theologian implicitly concedes that the propriety of belief in God is to be tested by its relationship to the deliverances of reason. Belief is right, or rational, or rationally acceptable only if it stands in the proper relationship to the deliverances of reason — only if, for example, it is more likely than not or at any rate not unlikely with respect to them.

Now to adopt the standpoint of unbelief is not, as Barth sees it, to reject belief in God. One who enthusiastically accepts and believes in the existence of God can nonetheless be in the standpoint of unbelief. To be in that standpoint it is sufficient to hold that belief in God is rationally permissible for a person *only if he or she has a good argument for it.* To be in the standpoint of unbelief is to hold that belief in God is rationally acceptable *only if it is more likely than not with respect to the deliverances of reason.* One who holds this belief, says Barth, is in the standpoint of unbelief; his ultimate commitment is to the deliverances of reason rather than to God. Such a person "makes reason a judge over Christ," or at any rate the Christian faith. And to do so, says Barth, is utterly improper for a Christian.

The horns of the Barthian dilemma, then, are bad faith or dishonesty on the one hand and the standpoint of unbelief on the other. Either the natural theologian accepts the standpoint of unbelief or he does not. In the latter case he misleads and deceives his unbelieving interlocutor and thus falls into bad faith. In the former case he makes his ultimate commitment to the deliverances of reason, a posture that is for a Christian totally inappropriate, a manifestation of sinful human pride.

> And this attempt to prove the existence of God certainly cannot end in any other way than with the affirmation that even apart from God's grace, already preceding God's grace, already anticipating it, he is ready for God, so that God is knowable to him otherwise than from and through himself. Not only does it end with this. In principle, it begins with it. For in what does it consist but in the arrogation, preservation and affirmation of the self-sufficiency of man and therefore his likeness with God? (135)

C. Rejecting Classical Foundationalism

Now I think the natural theologian has a sound response to Barth's dilemma: she can execute the maneuver known to dialectician and matador alike as "escaping between the horns." As a natural theologian she offers or endorses theistic arguments, but why suppose that her own belief in God must be based upon such argument? And if it is not, why suppose she must pretend that it is? Perhaps her aim is to point out to the unbeliever that belief in God follows from other things he already believes, so that he can continue in unbelief (and continue to accept these other beliefs) only on pain of inconsistency. We may hope this knowledge will lead him to give up his unbelief, but in any event she can tell him quite frankly that her belief in God is not based on its relation to the deliverances of reason. Indeed, she can follow Calvin in claiming that belief in God *ought* not to be based on arguments from the deliverances of reason or anywhere else. So even if "the standpoint of unbelief" is as reprehensible as Barth says it is, his dilemma seems to evaporate.

What is most interesting here is not Barth's claim that the natural theologian faces this dilemma; here he is probably wrong, or at any rate not clearly right. More interesting is his view that belief in God need not be based on argument. Barth joins Calvin and Bavinck in holding that the believer in God is entirely within his rights in believing as he does even if he does not know of any good theistic argument (deductive or inductive), even if he does not believe there is any such argument, and even if in fact no such argument exists. Like Calvin, Kuyper, and Bavinck, Barth holds that belief in God is properly basic — that is, such that it is rational to accept it without accepting it on the basis of any other propositions or beliefs at all. In fact, they think the Christian ought not to accept belief in God on the basis of argument; to do so is to run the risk of a faith that is unstable and wavering, subject to all the wayward whim and fancy of the latest academic fashion. What the Reformers held was that a believer is entirely rational, entirely within his epistemic rights, in *starting with* belief in God, in accepting it as basic, and in taking it as premise for argument to other conclusions.

In rejecting natural theology, therefore, these Reformed thinkers mean to say first of all that the propriety or rightness of belief in God in no way depends upon the success or availability of the sort of theistic arguments that form the natural theologian's stock in trade. I think this is their central claim here, and their central insight. As these Reformed thinkers see things, one who takes belief in God as basic is not thereby violating any epistemic duties or revealing a defect in his noetic structure; quite the reverse. The correct or proper way to believe in God, they thought, was not on the basis of arguments from natural theology or anywhere else; the correct way is to take belief in God as basic.

I spoke earlier of classical foundationalism, a view that incorporates the following three theses:

(1) In every rational noetic structure there is a set of beliefs taken as basic — that is, not accepted on the basis of any other beliefs,

(2) In a rational noetic structure nonbasic belief is proportional to support from the foundations,

and

(3) In a rational noetic structure basic beliefs will be self-evident or incorrigible or evident to the senses.

Now I think these three Reformed thinkers would be understood as rejecting classical foundationalism. They may have been inclined to accept (1); they show no objection to (2); but they were utterly at odds with the idea that the foundations of a rational noetic structure can at most include propositions that are self-evident or evident to the senses or incorrigible. In particular, they were prepared to insist that a rational noetic structure can include belief in God as basic. As Bavinck put it, "Scripture . . . does not make God the conclusion of a syllogism, leaving it to us whether we think the argument holds or not. But it speaks with authority. Both theologically and religiously it proceeds from God as the starting point." And of course Bavinck means to say that we must emulate Scripture here.

In the passages I quoted earlier, Calvin claims the believer does not need argument — does not need it, among other things, for epistemic respectability. We may understand him as holding, I think, that a rational noetic structure may very well contain belief in God among its foundations. Indeed, he means to go further, and in two separate directions. In the first place he thinks a Christian *ought* not believe in God on the basis of other propositions; a proper and well-formed Christian noetic structure will *in fact* have belief in God among its foundations. And in the second place Calvin claims that one who takes belief in God as basic can *know* that God exists. Calvin holds that one can *rationally accept* belief in God as basic; he also claims that one can *know* that God exists even if he has no argument, even if he does not believe on the basis of other propositions. A foundationalist is likely to hold that some properly basic beliefs are such that anyone who accepts them *knows* them. More exactly, he is likely to hold that among the beliefs properly basic for a person S, some are such that if S accepts them, S knows them. He could go on to say that *other* properly basic beliefs cannot be known if taken as basic, but only rationally believed; and he might think of the existence of God as a case in point. Calvin will have none of this; as he sees it, one needs no arguments to know that God exists.

IV. *Is* Belief in God Properly Basic?

According to the Reformed thinkers discussed in the last section the answer is "Yes indeed." I enthusiastically concur in this contention, and in this section I shall try to clarify and develop this view and defend it against some objections. I shall argue first that one who holds that belief in God is properly basic is not thereby committed to the view that just about *anything* is; I shall argue secondly that even if belief in God is accepted as basic, it is not *groundless;* I shall argue thirdly that one who accepts belief in God as basic may nonetheless be open to arguments *against* that belief; and finally I shall argue that the view I am defending is not plausibly thought of as a species of *fideism.*

A. The Great Pumpkin Objection

It is tempting to raise the following sort of question. If belief in God is properly basic, why cannot *just any* belief be properly basic? Could we not say the same for any bizarre aberration we can think of: What about voodoo or astrology? What about the belief that the Great Pumpkin returns every Halloween? Could I properly take *that* as basic? Suppose I believe that if I flap my arms with sufficient vigor, I can take off and fly about the room; could I defend myself against the charge of irrationality by claiming this belief is basic? If we say that belief in God is properly basic, will we not be committed to holding that just anything, or nearly anything, can properly be taken as basic, thus throwing wide the gates to irrationalism and superstition?

Certainly not. According to the Reformed epistemologist certain beliefs are properly basic in certain circumstances; those same beliefs may *not* be properly basic in other circumstances. Consider the belief that I see a tree: this belief is properly basic in circumstances that are hard to describe in detail, but include my being appeared to in a certain characteristic way; that same belief is not properly basic in circumstances including, say, my knowledge that I am sitting in the living room listening to music with my eyes closed. What the Reformed epistemologist holds is that there are widely realized circumstances in which belief in God is properly basic; but why should that be thought to commit him to the idea that just about *any* belief is properly basic in any circumstances, or even to the vastly weaker claim that for any belief there are circumstances in which it is properly basic? Is it just that he rejects the criteria for proper basicality purveyed by classical foundationalism? But why should *that* be thought to commit him to such tolerance of irrationality? Consider an analogy. In the palmy days of positivism the positivists went about confidently wielding their verifiability criterion and declaring meaningless much that was clearly meaningful. Now suppose someone rejected a formulation of that criterion — the one to be found in the second edition of A. J. Ayer's *Language, Truth and Logic,* for example. Would that mean she was committed to holding that

(1) 'Twas brillig, and the slithy toves did gyre and gimble in the wabe,

contrary to appearances, makes good sense? Of course not. But then the same goes for the Reformed epistemologist: the fact that he rejects the criterion for proper basicality purveyed by classical foundationalism does not mean that he is committed to supposing just anything is properly basic.

But what then is the problem? Is it that the Reformed epistemologist not only rejects those criteria for proper basicality but seems in no hurry to produce what he takes to be a better substitute? If he has no such criterion, how can he fairly reject belief in the Great Pumpkin as properly basic?

This objection betrays an important misconception. How *do* we rightly arrive at or develop criteria for meaningfulness, or justified belief, or proper basicality? Where do they come from? Must one have such a criterion before one can sensibly make any judgments — positive or negative — about proper basicality? Surely not. Suppose I do not know of a satisfactory substitute for the criteria proposed by classical foundationalism; I am nevertheless entirely within my epistemic rights in holding that certain propositions in certain conditions are not properly basic.

Some propositions seem self-evident when in fact they are not; that is the lesson of some of the Russell paradoxes. Nevertheless it would be irrational to take as basic the denial of a proposition that seems self-evident to you. Similarly, suppose it seems to you that you see a tree; you would then be irrational in taking as basic the proposition that you do not see a tree or that there are no trees. In the same way, even if I do not know of some illuminating criterion of meaning, I can quite properly declare (1) (above) meaningless.

And this raises an important question — one Roderick Chisholm has taught us to ask.[32] What is the status of criteria for knowledge, or proper basicality, or justified belief? Typically these are universal statements. The modern foundationalist's criterion for proper basicality, for example, is doubly universal:

(2) For any proposition A and person S, A is properly basic for S if and only if A is incorrigible for S or self-evident to S.

But how could one know a thing like that? What are its credentials? Clearly enough, (2) is not self-evident or just obviously true. But if it is not, how does one arrive at it? What sorts of arguments would be appropriate? Of course a foundationalist might find (2) so appealing he simply takes it to be true, neither offering argument for it nor accepting it on the basis of other things he believes. If he does so, however, his noetic structure will be self-referentially incoherent. (2) itself is neither self-evident nor incorrigible; hence if he accepts (2) as basic, the modern foundationalist violates in accepting it the condition of proper basicality he himself lays down. On the other hand, perhaps the foundationalist will try to produce some argument for it from premises that are self-evident or incorrigible: it is exceeding hard to see, however, what such an argument might be like. And until he has produced such arguments, what shall the rest of us do — we who do not find (2) at all obvious or compelling? How could he use (2) to show us that belief in God, for example, is not properly basic? Why should we believe (2) or pay it any attention?

The fact is, I think, that neither (2) nor any other revealing necessary

32. Roderick Chisholm, *The Problem of the Criterion* (Milwaukee: Marquette University Press, 1973), pp. 14ff.

and sufficient condition for proper basicality follows from clearly self-evident premises by clearly acceptable arguments. And hence the proper way to arrive at such a criterion is, broadly speaking, *inductive*. We must assemble examples of beliefs and conditions such that the former are obviously properly basic in the latter, and examples of beliefs and conditions such that the former are obviously *not* properly basic in the latter. We must then frame hypotheses as to the necessary and sufficient conditions of proper basicality and test these hypotheses by reference to those examples. Under the right conditions, for example, it is clearly rational to believe that you see a human person before you: a being who has thoughts and feelings, who knows and believes things, who makes decisions and acts. It is clear, furthermore, that you are under no obligations to reason to this belief from others you hold; under those conditions that belief is properly basic for you. But then (2) must be mistaken; the belief in question, under those circumstances, is properly basic, though neither self-evident nor incorrigible for you. Similarly, you may seem to remember that you had breakfast this morning, and perhaps you know of no reason to suppose your memory is playing you tricks. If so, you are entirely justified in taking that belief as basic. Of course it is not properly basic on the criteria offered by classical foundationalists, but that fact counts not against you but against those criteria.

Accordingly, criteria for proper basicality must be reached from below rather than above; they should not be presented *ex cathedra* but argued to and tested by a relevant set of examples. But there is no reason to assume, in advance, that everyone will agree on the examples. The Christian will of course suppose that belief in God is entirely proper and rational; if he does not accept this belief on the basis of other propositions, he will conclude that it is basic for him and quite properly so. Followers of Bertrand Russell and Madelyn Murray O'Hare may disagree; but how is that relevant? Must my criteria, or those of the Christian community, conform to their examples? Surely not. The Christian community is responsible to *its* set of examples, not to theirs.

So, the Reformed epistemologist can properly hold that belief in the Great Pumpkin is not properly basic, even though he holds that belief in God is properly basic and even if he has no full-fledged criterion of proper basicality. Of course he is committed to supposing that there is a relevant *difference* between belief in God and belief in the Great Pumpkin if he holds that the former but not the latter is properly basic. But this should prove no great embarrassment; there are plenty of candidates. These candidates are to be found in the neighborhood of the conditions that justify and ground belief in God — conditions I shall discuss in the next section. Thus, for example, the Reformed epistemologist may concur with Calvin in holding that God has implanted in us a natural tendency to see his hand in the world around us; the same cannot be said for the Great Pumpkin, there being no Great Pumpkin and no natural tendency to accept beliefs about the Great Pumpkin.[33]

B. The Ground of Belief in God

My claim is that belief in God is properly basic; it does not follow, however, that it is *groundless*. Let me explain. Suppose we consider perceptual beliefs, memory beliefs, and beliefs ascribing mental states to other persons, such beliefs as:

(3) I see a tree,
(4) I had breakfast this morning,

and

(5) That person is in pain.

Although beliefs of this sort are typically taken as basic, it would be a mistake to describe them as *groundless*. Upon having experience of a certain sort, I believe that I am perceiving a tree. In the typical case I do not hold this belief on the basis of other beliefs; it is nonetheless not groundless. My having that characteristic sort of experience — to use Professor Chisholm's language, my being appeared treely to — plays a crucial role in the formation of that belief. It also plays a crucial role in its *justification*. Let us say that a belief is *justified* for a person at a time if (a) he is violating no epistemic duties and is within his epistemic rights in accepting it then and (b) his noetic structure is not defective by virtue of his then accepting it.[34] Then my being appeared to in this characteristic way (together with other circumstances) is what confers on me the right to hold the belief in question; this is what justifies me in accepting it. We could say, if we wish, that this experience is what justifies me in holding it; this is the *ground* of my justification, and, by extension, the ground of the belief itself.

If I see someone displaying typical pain behavior, I take it that he or she is in pain. Again, I do not take the displayed behavior as *evidence* for that belief; I do not infer that belief from others I hold; I do not accept it on the basis of other beliefs. Still, my perceiving the pain behavior plays a unique role in the formation and justification of that belief; as in the previous case it forms the ground of my justification for the belief in question. The same holds

33. For further comment on the Great Pumpkin objection see Alvin Plantinga, "On Reformed Epistemology," *Reformed Journal,* January 1982.

34. I do not mean to suggest, of course, that if a person believes a true proposition and is justified (in this sense) in believing it, then it follows that he *knows* it; that is a different (and stronger) sense of the term.

for memory beliefs. I seem to remember having breakfast this morning; that is, I have an inclination to believe the proposition that I had breakfast, along with a certain past-tinged experience that is familiar to all but hard to describe. Perhaps we should say that I am appeared to pastly; but perhaps that insufficiently distinguishes the experience in question from those accompanying beliefs about the past not grounded in my own memory. The phenomenology of memory is a rich and unexplored realm; here I have no time to explore it. In this case as in the others, however, there is a justifying circumstance present, a condition that forms the ground of my justification for accepting the memory belief in question.

In each of these cases a belief is taken as basic, and in each case *properly* taken as basic. In each case there is some circumstance or condition that confers justification; there is a circumstance that serves as the *ground* of justification. So in each case there will be some true proposition of the sort

(6) In condition C, S is justified in taking p as basic.

Of course C will vary with p. For a perceptual judgment such as

(7) I see a rose-colored wall before me

C will include my being appeared to in a certain fashion. No doubt C will include more. If I am appeared to in the familiar fashion but know that I am wearing rose-colored glasses, or that I am suffering from a disease that causes me to be thus appeared to, no matter what the color of the nearby objects, then I am not justified in taking (7) as basic. Similarly for memory. Suppose I know that my memory is unreliable; it often plays me tricks. In particular, when I seem to remember having breakfast, then more often than not, I have not had breakfast. Under these conditions I am not justified in taking it as basic that I had breakfast, even though I seem to remember that I did.

So being appropriately appeared to, in the perceptual case, is not sufficient for justification; some further condition — a condition hard to state in detail — is clearly necessary. The central point here, however, is that a belief is properly basic only in certain conditions; these conditions are, we might say, the ground of its justification and, by extension, the ground of the belief itself. In this sense basic beliefs are not, or are not necessarily, *groundless* beliefs.

Now similar things may be said about belief in God. When the Reformers claim that this belief is properly basic, they do not mean to say, of course, that there are no justifying circumstances for it, or that it is in that sense groundless or gratuitous. Quite the contrary. Calvin holds that God "reveals and daily discloses himself in the whole workmanship of the universe," and the divine art "reveals itself in the innumerable and yet distinct and well-ordered variety of the heavenly host." God has so created us that we have a tendency or disposition to see his hand in the world about us. More precisely, there is in us a disposition to believe propositions of the sort *this flower was created by God* or *this vast and intricate universe was created by God* when we contemplate the flower or behold the starry heavens or think about the vast reaches of the universe.

Calvin recognizes, at least implicitly, that other sorts of conditions may trigger this disposition. Upon reading the Bible, one may be impressed with a deep sense that God is speaking to him. Upon having done what I know is cheap, or wrong, or wicked, I may feel guilty in God's sight and form the belief *God disapproves of what I have done*. A person in grave danger may turn to God, asking for his protection and help; and of course he or she then has the belief that God is indeed able to hear and help if he sees fit. When life is sweet and satisfying, a spontaneous sense of gratitude may well up within the soul; someone in this condition may thank and praise the Lord for his goodness, and will of course have the accompanying belief that indeed the Lord is to be thanked and praised.

There are therefore many conditions and circumstances that call forth belief in God: guilt, gratitude, danger, a sense of God's presence, a sense that he speaks, perception of various parts of the universe. A complete job would explore the phenomenology of all these conditions and of more besides. This is a large and important topic, but here I can only point to the existence of these conditions.

Of course none of the beliefs I mentioned a moment ago is the simple belief that God exists. What we have instead are such beliefs as:

(8) God is speaking to me,
(9) God has created all this,
(10) God disapproves of what I have done,
(11) God forgives me,

and

(12) God is to be thanked and praised.

These propositions are properly basic in the right circumstances. But it is quite consistent with this to suppose that the proposition *there is such a person as God* is neither properly basic nor taken as basic by those who believe in God. Perhaps what they take as basic are such propositions as (8)-(12), believing in the existence of God on the basis of propositions such as those. From this point of view it is not wholly accurate to say that it is belief in God that is properly basic; more exactly, what are properly basic are such propositions as (8)-(12), each of which self-evidently entails that God exists. It is not the relatively high-level and general proposition *God exists* that is properly basic, but instead propositions detailing some of his attributes or actions.

Suppose we return to the analogy between belief in God and belief in the existence of perceptual objects, other persons, and the past. Here too it is relatively specific and concrete propositions rather than their more general and abstract colleagues that are properly basic. Perhaps such items as:

(13) There are trees,

(14) There are other persons,

and

(15) The world has existed for more than five minutes

are not in fact properly basic; it is instead such propositions as:

(16) I see a tree,

(17) That person is pleased,

and

(18) I had breakfast more than an hour ago

that deserve that accolade. Of course propositions of the latter sort immediately and self-evidently entail propositions of the former sort, and perhaps there is thus no harm in speaking of the former as properly basic, even though so to speak is to speak a bit loosely.

The same must be said about belief in God. We may say, speaking loosely, that belief in God is properly basic; strictly speaking, however, it is probably not that proposition but such propositions as (8)-(12) that enjoy that status. But the main point, here, is this: belief in God, or (8)-(12), are properly basic; to say so, however, is not to deny that there are justifying conditions for these beliefs, or conditions that confer justification on one who accepts them as basic. They are therefore not groundless or gratuitous.

C. Is Argument Irrelevant to Basic Belief in God?

Suppose someone accepts belief in God as basic. Does it not follow that he will hold this belief in such a way that no argument could move him or cause him to give it up? Will he not hold it come what may, in the teeth of any evidence or argument with which he could be presented? Does he not thereby adopt a posture in which argument and other rational methods of settling disagreement are implicitly declared irrelevant? Surely not. Suppose someone accepts

(19) There is such a person as God

as basic. It does not for a moment follow that he will regard argument irrelevant to this belief of his; nor is he committed in advance to rejecting every argument against it. It could be, for example, that he accepts (19) as basic but also accepts as basic some propositions from which, by arguments whose corresponding conditionals he accepts as basic, it follows that (19) is false. What happens if he is apprised of this fact, perhaps by being presented with an argument from those propositions to the denial of (19)? Presumably some change is called for. If he accepts these propositions more strongly than (19), presumably he will give the latter up.

Similarly, suppose someone believes there is no God but also believes some propositions from which belief in God follows by argument forms he accepts. Presented with an argument from these propositions to the proposition that God exists, such a person may give up this atheism and accept belief in God. On the other hand, his atheistic belief may be stronger than his belief in some of the propositions in question, or his belief in their conjunction. It is possible, indeed, that he *knows* these propositions, but believes some of them less firmly than he believes that there is no God; in that case, if you present him with a valid argument from these propositions to the proposition that God exists, you may cause him to give up a proposition he knows to be true. It is thus possible to reduce the extent of someone's knowledge by giving him a sound argument from premises he knows to be true.

So a person can accept belief in God as basic without accepting it dogmatically — that is, in such a way that he will ignore any contrary evidence or argument. And now a second question: Suppose that belief in God *is* properly basic. Does it follow that one who accepts it dogmatically is within his epistemic rights? Does it follow that someone who is within his rights in accepting it as basic *remains* justified in this belief, no matter what counter-argument or counterevidence arises?

Again, surely not. The justification-conferring conditions mentioned above must be seen as conferring *prima facie* rather than *ultima facie,* or all-things-considered, justification. This justification can be overridden. My being appeared to treely gives me a *prima facie* right to take as basic the proposition *I see a tree.* But of course this right can be overridden; I might know, for example, that I suffer from the dreaded dendrological disorder, whose victims are appeared to treely only when there are no trees present. If I know this, then I am not within my rights in taking as basic the proposition *I see a tree* when I am appeared to treely. The same goes for the conditions that confer justification on belief in God. Like the fourteen-year-old theist (above, p. 117), perhaps I have been brought up to believe in God and am initially within my rights in so doing. But conditions can arise in which perhaps I am no longer justified in this belief. Perhaps you propose to me an argument for the conclusion that it is impossible that there be such a person as God. If this argument is convincing for me — if it started from premises that seem self-evident to me and proceeds by argument forms that seem self-evidently valid — then perhaps I am no longer justified in accepting theistic belief. Following John Pollock, we may say that a condition that overrides my *prima facie* justification for p is a *defeating condition* or *defeater* for p (for me). Defeaters, of course, are themselves *prima facie* defeaters, for the defeater can be defeated. Perhaps I spot a fallacy in the initially convincing argument; perhaps I discover a convincing argument for the denial of one of its premises; perhaps I learn on reliable authority that someone else has done one of those things. Then the defeater is defeated, and I am once again within my rights in accepting p. Of course a similar remark must be made about defeater-defeaters: they are subject to defeat by defeater-defeater-defeaters and so on.

Many believers in God have been brought up to believe, but then encountered potential defeaters. They have read books by skeptics, been apprised of the atheological argument from evil, heard it said that theistic belief is just a matter of wish fulfillment or only a means whereby one socioeconomic class keeps another in bondage. These circumstances constitute potential defeaters for justification in theistic belief. If the believer is to remain justified, something further is called for — something that *prima facie* defeats the defeaters. Various forms of theistic apologetics serve this function (among others). Thus the *free-will defense* is a defeater for the atheological argument from evil, which is a potential defeater for theistic belief. Suppose I am within my epistemic rights in accepting belief in God as basic, and suppose I am presented with a plausible argument — by Democritus, let's say — for the conclusion that the existence of God is logically incompatible with the existence of evil. (Let us add that I am strongly convinced that there *is* evil.) This is a potential defeater for my being rational in accepting theistic belief. What is required, if I am to continue to believe rationally, is a defeater for that defeater. Perhaps I discover a flaw in Democritus's argument, or perhaps I have it on reliable authority that Augustine, say, has discovered a flaw in the argument; then I am once more justified in my original belief.

D. Fideism

I take up one final question. In *Reflections on Christian Philosophy* Ralph McInerny suggests that what I have been calling Reformed epistemology is *fideism*. Is he right? Is the Reformed epistemologist perforce a fideist? That depends: it depends, obviously enough, on how we propose to use the term 'fideism.' According to my dictionary fideism is "exclusive or basic reliance upon faith alone, accompanied by a consequent disparagement of reason and utilized especially in the pursuit of philosophical or religious truth." A fideist therefore urges reliance on faith rather than reason, in matters philosophical and religious; and he may go on to disparage and denigrate reason. We may thus distinguish at least two grades of fideism: moderate fideism, according to which we must rely upon faith rather than reason in religious matters, and extreme fideism, which disparages and denigrates reason.

Now let us ask first whether the Reformed epistemologist is obliged to be an extreme fideist. Of course there is more than one way of disparaging reason. One way to do it is to claim that to take a proposition on faith is higher and better than accepting it on the basis of reason. Another way to disparage reason is to follow Kant in holding that reason left to itself inevitably falls into paradox and antinomy on ultimate matters. According to Kant pure reason offers us conclusive argument for supposing that the universe had no beginning, but also, unfortunately, conclusive arguments for the denial of that proposition. I do not think any of the alleged arguments are anywhere nearly conclusive, but if Kant were right, then presumably reason would not deserve to be paid attention to, at least on this topic. According to the most common brand of extreme fideism, however, reason and faith *conflict* or *clash* on matters of religious importance; and when they do, faith is to be preferred and reason suppressed. Thus according to Kierkegaard faith teaches "the absurdity that the eternal is the historical." He means to say, I think, that this proposition is among the deliverances of faith but absurd from the point of view of reason; and it should be accepted despite this absurdity. The turn-of-the-century Russian theologian Shestov carried extreme fideism even further; he held that one can attain religious truth only by rejecting the proposition that $2 + 2 = 4$ and accepting instead $2 + 2 = 5$.

Now it is clear, I suppose, that the Reformed epistemologist need not be an extreme fideist. His views on the proper basicality of belief in God surely do not commit him to thinking that faith and reason conflict. So suppose we ask instead whether the Reformed epistemologist is committed to *moderate* fideism. And again that depends; it depends upon how we propose to use the terms 'reason' and 'faith.' One possibility would be to follow Abraham Kuyper, who proposes to use these terms in such a way that one takes on faith whatever one accepts but does not accept on the basis of argument or inference or demonstration:

> There is thus no objection to the use of the term 'faith' for that function of the soul by which it attains certainty immediately or directly, without the aid of discursive demonstration. This places faith over against demonstration, but *not* over against knowing.[35]

On this use of these terms, anything taken as basic is taken on faith; anything believed on the basis of other beliefs is taken on reason. I take $2 + 1 = 3$ as

---

35. Abraham Kuyper, *Encyclopedia of Sacred Theology,* tr. J. DeVries (New York: Charles Scribner's Sons, 1898), pp. 128-29.

basic; accordingly, I take it on faith. When I am appropriately appeared to, I take as basic such propositions as *I see a tree before me* or *there is a house over there;* on the present construal I take these things on faith. I remember that I had lunch this noon, but do not accept this belief on the basis of other propositions; this too, then, I take on faith. On the other hand, what I take on the basis of reason is what I believe on the basis of argument or inference from other propositions. Thus I take $2 + 1 = 3$ on faith, but $21 \times 45 = 945$ by reason; for I accept the latter on the basis of calculation, which is a form of argument. Further, suppose I accept supralapsarianism or premillennialism or the doctrine of the virgin birth on the grounds that God proposes these doctrines for our belief and God proposes only truths; then on Kuyper's use of these terms I accept these doctrines not by faith but by reason. Indeed, if with Kierkegaard and Shestov I hold that the eternal is the historical and that $2 + 2 = 5$ because I believe God proposes *these* things for my belief, then on the present construal I take them not on faith but on the basis of reason.

And here we can see, I think, that Kuyper's use of these terms is not the relevant one for the discussion of fideism. For consider Shestov. Shestov is an extreme fideist because he thinks faith and reason conflict; and when they do, he says, it is reason that must be suppressed. To paraphrase the poem, "When faith and reason clash, let reason go to smash!" But he is not holding that faith teaches something — $2 + 2 = 5$, for example — that conflicts with a belief — $2 + 2 = 4$ — that one arrives at by reasoning from other propositions. On the contrary, the poignancy of the clash is just that what faith teaches conflicts with an *immediate* teaching of reason — a proposition that is apparently self-evident. On the Kuyperian use of these terms Shestov would be surprised to learn that he is not a fideist after all. For what he takes faith to conflict with here is not something one accepts by reason — that is, on the basis of other propositions. Indeed, on the Kuyperian account Shestov not only does not qualify as a fideist; he probably qualifies as an antifideist. Shestov probably did not recommend taking $2 + 2 = 5$ as basic; he probably held that God proposes this proposition for our belief and that we should therefore accept it. On the other hand, he also believed, no doubt, that $2 + 2 = 4$ is apparently self-evident. So given the Kuyperian use, Shestov would be holding that faith and reason conflict here, but it is $2 + 2 = 4$ that is the deliverance of faith and $2 + 2 = 5$ the deliverance of reason! Since he recommends accepting $2 + 2 = 5$, the deliverance of reason, he thus turns out to be a rationalist or antifideist, at least on this point.

And this shows that Kuyper's use of these terms is not the relevant use. What we take on faith is not simply what we take as basic, and what we accept by reason is not simply what we take on the basis of other propositions. The deliverances of reason include propositions taken as basic, and the deliverances of faith include propositions accepted on the basis of others.

The Reformed epistemologist, therefore, is a fideist only if he holds that some central truths of Christianity are not among the deliverances of reason and must instead be taken on faith. But just what are the deliverances of reason? What do they include? First, clearly enough, self-evident propositions and propositions that follow from them by self-evidently valid arguments are among the deliverances of reason. But we cannot stop there. Consider someone who holds that according to correct scientific reasoning from accurate observation the earth is at least a couple of billion years old; nonetheless, he adds, it is really no more than some 6,000 years old, because that is what faith teaches. Such a person is a fideist, even though the proposition *the earth is more than 6,000 years old* is neither self-evident nor a consequence of what is self-evident. So the deliverances of reason include more than the self-evident and its consequences. They also include basic perceptual truths (propositions "evident to the senses"), incorrigible propositions, certain memory propositions, certain propositions about other minds, and certain moral or ethical propositions.

But what about the belief that there is such a person as God and that we are responsible to him? Is that among the deliverances of reason or an item of faith? For Calvin it is clearly the former. "There is within the human mind, and indeed by natural instinct, an awareness of divinity. . . . God himself has implanted in all men a certain understanding of his divine majesty. . . . Men one and all perceive that there is a God and that he is their Maker" (*Institutes* I, 3, 1). According to Calvin everyone, whether in the faith or not, has a tendency or nisus, in certain situations, to apprehend God's existence and to grasp something of his nature and actions. This natural knowledge can be and is suppressed by sin, but the fact remains that a capacity to apprehend God's existence is as much part of our natural noetic equipment as is the capacity to apprehend perceptual truths, truths about the past, and truths about other minds. Belief in the existence of God is in the same boat as belief in other minds, the past, and perceptual objects; in each case God has so constructed us that in the right circumstances we form the belief in question. But then the belief that there is such a person as God is as much among the deliverances of reason as those other beliefs.

From this vantage point we can see, therefore, that the Reformed epistemologist is not a fideist at all with respect to belief in God. He does not hold that there is any conflict between faith and reason here, and he does not even hold that we cannot attain this fundamental truth by reason; he holds, instead, that it is among the deliverances of reason.

Of course the nontheist may disagree; he may deny that the existence of God is part of the deliverances of reason. A former professor of mine for whom I had and have enormous respect once said that theists and nontheists have different conceptions of reason. At the time I did not know what he meant, but now I think I do. On the Reformed view I have been urging, the deliverances of reason include the existence of God just as much as perceptual truths, self-evident truths, memory truths, and the like. It is not that theist and nontheist agree as to what reason delivers, the theist then going on to accept the existence of God by faith; there is, instead, disagreement in the first place as to what are the deliverances of reason. But then the Reformed epistemologist is no more a fideist with respect to belief in God than is, for example, Thomas Aquinas. Like the latter, he will no doubt hold that there are other truths of Christianity that are not to be found among the deliverances of reason — such truths, for example, as that God was in Christ, reconciling the world to himself. But he is not a fideist by virtue of his views on our knowledge of God.

By way of summary: I have argued that the evidentialist objection to theistic belief is rooted in classical foundationalism; the same can be said for the Thomistic conception of faith and reason. Classical foundationalism is attractive and seductive; in the final analysis, however, it turns out to be both false and self-referentially incoherent. Furthermore, the Reformed objection to natural theology, unformed and inchoate as it is, may best be seen as a rejection of classical foundationalism. As the Reformed thinker sees things, being self-evident, or incorrigible, or evident to the senses is not a necessary condition of proper basicality. He goes on to add that belief in God is properly basic. He is not thereby committed to the idea that just any or nearly any belief is properly basic, even if he lacks a criterion for proper basicality. Nor is he committed to the view that argument is irrelevant to belief in God if such a belief is properly basic. Furthermore, belief in God, like other properly basic beliefs, is not groundless or arbitrary; it is grounded in justification-conferring conditions. Finally, the Reformed view that belief in God is properly basic is not felicitously thought of as a version of fideism.

CHAPTER SIX

Justification and Theism

According to an ancient and honorable tradition, knowledge is *justified true belief.* But what is this "justification"? Theologians of the Protestant Reformation (however things may stand with their contemporary epigoni) had a clear conception of justification; justification, they held, is by faith. Contemporary epistemologists, sadly enough, do not thus speak with a single voice. They don't often subject the concept in question — the concept of epistemic justification — to explicit scrutiny; while there are many discussions of the conditions under which a person is justified in believing a proposition, there are few in which the principal topic is the *nature* of justification. But when they do discuss it, they display a notable lack of unanimity. Some claim that justification is by *epistemic dutifulness,* others that it is by *coherence,* and still others that it is by *reliability.*[1] The differences among these views are enormous; this is by no means a case of variations on the same theme. Indeed, disagreement is so deep and radical it is sometimes hard to be sure the various disputants are discussing the same issue. Now what should a Christian, or more broadly, a theist, make of this situation? How should such a person react to this baffling welter of conflict, this babble or Babel of confusion? In what follows I shall try to get a clearer look at epistemic justification and allied conceptions. In particular, I propose to examine this topic from an explicitly Christian, or more broadly, theistic point of view: how shall we think of epistemic justification from a theistic perspective? What can Christianity or theism contribute to our understanding of epistemic justification?

But here we need a preliminary word as to what it is, more exactly, I mean

---

1. See my "Positive Epistemic Status and Proper Function," in *Philosophical Perspectives 2: Epistemology,* ed. James Tomberlin (Northridge: California State University, 1988). [Ed. note: See bibliography #49.]

162

to be talking about. How shall we initially locate epistemic justification? First, such terms as 'justification' and 'justified' are, as Roderick Chisholm[2] suggests, terms of epistemic appraisal; to say that a proposition is *justified* for a person is to say that his believing or accepting it (here I shall not distinguish these two) has *positive epistemic status* for him. What we appraise here are a person's *beliefs:* more exactly, his *believings.* Someone's belief that there is such a person as God may be thus appraised, as well as her belief that human life evolved from unicellular life by way of the mechanisms suggested by contemporary evolutionary theory, and the less spectacular beliefs of everyday life. We may speak of a person's beliefs as *warranted,* or *justified,* or *rational,* or *reasonable,* contrasting them with beliefs that are unwarranted, unjustified, irrational, or unreasonable. The evidentialist objector to theistic belief, for example, argues that those who believe in God without evidence are unjustified in so doing, and are accordingly somehow unreasonable — guilty of an intellectual or cognitive impropriety, perhaps, or, alternatively and less censoriously, victims of some sort of intellectual dysfunction. Secondly, epistemic justification or positive epistemic status clearly comes in degrees: at any rate some of my beliefs have more by way of positive epistemic status for me than others.

And thirdly, among the fundamental concepts of epistemology, naturally enough, we find the concept of *knowledge.* It is widely agreed that true belief, while necessary for knowledge, is not sufficient for it. What more is required? It is widely agreed, again, that whatever exactly this further element may be, it is either epistemic justification or something intimately connected with it. Now it would be convenient just to *baptize* that quantity as 'justification,' thus taking that term as a proper name of the element, whatever exactly it is, enough of which (Gettier problems, perhaps, aside) distinguishes knowledge from mere true belief. The term 'justification,' however, has a deontological ring; it is redolent of duty and permission, obligation and rights. Furthermore, according to the long and distinguished tradition of Cartesian internalism (represented at its contemporary best by Roderick Chisholm's work[3]), aptness for epistemic duty fulfillment is indeed what distinguishes true belief from knowledge; using this term as a mere proper name of what distinguishes true belief from knowledge, therefore, can be confusing. Accordingly, I shall borrow Chisholm's term 'positive epistemic status' as my official name of the quantity in question — the quantity enough of which distinguishes mere true belief from knowledge.* (Of course we cannot initially assume that positive

---

2. See R. Chisholm, *Theory of Knowledge,* 2nd edition (New York: Prentice-Hall, 1977), pp. 5ff.

3. See my "Chisholmian Internalism," in *Philosophical Analysis: A Defense by Example,* ed. David Austin (Dordrecht: D. Reidel, 1988).

*Editor's Note: It is this property to which Plantinga later gives the name "warrant" (see Bibliography #28, 29, and 39).

epistemic status is a *single* or *simple* property; perhaps it is an amalgam of several others.) Initially, then, and to a first approximation, we can identify justification or positive epistemic status as a normative (possibly complex) property that comes in degrees, and which is such that enough of it (ignoring Gettier problems for the moment) is what distinguishes true belief from knowledge.

I. Positive Epistemic Status and Theism

Now how shall we think of positive epistemic status, or, indeed, the whole human cognitive enterprise, from a Christian theistic point of view? What bearing does theism have on the human cognitive enterprise? What features of theism bear on this topic? The central point, I think, is this: according to the theistic way of looking at the matter, we human beings, like ropes and linear accelerators, have been designed; we have been designed and created by God. We have been created by God; furthermore, according to Christian and Jewish versions of theism, we have been created by him *in his own image;* in certain crucial respects we resemble him. Now God is an actor, an agent, a creator: one who chooses certain ends and takes action to accomplish them. God is therefore a *practical* being. But he is also an *intellectual* or *intellecting* being. He has knowledge; indeed, he has the maximal degree of knowledge. He holds beliefs (even if his way of holding a belief is different from ours); and because he is omniscient, he believes every truth and holds only true beliefs. He therefore has the sort of grasp of concepts, properties, and propositions necessary for holding beliefs; and since he believes every true proposition, he has a grasp of every property and proposition.[4]

In setting out to create human beings in his image, then, God set out to create them in such a way that they could reflect something of his capacity to grasp concepts and hold beliefs. Furthermore, as the whole of the Christian tradition suggests, his aim was to create them in such a way that they can reflect something of his capacity for holding *true* beliefs, for attaining *knowledge.* This has been the nearly unanimous consensus of the Christian tradition; but it is worth noting that it is not inevitable. God's aim in creating us with the complicated, highly articulated establishment of faculties we do in fact display *could* have been something quite different; in creating us with these

4. Indeed, it is ludicrous understatement to say that God has a grasp of every proposition and property: from a theistic point of view the natural way to view propositions and properties is as God's thoughts and concepts. (See my "How to Be an Anti-Realist," *Proceedings of the American Philosophical Association,* vol. 56, no. 1, 1983.)

faculties he could have been aiming us, not at truth, but at something of some other sort — survival, for example, or a capacity to appreciate art, poetry, beauty in nature,[5] or an ability to stand in certain relationships with each other and with him. But the great bulk of the tradition has seen our imaging God in terms (among other things) of knowledge: knowledge of ourselves, of God himself, and the world in which he has placed us; and here I shall take for granted this traditional understanding of the *imago dei.*

God has therefore created us with cognitive faculties designed to enable us to achieve true beliefs with respect to a wide variety of propositions — propositions about our immediate environment, about our own interior lives, about the thoughts and experiences of other persons, about our universe at large, about right and wrong, about the whole realm of abstracta — numbers, properties, propositions, states of affairs, possible worlds, and their like; about modality — what is necessary and possible — and about himself. These faculties work in such a way that under the appropriate circumstances we form the appropriate belief. More exactly, the appropriate belief is *formed in us;* in the typical case we do not *decide* to hold or form the belief in question, but simply find ourselves with it. Upon considering an instance of *modus ponens,* I find myself believing its corresponding conditional; upon being appeared to in the familiar way, I find myself holding the belief that there is a large tree before me; upon being asked what I had for breakfast, I reflect for a moment and then find myself with the belief that what I had was eggs on toast. In these and other cases I do not *decide* what to believe; I don't total up the evidence (I'm being appeared to redly; on most occasions when thus appeared to I am in the presence of something red; so most probably in this case I am) and make a decision as to what seems best supported; I simply find myself believing. Of course in *some* cases I may go through such a procedure. For example, I may try to assess the alleged evidence in favor of the theory that human life evolved by means of the mechanisms of random genetic mutation and natural selection from unicellular life (which itself arose by substantially similar random mechanical processes from nonliving material); I may try to determine whether the evidence is in fact compelling or, more modestly, such as to make the theory plausible. Then I may go through a procedure of that sort. Even in this sort of case I still don't really *decide* anything: I simply call the relevant evidence to mind, try in some way to weight it up, and find myself with the appropriate belief. But in more typical and less theoretical cases of belief formation nothing like this is involved.

Experience, obviously enough, plays a crucial role in belief formation.

---

5. In C. S. Lewis's novel *Out of the Silent Planet* the creatures on Mars are of several different types displaying several different kinds of cognitive excellences: some are particularly suited to scientific endeavors, some to poetry and art, and some to interpersonal sensitivity.

Here it is important to see, I think, that two rather different sorts of experience are involved. In a typical perceptual case there is sensuous experience; I look out at my back yard and am appeared to greenly, perhaps. But in many cases of belief formation, there is present another sort of experiential component as well. Consider a memory belief, for example. Here there may be a sort of sensuous imagery present — I may be appeared to in a certain indistinct fleeting sort of way in trying to recall what I had for breakfast, for example. But this sort of sensuous imagery is in a way (as Wittgenstein never tired of telling us) inessential, variable from person to person, and perhaps in the case of some persons altogether absent. What seems less variable is a different kind of experience not easy to characterize: it is a matter, not so much of sensuous imagery, as of feeling impelled, or inclined, or moved towards a certain belief — in the case in question, the belief that what I had for breakfast was eggs on toast. (Perhaps it could be better put by saying that the belief in question has a sort of experienced attractiveness about it, a sort of drawing power.) Consider an *a priori* belief: *if all men are mortals and Socrates is a man, then Socrates is mortal.* Such a belief is not, as the denomination *a priori* mistakenly suggests, formed *prior to* or in the absence of experience; it is rather formed *in response to experience.* Thinking of the corresponding conditional of *modus ponens* feels different from thinking of, say, the corresponding conditional of *affirming the consequent;* thinking of $2 + 1 = 3$ feels different from thinking of $2 + 1 = 4$; and this difference in experience is crucially connected with our accepting the one and rejecting the other. Again, when I entertain or think of an example of *modus ponens,* there is both sensuous imagery — Descartes' clarity and distinctness, the luminous brightness of which Locke spoke; but there is also the feeling of being impelled to believe or accept the proposition; there is a sort of inevitability about it. (As I said, this isn't easy to describe.) Of course experience plays a different role here from the role it plays in the formation of perceptual beliefs; it plays a still different role in the formation of moral beliefs, beliefs about our own mental lives, beliefs about the mental lives of other persons, beliefs we form on the basis of inductive evidence, and so on. What we need here is a full and appropriately subtle and sensitive description of the role of experience in the formation of these various types of beliefs; but that project will have to await another occasion, as one says when one really has no idea how to accomplish the project.

God has therefore created us with an astonishingly complex and subtle establishment of cognitive faculties. These faculties produce beliefs on an enormously wide variety of topics — our everyday external environment, the thoughts of others, our own internal life (someone's internal musings and soliloquies can occupy an entire novel), the past, mathematics, science, right and wrong, our relationships to God, what is necessary and possible, and a host of other topics. They work with great subtlety to produce beliefs of many different degrees of strength ranging from the merest inclination to believe to absolute dead certainty. Our beliefs and the strength with which we hold them, furthermore, are delicately responsive to changes in experience — to what people tell us, to perceptual experience, to what we read, to further reflection, and so on.

Now: how shall we think of positive epistemic status from this point of view? Here is a natural first approximation: a belief has positive epistemic status for a person only if his faculties are *working properly,* working the way they ought to work, working the way they were designed to work (working the way God designed them to work), in producing and sustaining the belief in question. I therefore suggest that a necessary condition of positive epistemic status is that one's cognitive equipment, one's belief-forming and belief-sustaining apparatus, be free of cognitive malfunction. It must be functioning in the way it was designed to function by the being who designed and created us. Initially, then, let us say that a belief has positive epistemic status, for me, to the degree that my faculties are functioning properly in producing and sustaining that belief; and my faculties are working properly if they are working in the way they were designed to work by God.

The first thing to see here is that this condition — that of one's cognitive equipment functioning properly — is not the same thing as one's cognitive equipment functioning *normally,* or in normal conditions — not, at any rate, if we take the term 'normally' in a broadly statistical sense. If I give way to wishful thinking, forming the belief that I will soon be awarded a Nobel Prize for literature, then my cognitive faculties are not working properly — even though wishful thinking may be widespread among human beings. Your belief's being produced by your faculties working normally or in normal conditions — i.e., the sorts of conditions that obtain for the most part — must be distinguished from their working *properly.* It may be (and in fact is) the case that it is not at all abnormal for a person to form a belief out of pride, jealousy, lust, contrariness, desire for fame, wishful thinking, or self-aggrandizement; nevertheless when I form a belief in this way my cognitive equipment is not functioning properly. It is not functioning the way it ought to.

I shall have more to say about the notion of proper functioning below. For the moment, let us provisionally entertain the idea that the one necessary condition of a belief's having positive epistemic status for me is that the relevant portion of my noetic equipment involved in its formation and sustenance be functioning properly. It is easy to see, however, that this cannot be the whole story. Suppose you are suddenly and without your knowledge transported to an environment wholly different from earth; you awake on a planet near Alpha Centauri. Conditions there are quite different; elephants, we may suppose, are invisible to human beings, but emit a sort of radiation unknown on earth, a sort of radiation that causes human beings to form the belief that a trumpet is sounding nearby. An Alpha Centaurian elephant wanders by; you are subjected to the radiation, and form the belief that a trumpet is sounding nearby. There is nothing wrong with your cognitive faculties; but this belief has little by way of positive epistemic status for you. Nor is the problem merely that the belief is false; even if we can add that a trumpet really *is* sounding nearby (in a soundproof telephone booth, perhaps, so that it isn't audible to you), your belief will have little by way of positive epistemic status for you. To vary the example, imagine that the radiation emitted causes human beings to form the belief, not that a trumpet is sounding, but that there is a large gray object in the neighborhood. Again, an elephant wanders by: while seeing nothing of any particular interest, you suddenly find yourself with the belief that there is a large gray object nearby. A bit perplexed at this discovery, you examine your surroundings more closely: you still see no large gray object. Your faculties are displaying no malfunction and you are not being epistemically careless or slovenly; nevertheless you don't know that there is a large gray object nearby. That belief has little by way of positive epistemic status for you.

The reason is that your cognitive faculties and the environment in which you find yourself are not properly attuned. The problem is not with your cognitive faculties; they are in good working order. The problem is with the environment. In approximately the same way, your automobile might be in perfect working order, despite the fact that it will not run well at the top of Pike's Peak, or under water, or on the moon. We must therefore add another component to positive epistemic status: your faculties must be in good working order and the environment must be appropriate for your particular repertoire of epistemic powers. (Perhaps there are creatures native to the planet in question who are much like human beings, but whose cognitive powers differ from ours in such a way that Alpha Centaurian elephants are not invisible to them.)

It is tempting to suggest that positive epistemic status *just is* proper functioning (in an appropriate environment), so that one has warrant for a given belief to the degree that one's faculties are functioning properly (in producing and sustaining that belief) in an environment appropriate for one's cognitive equipment: the better one's faculties are functioning, the more positive the epistemic status. But it is easy to see that this cannot be correct. Couldn't it happen that my cognitive faculties are working properly (in an appropriate environment) in producing and sustaining a certain belief in me, while nonetheless that belief has very little by way of positive epistemic status for me? Say that a pair of beliefs are (for want of a better term) *productively equivalent* if they are produced by faculties functioning properly to the same degree and in environments of equal appropriateness. Then couldn't it be that a pair of my beliefs should be productively equivalent while nonetheless one of them has more by way of positive epistemic status — even a great deal more — than the other? Obviously enough, that could be; as a matter of fact it is plausible to think that *is* the case. *Modus ponens* has more by way of positive epistemic status for me than does the memory belief, now rather dim and indistinct, that forty years ago I owned a second hand 16-gauge shotgun and a red bicycle with balloon tires; but both, I take it, are produced by cognitive faculties functioning properly in a congenial environment. Although both epistemic justification and *being properly produced* come in degrees, there seems to be no discernible functional relationship between them: but then we can't see positive epistemic status as simply a matter of a belief's being produced by faculties working properly in an appropriate environment. We still have no real answer to the question *what is positive epistemic status?;* that particular frog is still grinning residually up from the bottom of the mug.

Fortunately there is an easy response. Not only does the first belief, the belief in the corresponding conditional of *modus ponens,* have more by way of positive epistemic status for me than the second; it is also one I accept much more firmly. It seems much more obviously true; I have a much stronger inclination or impulse to accept that proposition than to accept the other. When my cognitive establishment is working properly, the strength of the impulse towards believing a given proposition will be proportional to the degree it has of positive epistemic status — or if the relationship isn't one of straightforward proportionality, the appropriate functional relationship will hold between positive epistemic status and this impulse. So when my faculties are functioning properly, a belief has positive epistemic status to the degree that I find myself inclined to accept it; and this (again, if my faculties are functioning properly and I do not interfere or intervene) will be the degree to which I *do* accept it.

As I see it then, positive epistemic status accrues to a belief B for a person S only if S's cognitive environment is appropriate for his cognitive faculties and only if these faculties are functioning properly in producing this belief in him; and under these conditions the degree of positive epistemic status enjoyed by B is proportional to the strength of his inclination to accept B. To state the same claim a bit differently: a belief B has positive epistemic status for S if and only if that belief is produced in S by his epistemic faculties working properly (in an appropriate environment); and B has more positive epistemic status than B^* for S if (1) B has positive epistemic status for S and (2) either B^* does not or else S is more strongly inclined to believe B than B^*.

II. Eight Objections, Qualifications, or Applications

So far, of course, what I have said is merely programmatic, just a picture. Much more needs to be said by way of qualification, development, articulation. Let me therefore respond to some objections, make some qualifications and additions, and mention some topics for further study.

(1) Aren't such ideas as that of *working properly* and related notions such as *cognitive dysfunction* deeply problematic? What is it for a natural organism — a tree, for example, or a horse — to be in good working order, to be functioning properly? Isn't "working properly" relative to our aims and interests? A cow is functioning properly when she gives the appropriate milk; a garden patch is as it ought to be when it displays a luxuriant preponderance of the sorts of vegetation we propose to promote. But here it seems patent that what constitutes proper functioning depends upon our aims and interests. So far as nature herself goes, isn't a fish decomposing in a hill of corn functioning just as properly, just as excellently, as one happily swimming about chasing minnows? But then what could be meant by speaking of "proper functioning" with respect to our cognitive faculties? A chunk of reality — an organism, a part of an organism, an ecosystem, a garden patch — "functions properly" only with respect to a sort of grid *we* impose on nature — a grid that incorporates *our* aims and desires.

Reply: from a *theistic* point of view, of course, there is no problem here. The idea of my faculties functioning properly is no more problematic than, say, that of a Boeing 747's working properly. Something we have constructed — a heating system, a rope, a linear accelerator — is functioning properly when it is functioning in the way in which it was designed to function. But according to theism, human beings, like ropes, linear accelerators, and ocean liners, have been designed; they have been designed and created by God. Our faculties are working properly, then, when they are working in the way they were designed to work by the being who designed and created us and them. Of course there may be considerable room for disagreement and considerable difficulty in determining just how our faculties have in fact been designed to function, and consequent disagreement as to whether they are functioning properly in a given situation. There is disease, disorder, and dysfunction — malfunction of the mind as well as of the body. This can range from the extreme case of Descartes' lunatics (who thought their heads were made of glass or that they themselves were gourds) to cases where it isn't clear whether or not cognitive dysfunction is present at all. I stubbornly cling to my theory, long after wiser heads have given it up as a bad job. Is this a matter of cognitive dysfunction brought about by excessive pride or desire for recognition on my part? Or is it a perfectly natural and proper display of the sort of cognitive inertia built into our cognitive faculties (in order, perhaps, that we may not be blown about by every wind of doctrine)? Or a display of some other part of our cognitive design whose operation guarantees that new and unfamiliar ideas will persist long enough to get a real run for their money? Or what? So there may be great difficulty in discerning, in a particular instance, whether my faculties are or are not functioning properly; but from a theistic point of view there is no trouble in principle with the very *idea* of proper function.

But can a nontheist also make use of this notion of working properly? Is the idea of proper functioning tightly tied to the idea of design and construction in such a way that one can use it in the way I suggest only if one is prepared to agree that human beings have been designed? This is a topic I shall have to leave for another occasion;[6] here let me say just this much. This notion of proper functioning is, I think, more problematic from a nontheistic perspective — more problematic, but by no means hopeless. Can't anyone, theist or not, see that a horse, let's say, suffering from a disease, is displaying a pathological condition? Can't anyone see that an injured bird has a wing that isn't working properly? The notions of proper function and allied notions (sickness, dysfunction, disorder, malfunction, and the like) are ones we all or nearly all have and use. If in fact this notion is ultimately inexplicable or unacceptable from a nontheistic point of view, then there lurks in the neighborhood a powerful theistic argument — one that will be attractive to all those whose inclination to accept and employ the notion of proper function is stronger than their inclinations to reject theism.*

(2) Roderick Chisholm[7] sees fulfillment of epistemic duty as crucial to positive epistemic status; in fact he analyzes or explains positive epistemic status in terms of aptness for fulfillment of epistemic duty. Must we go with him, at least far enough to hold that a belief has positive epistemic status for me only if I am appropriately discharging my epistemic duty in forming and holding that belief in the way I do form and hold it? This is a difficult question. No doubt there *are* epistemic duties, duties to the truth, duties we have as cognitive beings; but the question is whether a necessary condition of my knowing a proposition is my violating or flouting no such duties in forming the belief in question. I am inclined to doubt that there is an element of this kind in positive epistemic status. It seems that that belief may constitute knowledge even if I am flouting an intellectual duty in the process of forming and holding it. Suppose I am thoroughly jaundiced and relish thinking the worst about you. I know that I suffer from this aberration, and ought to combat it, but do nothing whatever to correct it, taking a malicious pleasure in it. I

6. See my "Positive Epistemic Status and Proper Function" (footnote 1).

*Editor's Note: Cf. the argument developed in chapter 4 above.

7. See his *Theory of Knowledge,* p. 14, and *Foundations of Knowing* (Minneapolis: University of Minnesota Press, 1982), p. 7. See also my "Chisholmian Internalism" in *Philosophical Analysis: A Defense by Example* (footnote 3).

barely overhear someone make a derogatory comment about you; I can barely make out his words, and, were it not for my ill will, I would not have heard them correctly. (Others thought he said your thought was deep and rigorous; because of my ill will I correctly heard him as saying that your thought is weak and frivolous.) In this case perhaps I am not doing my cognitive duty in forming the belief in question; I am flouting my duty to try to rid myself of my inclination to form malicious beliefs about you, and it is only because I am not doing my duty that I do form the belief in question. Yet surely it seems to have positive epistemic status for me.

Consider another kind of example. Suppose I am convinced by a distinguished epistemologist that (like everyone else) I have a duty to do my best to try to bring it about that for every proposition I consider, I believe the proposition if and only if it is true. Suppose he also convinces me that on most of the occasions when we form ordinary perceptual beliefs, these beliefs are false. I therefore undergo a strenuous, difficult regimen enabling me, at considerable cost in terms of effort and energy, to inhibit my ordinary belief-forming impulses so that I am able to withhold most ordinary perceptual beliefs. Now suppose I hear a siren: I take a quick look and am appeared to in the familiar way in which one is appeared to upon perceiving a large red fire truck. The thought that I must withhold the natural belief here flashes through my mind. I have been finding the regimen burdensome, however, and say to myself: "This is entirely too much trouble; I am sick and tired of doing my epistemic duty." I let nature take its course, forming the belief that what I see is a large red fire truck. Then (assuming that my beliefs do in fact induce in me a duty to try to inhibit the natural belief) I am forming a belief in a way that is contrary to duty; but don't I nonetheless know that there is a red fire truck there? I think so. I am therefore inclined to think that I could know a proposition even if I came to believe it in a way that is contrary to my epistemic duty. The matter is delicate and unclear, however, and complicated by its involvement with difficult questions about the degree to which my beliefs are under my voluntary control. I am inclined to think that fulfillment of epistemic duty, while of course an estimable condition, is neither necessary nor sufficient for positive epistemic status; but the relationship between positive epistemic status and epistemic duty fulfillment remains obscure to me.*

(3) If a belief is to have positive epistemic status for me, then my faculties must be functioning properly in producing the *degree* of belief with which I hold A, as well as the belief A itself. I am driving down a freeway in Washington, D.C.; as I roar by, I catch a quick glimpse of what seems to be a camel

---

*Editor's Note: See chapters 1-3 of Bibliography #28 for more detailed examinations of and Plantinga's mature views on the relationship between warrant (positive epistemic status) and epistemic duty.

in the median strip. If my faculties are functioning properly, I may believe that I saw a camel, but I won't believe it very firmly — not nearly as firmly, for example, as that I am driving a car. If, due to cognitive malfunction (I am struck by a sudden burst of radiation from a Pentagon experiment gone awry), I do believe the former as firmly as the latter, it will have little by way of positive epistemic status for me.[8]

(4) When my epistemic faculties are functioning properly, I will often form one belief *on the evidential basis of* another. The notion of proper function does not apply, of course, only to basic beliefs, that is, beliefs not formed on the evidential basis of other beliefs; my faculties are also such that under the right conditions I will believe one proposition on the basis of some other beliefs I already hold. I may know that either George or Sam is in the office; you inform me that Sam is not there; I then believe that George is in the office on the basis of these other two beliefs. And of course if my faculties are functioning properly, I won't believe a proposition on the evidential basis of just *any* proposition. I won't, for example, believe a proposition on the evidential basis of itself (and perhaps this is not even possible). I won't believe that Homer wrote the *Iliad* on the evidential basis of my belief that the population of China exceeds that of Japan. Nor will I believe that Feike can swim on the basis of the proposition that 99 out of 100 Frisians cannot swim and Feike is a Frisian. Proper functioning here involves believing a proposition on the basis of *the right kind* of proposition.

(5) A very important notion here is the idea of *specifications,* or *design plan.* We take it that when human beings (and other creatures) function properly, they function *in a particular way.* That is, they not only function in such a way as to fulfill their purpose (in the way in which it is the purpose of the heart to pump blood), but they function to fulfill that purpose in just one of an indefinitely large number of possible ways. Our cognitive faculties have been designed, no doubt, with reliability in mind; they have been designed in such a way as to produce beliefs that are for the most part true. But they are not designed to produce true beliefs in just any old way. There is a proper way for them to work; we suppose there is something like a set of plans for us and our faculties. A house is designed to produce shelter — but not in just any old way. There will be plans specifying the length and pitch of the rafters, what kind of shingles are to be applied, the kind and quantity of insulation to be used, and the like. Something similar holds in the case of us and our faculties; we have been designed in accordance with a specific set

---

8. Must *all* of my cognitive faculties be functioning properly for any belief to have positive epistemic status for me? Surely not. And what about the fact that proper function comes in degrees? How well must the relevant faculties be working for a belief to have positive epistemic status for me? On these questions see "Positive Epistemic Status and Proper Function" (footnote 1).

of plans. Better (since this analogy is insufficiently dynamic) we have been designed in accordance with a set of specifications, in the way in which there are specifications for, for example, a 1983 GMC van. According to these specifications (here I am just guessing), after a cold start the engine runs at 1500 rpm until the engine temperature reaches 140 degrees F; it then throttles back to 750 rpm. In the same sort of way, our cognitive faculties are designed to function in a certain specific way — a way that may include development and change over time. It is for this reason that it is possible for a belief to be produced by a belief-producing process that is *accidentally* reliable. This notion of specifications or design plan is also the source of counterexamples to the reliabilist claim that a belief has positive epistemic status if it is produced by a reliable belief-producing mechanism.[9]

(6) We do have the idea of our cognitive faculties working properly in an appropriate environment and we also have the idea of positive epistemic status as what accrues to a belief for someone whose epistemic faculties are thus functioning properly. Still, there are cases in which our faculties are functioning perfectly well, but where their working in that way does not seem to lead to truth — indeed, where it may lead away from it. Perhaps you remember a painful experience as less painful than it was. (Some say it is thus with childbirth.) Or perhaps you continue to believe in your friend's honesty after evidence and objective judgment would have dictated a reluctant change of mind. Perhaps your belief that you will recover from a dread disease is stronger than the statistics justify. In all of these cases, your faculties may be functioning just as they ought to, but nonetheless their functioning in that way does not obviously seem to lead to truth.

The answer here is simplicity itself: what confers positive epistemic status is one's cognitive faculties working properly or working as designed to work *insofar as that segment of design is aimed at producing true beliefs.* Not all aspects of the design of our cognitive faculties need be aimed at the production of truth; some might be such as to conduce to survival, or relief from suffering, or the possibility of loyalty, and the like. But someone whose holding a certain belief is a result of an aspect of our cognitive design that is aimed not at truth but at something else won't properly be said to know the proposition in question, even if it turns out to be true. (Unless, perhaps, the same design would conduce both to truth and to the other state of affairs aimed at.)

(7a) Consider Richard Swinburne's "Principle of Credulity": "So generally, . . . I suggest that it is a principle of rationality that (in the absence of special considerations) if it seems (epistemically) to a subject that x is present, then probably x is present; what one seems to perceive is probably so. How things seem to be is good grounds for a belief about how things

9. See below, pp. 184-85.

are."[10] This principle figures into his theistic argument from religious experience: "From this it would follow that, in the absence of special considerations, all religious experiences ought to be taken by their subjects as genuine, and hence as substantial grounds for belief in the apparent object — God, or Mary, or Ultimate Reality or Poseidon" (254). Swinburne understands this "principle of rationality" in such a way that it relates *propositions:* the idea is that on any proposition of the form *S seems (to himself) to be experiencing a thing that is F,* the corresponding proposition of the form *S is experiencing a thing that is F* is more probable than not: "If it seems epistemically to *S* that *x* is present, then that is good reason for *S* to believe that it is so, in the absence of special considerations. . . . And it is good reason too for anyone else to believe that *x* is present. For if *e* is evidence for *h,* this is a relation which holds quite independently of who knows about *e*" (260).

To understand Swinburne's thought here we must briefly consider how he thinks of probability. He accepts a version of the logical theory of probability developed by Jeffrey, Keynes, and Carnap; Swinburne himself develops a version of this theory in *An Introduction to Confirmation Theory.*[11] On this theory, for any pair of propositions [A, B] there is an objective, logical probability relation between them: the probability of *A* conditional on *B,* i.e., *P(A/B).* This relation is *objective* in that it does not depend in any way upon what anyone (any human being, anyway) knows or believes; it is *logical* in that if *P(A/B)* is *n,* then it is necessary (true in every possible world) that *P(A/B)* is *n.* (Of course logical probability conforms to the Calculus of Probability.) Carnap spoke of the probabilistic relation between a pair of propositions as *partial entailment;* we may think of the logical probability of *A* on *B* as the degree to which *B* entails *A,* with entailment *simpliciter* as the limiting case. We could also think of the logical probability of *A* on *B* as follows: imagine the possible worlds as uniformly distributed throughout a logical space: then P(*A/B*) is the ratio between the volume of the space occupied by worlds in which both *A* and *B* hold and the volume of the space occupied by worlds in which *B* holds. And Swinburne's suggestion, as we have seen, is that on any proposition of the form *S seems (to himself) to be experiencing a thing that is F,* the corresponding proposition of the form *S is experiencing a thing that is F* is more probable (logically probable) than not.

I find this dubious. First there are notorious difficulties with the very notion of probability thought of this way. (I'll mention one a couple of paragraphs further down.) But second, even if we embrace a logical theory

10. R. Swinburne, *The Existence of God* (Oxford: Clarendon Press, 1979), p. 254. Subsequent references to Swinburne's work will be to this volume.

11. See R. Swinburne, *An Introduction to Confirmation Theory* (London: Methuen & Co. Ltd., 1973).

of probability of this kind we are still likely to have grave problems here. Why suppose that on the proposition *It seems to Sam that Zeus is present* it is more probable than not (probability taken as logical probability) that Zeus really is present? Here we are not to rely on our having discovered that as a matter of fact most of what most people think is true; what we must consider is the probability of Zeus's presence on the proposition *it seems to Sam that Zeus is present* alone, apart from any background knowledge or beliefs we might have. (Alternatively, this is a case where our background information "consists of nothing but tautologies," as it is sometimes put.) But if all we have for background information is tautologies (and other necessary truths) why think a thing like that? Wouldn't it be just as likely that Sam was mistaken, the victim of a Cartesian demon, or an Alpha Centaurian scientist, or any number of things we can't even think of? What would be a reason for thinking this? That in most possible worlds, most pairs of such propositions are such that the second number is true if the first is? But is there any reason to think that? (That is, is there any reason apart from *theism* to think that? If theism is true, then perhaps most beliefs in most possible worlds are indeed true, if only because God does most of the believing.)

But there is a quite different way in which we might think of this principle. Suppose we think of it from the perspective of the idea that positive epistemic status is a matter of the proper function of our epistemic faculties. It is of course true that when our faculties are functioning properly, then for the most part we do indeed believe what seems to us to be true. This isn't inevitable: consider the Russell paradoxes, where we wind up rejecting what seems true (and what still seems true even after we see where it leads). A madman, furthermore, might find himself regularly believing what didn't seem to him true; and an incautious reader of Kant, intent upon accentuating his free and rational autonomy, might undertake a regimen at the conclusion of which he was able to reject what he finds himself inclined by nature to believe. But all else being equal, we ordinarily believe what seems to us to be true, and what seems to us true (when our faculties are functioning properly in a suitable environment) will have more by way of positive epistemic status for us than what does not. The explanation, I suggest, is not that *p* is logically probable on the proposition *p seems to Sam to be true;* the explanation is much simpler; it is the fact that when my faculties are functioning properly, the degree of positive epistemic status a proposition has for me just is (*modulo* a constant of proportionality) the degree to which I am inclined to believe that proposition.

(7b) Similar comments apply to Swinburne's "Principle of Testimony": "the principle that (in the absence of special considerations) the experiences of others are probably as they report them" (272). Here again Swinburne apparently understands this principle in terms of his understanding of probability:

the proposition *Sam's experience is F* is more probable than not, in the logical sense, on the proposition *Sam testifies that his experience is F.* But this seems dubious: is there any reason to think that in most possible worlds in which Sam claims to have a headache, he really does have a headache? Or that the volume of "logical space" occupied by worlds in which Sam testifies that he has a headache and in fact does, is more than half of the volume of worlds in which Sam testifies that he has a headache but in fact doesn't? What could be the basis of such a claim? Swinburne's suggestion is that if we do not accept principles of this sort, we shall land in the "morass of skepticism." But we can avoid that morass without accepting these implausible claims about logical probability. Thomas Reid[12] speaks of "Credulity" — the tendency to believe what we are told by others. This tendency is of course subject to modification by experience: we learn to trust some people on some topics and distrust others on others; we learn never to form a judgment about a marital altercation until we have spoken to both parties; we learn that people's judgment can be skewed by pride, selfishness, desire to exalt oneself at the expense of one's fellows, love, lust, and much else. Nonetheless there is this tendency, and under the right circumstances when you tell me p (that your name is Sam, for example), then if p is true, and I believe p sufficiently firmly and my faculties are functioning properly in the formation of this belief, I know p. And here we need not try to account for this fact in terms of the logical probability of one proposition on another; we can note instead that (1) when our faculties are functioning properly, we are typically inclined to believe what we are told and (2) if we believe what is true and what we are sufficiently strongly inclined to believe, then if our faculties are functioning properly (and the cognitive environment is congenial) what we believe is something we know.

(7c) Finally, consider Swinburne's claim that *simplicity* is a prime determinant of *a priori* or intrinsic probability, at least for explanatory theories: "Prior probability depends on simplicity, fit with background knowledge, and scope. A theory is simple in so far as it postulates few mathematically simple laws holding between entities of an intelligible kind. . . . I am saying merely that a theory which postulates entities of an intelligible kind, as opposed to other entities, will have a greater prior probability, and so, *other things being equal,* will be more likely to be true. . . . For large-scale theories the crucial determinant of prior probability is simplicity" (52-53). Here Swinburne is speaking of *prior* probability, not *a priori* or intrinsic probability: "The prior probability of a theory is the probability before we consider the detailed

---

12. My whole account of positive epistemic status, not just this example, owes much to Thomas Reid with his talk of faculties and their functions and his rejection of the notion (one he attributes to Hume and his predecessors) that self-evident propositions and propositions about one's own immediate experience are the only properly basic propositions.

evidence of observation cited in its support" (52). The prior probability of a theory also depends on its fit with our background knowledge. But if we consider the *a priori* or *intrinsic* probability of the theory, then fit with background information drops outs, so that we are left with content (or "scope" as Swinburne calls it in *The Existence of God*) and simplicity as the determinants of intrinsic probability; and of these two, it is simplicity that is the more important: ". . . sometimes it is convenient to let *e* be all observational evidence and let *k* be mere 'tautological evidence.' In the latter case the prior probability *P(h/k)* will depend mainly on the simplicity of *h* (as well as to a lesser extent on its narrowness of scope)" (65).

Now I believe there are real problems here. The chief problem, it seems to me, is with the very notion of intrinsic, logical probability. On the theory in question, as we have seen, for any pair of propositions there is an objective, logical probability between them. As a special case of this relation we have intrinsic probability: the probability of a proposition conditional on nothing but necessary truths. Take such a contingent proposition as *Paul Zwier owns an orange shirt;* on this view, there is such a thing as the probability of that proposition conditional on the proposition $7 + 5 = 12$. And the problem here is substantially twofold. In the first place there is no reason, so far as I can see, to think that contingent propositions *do* in general have an intrinsic logical probability; and if they do, there seems to be no way to determine, even within very broad limits, what it might be.

But second and more important: there are many large classes of propositions such that there seems to be no way in which intrinsic probability can be distributed over their members in a way that accords both with the calculus of probability and with intuition. Consider, for example, a countably infinite set S of propositions that are mutually exclusive in pairs and such that necessarily, exactly one of them is true: S might be, for example, the set of propositions such that for each natural number n (including 0), S contains the proposition *there exist exactly n flying donkeys.* Given nothing but necessary truths, none of these propositions should be more likely to be true than any others; if there is such a thing as a logical probability on nothing but necessary truths, one number should be as probable as another to be the number of flying donkeys. But the members of this countably infinite set can have the same probability only if each has probability 0.* That means, however, that the

---

*Editor's Note: The proof of this conclusion is as follows (adapted from "The Probabilistic Argument from Evil," bibliography #83).

Let 'D$_0$' designate *There are exactly 0 flying donkeys;* 'D$_1$', *There is exactly 1 flying donkey;* 'D2', *There are exactly 2 flying donkeys;* and so forth. And let 'D' designate the countably infinite set $\{D_0, D_1, D_2, \ldots\}$.

1. For any real number r such that r is greater than 0, there is some natural number n such that $r_1 + r_2 + \ldots + r_n > 1$. (from arithmetic)

proposition *there are no flying donkeys* has intrinsic probability 0; hence its denial — *there are some flying donkeys* — has an intrinsic probability of 1. Further, according to the probability calculus, if a proposition has an intrinsic probability of 1 then its probability on any evidence is also 1; hence no matter what our evidence, the probability on our evidence that there are flying donkeys is 1. Still further, it is easy to see that (under these assumptions) for any number n, the probability that there are at least n flying donkeys also has an intrinsic probability of 1 and hence a probability of 1 on *any* evidence.[13] And of course this result is not limited to flying donkeys; for any kind of object such that for any number n it is possible that there be n objects of that kind — witches, demons, Siberian Cheesehounds — the probability that there are at least n of them (for any n) is 1 on any evidence whatever.[14]

The only way to avoid this unsavory result is to suppose that intrinsic probabilities are distributed in accordance with some series that converges to 0: for example, *there are no flying donkeys* has an intrinsic probability of ½, *there is just one flying donkey* gets ¼, and so on. But then we are committed to the idea that some numbers are vastly more likely (conditional on necessary truths alone) than others to be the number of flying donkeys. In fact we are committed to the view that for any number n you please, there will be a pair of natural numbers m and m^* such that is m^* is n times more likely (conditional on necessary truths alone) to be the number of donkeys than m. And this seems just as counterintuitive as the suggestion that for any number n you pick, the probability (on any evidence) that there are at least n flying donkeys is 1.

It therefore seems to me unlikely that such propositions have intrinsic probability at all; but similar arguments can be brought to bear on many other

---

2. Therefore, if all members of D have the same *a priori* probability and that probability is greater than 0, then there is some number n such that $P(D_0) + P(D_1) + P(D_2) + \ldots + P(D_n) > 1$. (from 1)

3. It is an axiom of the Probability Calculus that, if A and B are mutually exclusive propositions (i.e., each entails the falsehood of the other), then $P(A \vee B) = P(A) + P(B)$.

4. Therefore, since each member of D entails the falsehood of all other members, $P(D_0 \vee D_1 \vee D_2 \vee \ldots \vee D_n) > 1$. (from 2 and 3)

5. However, under the Probability Calculus, the probability assignment of any proposition must be some real number r such that $0 \le r \le 1$.

6. Therefore, all members of D have the same probability only if that probability is 0. (from 4 and 5)

13. The proposition *there are at least n flying donkeys* is equivalent to the denial of (a) *There are 0 flying donkeys* or *there is just 1 flying donkey,* or *there are just 2 flying donkeys* or . . . *there are just n-1 flying donkeys*. By hypothesis, the probability of each disjunct of (a) is 0; hence by the Additive Axiom the probability of the disjunction is 0, so that the probability of its denial is 1.

14. See my "The Probabilistic Argument from Evil," *Philosophical Studies,* 1979.

classes of propositions. Accordingly, I think the whole idea of intrinsic probability is at best dubious. But even if there is such a thing, why should we suppose that *simpler* propositions, all else being equal, have more of it than complex propositions? Is there some *a priori* reason to suppose that reality prefers simplicity? Where would this notion come from? Swinburne, again, believes that if we don't accept some such principle as this, we shall fall into that skeptical bog: if we don't accept some such principle, we will have no reason for preferring simple to complex hypotheses, but in many contexts all that our favored hypotheses have going for them (as compared to others that fit the same data just as well) is simplicity.

But suppose we look at the matter from the point of view of the present conception of positive epistemic status. Despite the real problems in saying just what simplicity is (and in saying in any sort of systematic way when one theory is simpler than another) there clearly *is* such a thing as simplicity, and it clearly does contribute to the positive epistemic status a theory or explanation has for us. But why think of this in terms of the problematic notion of intrinsic logical probability? Why not note instead that when our faculties are functioning properly, we do opt for simple theories as opposed to complex ones (all else being equal); we can therefore see the greater positive epistemic status of simple theories (again, all else being equal) as resulting from the fact that when our faculties are functioning properly, we are more strongly inclined to accept simple theories than complex ones.

(8) There are presently three main views as to the nature of positive epistemic status: Chisholmian internalism, coherentism, and reliabilism. The present conception of positive epistemic status as a matter of degree of inclination towards belief when epistemic faculties are functioning properly — the conception that seems to me to go most naturally with theism — provides a revealing perspective from which, as it seems to me, we can see that none of these three views is really viable. For each we can easily see that the proposed necessary and sufficient condition for positive epistemic status is not in fact sufficient (and in some cases not necessary either) — and not sufficient just because a belief could meet the condition in question but still have little by way of positive epistemic status because of cognitive pathology, failure to function properly. I don't have the space here to go into the matter with the proper thoroughness;[15] I shall say just the following.

First, the Chisholmian internalist (or at any rate its most distinguished exemplar) sees positive epistemic status as a matter of aptness for epistemic

---

15. See my "Chisholmian Internalism" (footnote 3) for detailed criticism of Chisholmian internalism; see my "Coherentism and the Evidentialist Objection to Belief in God" in *Rationality, Religious Belief, and Moral Commitment,* ed. William Wainwright and Robert Audi (Ithaca: Cornell University Press, 1986), for detailed criticism of coherentism, and see my "Positive Epistemic Status and Proper Function" (footnote 1) for criticism of reliabilism.

duty fulfillment. Chisholm begins by introducing an undefined technical locution: p is more reasonable than q for S at t; here the values for p and q will be such states of affairs as *believing that all men are mortal* and *withholding the belief that all men are mortal* — that is, believing neither the proposition in question nor its denial. Given "is more reasonable than" as an undefined locution, he goes on to define a battery of "terms of epistemic appraisal" as he calls them: "certain," "beyond reasonable doubt," "evident," "acceptable," and so on. A proposition A is beyond reasonable doubt for a person at a time t, for example, if at that time it is more reasonable for him to accept that proposition than to withhold it; A has some presumption in its favor for him at t just if accepting it then is more reasonable than accepting its negation. Now Chisholm introduces "is more reasonable than" as an undefined locution; but of course he intends it to have a sense, and to have a sense reasonably close to the sense it has in English. In *Foundations of Knowing,* his most recent full-dress presentation of his epistemology, he says that "Epistemic reasonability could be understood in terms of the general requirement to try to have the largest possible set of logically independent beliefs that is such that the true beliefs outnumber the false beliefs. The principles of epistemic preferability are the principles one should follow if one is to fulfill this requirement."[16] In his earlier *Theory of Knowledge* Chisholm is a bit more explicit about intellectual requirements: "We may assume," he says,

> that every person is subject to a purely intellectual requirement: that of trying his best to bring it about that for any proposition p he considers, he accepts p if and only if p is true;[17]

and he adds that

> One might say that this is the person's responsibility qua intellectual being. . . . One way, then, of re-expressing the locution 'p is more reasonable than q for S at t' is to say this: 'S is so situated at t that his intellectual requirement, his responsibility as an intellectual being, is better fulfilled by p than by q.'

Reasonability, therefore, is a *normative* concept; more precisely, it pertains to requirement, duty, or obligation. And Chisholm's central claim here is that a certain epistemic requirement, or responsibility, or duty, or obligation lies at the basis of such epistemic notions as evidence, justification, positive epistemic status, and knowledge itself. To say, for example, that a proposition p is *acceptable* for a person at a time is to say that he is so situated, then, that

16. P. 7.
17. P. 14.

it is not the case that he can better fulfill his epistemic duty by withholding than by accepting $p;$ to say that p is *beyond reasonable doubt* for him is to say that he is so situated, then, that he can better fulfill his intellectual responsibility by accepting p than by withholding it. The basic idea is that our epistemic duty or requirement is to try to achieve and maintain a certain condition — call it 'epistemic excellence' — which may be hard to specify in detail, but consists fundamentally in standing in an appropriate relation to truth. A proposition has positive epistemic status for me, in certain circumstances, to the extent that I can fulfill my epistemic duty by accepting it in those circumstances. This duty or obligation or requirement, furthermore, is one of *trying* to bring about a certain state of affairs. My requirement is not to *succeed* in achieving and maintaining intellectual excellence; my requirement is only to *try* to do so. Presumably the reason is that it may not be within my power to succeed. Perhaps I don't know how to achieve intellectual excellence; or perhaps I do know how but simply can't do it. So my duty is only to *try* to bring about this state of affairs.

There is a simple and attractive picture of the nature of justification and positive epistemic status. I think it is easy to see, however, that it is deeply flawed: for it is utterly clear that aptness for the fulfillment of epistemic duty or obligation is not sufficient for positive epistemic status. Suppose Paul is subject to cognitive dysfunction: then there could be a proposition A that has little by way of positive epistemic status for him, but is nonetheless such that believing it is maximally apt for epistemic duty fulfillment for him. Suppose Paul is subject to a cerebral disturbance that causes far-reaching cognitive dysfunction: when he is appeared to in one sense modality, he forms beliefs appropriate to another. When he is aurally appeared to in the way in which one is appeared to upon hearing church bells, for example, he has a nearly ineluctable tendency to believe that there is something that is appearing to him in that fashion, and that that thing is orange — bright orange. This belief, furthermore, seems utterly convincing; it has for him, all the phenomenological *panache* of *modus ponens* itself. He knows nothing about this defect in his epistemic equipment, and his lack of awareness is in no way due to dereliction of epistemic duty. As a matter of fact, Paul is unusually dutiful, unusually concerned about doing his epistemic duty; fulfilling this duty is the main passion of his life. Add that those around him suffer from a similar epistemic deficiency: Paul lives in Alaska and he and all his neighbors have suffered all their lives from similar lesions due to radioactive fallout from a Soviet missile test. Now suppose Paul is aurally appeared to in the way in question and forms the belief that he is being appeared to in that way by something that is orange. Surely this proposition is such that believing it is the right thing to do from the point of view of epistemic duty; nevertheless the proposition has little by way of positive epistemic status for him. Paul is beyond reproach; he has done his duty as he saw it; he is within his epistemic rights; he is permissively justified, and more. Nevertheless there is a kind of positive epistemic status this belief lacks — a kind crucial for knowledge. For that sort of positive epistemic status, it isn't sufficient to satisfy one's duty and do one's epistemic best. Paul can be ever so conscientious about his epistemic duties and still be such that his beliefs do not have that kind of positive epistemic status.

Clearly enough, we can vary the above sorts of examples. Perhaps you think that what goes *in excelsis* with satisfying duty is *effort;* perhaps (in a Kantian vein) you think that genuinely dutiful action must be contrary to inclination. Very well; alter the above cases accordingly. Suppose, for example, that Paul (again, due to cognitive malfunction) nonculpably believes that his nature is deeply misleading. Like the rest of us, he has an inclination, upon being appeared to redly, to believe that there is something red lurking in the neighborhood; unlike the rest of us, he believes that this natural inclination is misleading and that on those occasions there really isn't anything that is thus appearing to him. He undertakes a strenuous regimen to overcome this inclination; after intense and protracted effort he succeeds: upon being appeared to redly he no longer believes that something red is appearing to him. His devotion to duty costs him dearly. The enormous effort he expends takes its toll upon his health; he is subject to ridicule and disapprobation on the part of his fellows; his wife protests his unusual behavior and finally leaves him for someone less epistemically nonstandard. Nonetheless he persists in doing what he nonculpably takes to be his duty. It is obvious, I take it, that even though Paul is unusually dutiful in accepting, on a given occasion, the belief that nothing red is appearing to him, he has little by way of positive epistemic status for that belief.

We may therefore conclude, I think, that positive epistemic status is not or is not merely a matter of aptness for fulfillment of epistemic duty or obligation. Could it be *coherence,* as with Lehrer,[18] Bonjour,[19] and several Bayesians? Coherentism, of course, comes in many varieties; here I don't have the space to discuss any of them properly. From the present perspective, however, there is at least one crucial difficulty with them all: they all neglect the crucial feature of proper function. According to coherentism, all that is relevant to my beliefs having positive epistemic status for me is a certain internal relationship among them. But surely this is not so. Consider, for example, the case of the Epistemically Inflexible Climber. Paul is climbing Guide's Wall, in the Grand Tetons; having just led the next-to-last pitch, he is seated on a comfortable ledge, belaying his partner. He believes that Cascade Canyon is down to his left, that

18. Keith Lehrer, *Knowledge* (Oxford: Oxford University Press, 1974).

19. Lawrence Bonjour, *The Structure of Empirical Knowledge* (Cambridge, Mass.: Harvard University Press, 1986).

the cliffs of Mt. Owen are directly in front of him, that there is a hawk flying in lazy circles 200 feet below him, that he is wearing his new *Fire* rock shoes, and so on. His beliefs, we may stipulate, are coherent. Now imagine that Paul is struck by a burst of high-energy cosmic radiation, causing his beliefs to become fixed, no longer responsive to changes in experience. His partner gets him down the wall and, in a last ditch attempt at therapy, takes him to the opera in Jackson, where the Metropolitan Opera on tour is performing "La Traviata" with Pavarotti singing the tenor lead. Paul is appeared to in the same way as everyone else there; he is inundated by waves of golden sound. Sadly enough, the effort at therapy fails; Paul still believes that he is on the belay ledge at the top of the next to last pitch of Guide's Wall, that Cascade Canyon is down to his left, that there is a hawk flying in lazy circles 200 feet below him, and so on. Furthermore, since he believes the very same things he believed when seated on the ledge, his beliefs are coherent. But surely they have very little by way of positive epistemic status for him. Clearly, then, coherence is not sufficient for positive epistemic status.

I turn finally to reliabilism, the last of the three chief contemporary ideas as to the nature of positive epistemic status. The view I have suggested in this paper is closer to reliabilism, especially in the form suggested by William Alston,[20] than to either of the other two; indeed, perhaps you think it *is* a form of reliabilism. I don't propose to argue about labels; still, as I see it, that would be less than wholly accurate. Of course reliability crucially enters into the account I suggest. According to that account, we implicitly think of positive epistemic status as involving our faculties' functioning properly; but clearly we wouldn't think of positive epistemic status in this way if we didn't think that when our faculties function as they ought, then for the most part they are in fact reliable. Still there is more to a belief's having positive epistemic status than its being reliably produced. There are even more brands of reliabilism than of coherentism; and what is true of one may not be true of another. But the leading idea of at least many central brands of reliabilism is that a belief has positive epistemic status if and only if it is produced by a reliable belief-producing mechanism or process; and the degree of its positive epistemic status is determined by the degree of reliability of the process that produces it. Thus Alvin Goldman: "The justificational status of a belief," he says, "is a function of the reliability of the process or processes that cause it, where (as a first approximation) reliability consists in the tendency of a process to produce beliefs that are true rather than false."[21]

---

20. See his "Concepts of Epistemic Justification," *The Monist,* vol. 68, no. 1 (Jan. 1985), and "An Internalist Externalism" in *Synthese* 74 (1988): 265-83.

21. "What Is Justified Belief?" in *Justification and Knowledge: New Studies in Epistemology,* ed. George Pappas (Dordrecht: D. Reidel, 1979), p. 10.

Here there are problems of several sorts; one of the most important is the dreaded *problem of generality,* developed by Richard Feldman in "Reliability and Justification."[22] But there are other problems as well, problems that arise out of the neglect of the idea of proper function. As we saw above, a crucial part of our notion of positive epistemic status is the idea of a design plan or specifications. But then not just any reliable belief-producing process can confer positive epistemic status. Suppose I am struck by a burst of cosmic rays, resulting in the following unfortunate malfunction. Whenever I hear the word 'prime' in any context, I form a belief, with respect to one of the first 1,000 natural numbers, that it is not prime. So you say "Pacific Palisades is a prime residential area"; or "Prime rib is my favorite," or "First you must prime the pump," or "(17′) entails (14)," or "The prime rate is dropping again," or anything else in which the word occurs; in each case I form a belief, with respect to a randomly selected natural number, that it is not prime. This belief-producing process or mechanism is indeed reliable; in the vast majority of cases it produces truth. But it is only *accidentally* reliable; it just happens, by virtue of a piece of epistemic serendipity, to produce mostly true beliefs. And the force of the suggestion that the process in question is accidentally reliable, I suggest, is just that under the envisaged conditions my faculties are not working in accordance with the design plan or the specifications for human beings; that's what makes the reliability in question *accidental* reliability. Furthermore, it does not confer positive epistemic status. Here the process or mechanism in question is indeed reliable; but my belief — that, say, 41 is not prime — has little or no positive epistemic status. Nor is the problem simply that the belief is false; the same goes for my (true) belief that 631 is not prime, if it is formed in this fashion. So reliable belief formation is not sufficient for positive epistemic status.

By way of conclusion, then: from a theistic perspective, it is natural to see positive epistemic status, the quantity enough of which is sufficient, together with truth, for knowledge in the following way: positive epistemic status accrues to a belief B for a person S only if S's cognitive environment is appropriate for his cognitive faculties and only if these faculties are functioning properly in producing this belief in him — i.e., only if his cognitive faculties are functioning in the way God designed human cognitive faculties to function, and only if S is in the sort of cognitive environment for which human cognitive faculties are designed; and under these conditions the degree of positive epistemic status enjoyed by B is proportional to the strength of his inclination to accept B. Alternatively: a belief B has positive epistemic status for S if and only if that belief is produced in S by his epistemic faculties working properly (in an appropriate environment); and B has more positive epistemic status than B^* for S if B has positive epistemic status for S and either B^* does not or else S is more

22. *The Monist,* vol. 68, no. 2 (April 1985), 159ff.

strongly inclined to believe B than B^*. Still another way to put the matter: a belief B has degree d of positive epistemic status for a person S if and only if the faculties relevant to producing B in S are functioning properly (in an appropriate environment), and S is inclined to degree d to believe B.

There remains, of course, an enormous amount to be said and an enormous amount to be thought about. For example: (1) What about *God's* knowledge? God is the premier example of someone who knows; but of course his faculties are not designed either by himself or by someone else. So how shall we think of his knowledge? The answer, I think, lies in the following neighborhood: "Working properly" is used *analogically* when applied to God's cognitive faculties and ours, the analogy being located in the fact that a design plan for a *perfect* knower would specify cognitive powers of the very sort God displays. But of course this notion needs to be developed and worked out in detail. (2) Our spiritual forebears at Princeton used to speak of the *noetic effects of sin.* Clearly (from a Christian perspective) sin has had an important effect upon the function of our cognitive faculties; but just how does this work and how does it bear on specific questions about the degree of positive epistemic status enjoyed by various beliefs? (3) This way of thinking of positive epistemic status, I believe, makes it much easier to understand the degree of positive epistemic status enjoyed by *moral* beliefs and by *a priori* beliefs; but just what sort of account is correct here? (4) How, from this perspective, shall we think of the dreaded Gettier problem? (5) The present account is clearly an *externalist* account of positive epistemic status; but how do *internalist* factors fit in? (6) From the present perspective, how shall we think about skepticism? (7) How is the present account related to the broadly Aristotelian account of knowledge to be found in medieval thinkers? (8) How shall we construe *epistemic probability* — more exactly, how shall we construe the relationship between A and B when A is a good non-deductive reason for B, or where B is epistemically probable with respect to A? Here the present account of positive epistemic status is clearly suggestive;[23] but how, precisely, does it work? (9) Over the last few years several philosophers[24] have been arguing that rational belief in God does not require propositional evidence or argument, that it can be properly basic; how shall we think of that claim from the present perspective? These and many others are questions for another occasion.

23. See Richard Otte's "Theistic Conception of Probability," *Faith and Philosophy* 4 (1987): 427-47.

24. See, for example, William Alston's "Christian Experience and Christian Belief," Nicholas Wolterstorff's "Can Belief in God Be Rational If It Has No Foundations?" and my "Reason and Belief in God," all in *Faith and Rationality,* ed. N. Wolterstorff and A. Plantinga (Notre Dame: University of Notre Dame Press, 1983).

CHAPTER SEVEN

A Defense of Religious Exclusivism

When I was a graduate student at Yale, the philosophy department prided itself on diversity, and it was indeed diverse. There were idealists, pragmatists, phenomenologists, existentialists, Whiteheadians, historians of philosophy, a token positivist, and what could only be described as observers of the passing intellectual scene. In some ways, this was indeed something to take pride in; a student could behold and encounter real, live representatives of many of the main traditions in philosophy. However, it also had an unintended and unhappy side effect. If anyone raised a philosophical question inside, but particularly outside, of class, the typical response would be to catalog some of the various different answers the world has seen: There is the Aristotelian answer, the existentialist answer, the Cartesian answer, Heidegger's answer, perhaps the Buddhist answer, and so on. But the question "What is the truth about this matter?" was often greeted with disdain as unduly naïve. There are all these different answers, all endorsed by people of great intellectual power and great dedication to philosophy; for every argument *for* one of these positions, there is another *against* it; would it not be excessively naïve, or perhaps arbitrary, to suppose that one of these is in fact true, the others being false? Or, if even there really is a truth of the matter, so that one of them is true and conflicting ones false, wouldn't it be merely arbitrary, in the face of this embarrassment of riches, to *endorse* one of them as the truth, consigning the others to falsehood? How could you possibly know which was true?

A similar attitude is sometimes urged with respect to the impressive variety of religions the world displays. There are theistic religions but also at least some nontheistic religions (or perhaps nontheistic strands) among the enormous variety of religions going under the names Hinduism and Buddhism; among the theistic religions, there are strands of Hinduism and Buddhism and American Indian religion as well as Islam, Judaism, and Christianity; and all

187

differ significantly from each other. Isn't it somehow arbitrary, or irrational, or unjustified, or unwarranted, or even oppressive and imperialistic to endorse one of these as opposed to all the others? According to Jean Bodin, "Each is refuted by all";[1] must we not agree? It is in this neighborhood that the so-called problem of pluralism arises. Of course, many concerns and problems can come under this rubric; the specific problem I mean to discuss can be thought of as follows. To put it in an internal and personal way, I find myself with religious beliefs, and religious beliefs that I realize aren't shared by nearly everyone else. For example, I believe both

(1) The world was created by God, an almighty, all-knowing, and perfectly good personal being (one that holds beliefs; has aims, plans, and intentions; and can act to accomplish these aims).

(2) Human beings require salvation, and God has provided a unique way of salvation through the incarnation, life, sacrificial death, and resurrection of his divine son.

Now there are many who do not believe these things. First, there are those who agree with me on (1) but not (2): they are non-Christian theists. Second, there are those who don't accept either (1) or (2) but nonetheless do believe that there is something beyond the natural world, a something such that human well-being and salvation depend upon standing in a right relation to it. Third, in the West and since the Enlightenment, anyway, there are people — naturalists, we may call them — who don't believe any of these three things. And my problem is this: When I become really aware of these other ways of looking at the world, these other ways of responding religiously to the world, what must or should I do? What is the right sort of attitude to take? What sort of impact should this awareness have on the beliefs I hold and the strength with which I hold them? My question is this: How should I think about the great religious diversity the world in fact displays? Can I sensibly remain an adherent of just one of these religions, rejecting the others? And here I am thinking specifically of *beliefs*. Of course, there is a great deal more to any religion or religious practice than just belief, and I don't for a moment mean to deny it. But belief is a crucially important part of most religions; it is a crucially important part of *my* religion; and the question I mean to ask here is, What does the awareness of religious diversity mean or what should it mean for my religious beliefs?

Some speak here of a *new* awareness of religious diversity and speak of this new awareness as constituting (for us in the West) a crisis, a revolution,

---

1. Jean Bodin, *Colloquium Heptaplomeres de Rerum Sublimium Arcanis Abditis,* written in 1593 but first published in 1857. English translation by Marion Kuntz (Princeton: Princeton University Press, 1975). The quotation is from the Kuntz translation, p. 256.

an intellectual development of the same magnitude as the Copernican revolution of the sixteenth century and the alleged discovery of evolution and our animal origins in the nineteenth.[2] No doubt there is at least some truth to this. Of course, the fact is all along many Western Christians and Jews have known that there are other religions and that not nearly everyone shares *their* religion. The ancient Israelites — some of the prophets, say — were clearly aware of Canaanite religion; and the apostle Paul said that he preached "Christ crucified, a stumbling block to Jews and folly to the Greeks" (1 Cor. 1:23). Other early Christians, the Christian martyrs, say, must have suspected that not everyone believed as they did; and the church fathers, in offering defenses of Christianity, were certainly apprised of this fact. Thomas Aquinas, again, was clearly aware of those to whom he addressed the *Summa Contra Gentiles;* and the fact that there are non-Christian religions would have come as no surprise to the Jesuit missionaries of the sixteenth and seventeenth centuries or to the Methodist missionaries of the nineteenth. To come to more recent times, when I was a child, *The Banner,* the official publication of my church, contained a small column for children; it was written by "Uncle Dick," who exhorted us to save our nickels and send them to our Indian cousins at the Navaho mission in New Mexico. Both we and our elders knew that the Navahos had or had had a religion different from Christianity, and part of the point of sending the nickels was to try to rectify that situation.

Still, in recent years, probably more of us Christian Westerners have become aware of the world's religious diversity; we have probably learned more about people of other religious persuasions, and we have come to see that they display what looks like real piety, devoutness, and spirituality. What is new, perhaps, is a more widespread sympathy for other religions, a tendency to see them as more valuable, as containing more by way of truth, and a new feeling of solidarity with their practitioners.

Now there are several possible reactions to awareness of religious diversity. One is to continue to believe what you have all along believed; you learn about this diversity but continue to believe — that is, take to be true — such propositions as (1) and (2) above, consequently taking to be false any beliefs, religious or otherwise, that are incompatible with (1) and (2). Following current practice, I will call this *exclusivism;* the exclusivist holds that the tenets or some of the tenets of *one* religion — Christianity, let's say — are in fact true; he adds, naturally enough, that any propositions, including other religious beliefs, that are incompatible with those tenets are false. And there is a fairly widespread

2. Joseph Runzo: "Today, the impressive piety and evident rationality of the belief systems of other religious traditions, inescapably confronts Christians with a crisis — and a potential revolution." "God, Commitment, and Other Faiths: Pluralism vs. Relativism," *Faith and Philosophy* 5, no. 4 (October 1988): 343f.

apprehension that there is something seriously wrong with exclusivism. It is irrational, or egotistical and unjustified,[3] or intellectually arrogant,[4] or elitist,[5] or a manifestation of harmful pride,[6] or even oppressive and imperialist.[7] The claim is that exclusivism as such is or involves a vice of some sort: It is wrong or deplorable. It is this claim I want to examine. I propose to argue that exclusivism need not involve either epistemic or moral failure and that, furthermore, something like it is wholly unavoidable, given our human condition.

These objections, of course, are not to the *truth* of (1) or (2) or any other proposition someone might accept in this exclusivist way (although objections of that sort are also put forward); they are instead directed to the *propriety* or *rightness* of exclusivism. There are initially two different kinds of indictments of exclusivism: broadly moral, or ethical, indictments and other broadly intellectual, or epistemic, indictments. These overlap in interesting ways as we will see below. But initially, anyway, we can take some of the complaints about exclusivism as *intellectual* criticisms: It is *irrational* or *unjustified* to think in an exclusivistic way. The other large body of complaint is moral: There is something *morally* suspect about exclusivism — it is arbitrary, or intellectually arrogant, or imperialistic. As Joseph Runzo suggests, exclusivism is "neither tolerable nor any longer intellectually honest in the context of our contemporary knowledge of other faiths."[8] I want to consider both

3. Gary Gutting: "Applying these considerations to religious belief, we seem led to the conclusion that, because believers have many epistemic peers who do not share their belief in God . . . , they have no right to maintain their belief without a justification. If they do so, they are guilty of epistemological egoism." *Religious Belief and Religious Skepticism* (Notre Dame, Ind.: University of Notre Dame Press, 1982), p. 90 (but see the following pages for an important qualification).

4. Wilfred Cantwell Smith: "Here my submission is that on this front the traditional doctrinal position of the Church has in fact militated against its traditional moral position, and has in fact encouraged Christians to approach other men immorally. Christ has taught us humility, but we have approached them with arrogance. . . . This charge of arrogance is a serious one." *Religious Diversity* (New York: Harper & Row, 1976), p. 13.

5. Runzo: "Ethically, Religious Exclusivism has the morally repugnant result of making those who have privileged knowledge, or who are intellectually astute, a religious elite, while penalizing those who happen to have no access to the putatively correct religious view, or who are incapable of advanced understanding." "God, Commitment, and Other Faiths," p. 348.

6. John Hick: "But natural pride, despite its positive contribution to human life, becomes harmful when it is elevated to the level of dogma and is built into the belief system of a religious community. This happens when its sense of its own validity and worth is expressed in doctrines implying an exclusive or a decisively superior access to the truth or the power to save." "Religious Pluralism and Absolute Claims," *Religious Pluralism,* ed. Leroy Rouner (Notre Dame: University of Notre Dame Press, 1984), p. 197.

7. John Cobb: "I agree with the liberal theists that even in Pannenberg's case, the quest for an absolute as a basis for understanding reflects the long tradition of Christian imperialism and triumphalism rather than the pluralistic spirit." "The Meaning of Pluralism for Christian Self-Understanding," *Religious Pluralism,* p. 171.

8. Runzo, "God, Commitment, and Other Faiths," p. 357.

kinds of claims or criticisms; I propose to argue that the exclusivist as such is not necessarily guilty of any of these charges.

I. Moral Objections to Exclusivism

I turn to the moral complaints: that the exclusivist is intellectually arrogant, or egotistical or self-servingly arbitrary, or dishonest, or imperialist, or oppressive. But first, I provide three qualifications. An exclusivist, like anyone else, will probably be guilty of some or all three of these things to at least some degree, perhaps particularly the first two. The question, however, is whether she is guilty of these things just by virtue of being an exclusivist. Second, I will use the term *exclusivism* in such a way that you don't count as an exclusivist unless you are rather fully aware of other faiths, have had their existence and their claims called to your attention with some force and perhaps fairly frequently, and have to some degree reflected on the problem of pluralism, asking yourself such questions as whether it is or could be really true that the Lord has revealed himself and his programs to us Christians, say, in a way in which he hasn't revealed himself to those of other faiths. Thus, my grandmother, for example, would not have counted as an exclusivist. She had, of course, *heard* of the heathen, as she called them, but the idea that perhaps Christians could learn from them, and learn from them with respect to religious matters, had not so much as entered her head; and the fact that it *hadn't* entered her head, I take it, was not a matter of moral dereliction on her part. This same would go for a Buddhist or Hindu peasant. These people are not, I think, properly charged with arrogance or other moral flaws in believing as they do.

Third, suppose I am an exclusivist with respect to (1), for example, but nonculpably believe, like Aquinas, say, that I have a knock-down, drag-out argument, a demonstration or conclusive proof of the proposition that there is such a person as God; and suppose I think further (and nonculpably) that if those who don't believe (1) were to be apprised of this argument (and had the ability and training necessary to grasp it and were to think about the argument fairly and reflectively), they too would come to believe (1). Then I could hardly be charged with these moral faults. My condition would be like that of Gödel, let's say, upon having recognized that he had a proof for the incompleteness of arithmetic. True, many of his colleagues and peers didn't believe that arithmetic was incomplete, and some believed that it *was* complete; but presumably Gödel wasn't arbitrary or egotistical in believing that arithmetic is in fact incomplete. Furthermore, he would not have been at fault had he nonculpably but *mistakenly* believed that he had found such a proof. Accordingly, I will use the term *exclusivist* in such a way that you don't count as an exclusivist if you nonculpably think you know of a demonstration or conclusive argument for the beliefs with respect to which you are an exclusivist, or even if you nonculpably think you know of an argument that would convince all or most intelligent and honest people of the truth of that proposition. So an exclusivist, as I use the term, not only believes something like (1) and (2) and thinks false any proposition incompatible with it; she also meets a further condition C that is hard to state precisely and in detail (and in fact any attempt to do so would involve a long and presently irrelevant discussion of *ceteris paribus* clauses). Suffice it to say that C includes (a) being rather fully aware of other religions, (b) knowing that there is much that at the least looks like genuine piety and devoutness in them, and (c) believing that you know of no arguments that would necessarily convince all or most honest and intelligent dissenters.

Given these qualifications then, why should we think that an exclusivist is properly charged with these moral faults? I will deal first and most briefly with charges of oppression and imperialism: I think we must say that they are on the face of it wholly implausible. I daresay there are some among you who reject some of the things I believe; I do not believe that you are thereby oppressing me, even if you do not believe you have an argument that would convince me. It is conceivable that exclusivism might in some way *contribute to* oppression, but it isn't in itself oppressive.

The more important moral charge is that there is a sort of self-serving arbitrariness, an arrogance or egotism, in accepting such propositions as (1) or (2) under condition C; exclusivism is guilty of some serious moral fault or flaw. According to Wilfred Cantwell Smith, ". . . except at the cost of insensitivity or delinquency, it is morally not possible actually to go out into the world and say to devout, intelligent, fellow human beings: '. . . we believe that we know God and we are right; you believe that you know God, and you are totally wrong.' "9

So what can the exclusivist have to say for himself? Well, it must be conceded immediately that if he believes (1) or (2), then he must also believe that those who believe something incompatible with them are mistaken and believe what is false. That's no more than simple logic. Furthermore, he must

---

9. Smith, *Religious Diversity,* p. 14. A similar statement by John Hick: "Nor can we reasonably claim that our own form of religious experience, together with that of the tradition of which we are a part, is veridical whilst others are not. We can of course claim this; and indeed virtually every religious tradition has done so, regarding alternative forms of religion either as false or as confused and inferior versions of itself. . . . Persons living within other traditions, then, are equally justified in trusting their own distinctive religious experience and in forming their beliefs on the basis of it. . . . Let us avoid the implausibly arbitrary dogma that religious experience is all delusory with the single exception of the particular form enjoyed by the one who is speaking." *An Interpretation of Religion* (New Haven: Yale University Press, 1989), p. 235.

also believe that those who do not believe as he does — those who believe neither (1) nor (2), whether or not they believe their negations — *fail* to believe something that is deep and important and that he *does* believe. He must therefore see himself as *privileged* with respect to those others — those others of both kinds. There is something of great value, he must think, that *he* has and *they* lack. They are ignorant of something — something of great importance — of which he has knowledge. But does this make him properly subject to the above censure?

I think the answer must be no. Or if the answer is yes, then I think we have here a genuine moral dilemma; for in our earthly life here below, as my Sunday School teacher used to say, there is no real alternative; there is no reflective attitude that is not open to the same strictures. These charges of arrogance are a philosophical tar baby: Get close enough to them to use them against the exclusivist and you are likely to find them stuck fast to yourself. How so? Well, as an exclusivist, I realize that I can't convince others that they should believe as I do, but I nonetheless continue to believe as I do. The charge is that I am, as a result, arrogant or egotistical, arbitrarily preferring my way of doing things to other ways.[10] But what are my alternatives with respect to a proposition like (1)? There seem to be three choices.[11] I can continue to hold it; I can withhold it, in Roderick Chisholm's sense, believing neither it nor its denial; and I can accept its denial. Consider the third way, a way taken by those pluralists who, like John Hick, hold that such propositions as (1) and (2) and their colleagues from other faiths are literally false, although in some way still valid responses to the Real. This seems to me to be no advance at all with respect to the arrogance or egotism problem; this is not a way out. For if I do this, I will then be in the very same condition as I am now: I will believe many propositions others don't believe and will be in condition *C* with respect to those propositions. For I will then believe the denials of (1) and (2) (as well as the denials of many other propositions explicitly accepted by those of other faiths). Many others, of course, do not believe the denials of (1) and (2) and in fact believe (1) and (2). Further, I will not know of any arguments that can be counted on to persuade those who do believe (1) or (2) (or propositions accepted by the adherents of other

10. John Hick: ". . . The only reason for treating one's tradition differently from others is the very human but not very cogent reason that it is one's own!" *An Interpretation of Religion,* loc. cit.

11. To speak of choice here suggests that I can simply choose which of these three attitudes to adopt; but is that at all realistic? Are my beliefs to that degree within my control? Here I will set aside the question whether and to what degree my beliefs are within my control and within my power. Perhaps we have very little control over them; then the moral critic of exclusivism can't properly accuse the exclusivist of dereliction of moral duty, but he could still argue that the exclusivist's stance is unhappy, bad, a miserable state of affairs. Even if I can't help it that I am overbearing and conceited, my being that way is a bad state of affairs.

religions). I am therefore in the condition of believing propositions that many others do not believe and furthermore am in condition C. If, in the case of those who believe (1) and (2), that is sufficient for intellectual arrogance or egotism, the same goes for those who believe their denials.

So consider the second option: I can instead *withhold* the proposition in question. I can say to myself: "The right course here, given that I can't or couldn't convince these others of what I believe, is to believe neither these propositions nor their denials." The pluralist objector to exclusivism can say that the right course, under condition C, is to abstain from believing the offending proposition and also abstain from believing its denial; call him, therefore, "the abstemious pluralist." But does he thus really avoid the condition that, on the part of the exclusivist, leads to the charges of egotism and arrogance in this way? Think, for a moment, about disagreement. Disagreement, fundamentally, is a matter of adopting conflicting propositional attitudes with respect to a given proposition. In the simplest and most familiar case, I disagree with you if there is some proposition p such that I believe p and you believe $-p$. But that's just the simplest case; there are also others. The one that is presently of interest is this: I believe p and you withhold it, fail to believe it. Call the first kind of disagreement "contradicting"; call the second "dissenting."

My claim is that if contradicting others (under the condition C spelled out above) is arrogant and egotistical, so is dissenting (under that same condition). Suppose you believe some proposition p but I don't; perhaps you believe that it is wrong to discriminate against people simply on the grounds of race, but I, recognizing that there are many people who disagree with you, do not believe this proposition. I don't disbelieve it either, of course, but in the circumstances I think the right thing to do is to abstain from belief. Then am I not implicitly condemning your attitude, your *believing* the proposition, as somehow improper — naïve, perhaps, or unjustified, or in some other way less than optimal? I am implicitly saying that my attitude is the superior one; I think my course of action here is the right one and yours somehow wrong, inadequate, improper, in the circumstances at best second-rate. Of course, I realize that there is no question, here, of *showing* you that your attitude is wrong or improper or naïve; so am I not guilty of intellectual arrogance? Of a sort of egotism, thinking I know better than you, arrogating to myself a privileged status with respect to you? The problem for the exclusivist was that she was obliged to think she possessed a truth missed by many others; the problem for the abstemious pluralist is that he is obliged to think that he possesses a virtue others don't or acts rightly where others don't. If, in condition C, one is arrogant by way of believing a proposition others don't, isn't one equally, under those reflective conditions, arrogant by way of withholding a proposition others don't?

Perhaps you will respond by saying that the abstemious pluralist gets into trouble, falls into arrogance, by way of implicitly saying or believing that his way of proceeding is better or wiser than other ways pursued by other people; and perhaps he can escape by abstaining from *that* view as well. Can't he escape the problem by refraining from believing that racial bigotry is wrong and also refraining from holding the view that it is *better,* under the conditions that obtain, to withhold that proposition than to assert and believe it? Well, yes he can; then he has no *reason* for his abstention; he doesn't believe that abstention is better or more appropriate; he simply abstains. Does this get him off the egotistical hook? Perhaps. But then he can't, in consistency, also hold that there is something wrong with *not* abstaining, with coming right out and *believing* that bigotry is wrong; he loses his objection to the exclusivist. Accordingly, this way out is not available for the abstemious pluralist who accuses the exclusivist of arrogance and egotism.

Indeed, I think we can show that the abstemious pluralist who brings charges of intellectual arrogance against exclusivism is hoist with his own petard; he holds a position that in a certain way is self-referentially inconsistent in the circumstances. For he believes

(3) If S knows that others don't believe p and that he is in condition C with respect to p, then S should not believe p.

This or something like it is the ground of the charges he brings against the exclusivist. But the abstemious pluralist realizes that many do not accept (3); and I suppose he also realizes that it is unlikely that he can find arguments for (3) that will convince them; hence, he knows that condition C obtains. Given his acceptance of (3), therefore, the right course for him is to abstain from believing (3). Under the conditions that do in fact obtain — namely, his knowledge that others don't accept it and that condition C obtains — he can't properly accept it.

I am therefore inclined to think that one can't, in the circumstances, properly hold (3) or any other proposition that will do the job. One can't find here some principle on the basis of which to hold that the exclusivist is doing the wrong thing, suffers from some moral fault — that is, one can't find such a principle that doesn't, as we might put it, fall victim to itself.

So the abstemious pluralist is hoist with his own petard; but even apart from this dialectical argument (which in any event some will think unduly cute), aren't the charges unconvincing and implausible? I must concede that there are a variety of ways in which I can be and have been intellectually arrogant and egotistic; I have certainly fallen into this vice in the past and no doubt am not free of it now. But am I really arrogant and egotistic just by virtue of believing what I know others don't believe, where I can't show them that I am right? Suppose I think the matter over, consider the objections as carefully as I can, realize that I am finite and furthermore a sinner, certainly no better than those with whom I disagree; but suppose it still seems clear to me that the proposition in question is true. Can I really be behaving immorally in continuing to believe it? I am dead sure that it is wrong to try to advance my career by telling lies about my colleagues; I realize there are those who disagree; I also realize that in all likelihood there is no way I can find to show them that they are wrong; nonetheless I think they *are* wrong. If I think this after careful reflection, if I consider the claims of those who disagree as sympathetically as I can, if I try my level best to ascertain the truth here, and it *still* seems to me sleazy, wrong, and despicable to lie about my colleagues to advance my career, could I really be doing what is immoral by continuing to believe as before? I can't see how. If, after careful reflection and thought, you find yourself convinced that the right propositional attitude to take to (1) and (2) in the face of the facts of religious pluralism is belief or abstention from belief, how could you properly be taxed with egotism, either for so believing or for so abstaining? Even if you knew others did not agree with you?

II. Epistemic Objections to Exclusivism

I turn now to *epistemic* objections to exclusivism. There are many different specifically epistemic virtues and a corresponding plethora of epistemic vices. The ones with which the exclusivist is most frequently charged, however, are *irrationality* and *lack of justification* in holding his exclusivist beliefs. The claim is that as an exclusivist he holds unjustified beliefs and/or irrational beliefs. Better, *he* is unjustified or irrational in holding these beliefs. I will therefore consider those two claims, and I will argue that the exclusivist views need not be either unjustified or irrational. I will then turn to the question whether his beliefs could have *warrant* — that property, whatever precisely it is, that distinguishes knowledge from mere true belief — and whether they could have enough warrant for knowledge.

A. *Justification*

The pluralist objector sometimes claims that to hold exclusivist views, in condition *C,* is *unjustified — epistemically* unjustified. Is this true? And what does he mean when he makes this claim? As even a brief glance at the contemporary epistemological literature will show, justification is a protean and multifarious notion.[12] There are, I think, substantially two possibilities as to what he means. The central core of the notion, its beating heart, the paradigmatic center to which most of the myriad contemporary variations are related by way of analogical extension and family resemblance, is the notion of *being within one's intellectual rights,* having violated no intellectual or cognitive duties or obligations in the formation and sustenance of the belief in question. This is the palimpsest, going back to René Descartes and especially John Locke, that underlies the multitudinous battery of contemporary inscriptions. There is no space to argue that point here; but chances are, when the pluralist objector to exclusivism claims that the latter is unjustified, it is some notion lying in this neighborhood that he has in mind. (Here we should note the very close connection between the moral objections to exclusivism and the objection that exclusivism is epistemically unjustified.)

The duties involved, naturally enough, would be specifically *epistemic* duties: perhaps a duty to proportion degree of belief to (propositional) evidence from what is *certain,* that is, self-evident or incorrigible, as with Locke, or perhaps to try one's best to get into and stay in the right relation to the truth, as with Chisholm,[13] the leading contemporary champion of the justificationist tradition with respect to knowledge. But at present there is widespread (and as I see it, correct) agreement that there is no duty of the Lockean kind. Perhaps there is one of the Chisholmian kind;[14] but isn't the exclusivist conforming to that duty if, after the sort of careful, indeed prayerful consideration I mentioned in the response to the moral objection, it still seems to him strongly that (1), say, is true and he accordingly still believes it? It is therefore very hard to see that the exclusivist is necessarily unjustified in this way.

The second possibility for understanding the charge — the charge that exclusivism is epistemically unjustified — has to do with the oft-repeated claim that exclusivism is intellectually *arbitrary.* Perhaps the idea is that there is an intellectual duty to treat similar cases similarly; the exclusivist violates this duty by arbitrarily choosing to believe (for the moment going along with the fiction that we *choose* beliefs of this sort) (1) and (2) in the face of the

12. See my "Justification in the Twentieth Century," *Philosophy and Phenomenological Research,* vol. L, supplement (Fall 1990), pp. 45ff., and see chapter 1 of my *Warrant: The Current Debate* (New York: Oxford University Press, 1993).

13. See the three editions of *Theory of Knowledge* referred to in footnote 22.

14. Some people think there is and also think that withholding belief, abstaining from belief, is always and automatically the safe course to take with respect to this duty, whenever any question arises as to what to believe and withhold. But that isn't so. One can go wrong by withholding as well as by believing: there is no safe haven here, not even abstention. If there is a duty of the Chisholmian kind, and if I, out of epistemic pride and excessive scrupulosity, succeed in training myself not to accept ordinary perceptual judgments in ordinary perceptual circumstances, I am not performing works of epistemic supererogation; I am epistemically culpable.

plurality of conflicting religious beliefs the world presents. But suppose there is such a duty. Clearly you do not violate it if you nonculpably think the beliefs in question are *not* on a par. And as an exclusivist, I *do* think (nonculpably, I hope) that they are not on a par: I think (1) and (2) *true* and those incompatible with either of them *false*.

The rejoinder, of course, will be that it is not alethic parity (their having the same truth value) that is at issue: it is *epistemic* parity that counts. What kind of epistemic parity? What would be relevant, here, I should think, would be *internal* or internalist epistemic parity: parity with respect to what is internally available to the believer. What is internally available to the believer includes, for example, detectable relationships between the belief in question and other beliefs you hold; so internal parity would include parity of propositional evidence. What is internally available to the believer also includes the *phenomenology* that goes with the beliefs in question: the *sensuous* phenomenology but also the nonsensuous phenomenology involved, for example, in the belief's just having the feel of being *right*. But once more, then, (1) and (2) are not on an internal par, for the exclusivist, with beliefs that are incompatible with them. (1) and (2), after all, seem to me to be true; they have for me the phenomenology that accompanies that seeming. The same cannot be said for propositions incompatible with them. If, furthermore, John Calvin is right in thinking that there is such a thing as the *Sensus Divinitatis* and the Internal Testimony of the Holy Spirit, then perhaps (1) and (2) are produced in me by those belief-producing processes and have for me the phenomenology that goes with them; the same is not true for propositions incompatible with them.

But then the next rejoinder: Isn't it probably true that those who reject (1) and (2) in favor of other beliefs have propositional evidence for their beliefs that is on a par with mine for my beliefs? And isn't it also probably true that the same or similar phenomenology accompanies their beliefs as accompanies mine? So that those beliefs really are epistemically and internally on a par with (1) and (2), and the exclusivist is still treating like cases differently? I don't think so; I think there really are arguments available for (1), at least, that are not available for its competitors. And as for similar phenomenology, this is not easy to say; it is not easy to look into the breast of another; the secrets of the human heart are hard to fathom; it is hard indeed to discover this sort of thing even with respect to someone you know really well. I am prepared, however, to stipulate both sorts of parity. Let's agree for purposes of argument that these beliefs are on an epistemic par in the sense that those of a different religious tradition have the same sort of internally available markers — evidence, phenomenology, and the like — for their beliefs as I have for (1) and (2). What follows?

Return to the case of moral belief. King David took Bathsheba, made her pregnant, and then, after the failure of various stratagems to get her husband Uriah to think the baby was his, arranged for him to be killed. The prophet Nathan came to David and told him a story about a rich man and a poor man. The rich man had many flocks and herds; the poor man had only a single ewe lamb, which grew up with his children, "ate at his table, drank from his cup, lay in his bosom, and was like a daughter to him." The rich man had unexpected guests. Rather than slaughter one of his own sheep, he took the poor man's single ewe lamb, slaughtered it, and served it to his guests. David exploded in anger: "The man who did this deserves to die!" Then, in one of the most riveting passages in all the Bible, Nathan turns to David and declares, "You are that man!" And then David sees what he has done.

My interest here is in David's reaction to the story. I agree with David: Such injustice is utterly and despicably wrong; there are really no words for it. I believe that such an action is wrong, and I believe that the proposition that it *isn't* wrong — either because really *nothing* is wrong, or because even if *some* things are wrong, *this* isn't — is false. As a matter of fact, there isn't a lot I believe more strongly. I recognize, however, that there are those who disagree with me; and once more, I doubt that I could find an argument to show them that I am right and they wrong. Further, for all I know, their conflicting beliefs have for them the same internally available epistemic markers, the same phenomenology, as mine have for me. Am I then being arbitrary, treating similar cases differently in continuing to hold, as I do, that in fact that kind of behavior *is* dreadfully wrong? I don't think so. Am I wrong in thinking racial bigotry despicable, even though I know there are others who disagree, and even if I think they have the same internal markers for their beliefs as I have for mine? I don't think so. I believe in serious actualism, the view that no objects have properties in worlds in which they do not exist, not even nonexistence. Others do not believe this, and perhaps the internal markers of their dissenting views have for them the same quality as my views have for me. Am I arbitrary in continuing to think as I do? I can't see how.

And the reason here is this: in each of these cases, the believer in question doesn't really think the beliefs in question *are* on a relevant epistemic par. She may agree that she and those who dissent are equally convinced of the truth of their beliefs and even that they are internally on a par, that the internally available markers are similar, or relevantly similar. But she must still think that there is an important epistemic difference; she thinks that somehow the other person has *made a mistake,* or *has a blind spot,* or hasn't been wholly attentive, or hasn't received some grace she has, or is in some way epistemically less fortunate. And, of course, the pluralist critic is in no better case. He thinks the thing to do when there is internal epistemic parity is to withhold judgment; he knows that there are others who don't think so, and for all he knows that belief has internal parity with his; if he continues in that belief, therefore, he will be in the same condition as the exclusivist; and if he doesn't continue in this belief, he no longer has an objection to the exclusivist.

But couldn't I be wrong? Of course I could! But I don't avoid that risk by withholding all religious (or philosophical or moral) beliefs: I can go wrong that way as well as any other, treating all religions, or all philosophical thoughts, or all moral views as on a par. Again, there is no safe haven here, no way to avoid risk. In particular, you won't reach a safe haven by trying to take the same attitude toward all the historically available patterns of belief and withholding; for in so doing, you adopt a particular pattern of belief and withholding, one incompatible with some adopted by others. "You pays your money and you takes your choice," realizing that you, like anyone else, can be desperately wrong. But what else can you do? You don't really have an alternative. And how can you do better than believe and withhold according to what, after serious and responsible consideration, seems to you to be the right pattern of belief and withholding?

B. Irrationality

I therefore can't see how it can be sensibly maintained that the exclusivist is unjustified in his exclusivist views; but perhaps, as is sometimes claimed, he or his view is *irrational*. Irrationality, however, is many things to many people; so there is a prior question: What is it to be irrational? More exactly, precisely what quality is it that the objector is attributing to the exclusivist (in condition C) when the former says the latter's exclusivist beliefs are irrational? Since the charge is never developed at all fully, it isn't easy to say. So suppose we simply consider the main varieties of irrationality (or, if you prefer, the main senses of 'irrational') and ask whether any of them attach to the exclusivist just by virtue of being an exclusivist. I believe there are substantially five varieties of rationality, five distinct but analogically[15] connected senses of the term *rational;* fortunately not all of them require detailed consideration.

1. Aristotelian Rationality

This is the sense in which man is a rational animal, one that has *ratio,* one that can look before and after, can hold beliefs, make inferences and is capable of knowledge. This is perhaps the basic sense, the one of which the others are analogical extensions. It is also, presumably, irrelevant in the present

15. In Aquinas's sense, so that analogy may include causality, proportionality, resemblance, and the like.

context; at any rate I hope the objector does not mean to hold that an exclusivist will by that token no longer be a rational animal.

2. The Deliverances of Reason

To be rational in the Aristotelian sense is to possess reason: the power of thinking, believing, inferring, reasoning, knowing. Aristotelian rationality is thus *generic*. But there is an important more specific sense lurking in the neighborhood; this is the sense that goes with reason taken more narrowly, as the source of a priori knowledge and belief.[16] An important use of *rational* analogically connected with the first has to do with reason taken in this more narrow way. It is by reason thus construed that we know *self-evident* beliefs — beliefs so obvious that you can't so much as grasp them without seeing that they couldn't be false. These will be among the *deliverances of reason*. Of course there are other beliefs — $38 \times 39 = 1,482$, for example — that are not self-evident but are a consequence of self-evident beliefs by way of arguments that are self-evidently valid; these too are among the deliverances of reason. So say that the deliverances of reason is the set of those propositions that are self-evident for us human beings, closed under self-evident consequence. This yields another sense of rationality: a belief is *rational* if it is among the deliverances of reason and *irrational* if it is contrary to the deliverances of reason. (A belief must therefore be either rational or irrational, in this sense.) This sense of *rational* is an analogical extension of the fundamental sense, but it is itself extended by analogy to still other senses. Thus, we can broaden the category of reason to include memory, experience, induction, probability, and whatever else goes into science; this is the sense of the term when reason is sometimes contrasted with faith. And we can also soften the requirement for self-evidence, recognizing both that self-evidence or a priori warrant is a matter of degree and that there are many propositions that have a priori warrant, but are not such that no one who understands them can fail to believe them.[17]

16. See my *Warrant and Proper Function* (New York: Oxford University Press, 1993), chapter 7.

17. See my *Warrant and Proper Function,* chapter 7. Still another analogical extension: A person can be said to be irrational if he won't listen to or pay attention to the deliverances of reason. He may be blinded by lust, or inflamed by passion, or deceived by pride; he might then act contrary to reason — *act* irrationally but also *believe* irrationally. John Locke: "Let ever so much probability land on one side of a covetous man's reasoning, and money on the other, it is easy to foresee which will outweigh. Tell a man, passionately in love, that he is jilted; bring a score of witnesses of the falsehood of his mistress, 'tis ten to one but three kind words of hers, shall invalidate all their testimonies. . . . And though men cannot always openly gainsay, or resist the force of manifest probabilities, that make against them; yet yield they not to the argument." *An Essay Concerning Human Understanding,* ed. A. D. Woozley (New York: World Publishing, 1963), bk. IV, sec. xx, p. 439.

Is the exclusivist irrational in *these* senses? I think not; at any rate, the question whether he is isn't the question at issue. His exclusivist beliefs are irrational in these senses only if there is a good argument from the deliverances of reason (taken broadly) to the denials of what he believes. I do not believe that there are any such arguments. Presumably, the same goes for the pluralist objector; at any rate, his objection is not that (1) and (2) are demonstrably false or even that there are good arguments against them from the deliverances of reason; his objection is instead that there is something wrong or subpar with believing them in condition C. This sense too, then, is irrelevant to our present concerns.

3. The Deontological Sense

This sense of the term has to do with intellectual *requirement,* or *duty,* or *obligation;* a person's belief is irrational in this sense if in forming or holding it she violates such a duty. This is the sense of *irrational* in which, according to many contemporary evidentialist objectors to theistic belief, those who believe in God without propositional evidence are irrational.[18] Irrationality in this sense is a matter of failing to conform to intellectual or epistemic duties; the analogical connection with the first, Aristotelian sense is that these duties are thought to be among the deliverances of reason (and hence among the deliverances of the power by virtue of which human beings are rational in the Aristotelian sense). But we have already considered whether the exclusivist is flouting duties; we need say no more about the matter here. As we saw, the exclusivist is not necessarily irrational in this sense either.

4. Zweckrationalität

A common and very important notion of rationality is *means-end rationality* — what our continental cousins, following Max Weber, sometimes call *Zweckrationalität,* the sort of rationality displayed by your actions if they are well calculated to achieve your goals. (Again, the analogical connection with the first sense is clear: The calculation in question requires the power by virtue of which we are rational in Aristotle's sense.) Clearly, there is a whole con-

---

18. Among those who offer this objection to theistic belief are, for example, Brand Blanshard, *Reason and Belief* (London: Allen & Unwin, 1974), pp. 400ff.; Anthony Flew, *The Presumption of Atheism* (London: Pemberton, 1976), pp. 22ff.; Michael Scriven, *Primary Philosophy* (New York: McGraw-Hill, 1966), pp. 102ff., and others. See my "Reason and Belief in God" [Ed. note: chapter 5 above] in *Faith and Rationality* (Notre Dame: University of Notre Dame Press, 1983), pp. 17ff.

stellation of notions lurking in the nearby bushes: What would *in fact* contribute to your goals? What you *think* would contribute to your goals? What you *would* think would contribute to your goals if you were sufficiently acute, or knew enough, or weren't distracted by lust, greed, pride, ambition, and the like? What you would think would contribute to your goals if you weren't thus distracted and were also to reflect sufficiently? and so on. This notion of rationality has assumed enormous importance in the last 150 years or so; among its laurels, for example, is the complete domination of the development of the discipline of economics. Rationality thus construed is a matter of knowing how to get what you want; it is the cunning of reason. Is the exclusivist properly charged with irrationality in this sense? Does his believing in the way he does interfere with his attaining some of his goals, or is it a markedly inferior way of attaining those goals?

An initial *caveat:* It isn't clear that this notion of rationality applies to belief at all. It isn't clear that in *believing* something, I am acting to achieve some goal. If believing is an action at all, it is very far from being the paradigmatic kind of action taken to achieve some end; we don't have a choice as to whether to have beliefs, and we don't have a lot of choice with respect to which beliefs we have. But suppose we set this *caveat* aside and stipulate for purposes of argument that we have sufficient control over our beliefs for them to qualify as actions. Would the exclusivist's beliefs then be irrational in this sense? Well, that depends upon what his goals *are;* if among his goals for religious belief is, for example, not believing anything not believed by someone else, then indeed it would be. But, of course, he needn't have *that* goal. If I do have an end or goal in holding such beliefs as (1) and (2), it would presumably be that of believing the truth on this exceedingly important matter or perhaps that of trying to get in touch as adequately as possible with God, or more broadly with the deepest reality. And if (1) and (2) are *true,* believing them will be a way of doing exactly that. It is only if they are *not* true, then, that believing them could sensibly be thought to be irrational in this means-ends sense. Because the objector does not propose to take as a premise the proposition that (1) and (2) are false — he holds only that there is some flaw involved in *believing* them — this also is presumably not what he means.

5. Rationality as Sanity and Proper Function

One in the grip of pathological confusion, or flight of ideas, or certain kinds of agnosia, or the manic phase of manic-depressive psychosis will often be said to be irrational; the episode may pass, after which he has regained rationality. Here *rationality* means absence of dysfunction, disorder, impairment, or pathology with respect to rational faculties. So this variety of rationality is again analogically related to Aristotelian rationality; a person is rational in this sense when no malfunction obstructs her use of the faculties by virtue of which she is rational in the Aristotelian sense. Rationality as sanity does not require possession of particularly exalted rational faculties; it requires only normality (in the nonstatistical sense), or health, or proper function. This use of the term, naturally enough, is prominent in psychiatric discussions — Oliver Sack's male patient who mistook his wife for a hat,[19] for example, was thus irrational.[20] This fifth and final sense of rationality is itself a family of analogically related senses. The fundamental sense here is that of sanity and proper function, but there are other closely related senses. Thus, we may say that a belief (in certain circumstances) is irrational, not because no sane person would hold it, but because no person who was sane and had also undergone a certain course of education would hold it or because no person who was sane and furthermore was as intelligent as we and our friends would hold it; alternatively and more briefly, the idea is not merely that no one who was functioning properly in those circumstances would hold it, but rather no one who was functioning *optimally,* as well or nearly as well as human beings ordinarily do (leaving aside the occasional great genius), would hold it. And this sense of rationality leads directly to the notion of *warrant;* I turn now to that notion; in treating it, we will also treat *ambulando* — this fifth kind of irrationality.

C. Warrant

So we come to the third version of the epistemic objection: that at any rate the exclusivist doesn't have warrant, or anyway *much* warrant (enough warrant for knowledge) for his exclusivistic views. Many pluralists — for example, Hick, Runzo, and Cantwell Smith — unite in declaring that, at any rate, the exclusivist certainly can't *know* that his exclusivistic views are true.[21] But is this really true? I will argue briefly that it is not. At any rate, from the

---

19. *The Man Who Mistook His Wife for a Hat* (New York: Harper & Row, 1987).

20. In this sense of the term, what is properly called an *irrational impulse* may be perfectly rational: an irrational impulse is really one that goes contrary to the deliverances of reason; but undergoing such impulses need not be in any way dysfunctional or a result of the impairment of cognitive faculties. To go back to some of William James's examples, that I will survive my serious illness might be unlikely given the statistics I know and my evidence generally; perhaps we are so constructed, however, that when our faculties function properly in extreme situations, we are more optimistic than the evidence warrants. This belief, then, is irrational in the sense that it goes contrary to the deliverances of reason; it is rational in the sense that it doesn't involve dysfunction.

21. Runzo, "God, Commitment, and Other Faiths," p. 348; Smith, *Religious Diversity,* p. 16.

perspective of each of the major contemporary accounts of knowledge, it may very well be that the exclusivist knows (1) or (2) or both. First, consider the two main internalistic accounts of knowledge: the justified true belief accounts and the coherentist accounts. As I have already argued, it seems clear that a theist, a believer in (1), could certainly be *justified* (in the primary sense) in believing as she does: she could be flouting no intellectual or cognitive duties or obligations. But then on the most straightforward justified true belief account of knowledge, she can also *know* that it is true — if, that is, it *can* be true. More exactly, what must be possible is that both the exclusivist is justified in believing (1) and/or (2) and they be true. Presumably, the pluralist does not mean to dispute this possibility.

For concreteness, consider the account of justification given by the classical foundationalist Chisholm.[22] On this view, a belief has warrant for me to the extent that accepting it is apt for the fulfillment of my epistemic duty, which (roughly speaking) is that of trying to get and remain in the right relation to the truth. But if after the most careful, thorough, open, and prayerful consideration, it still seems to me — perhaps more strongly than ever — that (1) and (2) are true, then clearly accepting them has great aptness for the fulfillment of that duty.

A similarly brief argument can be given with respect to *coherentism,* the view that what constitutes warrant is coherence with some body of belief. We must distinguish two varieties of coherentism. On the one hand, it might be held that what is required is coherence with some or all of the other beliefs I actually hold; on the other, that what is required is coherence with my *verific* noetic structure (Keith Lehrer's term): the set of beliefs that remains when all the false ones are deleted or replaced by their contradictories. But surely a coherent set of beliefs could include both (1) and (2) together with the beliefs involved in being in condition *C;* what would be required, perhaps, would be that the set of beliefs contain some explanation of why it is that others do not believe as I do. And if (1) and (2) *are* true, then surely (and a fortiori) there can be coherent verific noetic structures that include them. Hence, neither of these versions of coherentism rules out the possibility that the exclusivist in condition *C* could know (1) and/or (2).

And now consider the main externalist accounts. The most popular externalist account at present would be one or another version of *reliabilism.* And there is an oft-repeated pluralistic argument that seems to be designed

---

22. See his *Perceiving: A Philosophical Study* (Ithaca: Cornell University Press, 1957), the three editions of *Theory of Knowledge* (New York: Prentice-Hall, first edition 1966, second edition 1977, third edition 1989), and *The Foundations of Knowing* (Minneapolis: University of Minnesota Press, 1982); and see my "Chisholmian Internalism," in *Philosophical Analysis: A Defense by Example,* ed. David Austin (Dordrecht: D. Reidel, 1988), and chapter 2 of *Warrant: The Current Debate.*

to appeal to reliabilist intuitions. The conclusion of this argument is not always clear, but here is its premise, in Hick's words:

> For it is evident that in some ninety-nine percent of cases the religion which an individual professes and to which he or she adheres depends upon the accidents of birth. Someone born to Buddhist parents in Thailand is very likely to be a Buddhist, someone born to Muslim parents in Saudi Arabia to be a Muslim, someone born to Christian parents in Mexico to be a Christian, and so on.[23]

As a matter of sociological fact, this may be right. Furthermore, it can certainly produce a sense of intellectual vertigo. But what is one to do with this fact, if fact it is, and what follows from it? Does it follow, for example, that I ought not to accept the religious views that I have been brought up to accept, or the ones that I find myself inclined to accept, or the ones that seem to me to be true: or that the belief-producing processes that have produced those beliefs in me are unreliable? Surely not. Furthermore, self-referential problems once more loom; this argument is another philosophical tar baby.

For suppose we concede that if I had been born of Muslim parents in Morocco rather than Christian parents in Michigan, my beliefs would have been quite different. (For one thing, I probably wouldn't believe that I was born in Michigan.) The same goes for the pluralist. Pluralism isn't and hasn't been widely popular in the world at large; if the pluralist had been born in Madagascar, or medieval France, he probably wouldn't have been a pluralist. Does it follow that he shouldn't be a pluralist or that his pluralist beliefs are produced in him by an unreliable belief-producing process? I doubt it. Suppose I hold the following, or something similar:

(4) If S's religious or philosophical beliefs are such that if S had been born elsewhere and elsewhen, she wouldn't have held them, then those beliefs are produced by unreliable belief-producing mechanisms and hence have no warrant.

Once more I will be hoist with my own petard. For in all probability, someone born in Mexico to Christian parents wouldn't believe (4) itself. No matter what philosophical and religious beliefs we hold and withhold (so it seems), there are places and times such that if we have been born there and then, then we would not have displayed the pattern of holding and withholding of religious and philosophical beliefs we *do* display. As I said, this can indeed be vertiginous; but what can we make of it? What can we infer from it about what has warrant and how we should conduct our intellectual lives? That's

---

23. *An Interpretation of Religion,* p. 2.

not easy to say. Can we infer *anything at all* about what has warrant or how we should conduct our intellectual lives? Not obviously.

To return to reliabilism then: For simplicity, let's take the version of reliabilism according to which S knows p if the belief that p is produced in S by a reliable belief-producing mechanism or process. I don't have the space here to go into this matter in sufficient detail, but it seems pretty clear that if (1) and (2) are true, then it *could be* that the beliefs that (1) and (2) be produced in me by a reliable belief-producing process. For either we are thinking of *concrete* belief-producing processes, like your memory or John's powers of a priori reasoning (tokens as opposed to types), or else we are thinking of *types* of belief-producing processes (type reliabilism). The problem with the latter is that there are an enormous number of *different* types of belief-producing processes for any given belief, some of which are reliable and some of which are not; the problem (and a horrifying problem it is) is to say which of these is the type the reliability of which determines whether the belief in question has warrant. So the first (token reliabilism) is a better way of stating reliabilism. But then clearly enough if (1) and (2) *are* true, they could be produced in me by a reliable belief-producing process. Calvin's *Sensus Divinitatis,* for example, could be working in the exclusivist in such a way as to reliably produce the belief that (1) is true; Calvin's Internal Testimony of the Holy Spirit could do the same for (2). If (1) and (2) are true, therefore, then from a reliabilist perspective there is no reason whatever to think that the exclusivist might not know that they are true.

There is another brand of externalism which seems to me to be closer to the truth than reliabilism: call it *(faute de mieux)* 'proper functionalism.' This view can be stated to a first approximation as follows: S knows p if (1) the belief that p is produced by S by cognitive faculties that are functioning properly (working as they ought to work, suffering from no dysfunction), (2) the cognitive environment in which p is produced is appropriate for those faculties, (3) the purpose of the module of the epistemic faculties producing the belief in question is to produce true beliefs (alternatively, the module of the design plan governing the production of p is aimed at the production of true beliefs), and (4) the objective probability of a belief's being true, given that it is produced under those conditions, is high.[24] All of this needs explanation, of course; for present purposes, perhaps, we can collapse the account into the first condition. But then clearly it *could* be, if (1) and (2) are true, that they are produced in me by cognitive faculties functioning properly under condition C. For suppose (1) is true. Then it is surely possible that God has created us human beings with something like Calvin's *Sensus Divinitatis,* a

---

24. See chapter 10 of *Warrant: The Current Debate* and the first couple of chapters of *Warrant and Proper Function* for exposition and defense of this way of thinking about warrant.

belief-producing process that in a wide variety of circumstances functions properly to produce (1) or some very similar belief. Furthermore, it is also possible that in response to the human condition of sin and misery, God has provided for us human beings a means of salvation, which he has revealed in the Bible. Still further, perhaps he has arranged for us to come to believe what he means to teach there by way of the operation of something like the Internal Testimony of the Holy Spirit of which Calvin speaks. So on this view, too, if (1) and (2) are true, it is certainly possible that the exclusivist *knows* that they are. We can be sure that the exclusivist's views are irrational in this sense, then, only if they are false; but the pluralist objector does not mean to claim that they *are* false; this version of the objection, therefore, also fails. The exclusivist isn't necessarily irrational, and indeed might *know* that (1) and (2) are true, if indeed they *are* true.

All this seems right. But don't the realities of religious pluralism count for anything at all? Is there nothing at all to the claims of the pluralists? Could that really be right? Of course not. For many or most exclusivists, I think, an awareness of the enormous variety of human religious response functions as a *defeater* for such beliefs as (1) and (2) — an *undercutting* defeater, as opposed to a rebutting defeater. It calls into question, to some degree or other, the sources of one's belief in (1) or (2). It doesn't or needn't do so by way of an *argument;* and indeed there isn't a very powerful argument from the proposition that many apparently devout people around the world dissent from (1) and (2) to the conclusion that (1) and (2) are false. Instead, it works more directly; it directly reduces the level of confidence or degree of belief in the propositions in question. From a Christian perspective, this situation of religious pluralism and our awareness of it is itself a manifestation of our miserable human condition; and it may deprive us of some of the comfort and peace the Lord has promised his followers. It can also deprive the exclusivist of the *knowledge* that (1) and (2) are true, even if they *are* true and he *believes* that they are. Because degree of warrant depends in part on degree of belief, it is possible, though not necessary, that knowledge of the facts of religious pluralism should reduce an exclusivist's degree of belief and hence of warrant for (1) and (2) in such a way as to deprive him of knowledge of (1) and (2). He might be such that if he *hadn't* known the facts of pluralism, then he would have known (1) and (2), but now that he *does* know those facts, he doesn't know (1) and (2). In this way, he may come to know less by knowing more.

Things *could* go this way with the exclusivist. On the other hand, they *needn't* go this way. Consider once more the moral parallel. Perhaps you have always believed it deeply wrong for a counselor to use his position of trust to seduce a client. Perhaps you discover that others disagree; they think it more like a minor peccadillo, like running a red light when there's no traffic; and you realize that possibly these people have the same internal markers for their beliefs that you have for yours. You think the matter over more fully, imaginatively re-create and rehearse such situations, become more aware of just what is involved in such a situation (the breach of trust, the breaking of implied promises, the injustice and unfairness, the nasty irony of a situation in which someone comes to a counselor seeking help but receives only hurt), and come to believe even more fully that such an action is wrong — and indeed to have more warrant for that belief. But something similar can happen in the case of religious beliefs. A fresh or heightened awareness of the facts of religious pluralism could bring about a reappraisal of one's religious life, a reawakening, a new or renewed and deepened grasp and apprehension of (1) and (2). From Calvin's perspective, it could serve as an occasion for a renewed and more powerful working of the belief-producing processes by which we come to apprehend (1) and (2). In that way, knowledge of the facts of pluralism could initially serve as a defeater, but in the long run have precisely the opposite effect.

SECTION III

Divine Nature and Attributes

Introduction

When one thinks of "philosophy of religion" today one most often thinks of the kinds of issues dealt with in the first two sections of this collection: arguments for and against the existence of God, and discussions regarding the nature of theistic knowledge and the conditions for rationality or justification of theistic belief. Perhaps this inclination is the result of a phenomenon Plantinga so often refers to in his writings: the virtual eviction of religious topics from "respectable" philosophical circles that took place through the early and middle decades of this century. (See, for example, chapter 5 above, pp. 106-14.) When Christian philosophers in the 1950s and 1960s attempted to resurrect the philosophical study of religion, their concentration quite naturally was on natural theology, apologetics, and religious epistemology. They had first to win back the respectability lost before they could venture into deeper and meatier topics of religious philosophy.

But when Christian philosophy was in its heyday — in the high Middle Ages, through the Renaissance, and even well into the modern period — philosophy of religion played a more noble role, examining many of the important doctrines of the church and the philosophical implications of those doctrines. This discipline, referred to often as "philosophical theology," has only recently begun to wind its way back to the center stage in philosophy of religion. In "Christian Philosophy at the End of the Twentieth Century" Plantinga surveys some of the more significant contemporary projects of this genre (chapter 13).

While his major concern (as a leader in the resurgence movement) has been with the more fundamental topics discussed in the initial paragraph of this introduction, Plantinga has, on occasion, stepped out to do serious philo-

211

sophical theology of his own. The chapters of this section are representative of these forays. As I mentioned in my "Appreciation" essay at the beginning of this volume, these chapters have received the least attention in philosophical literature of all of Plantinga's work, and I consider this to be an oversight that can only be detrimental to the maturation of contemporary philosophy of religion. I reprint them here with the hope that they will engender new debate over some old but timeless issues.

Chapter 8 is an early work, published in the 1964 collection *Faith and Philosophy,* edited by Plantinga (Bibliography #120). It considers the charge that the concept of "necessary being" is incoherent, so that God either does not exist or is not a necessary being. Plantinga argues that, while it is perhaps best not to think of the proposition *God exists* as a necessary truth, there is nonetheless a quite adequate way to think of God as a necessary being. While Plantinga comes in his later work to consider *God exists* a necessary truth, the conception of necessary being offered here is still quite useful, and seems to lay to rest once for all the claim that there is no coherent way to think about necessary being.

Chapter 9 is excerpted from Plantinga's presentation of the 1980 Aquinas Lecture at Marquette University, titled "Does God Have a Nature?" Here Plantinga considers the age-old tension felt between the concepts of God's aseity (his self-sufficiency and total independence) and his supposed essential qualities (e.g., omnipotence, omniscience, moral perfection). If God does bear any properties essentially, then it seems that in some important sense he is dependent on them for his existence (if God is essentially omnipotent, then God exists only if the property of omnipotence exists). But if this is so, then God is not independent of the property of omnipotence; hence his aseity is nullified. Plantinga investigates Thomistic and Cartesian responses to this problem before presenting his own views, which include the provocative claim that "exploring the realm of abstract objects can be seen as exploring the nature of God."

Chapter 10, "On Ockham's Way Out," addresses the problem of divine foreknowledge and human freedom. Plantinga identifies a strong formulation of the argument that these concepts are incompatible and then explores Ockham's attempt to circumvent the argument. Embracing Ockham's concepts of accidental necessity and propositions "strictly about the past," Plantinga offers a solution to the problem that explicates and makes use of critical differences between the past and the future; most notably that the future is under our control in a way that the past is not. This chapter may be the most technical and arduous of the book, but it certainly rewards careful study.

Plantinga's best work in philosophical theology may be yet to come in his forthcoming third warrant volume, *Warranted Christian Belief.* Given past work, it is a safe bet that Plantinga will relate our knowledge of God closely to the doctrine of the image of God. This will undoubtedly raise many questions regarding the structure of divine knowledge and the nature of God in general. And it is safe to say that Plantinga will not let these questions lie for long.

CHAPTER EIGHT

Necessary Being

It is often said that the important philosophical questions about religious belief are not questions of proof but questions of meaning. The skeptic used to insist that "it is wrong always, everywhere, and for anyone, to believe anything upon insufficient evidence"[1] and that the evidence for religious or theological teachings is insufficient indeed; he now claims that the teachings themselves are logically questionable or out of order or even senseless. A case in point is the assertion that God is the *necessary being*. Theologians and religious persons do say in fact that God is the necessary being. In this respect, they say, God is to be contrasted with all other beings whatever; these others are merely *contingent*. Some have argued that from the very concept of God it follows that He is a necessary being; and a necessary being, they point out, necessarily exists.[2] On the other hand, it has been argued that God must indeed be a necessary being. . . . But since the concept of necessary being is self-contradictory, God necessarily does not exist.[3] And many philosophers have claimed that the locution "necessary being" is a piece of straight nonsense; hence if there is a God, He cannot possibly be a necessary being. The claim that God is the necessary being, then, is troublesome. My purpose in this paper is to discover whether that claim can be construed in a way which is both logically proper and religiously adequate.

What requirements must a "religiously adequate" account of necessary being meet? First, by "religiously adequate" I mean "adequate to the demands

1. W. K. Clifford, "The Ethics of Belief," in *Lectures and Essays* (London, 1901).

2. Anselm, in one formulation of the ontological argument. Cf. N. Malcolm, "Anselm's Ontological Arguments," *Philosophical Review,* Jan., 1960.

3. J. N. Findlay, "Can God's Existence Be Disproved?" *Mind,* 1949. Reprinted in *New Essays in Philosophical Theology,* edited by Anthony Flew and Alasdair MacIntyre (London: SCM, 1955).

of the Christian religion." The doctrine that God is the necessary being perhaps occurs in other religions as well, particularly in Judaism and Islam. But whether this is so is not my concern here. So to see what requirements a religiously adequate account of God's necessity must meet, we must see what it is about Christianity that leads the believer to hold this doctrine. The answer is at least twofold. First, there is the pressure in theistic religions to ascribe *unlimited superiority* to God. The object of worship (as opposed to surpassing admiration or limitless respect), God is not merely very great; He is the greatest of all beings. Nor is He merely the greatest of all beings as a matter of fact; God is the greatest possible being; He is "that than which none greater can be conceived." Now mere creatures have, so to speak, a tenuous and uneasy hold upon their existence. They are made by God and can be unmade by Him. They exist only by courtesy and their continued existence depends upon the continued favor of their creator. And God's superiority to His creatures is manifested, not merely in the fact that this dependence is not reciprocal, but in the fact that He alone has always existed, will always exist, cannot cease to exist. "From everlasting to everlasting, thou art."4

A second feature of Christian theism leads to the same conclusion. For the believer, God is the being in whom *absolute trust* may be placed; He is an invincible and utterly reliable ally. Earthly fathers, in spite of good intentions, may fail in various ways; but the Heavenly Father cannot be defeated by any eventuality whatever. Earthly parents are sometimes thwarted in their efforts, and as the child discovers to his dismay, parents are subject to death. But God differs from any earthly parent in just this respect; nothing can thwart His purposes, and the threat of nonexistence does not confront Him. Hence, the believer claims, God exists in some necessary manner; He *cannot* cease to exist. These two features of Christian theism (and perhaps others as well) lead the believer to assert that God is the necessary being. A religiously adequate account of God's necessity, therefore, must allow the believer to say, in some non-Pickwickian sense of "cannot," that God cannot cease existing.

An example of an account of God's necessity that does not seem to meet this requirement is to be found in J. J. C. Smart's "The Existence of God."5 After asserting that the existence of God cannot be *logically* necessary, Smart makes the following suggestion:

> I think I can see roughly what sort of necessity theological necessity might be. Let me give an analogy from physics. It is not a logical necessity that the velocity of light in a vacuum should be constant. It would, however,

---

4. See Findlay's article mentioned above. Findlay puts this very well.
5. *Church Quarterly Review,* 1955. Reprinted in Flew and MacIntyre, *New Essays in Philosophical Theology.*

upset physical theory considerably if we denied it. Similarly it is not a logical necessity that God exists. But it would clearly upset the structure of our religious attitudes in the most violent way if we denied it or even entertained the possibility of its falsehood.[6]

It is indeed true that the believer's attitude of worship would be upset in the most violent way if he denied or were doubtful of the existence of God. Engaging in Christian worship without believing in God is like admitting that Pegasus is a mere myth while eagerly scanning the heavens for a glimpse of him. The belief that God exists is a presupposition of the Christian's entire religious enterprise. But contrary to the apparent intent of Smart's suggestion, when the believer says that God is the necessary being he is not, surely, uttering the mere truism that his religious attitudes would be upset if he ceased to believe in God. For it is quite in accord with theism to admit the possibility of persons who believe that God is the necessary being and yet have no religious attitudes at all. "The devils also believe, and they tremble."[7] And one of the things the devils might well believe is that God is the necessary being; but, of course, there is no question of *their* religious attitudes being upset. More importantly, on Smart's account the assertion of God's necessity becomes an assertion about believers and their religious attitudes rather than an assertion about God. His account does not allow the believer to assert straightforwardly that God cannot cease to exist; and it thereby fails to do justice to the concept of necessary existence.

I

If Smart's explanation won't do, how *are* we to construe the assertion that God is the necessary being?

It has been argued that to speak of necessary *beings* (or for that matter of contingent beings) is to talk egregious nonsense. Locutions such as "necessary" and "contingent," so the claim goes, apply properly to statements or propositions only; to speak of a necessary being is like speaking of an unpunctual triangle. Argument for this view is distressingly scarce, however, and it is accordingly difficult to evaluate. But even if the proscription upon the phrase "necessary being" is correct, the theist will be happy to oblige, presumably, by holding instead that the statement "God exists" is necessary. We may begin by examining that claim.

6. In Flew and MacIntyre, *New Essays in Philosophical Theology*, p. 40.
7. James 2:19.

A fashionable view has it that a statement or proposition is necessary if and only if it is analytic. Whether that view is correct is a matter of controversy; but at any rate it is clear that all analytic propositions are necessary. We shall first inquire, therefore, whether the proposition "God exists" is analytic. And for present purposes a proposition is analytic if and only if its denial is self-contradictory. Now our proposition does not, at first glance anyway, seem to be analytic, for the proposition "God does not exist" does not seem to be contradictory. Indeed, many philosophers and even some theologians have cheerfully accepted the proposition that God does not exist. And this apparently leads J. N. Findlay to believe that "God exists" is not analytic, on the grounds, presumably, that if it were, no one who seriously considered it would deny it.[8] But, of course, often there *is* sensible disagreement as to whether a given proposition is analytic. Leaving aside such cases as complicated mathematical and logical propositions, we might note the controversy as to whether one can consistently assert the existence of a logically private language. Hence the fact that "God exists" does not prima facie appear analytic by no means settles the question. What is needed is some sort of argument to *show* that it is not analytic.

And such argument, I think, can be provided. Let us begin by recognizing a class of statements which assert or entail the existence of a thing or things of some specified kind, e.g., "There are female cab drivers," or "Some children are very noisy." We may refer to statements of this sort as "existential statements" and to their contradictories as "contra-existential statements." In making an existential statement, I assert that there is at least one thing which satisfies a certain description. Now it often happens that the description in question is complex in the sense that it comprises several logically independent properties or characteristics.[9] And if it is complex (as is, e.g., the description implied by "centaur"), then my assertion that at least one thing satisfies that description entails that at least one thing has all of the properties included in the description. If I say, "There are some centaurs," I am saying that there is at least one thing which has each of the properties included in the connotation of "centaur." My statement, therefore, entails that certain statements of the form "A has F" are true where what replaces A refers to some specific individual which in fact has all of the properties comprising the connotation of "centaur" and where F may be replaced by the names of those properties. Some of these statements would be the following: "A has a human head," "A has a human chest," "A has an equine

8. J. N. Findlay, "Can God's Existence Be Disproved?" See especially pp. 48 and 54. See also G. B. Hughes's comments on Findlay's paper, in Flew and MacIntyre, *New Essays in Philosophical Theology,* pp. 61, 62.

9. Properties A and B are logically independent if the statement that X has A neither entails nor is entailed by the statement that X has B.

lower body," etc. Some existential statements, therefore, are complex in the sense that they entail several logically independent propositions of the above form.

It is for this reason, of course, that existential statements may be self-contradictory. For our purposes, a self-contradictory statement may be characterized as one which entails two statements such that one of the entailed statements is the denial of the other. "Jones is a married bachelor," for example, entails that Jones is married and also that Jones is not married; similarly, such existential statements as "There are round squares" or "There are octogenarians under fifty years of age" are contradictory.

Contra-existential statements, on the other hand, are not in this sense complex. Suppose the connotation of "centaur" is comprised by properties A, B, C, D. In asserting that there are no centaurs I am not, of course, asserting that there are no individuals with the property "A." I am not, for example, asserting that nothing has the head of a man, or an equine lower body. What I am asserting is only that no individual satisfies the description in question by having all the properties comprising the connotation of "centaur"; I am saying that there is nothing which is ABCD. But that statement is not complex. For it may be regarded as asserting, of each individual, that either it is non-A or non-B or non-C or non-D (where "X is non-A" is to mean the same as "X is not A"). And the truth of any instantiation of such a statement requires only that one of its disjuncts be true. But if so, the statement in question does not and cannot entail two statements one of which is the denial of the other; hence it cannot be contradictory. And of course the point may be put more generally; to deny that there are any X's is to assert that no individual has all of the properties comprising the connotation of "X." But such an assertion is not complex in the above sense and cannot, therefore, be contradictory. And if no contra-existential statement is contradictory, no existential statement is analytic; accordingly, "God exists" is not analytic.

An objection might be directed against the specific thesis that the statement "God exists" is not analytic: if "is a man" is one of the properties included in the connotation of "bachelor," to deny that bachelors are men would be contradictory. So, if "is existent" is one of the properties included in the connotation of the term "God," it would be contradictory to deny that God exists. And, the argument might proceed, existence is one of the properties included in the concept of God. This line has been familiar since Anselm. And the answer, traditional since Kant, is that existence is not a property; it cannot, therefore, be one of the properties included in the connotation of "God." Kant's answer, someone might say, takes too short a way with Anselm's argument. For when I say "This chair exists," I am surely saying something that might not have been true; since what I say is true, I am saying something about something; and if not about this chair, then about what? But if I can say something about a chair by saying that it exists, there is good reason to hold that existence *is* a property or predicate.[10]

This argument is wrong on more than one count. But even if existence *is* a property, it is a property of a very special sort, and the features that distinguish it from other properties are just what make it impossible that existential statements be analytic. That this is the case may be suggested in the following way: Any synthetic non-existential statement of subject predicate form may be turned into an analytic statement by the simple expedient of redefining the subject term in such a way that the property mentioned in the predicate is annexed to the connotation of the subject term. For example, the statement, "All crows are black" (taken non-existentially), can be made analytic simply by annexing "black" to the normal connotation of "crow"; the proposition then says what "All black crows are black" says when the terms involved have their usual meanings. In like fashion we can convert "All potatoes are edible" into an analytic statement by adding "edible" to the normal connotation of potato. (A similar procedure can be specified for statements that do not yield to subject predicate analysis.) But existential statements cannot be made analytic by redefinition in this way. Consider, for example, the statement, "There are centaurs." Can this statement be rendered analytic by redefinition? Let's try. Presumably the thing to do is to annex the property of existence, ascribed to centaurs by the statement in question, to the connotation of "centaur." "Centaur" in our redefined sense means what "existent centaur" ordinarily means. "There are centaurs" then comes to "There are existent centaurs." Is that proposition analytic? It does not seem so. For the difference between a centaur and an existent centaur is far from clear. It might be argued that to say "Centaurs exist" and to say "Existent centaurs exist" is to say the same thing. And if so, of course there would be no contradiction in denying that there are existent centaurs. But even if there is a difference between centaurs and existent centaurs, even if the adjective "existent" marks off some special class of centaurs (e.g., existent centaurs as opposed to merely imaginary ones), we can still deny that there are existent centaurs without contradiction, for we can consistently deny that there are any centaurs at all. And if there are no centaurs at all, of course there are no existent ones. So the fact that existential propositions cannot be made analytic by redefinition indicates a crucial difference between existence, if it is a property at all, and other properties. It is in virtue of that difference, I suggest, that non-contradictory existential statements are all synthetic. It follows, then, that "God exists" is not analytic.

10. Cf. G. E. Moore, "Is Existence a Predicate?" *Proceedings of the Aristotelian Society,* Supplementary Volume XV, 1936. Reprinted in *Logic and Language,* Second Series, edited by A. Flew (Oxford, 1953), pp. 92-93.

And if not analytic, it may be asked, in what sense necessary? Some philosophers hold that propositions expressing the incompatibility of certain colors, or the relational properties of certain tones, or certain spatial and temporal relations are necessary though not analytic. The proposition, "Nothing can be green and red all over at the same time," e.g., is something said to be both synthetic and necessary. Is the assertion that God exists necessary in the way that such propositions are said to be? Surely not. For the distinguishing characteristic of synthetic necessary propositions, as explained by their defenders, is that their denials, while logically quite consistent, are nonetheless inconceivable. And the best evidence that "God exists" does not enjoy this characteristic is just that reasonable and intelligent people do in fact conceive its denial. This answer would be inappropriate to the suggestion that the proposition is analytic, for reasonable people do sometimes appear to hold beliefs revealed contradictory by subsequent investigation. But it is the best and only conclusive reply to the claim that though the statement in question is synthetic, its denial is nonetheless inconceivable. A secondary count against the claim is that all other propositions said to enjoy this status describe or report relationships between possible instances of two or more properties; none of them assert that any property *has* instances or that some description actually applies to anything. "Whatever is colored is extended" has been held to be both necessary and synthetic; that claim is not made for "There are colored objects." Hence, the claim that "God exists" is a synthetic necessary proposition is implausible.

The above discussion raises most acutely the question whether any meaning at all can be given to the assertion that God is the necessary being. In what follows, I shall try to explain the proposition that God is a necessary being in a way that is faithful to the conceptual scheme of theism but avoids the paradoxical conclusion that "God exists" is logically necessary.

II

We may begin by considering two somewhat peculiar questions. Suppose someone asked, "Why is it that all vacuums are empty?" The question is puzzling. It is indeed true and necessarily true that all vacuums are empty. But if the phrase, "Why is it that . . . ," is taken to have the same role here that it does in say, "Why is it that there are craters on the moon?", then the question seems senseless, for there seems to be no sensible way of answering it. "They just are" won't do; that suggests that perhaps they might not have been. "I don't know" won't do as a reply either, for there is nothing here we don't know — there is no room for some unknown fact which would serve as an answer to the question. One might possibly use this sentence to ask why we use the word "vacuum" to designate spaces entirely devoid of matter; presumably many other sequences of letters would do as well. But that question is about speakers and language habits; it is not about vacuums at all. Again, the question might be a misleading way of asking for the conditions under which vacuums occur. And other reinterpretations could be suggested. But one who repudiated all such reinterpretations and insisted that he meant the question in a perfectly straightforward manner would betray misunderstanding of one or another of the concepts involved. For in the case of any analytic statement A, the words "Why is it that A?" do not express a genuine query; since there is no room for an answer (since nothing *could* serve as an answer), nothing is being asked.

Now let us consider a different sort of question. Suppose someone, struck by the fact that his desk might not have existed, asks, "Why it is that this desk exists?" Perhaps there are several sorts of reply we could give him. One answer might be that the desk exists because a certain carpenter made it. But suppose our questioner is still puzzled; the carpenter, he says, also might not have existed, so why did *he* exist? We could answer again by referring to some other beings or states of affairs which were causally sufficient for the existence of the carpenter; but of course, the same question will arise about these beings, and about the causes of these beings, and so indefinitely. No matter how far back we push this series of questions and answers, our questioner may remain dissatisfied. It may appear to us that he is looking for a *final* answer, one which allows no further questions of the same sort. He seems to be seeking an answer which shares with the analytic statement above the characteristic that it leaves no room for a question of the form, "Why is it that p?" And in order to put an end to the series of questions and answers which, as he claims, never will be able to satisfy him, he may ask, "But why does anything exist at all?"

This is the second unusual question I wish to consider. It *is* an unusual question both in the sense that it is asked by some people only, and then only in certain uncommon moods, and in the sense that it is not easy to see what kind of answer is required. Now the context in which the question arises might suggest that the questioner would be satisfied only with an answer referring to some being that never could fail to exist. And such a being would be a necessary being. But if the kind of necessity involved is *logical* necessity, then (if my previous argument is correct) there *could be* no such being and hence no answer to the question. J. J. C. Smart so interprets the question: ". . . now let us ask, 'Why should anything exist at all?' Logic seems to tell us that the only answer which is not absurd is to say, 'Why shouldn't it?' "[11]

11. Op. cit., p. 46.

But, of course, that retort is a way of rejecting the question altogether; and Smart's argument that the question ought on logical grounds to be rejected rests upon the supposition that the question is "an absurd request for the nonsensical postulation of a logically necessary being."[12] But it need not be interpreted that way.

How then *is* it to be interpreted? Let us return to the context of the question. In asking "Why is there anything at all?" the questioner attempts to put an end to the indefinitely long series of questions and answers where the answer to each question mentions a being or state of affairs about which precisely the same question again may be asked. In seeking a *final* answer, he is seeking a statement which puts an end to the series of questions and answers. A necessary being, therefore, may be characterized as (a) a being such that some statement referring to it can serve as a final answer in this sort of question and answer series, an answer which puts an end to the series. But a final answer in the series would refer to a being of an unusual sort; such a being must be one about which the question "Why does it exist?" *does not arise* or cannot sensibly be asked. A necessary being, therefore, may be further characterized as (b) a being about which one cannot sensibly ask why it exists. But of course these two descriptions are not independent. For if a being satisfied description (a) it must also satisfy (b); the statement that a being satisfies (a) entails the statement that it satisfies (b). But similarly if the question "Why does X exist?" cannot sensibly be asked, then quite obviously some statement mentioning X can serve to put an end to the series of questions and answers under consideration. The entailment holds the other way as well. When the theist, therefore, asserts that God is the necessary being, we may construe his remark in the following way. He is pointing out that we cannot sensibly ask, "Why is it that God exists?" And he is holding that some assertion about God is the final answer in the series of questions and answers we have been considering.

Next, we should note that the question "Why does God exist?" never does, in fact, arise. Those who do not believe that God exists will not, of course, ask *why* He exists. But neither do believers ask that question. Outside of theism, so to speak, the question is nonsensical, and inside of theism, the question is never asked. But it is not that the religious person fails to ask why God exists through inadvertence or because of lack of interest. There may be many beings about which the question "Why do they exist?" is never *in fact* asked; and not all such beings are necessary in the sense in question. "Why does God exist?" is never in fact asked (either by religious or non-religious people) because it is a bogus question. If a believer were asked why God exists, he might take it as a request for his reasons for believing in God; but

12. Ibid.

if it is agreed that God exists, then it is less than sensible to ask why He does. And the explanation is not hard to find. Essential to theism is an assertion to the effect that there is a connection between God and all other beings, a connection in virtue of which these others are causally dependent upon God. And this proposition is analytic; it is part of the Hebraic-Christian concept of God that He is "Maker of heaven and earth." But it is also a necessary truth that if God exists, He is Himself uncreated and in no way causally dependent upon anything else. God is a causally necessary condition of the existence of anything else, whereas His existence has no necessary conditions. Now the absence of a necessary condition of the existence of anything is a sufficient condition of the nonexistence of that thing; and if a being has no causally necessary conditions, then its nonexistence has no causally sufficient conditions. And hence if God does exist, His going out of existence could have no causally sufficient conditions and is therefore causally impossible. If God has no necessary conditions, then it is analytic that His going out of existence, if it occurred, would be an uncaused event; for it is analytic that there can be no causally sufficient conditions of its occurrence. Similarly, His beginning to exist is causally impossible, for since it is analytic that God is not dependent upon anything, He has no cause; and hence His coming into existence would be an event which could have no causally sufficient conditions. So if God does exist, He cannot cease to exist; nor could He have begun to exist.

Now it becomes clear that it is absurd to ask why God exists. To ask that question is to presuppose that God does exist; but it is a necessary truth that if He has no cause, then there is no answer to a question asking for His causal conditions. The question "Why does God exist?" is, therefore, an absurdity. And in this respect there is an important analogy between the statement that God exists and any analytic statement such as "All vacuums are empty." In each case, the question "Why is it that . . . ?" cannot arise. A person who seriously asked why all vacuums are empty would betray failure to understand; in the same way someone who seriously asked why God exists would betray misapprehension of the concept of God. And this characteristic is one which the statement "God exists" or "There is a God" shares with necessary statements alone; it is in point to ask, with respect to any contingent assertion p, "Why is it that p?" That this is so may tempt one to conclude, misleadingly, that the proposition "God exists" is necessary though synthetic. This conclusion, though misleading, would serve to focus attention upon the unique role played by the assertion of God's existence in the conceptual scheme of theism. And if we bear in mind that such a conclusion could be no more than a summary way of indicating that role, perhaps no harm would result.

This account raises further questions. In particular, it leaves unexplained such notions as "dependence" and "causally necessary condition" as applied to God. And consideration of these would lead to an interesting and difficult constellation of questions regarding the Christian concepts of creation and divine omnipotence and timelessness. And so it is with any adequate explanation of any aspect of the conceptual system involved in Christianity. One aspect of it leads to and terminates in others. But to say this is only to say that the conceptual system involved in Christianity is a conceptual *system*.

CHAPTER NINE

Does God Have a Nature?

Introduction

Christians think of God as a being of incomparable greatness. He is the first being of the universe, one than whom it is not so much as possible that there be a greater. God's greatness is not just one step — even a big step — further along a scale measuring the greatness of things in general; his greatness is of a different order from that of his creatures. If the ordinary cardinal numbers — finite and infinite — measure *our* greatness then God must be compared to an inaccessible cardinal (though that might make him sound too much like an unduly reclusive candidate for Pope). God's greatness has many facets; preeminent among them are his love, justice, mercy, power, and knowledge. As important as any, however, are his *aseity* — his uncreatedness, self-sufficiency, and independence of everything else — and his *sovereignty* — his control over all things and the dependence of all else on his creative and sustaining activity. Most Christians claim that God is the uncreated creator of all things; all things depend on him, and he depends upon nothing at all.

Now the created universe presents no problem for this doctrine. Mountains, planets, stars, quarks, you and I and all the rest of us — we have all been created by God and we exist at his sufferance. On the other hand, he does not depend on us, either for his existence or for his properties. True, he accords some of his creatures *freedom,* and thus may be thought dependent, in a Pickwickian fashion, on their free actions. He may have certain aims and goals which can be attained only with the free and uncoerced cooperation of his creatures. But even here, every free action and hence every act of rebellion against him and his precepts is totally dependent upon him. Our every act of rebellion has his sustaining activity as a necessary substratum; the rebel's very existence depends from moment to moment on God's affirming activity. "The power, even of those who are hurtful," says Augustine, "is from God alone." This dependence upon God is not something we may hope one day to outgrow. Perhaps human technology will someday overcome suffering, want, disease, and, conceivably, death itself: perhaps so and perhaps not. But even if so, to declare ourselves independent of God would be at best a piece of laughable bravado; for the very causal laws on which we rely in any activity are no more than the record of God's regular, constant, and habitual dealings with the stuff of the universe he has created.

So God's creation creates no special problem here: it is dependent on him in myriad ways; he is in no way significantly dependent upon it. What does or might seem to create a problem are not these creatures of God, but the whole realm of abstract objects — the whole Platonic pantheon of universals, properties, kinds, propositions, numbers, sets, states of affairs, and possible worlds. It is natural to think of these things as *everlasting,* as having neither beginning nor end. There was a time before which there were no human beings, but no time before which there was not such a thing as the property of being human or the proposition *there are human beings.* That property and that proposition have always existed and have never *begun* to exist. Abstract objects are also naturally thought of as *necessary* features of reality, as objects whose nonexistence is impossible. There could have been no mountains or planets; but could there have been no such thing as the property of being a mountain or the proposition *there are nine planets?* That proposition could have been *false,* obviously, but could it have been *nonexistent?* It is hard to see how. Sets of contingent objects, perhaps, are as contingent as their members; but properties, propositions, numbers, and states of affairs, it seems, are objects whose nonexistence is quite impossible.

If so, however, how are they related to God? According to Augustine, God created everything distinct from him; did he then create these things? Presumably not; they have no beginnings. Are they dependent on him? But how could a thing whose nonexistence is impossible — the number 7, let's say, or the property of being a horse — depend upon anything for its existence? And what about the characteristics and properties these things display? Does God (so to speak) just find them constituted the way they are? Must he simply put up with their being thus constituted? Are these things, their existence and their character, outside his control? Augustine saw in Plato a *vir sapientissimus et eruditissimus* (*Contra Academicos* III, 17); yet he felt obliged to transform Plato's theory of ideas in such a way that these abstract objects become, obscurely, *part* of God — perhaps identical with his intellect. It is easy to see why Augustine took such a course, and easy to see why most later medieval thinkers adopted similar views. For the alternative seems to *limit* God in an important way; the existence and necessity of these things distinct from him seems incompatible with his sovereignty.

And what about his own properties — omnipotence, justice, wisdom, and the like? Did he create them? But if God has created wisdom, then he existed before it did, in which case, presumably, there was a time at which he was not wise. But surely he has *always* been wise; he has not *acquired* wisdom. Furthermore, he seems to be somehow conditioned and limited by these properties, and dependent upon them. Take the property *omniscience* for example. If that property didn't exist, then God wouldn't have it, in which case he wouldn't be omniscient. So the existence of omniscience is a necessary condition of God's being the way he is; in this sense he seems to be dependent upon it. Omniscience, furthermore, has a certain character: it is such that whoever has it, knows, for any proposition p, whether or not p is true. But its displaying this character is not up to God and is not within his control. God did not bring it about that omniscience has this character, and there is no action he could have taken whereby this property would have been differently constituted. Neither its existence nor its character seems to be within his control. Furthermore, its existence and its having the character it does are necessary conditions of God's being the way *he* is. But how is this compatible with his being truly sovereign? In this way God seems to be limited and conditioned by the properties he has.

Still further, suppose God has a *nature* — a property he has essentially that includes each property essential to him.[1] Perhaps God is essentially omniscient; that is, perhaps it's just not possible that he fail to be omniscient. If so, then it isn't up to him whether he has that property; his having it is in no way dependent upon his own decision or will. He simply finds himself with it; and that he has it is in no way up to him. So God's having a nature seems incompatible with his being in total control. As Hendrick Hart says,

> As far as I can see, a view that commits one to holding that God is subject to laws (exemplifies predicables) that are neither created by him nor identical with him, is a view that commits one to holding that God is neither sovereign nor omnipotent.[2]

If abstract objects such as propositions and properties are necessarily existent, then affirming their existence and knowing that they exist will be part of God's nature — at any rate if omniscience is. If God is essentially omniscient, then

---

1. One property includes another if it is not possible that there be an object that has the first but not the second. Thus the property of being a horse includes the property of being an animal. The nature of an object can be thought of as a conjunctive property, including as conjuncts just those properties essential to that object. Accordingly, an object has a nature if it has any essential properties at all. For more about natures, see my book *The Nature of Necessity* (Oxford: Oxford University Press, 1974), chapter V.

2. "On the Distinction Between Creator and Creature," *Philosophia Reformata*, 1979, p. 184.

for any abstract object you pick, that object will be a necessary being only if it is part of God's nature to know of and affirm its existence. So our questions can be put this way: does God have a nature? And if he does, is there a conflict between God's sovereignty and his having a nature? How is God related to such abstract objects as properties and propositions? These are the questions I want to explore.

These questions may sound unduly recondite or even a bit arcane to contemporary ears. The fact is, however, that nearly all of the great theistic thinkers of the past have addressed them, and for good reason: they are crucially important for any deep understanding of what it is to see God as the sovereign first being of the universe.

II. Divine Simplicity*

Historically the most widely accepted answer to our question is *Yes*. God does indeed have a nature; but he is identical with it. God is somehow simple, utterly devoid of complexity. He has a nature; but he and it are the very same thing. But then of course it is not prior to him; and if he is dependent upon it, this is no more than a harmless case of self-dependence. This mysterious doctrine has its roots deep in antiquity, going all the way back to Parmenides, with his vision of reality as an undifferentiated plenum in which no distinctions can be made. The idea that God is simple has been embraced by thinkers as diverse as Duns Scotus and Louis Berkhof; it is to be found both in the ancient creeds of the church and in such relatively recent declarations as the Belgic Confession.

The basic idea of this doctrine is that no distinctions can be made in God. We cannot distinguish him from his nature, or his nature from his existence, or his existence from his other properties; he is the very same thing as his nature, existence, goodness, wisdom, power, and the like. And this is a dark saying indeed. The difficulty is twofold. In the first place, it is exceedingly hard to grasp or construe this doctrine, to see just what divine simplicity *is*. Secondly, insofar as we do have a grasp of this doctrine, it is difficult to see why anyone would be inclined to accept it; the motivation for this doctrine seems shrouded in obscurity. Why should anyone want to hold that God just is the same thing as, say, goodness? Why hold that no distinctions can be made in God? Suppose we start with this second perplexity.

*Editor's Note: Section I, "Can We Discuss the Question?", is omitted.

A. Why Simplicity?

When Thomas Aquinas embarks on the task of characterizing God's attributes, simplicity is the first item on his list.[3] He is quite clear, furthermore, as to his reasons for holding this doctrine; the fundamental reason is to accommodate God's aseity and sovereignty. Aquinas believes that if God had a nature and properties distinct from him, then there would be beings distinct from him to which he is subsequent and on which he depends; this would compromise his aseity and ill befits the status of the First Being. "Secondly," he says, "everything composite is subsequent to its components and dependent upon them; whilst God, as we have seen, is the first of all beings."[4] But how or why is a thing *dependent* on its components? What is it for a thing to be *subsequent* to its components? And what sorts of things does Aquinas think of as components of an object? The spatial parts of a material object, he thinks, are components of it; the *nature* or essence of an object is a component of it, as are its existence and any other property — essential or accidental — it may have.

So a fundamental — perhaps *the* fundamental — reason for the simplicity doctrine is that it seems implied by God's sovereignty and aseity. But why should an object be thought of as dependent on its properties? Aquinas clearly says *that* this is so; he is less explicit as to why. Among a thing's properties is its nature or essence. But he holds that the essence of an object

> is either the thing itself or related to the thing in some way as its cause; for a thing derives its species through its essence. But nothing can in any way be the cause of God, since as we have shown, He is the first being. (SCG I, 21, 5)

If an object is distinct from its essence, then its essence is in some way a *cause* of that thing, so that the latter is dependent — causally dependent — on the former. Aquinas argues that the same considerations apply to a thing's goodness, existence, and, by implication, any other properties it may have. For example,

> . . . anything that exists either is itself existence or is a being [existent] by participation. Now God, as we have seen, exists. If then he is not himself existence, and thus not by nature existent, he will be a being [existent] only by participation. And so he will not be the first being. (ST Ia, 3, 4)

3. *Summa Theologiae* (hereafter ST) Ia, Question 3.
4. ST Ia, 3, 8; see also *Summa Contra Gentiles* (hereafter SCG) I, 18, 3.

And

> ... each good thing that is not its goodness is called good by participation. But that which is named by participation has something prior to it from which it receives the character of goodness. This cannot proceed to infinity, since among final causes there is no regress to infinity. . . . We must therefore reach some first good, that is not by participation good through an order towards some other good, but is good through its own essence. This is God. God is therefore His own goodness. (SCG I, 38)

In the same way God is his wisdom, his knowledge, his blessedness, and each of the rest of his virtues.

The essential idea, then, is that if God were good, or blessed, or knowledgeable or wise by *participation* in the properties goodness, knowledge, blessedness, or wisdom, then he would be *subsequent* to these properties; and if he *had* an essence (or nature), as opposed to being *identical* with it, then that essence would be his cause. These two considerations are linked in the last passage, which suggests that if a thing has a property by participation (by having it without being identical with it) then *it is subsequent to that property in the order of final causation.* And what this means, I think, is the following. If God were distinct from such properties as wisdom, goodness, and power but nonetheless *had* these properties, then he would be *dependent* on them. He would be dependent on them in a dual way. First, if, as Aquinas thinks, these properties are essential to him, then it is not possible that he should have existed and they not be "in" him. But if they had not existed, they could not have been in him. Therefore he would not have existed if they had not. This connection between his existence and theirs, furthermore, is necessary; it is not due to his will and it is not within his power to abrogate it. That it holds is not up to him or within his control. He is obliged simply to put up with it. No doubt he wouldn't *mind* being thus constrained, but that is not the point. The point is that he would be dependent upon something else for his existence, and dependent in a way outside his control and beyond his power to alter; this runs counter to his aseity.

Secondly, under the envisaged conditions God would be dependent upon these properties for his character. He is, for example, *wise.* But then if there had been no such thing as wisdom, he would not have been wise. He is thus dependent upon these properties for his being the way he is, for being what he is like. And again he didn't bring it about that he is thus dependent; this dependence is not a result of his creative activity; and there is nothing he can do to change or overcome it. If he had properties and a nature distinct from him, then he would exist and display the character he does display because of a relation in which he stands to something other than himself. And this doesn't fit with his existence *a se.* Aquinas therefore concludes that these properties are indeed "in" God, but in such a way that he is identical with them. He just is his nature.

Now I think the intuition — call it the sovereignty-aseity intuition — underlying the doctrine of divine simplicity must be taken with a real seriousness. Suppose God has essentially the property of being omnipotent and suppose that property is an object distinct from him, is uncreated by him and exists necessarily. Then in some sense he does depend on that property. For in the first place he could not have existed if it had not; its existence is a necessary condition of his existence. And secondly he couldn't have the character he does have, couldn't be the way he is, if omnipotence didn't exist or weren't the way *it* is. If omnipotence were of a different character — if, for example, it couldn't be *had* by anything, or were such that nothing could both have it and be wise — then God would not have existed or would not have been the way he is: either he wouldn't have been omnipotent or he wouldn't have been wise. Further, this connection between him and the nature and existence of omnipotence is not owing to his decision or activity; nor is it within his power to cancel or alter it. And, initially, at least, this seems incompatible with his aseity.

Still further, we have been speaking only of his own properties; but of course there is the rest of the Platonic menagerie — the propositions, properties, numbers, sets, possible worlds, and all the rest. If these things are distinct from God, if they exist necessarily and have their characters essentially, then there is a vast and enormous structure that seems to be independent of God. That there are natural numbers, for example, is not up to God; he didn't create them and couldn't destroy them. They do not owe their character to him. The properties they have and the relations in which they stand are not within his control, so if God has a nature distinct from him, then there are things distinct from him on which he depends; and if the rest of the Platonic menagerie are distinct from him, then there are innumerable beings whose existence and character are independent of God. And doesn't it seem that this compromises his sovereignty?

That this swarm of Platonic paraphernalia infringes on the sovereignty of God is the best argument I know for nominalism. God exists, is the sovereign first being, depends upon nothing else, and is such that everything else depends on him; if there were such things as properties, numbers, propositions, and the rest of the Platonic *mélange,* they would exist necessarily and have their properties essentially; but then there would be an uncountable host of beings intuitively independent of God, on some of which he depends. So there aren't any such things. Surely this is a better argument for nominalism than any based on the hankering for ontological penury or a taste for desert landscapes. After all, the Olympic peninsula is just as impressive as the Sonora desert. The theistic argument for nominalism is at any rate based on more than personal preference. If the Platonic pantheon infringes on the divine sovereignty, perhaps we should hold that there just aren't any such things as properties and their ilk. There are concrete objects — God, persons, material objects — but no abstract objects. There are red houses and red sunsets, but no such thing as the property of being red; there may be five chairs and three dogs in the room, but no such thing as the number three or the set of dogs or the proposition *there are three dogs in the room.*

B. The Nature of Simplicity

But of course this is not the conclusion Aquinas draws; he argues that in some way all these things are identical with God. God is identical with his properties and with his essence. The latter, furthermore, is in some obscure way identical with the Divine Ideas, among which are to be found properties, kinds, and exemplars. What Aquinas says on this head (ST Ia, 15; SCG I, 51-54) is desperately difficult; but the conclusion is that the whole Platonic realm is identical with God's essence and thus with God himself. How this is to be construed I do not know; it is far from clear that this is compatible with the obvious fact that, for example, the property of being a horse is distinct from that of being a turkey and both are distinct from God and his essence. But suppose we turn from the Platonic swarm to consider those properties God himself exemplifies; here divine simplicity is on strongest ground. Aquinas develops this doctrine by denying various salient kinds of complexity of God. He is not composed of extended parts (he is not a physical object); he is not composed of form and matter; there is no composition of substance and nature in him — that is, he is identical with his nature; there is no composition of nature and existence in him, nor of genus and difference, or substance and accident or potentiality and actuality (ST Ia, 3, 1-7). Aquinas adds that God is identical with goodness itself and with his goodness (SCG I, 38), with his act of understanding (SCG I, 45), his will (SCG I, 73), and his justice (ST Ia, 21, 1 ad 4). Now some of these claims are quite unproblematic. Everyone (with the possible exceptions of David of Dinant and Thomas Hobbes) agrees both that God is immaterial — not a physical or material object — and that he has no body. Accordingly, there is no composition of spatial parts in him; nor is there composition of matter and form in him, if, as seems plausible, an object contains matter only if it is a material object.

The claim that there are no accidents in God is more troublesome. Presumably this must be understood as the claim that God has no accidental properties. All of God's properties are essential to him; each property he has is one he couldn't possibly have lacked. You and I have accidental as well as essential properties; *living in Milwaukee,* for example, is a property some of us have and have accidentally. *Being a bit corpulent* is a property Aquinas is alleged to have had, and one he could have lacked. But all of God's properties are essential to him.

What are Aquinas's reasons for holding that all of God's properties are thus essential to him? One reason — the one presently relevant — perhaps goes as follows. If God had a property P accidentally — had it but could have lacked it — then he could not be identical with P. For suppose he were identical with P. Then it would be impossible that he exist and be distinct from P; if an object x is identical with an object y, then x is essentially identical with y. But by hypothesis he could have existed and not had P. So he could have existed and been identical with a property that he didn't even have. So if he were identical with P, then it would be possible that he be identical with a property he didn't have. But that is clearly *not* possible. Accordingly, God is not identical with any property accidental to him. But then if he has an accidental property, there is something distinct from him that limits and conditions him; for then he could not be the way he is if that property did not exist. Hence each property he has must be essential to him.

Now if we take the term 'property' in the very broad sense presently customary, this is of course paradoxical and plainly false. In that broad use of the term, one property God has is *being such that Adam sinned;* and surely this property is not essential either to Adam or to God. Of course Aquinas would reply that there is no such property as *being such that Adam sinned.* The singular term 'being such that Adam sinned' does not denote a property, and the open sentence 'x is such that Adam sinned' while it has true substitution instances, does not express a property. One who asserts that God is such that Adam sinned speaks the truth, no doubt, but does not predicate a property of God. This response is plausible. In claiming that God has no accidents, Aquinas meant to make no claims at all about *being such that Adam sinned.* As we have seen, his reason for holding that God has no accidental properties is that if he did, then he would be dependent for being the way he is, for being what he is like, upon some object distinct from him. But *being such that Adam sinned* doesn't really characterize God, so that he couldn't plausibly be said to be dependent upon it for being the way he is. *Being such that Adam sinned* is relevant to the way *Adam* is; it has nothing to do with God's being the way *he* is.

But what about such alleged properties as *having created Adam* and *knowing that Adam sinned?* Aren't these properties God has, and isn't it possible that he should have lacked them? Aquinas's answer here, I think, would be the same as in the previous case; 'having created Adam' and 'knowing that Adam sinned' do not denote properties. It is of course true that God has created Adam and true that God knows that Adam sinned; but one who affirms these propositions predicates no property of God. *God has created*

Adam signifies a *relation* — a relation that is to be found in Adam but not in God. A real property of God, unlike *having created Adam* will be *non-relational.*

I think this reply leaves a good deal to be desired. In essence Aquinas (as I am representing him) rejects the claim that God has accidental properties by denying that such items as *having created Adam* or *knowing that Adam sinned* are properties. I can't see that this is helpful; for even if *having created Adam* isn't a *property* it is at any rate something that *characterizes* God, and it is something such that its characterizing him makes him different from what he would have been had it not characterized him. It seems plainly mistaken to say that the proposition *God created Adam* characterizes Adam but not God or says something about the former but not the latter. If I know that God created Adam, then I know something about God as well as Adam; I know that he has the attribute or characteristic of having created Adam. Whether we call this characteristic a 'property' or not is really of no consequence; if it isn't a property it is at any rate very much like a property. And among God's characteristics, we will find some that he could not have lacked and some (*having created Adam,* e.g.) that he could have. We needn't call this a composition of essence and accident, but the distinction remains: some of God's characteristics characterize him in every possible world and some do not. And if there is something objectionable, from the point of view of the sovereignty-aseity intuition, in God's having both essential and accidental properties, there will be something equally objectionable in his having two kinds of characteristics: those he couldn't have lacked and those he could have. But suppose we waive this difficulty for the moment.

The question of actuality-potentiality complexity inherits all the difficulty connected with essence-accident complexity and is furthermore vexed in its own right. Just as it seems right to suppose there are characteristics God has but could have lacked, so it seems right to think there are characteristics he lacks but could have. It is natural to think, furthermore, that among these there are some he hasn't yet acquired but could acquire. No doubt he hasn't yet created all the persons he will create; he will create persons distinct from all those that have so far existed. If so, there is at least one individual essence E such that God does not now but will have the characteristic of causing E to be instantiated. If so, he is in potentiality with respect to that characteristic.

Here, of course, things are complicated by Aquinas's doctrine of God's eternity or timelessness. He holds that God is not in time at all; then presumably it isn't correct to say that he hasn't yet caused E to be exemplified, but will do so at some future time. This is a large and complex question.[5]

---

5. N. Wolterstorff unravels some of the complexities in "God Everlasting," in C. Orlebeke and L. Smedes (eds.), *God and the Good* (Grand Rapids: Eerdmans, 1975).

Here I shall say only that I think Aquinas, in company with much of the theistic tradition, is mistaken in taking God to be thus timeless. God's life is of endless (and beginningless) duration; he has always existed and always will. His knowledge, furthermore, is not temporally limited; he knows the future in the same minute detail as he knows the present and the past. But to add that he is somehow timeless, somehow not in time at all, is to court a host of needless perplexities. There is nothing in Scripture or the essentials of the Christian message to support this utterly opaque addition, and much that seems *prima facie* to militate against it. God spoke to Abraham and did so, naturally enough, during the latter's life time. God created Adam and Eve and did so well before he created, say, Bertrand Russell. God led the children of Israel out of Egypt; he did so after he created Abraham and before he spoke to Samuel. On the face of it, then, God acts in time, acts at various times, and has done some things before he did others. It is at best Quixotic to deny this *prima facie* truth on the tenuous sorts of grounds alleged by those who do deny it.

Potentiality-actuality complexity, therefore, raises deep and difficult questions. Rather than pursue them here, let us turn to the most important and most perplexing denial of divine composition: the claim that there is no complexity of properties in him and that he is identical with his nature and each of his properties. God isn't merely good, on this view; he is goodness, or his goodness, or goodness itself. He isn't merely alive; he is identical with his life. He doesn't merely have a nature or essence; he just *is* that nature, is the very same thing as it is. And this is a hard saying. There are two difficulties, one substantial and the other truly monumental. In the first place if God is identical with each of his properties, then each of his properties is identical with each of his properties, so that God has but one property. This seems flatly incompatible with the obvious fact that God has several properties; he has both power and mercifulness, say, neither of which is identical with the other. In the second place, if God is identical with each of his properties, then, since each of his properties is a property, he is a property — a self-exemplifying property. Accordingly God has just one property: himself. This view is subject to a difficulty both obvious and overwhelming. No property could have created the world; no property could be omniscient, or indeed, know anything at all. If God is a property, then he isn't a person but a mere abstract object; he has no knowledge, awareness, power, love, or life. So taken, the simplicity doc-trine seems an utter mistake.

But perhaps we can take it another way. Aquinas also says of God, not that he is identical with *life,* but that he is identical with *his* life. Perhaps the idea is that God is identical, not with power and knowledge, but with *his* power and *his* knowledge. The view would thus imply, not indeed that power and knowledge are identical, but that they are, we might say, identical in God; his knowledge is identical with his power. His essence or nature, furthermore, would be identical with his knowledge and power; but (where 'E' names his essence) E is identical neither with knowledge nor power. How can we understand this? Perhaps as follows. Suppose we consider Socrates and wisdom: we can distinguish Socrates from wisdom and each of them from the state of affairs *Socrates' being wise* — a state of affairs that obtains or is actual if and only if Socrates displays wisdom. Perhaps we could refer to *Socrates' being wise* by the locutions 'Socrates' having wisdom' or 'the wisdom of Socrates' or even 'Socrates' wisdom.' And when Aquinas speaks of God's life or God's wisdom, perhaps we may take him as speaking of the states of affairs consisting in God's being wise and having life. Then his simplicity doctrine could be construed as making the following claim:

(1) For any properties P and Q in God, *God's having P* is identical with *God's having Q* and each is identical with God.

More plausibly, since Aquinas never spoke of states of affairs, perhaps *we* might try thus to outline a sensible defense of a simplicity doctrine similar to his.

This suggestion is indeed of some help with respect to the first difficulty I mentioned above. For while it is obviously absurd to claim that wisdom and power are the very same property, it is not obviously absurd to hold that *God's being wise* is the same state of affairs as *God's being powerful*. If, as Aquinas holds, God is *essentially* wise and *essentially* powerful — is wise and powerful in every possible world in which he exists — then the states of affairs *God's being wise* and *God's being powerful* are equivalent in the broadly logical sense: they obtain or are actual in the very same possible worlds. Several philosophers hold that *propositions* are identical if equivalent in this sense; they hold that if propositions A and B are logically equivalent, i.e., true in the same possible worlds, then A is identical with B. And if this can be held with some show of plausibility for propositions, then surely the same goes for states of affairs. And if you think this can't plausibly be held for propositions, take heart; we can tighten up the relevant criterion of identity as follows:

(2) States of affairs *x's having P* and *y's having Q* are identical if and only if *x's having P* is equivalent to (obtains in the same possible worlds as) *y's having Q* and $x = y$.

On this criterion *God's having power* is identical with *God's having wisdom* and (where 'E' names God's essence) *God's having E*. Each of the mentioned properties is essential to him, so that he has each of these properties in every possible world in which he exists; hence the mentioned states of affairs obtain in the same possible worlds and are thus equivalent. True, this criterion has a mildly annoying consequence with respect to Socrates: his having P and his having Q will be the same state of affairs for any properties P and Q essential to him. Thus *Socrates' being a person, Socrates' being a non-number,* and *Socrates' being self-identical* will be the very same state of affairs. But this consequence is only mildly annoying, and perhaps we can accept it with a certain equanimity. This version of the simplicity doctrine can thus be defended against the first sort of objection.

Still, the view in question is totally unsatisfactory. First, it does not resolve the difficulty the simplicity doctrine was invoked to resolve. The underlying motivation for that doctrine was to provide a way out of the dilemma whose horns were: either God has no nature or else God isn't genuinely sovereign. The simplicity doctrine aims to escape between the horns by holding that God has a nature and properties, all right, but they aren't distinct from him, so that he cannot rightly be said to be limited by something distinct from himself. But on the present suggestion, he does have a nature and properties distinct from him. On this view, God is identical with a certain state of affairs; even so, on the view in question, he has essentially such properties as goodness and knowledge and is distinct from them. Since they are essential to him, furthermore, they exist in every world he does. But Aquinas holds that God is a necessary being; he exists in every possible world. If so, the same must be said for these properties. But then how can they be dependent on him? That they exist and have the characteristics they have is not up to him. And won't he be dependent upon them for his nature and character? The dilemma remains untouched.

Second and more important: on this view God is a state of affairs. If he is identical with his being wise, for example, then he is the state of affairs consisting in God's being wise. And this is every bit as outrageous as the claim that God is a property. If God is a state of affairs, then he is a mere abstract object and not a person at all; he is then without knowledge or love or the power to act. But this is clearly inconsistent with the claims of Christian theism at the most basic level.

So initially, at least, it looks as if Aquinas means to suggest that God is identical with some property or perhaps with a certain state of affairs. Both of these suggestions are eminently rejectable. What Aquinas says here, however, is at times terse and enigmatic; perhaps I haven't completely understood him. Perhaps when he argues that God is identical with his essence, with his goodness, with goodness itself, and the like, he doesn't mean to identify God with a property or state of affairs at all, but with something quite different. If so, it isn't easy to see what sort of thing it might be. Taken at face value, the Thomistic doctrine of divine simplicity seems entirely unacceptable. Like the view that our concepts do not apply to God, it begins in a pious and proper concern for God's sovereignty; it ends by flouting the most fundamental claims of theism.

Or perhaps it is something else that simplicity flouts. Suppose we take a more careful look at the logic of the situation. In company with nearly all theists, Aquinas accepts

(3) God is sovereign and exists *a se* (has aseity).

He also holds

(4) God is alive, knowledgeable, capable of action, powerful, and good,

a proposition essential to any brand of theism. In addition, I think he means to endorse

(5) If (3), then (a) God has created everything distinct from himself, (b) everything distinct from God is dependent upon him, (c) he is not dependent on anything distinct from himself, and (d) everything is within his control.

(5) is what we have been calling the "sovereignty-aseity intuition"; it lays down allegedly necessary conditions of the conjunction of sovereignty with aseity. Furthermore, I think Aquinas accepts

(6) If (4), then there are such properties as life, knowledgeability, capability of action, power, and goodness; and God has these properties.

Now Aquinas speaks, not of God's *having* properties, but of properties being *in* God; he thinks of God's properties as *constituents* of him. There is a difference between thinking of God as *having* properties and thinking of his properties as *constituents* of him. In some contexts this difference may be significant and we must bear it in mind. Here, however, I think it is not significant, and for ease of exposition I shall use 'having properties' to cover having properties as constituents. Aquinas also endorses, I believe, all of the following:

(7) If God has properties distinct from him, then he is dependent on them.

(8) God is a necessary being.

(9) God is essentially alive, knowledgeable, capable of action, powerful, and good.

(10) If (9), then there are such properties as life, knowledge, capability of action, power, and goodness, and God could not have failed to have them.

(11) If (8) and God could not have failed to have these properties, then they could not have failed to exist, are necessary beings.

(12) If God has some properties that exist necessarily and are distinct from him, then God is dependent on these properties and they are independent of him, uncreated by him and outside his control.

Aquinas accepts all of these propositions, I think; and together they entail that God's properties are not distinct from him. In fact they entail this at least twice over; (3)-(7) entail this conclusion as do (3) and (5) together with (8)-(12). And as I have argued above, all these propositions have a certain intuitive appeal for the theist. But there are other relevant propositions lurking in the neighborhood — propositions that have at least as much intuitive support:

(13) If there is a property with which God is identical, then God is a property

and

(14) No property is alive, knowledgeable, capable of action, powerful, or good.

(13) is a truth of logic; and (14) seems very secure. If God is a living, conscious being who knows, wills, and acts — if, in a word, God is a *person* — then God is not a property or state of affairs or set or proposition or any other abstract object.

Someone might object that our language about God, according to Aquinas, is *analogical* rather than univocal, so that when we predicate 'being a property' or 'being identical with his nature' of God, what we say doesn't mean the same as when we predicate these things of other beings. He might add that since this is so, we cannot properly draw the above inferences; we cannot properly claim, for example, that if God is a person, then he is not a property or state of affairs. The sentences 'Socrates is a person' and 'Socrates is a property (or state of affairs)' express incompatible propositions; but 'God is a person' and 'God is a property (or state of affairs)' do not — or at any rate we have no reason to suppose that they do. Since our language about God is merely analogical, we cannot rely on the usual sorts of inferences in talking and thinking about God.

The teaching that our language about God is analogical rather than literal is another large and difficult topic — one I cannot discuss here. What is crucially important to see, however, is that the present objection is a two-edged sword. The claim is we cannot rely on our usual styles of inference in reasoning about God; hence we can't object to the simplicity doctrine by arguing that *God is a person* entails *God is not a property.* But if this claim is true, then we are equally handicapped when it comes to the arguments *for* divine simplicity. If we can't rely on our usual modes of inference in reasoning about God, by what right do we argue from (3)-(7), say, to the conclusion that God is not distinct from his properties? Suppose it is a fact that our language about God is analogical: if that fact vitiates the argument *against* divine simplicity, it pays the same compliment to the arguments *for* this doctrine.

All of (3)-(14), I think, have at least some intuitive appeal for the theist. Sadly enough, we cannot accept them all; (3)-(12) entail that God is identical with each of his properties, while (4), (13), and (14) entail that God is not identical with any property at all. Thus (3)-(14) are jointly incompatible; we can't, it seems, hold to them all.

Of course there is one further possibility. Hilary Putnam has claimed that the logical law of distribution is incompatible with quantum mechanics, so that we must give up one or the other.[6] A possible course he doesn't mention is that of giving up their incompatibility; perhaps each of quantum mechanics, distribution, and the idea that incompatibles can't both be true is more secure than the claim that quantum mechanics is incompatible with distribution. Here too then; if we are desperately attached to all of (3)-(14) a possible course would be to reject the laws of logic according to which (3)-(14) are jointly inconsistent. This would be a heroic course indeed; it will probably find few takers. But it does highlight the main point: the point that what we have here is a conflict of intuitions. Something has to go: either (3)-(14) or their incompatibility. (3) and (4), however, are non-negotiable from a theistic point of view. (13) and (14), furthermore, each have at least as much intuitive support as any of (5)-(12). (13) is a truth of logic and about as obvious as anything could be. But surely (14) is equally clear; no properties are persons. Given (3), (4), (13), and (14), however, it follows that (5)-(12) are not all true; the former entail that God is not a property and the latter entail that he is. Accordingly, we must conclude that at least one of (5)-(12) is false. And the fact is, several of (5)-(12) seem fairly plausible candidates for that post. Is it really clear, for example, that (7) is true, that if God has properties distinct from himself, then he is dependent upon them? And what about (5), the sovereignty-aseity intuition itself? As I conceded earlier, it does have intuitive support. But (5) isn't totally easy to grasp. How, for example, are we to understand *dependence* and *control?* And is it obvious that if God is sovereign, then he has created *everything* distinct from himself — even his own properties and the fact that he has always existed? I think not. This requires further discussion and isn't obvious — not nearly as obvious, anyway, as that no properties are persons. Divine simplicity, therefore, is not the way out; for while it does indeed have a certain intuitive grounding, it scouts intuitions much firmer than those that support it.

6. "Is Logic Empirical?" in *Boston Studies in Philosophy of Science,* vol. 5 (Dordrecht: D. Reidel, 1969), pp. 216-41.

IV. Universal Possibilism*

If there is no composition in God, then he won't have a nature distinct from himself on which he depends, but there will still be many truths outside his control. *Being red* and *being colored* will be divine ideas and in some obscure way identical with God; but the truth *whatever is red is colored* will not be within his control. In the same way, the natural numbers will be among the divine ideas and hence obscurely identical with God; but it will not be up to him whether or not every even number is the sum of two primes. The claim that God is simple pays a high philosophical price for a doctrine that is ultimately beside the point.

The real issue, therefore, is control. What the sovereignty-aseity intuition demands is

(15) If God is sovereign and exists *a se,* then every truth is within his control.

Suppose we say that God is *absolutely omnipotent* if and only if every truth is within his control — alternatively, if and only if every proposition is such that it is within God's power to cause it to be true and within his power to cause it to be false. What the sovereignty-aseity intuition requires, then, is that God be absolutely omnipotent. But if God is absolutely omnipotent, then in the first place, God will have no nature. There will be no properties he could not have lacked; for any property you pick it is within God's power to bring it about that he lacks that property. And in the second place, there will be no necessary truths; if God is absolutely omnipotent, then *every* proposition is such that he could cause it to be false. But then every proposition could be false, so that there aren't any that are necessarily true. What the sovereignty-aseity intuition really requires, therefore, is universal possibilism.

A. Descartes and Possibilism

This implication of the sovereignty-aseity intuition was, I think, clearly evident to Descartes; there is good reason to think, moreover, that he was prepared to bite the bullet and accept the consequence that there are no necessary truths. Suppose we consider the class of truths alleged to be necessary. This class would include truths of logic, truths of mathematics, and a host of homelier items such as

(16) Red is a color,

---

*Editor's Note: Section III, "Nominalism," is omitted.

(17) The proposition *all dogs are animals* is distinct from the proposition *all animals are dogs,*

and

(18) No numbers are persons.

Suppose we choose a name for all these truths; following Descartes, let's say these are *eternal* truths, leaving open for the moment the question whether they are necessary as well as eternal. Now Descartes, clearly enough, believed that these eternal truths were created, or instituted, or caused to be true by God's activity:

The mathematical truths which you call eternal have been laid down by God and depend on Him entirely no less than the rest of his creatures. . . . Please do not hesitate to assert and proclaim everywhere that it is God who has laid down these laws in nature just as a king lays down laws in his kingdom.[7]

As for the eternal truths, I say once more that *they are true or possible only because God knows them as true or possible. They are not known as true by God in any way which would imply that they are true independently of Him.* If men really understood the sense of their words they could never say without blasphemy that the truth of anything is prior to the knowledge which God has of it. In God willing and knowing are a single thing in such a way that *by the very fact of willing something he knows it and it is only for this reason that such a thing is true.* So we must not say that if *God did not exist nonetheless these truths would be true;* for the existence of God is the first and the most eternal of all possible truths and the one from which alone all others derive. (To Mersenne, May 6, 1630)

You ask me *by what kind of causality God established the eternal truths.* I reply: *by the same kind of causality* as he created all things, that is to say, as their *efficient and total cause.* For it is certain that he is no less the author of creatures' essence than he is of their existence; and this essence is nothing other than the eternal truths. I do not conceive them as emanating from God like rays from the sun; but I know that God is the author of everything and that these truths are something and consequently that he is their author. (To Mersenne, May 27, 1630)

It is because He willed the three angles of a triangle to be necessarily equal to two right angles that this is true and cannot be otherwise; and so in other cases.[8]

---

7. Letter from Descartes to Mersenne, April 15, 1630. In *Descartes' Philosophical Letters,* trans. and ed. by Anthony Kenny (Oxford: Clarendon Press, 1970), p. 11.

8. Reply to Objections to Meditation VI, in *The Philosophical Works of Descartes,* tr. E. Haldane and G. Ross (Cambridge: Cambridge University Press, 1967), vol. II, p. 250.

To one who pays attention to God's immensity, it is clear that nothing at all can exist which does not depend on Him. This is true not only of everything that subsists, but of all order, of every law, and of every reason of truth and goodness; for otherwise God, as has been said just before, would not have been wholly indifferent to the creation of what he has created. (Reply to Objections VI, p. 250)

It is therefore plain that on Descartes' view God has instituted, caused, authored, or created the eternal truths. His reasons for saying so would extend beyond these truths to allegedly necessary beings generally — to all the abstract objects such as properties, numbers, propositions, states of affairs, possible worlds, and the like.[9] It doesn't obviously follow from what he says, however, that there was a time when abstract objects did not exist or that they had a beginning. Descartes suggests that God's instituting or causing these things consists in his willing them — perhaps *affirming* them:

You ask what God did in order to produce them. I reply that from all eternity he willed and understood them to be, and by that very fact he created them. (To Mersenne, May 27, 1630)

Perhaps for any Platonic entity you pick and any time, at that time God was affirming that Platonic entity. In the case of numbers and properties, what he affirms is their *existence;* in the case of eternal truths what he affirms is both their existence and their *truth.*

According to Descartes, then, God establishes the eternal truths, and they are dependent upon him for their existence and properties. This suggests that it was within God's power to *refrain* from affirming the eternal truths, so that he could have brought it about that they should not have been true. It suggests that it was within God's power to cause them to be false, causing their negations to be true. But if God could have done this, then the eternal truths could have been false; and if they could have been false, then they aren't necessary.

Descartes' central claim is that God's power and freedom must be infinite, i.e., without limits; "the power of God," he says, "cannot have any limits." Why does he think God's power cannot have any limits? Because, I suggest, he believes that God is the sovereign first being of the universe on whom *everything* depends, including the eternal truths:

The mathematical truths which you call eternal have been laid down by God and depend on Him entirely no less than the rest of his creatures. Indeed, to say that these truths are independent of God is to talk of Him as

9. ". . . I know that God is the author of everything and that these truths are something and consequently that he is their author." Descartes to Mersenne, May 27, 1630.

if He were Jupiter or Saturn and to subject Him to the Styx and the Fates. (To Mersenne, April 15, 1630)

Elsewhere he adds that the eternal truths "are true or possible only because God knows them as true or possible. They are not known by God in any way that would imply that they are true independently of Him" (to Mersenne, May 6, 1630). They are dependent upon God, first, for their existence: "You ask what God did in order to produce them. I reply that from all eternity he willed and understood them to be, and by that very fact he created them" (to Mersenne, May 27, 1630). But they are also dependent upon God for their *truth.* And here, I think, Descartes clearly sees the intimate connection between dependence and *power* or *control.* Descartes does not shrink from the indicated inference: if the eternal truths are genuinely dependent upon God, then they must be within his control. Each eternal truth must then be such that it was (and is) within God's power to make it false. Accordingly, God was "free to make it untrue that all the lines drawn from the center of a circle to its circumference are equal"; his power isn't limited even by the eternal truths of logic and mathematics.

Descartes means to hold that *everything* is dependent upon God. But then the eternal truths are thus dependent. He sees further that if they are dependent upon God, then they are within his control; he could have made them false. According to limited possibilism, *modal* propositions — propositions that ascribe a modality to another proposition — are within God's control; it is up to him whether a proposition is necessary, contingent, or impossible. The eternal truths themselves, however, are not within God's control. On this interpretation, God could not have made

(19) $2 \times 4 = 8$

false; what he could have done is only this: he could have made it the case that he *could have* made (19) false. He could have made it *possibly* false. But this is at most a trifling and churlish concession to Descartes' deep conviction that *all* things are dependent upon God and hence within his control. What he really meant to say, I think, is not just that God could have made (19) *possibly* false; he could have made it *false,* and, indeed *necessarily* false.

And here Descartes is not speaking just of mathematical truths; he means to say, I think, that *all* truths are within the control of God. For example, God could have made

(20) God has created Descartes, but Descartes has not been created

true. He could have made "contradictories true together." *Every* truth is within his control; and hence no truth is necessary.

Descartes concedes that there is a problem here: "I turn to the difficulty of conceiving how it was free and indifferent for God to make it not be true that the three angles of a triangle were equal to two right angles, or in general that contradictories could not be true together." The difficulty is that some propositions seem obviously impossible; we cannot entertain them without judging them impossible: "I agree that there are contradictions which are so evident, that we cannot put them before our minds without judging them entirely impossible, like the one you suggest: *That God might have made creatures independent of him*" (to Mersenne, May 26, 1630). We are so constructed, by God, that we cannot entertain (20) or hold it before our minds without thinking it quite impossible — not just false, but impossible. The fact is, however, that it is not impossible; and if we want to know the truth here, we should *not* hold it before our minds. "But if we would know the immensity of his power, we should not put these thoughts before our minds"; for to do so is to be compelled to believe falsehood. To paraphrase Raskolnikov, if God does not exist everything is possible; according to Descartes, the same holds if God *does* exist.

B. Descartes Defended

What shall we say about Descartes' universal possibilism? There is no denying its widespread popular appeal. Undergraduates by the hundred have thought it obvious that God is sovereign, and that if he is sovereign, then everything — absolutely everything — is within his control. And, of course, any view endorsed by a philosopher as great as Descartes has something to be said for it. But it also has its unlovely features. Harry Frankfurt, for example, suggests reasons for thinking Descartes' claim — that since God's power is infinite, no proposition is necessary — is *unintelligible:*

> Now a person's assertion that there is something he cannot understand is often entirely comprehensible, and there may be quite good evidence that it is true. In the present instance, however, the assertion is peculiar and problematical. That there is a deity with infinite power is supposed by Descartes to entail the possibility of what is logically impossible. But if it must entail this, then the assertion that God has infinite (and hence unintelligible) power seems itself unintelligible. For it appears that no coherent meaning can be assigned to the notion of an infinitely powerful being as Descartes employs it — that is, to the notion of a being for whom the logically impossible is possible. And if this is so, then it is no more possible for us to know or to believe that God *has* infinite power than it is, according to Descartes, for us to understand that power. If we cannot understand "infinite power," we also cannot understand and hence cannot believe or know, the proposition that God's power is infinite.[10]

10. "Descartes on the Creation of the Eternal Truths," *Philosophical Review,* 1977, p. 44.

But this seems incorrect. First, Descartes does not intend to say that for God, the logically impossible is possible; he means to say instead that nothing is logically impossible. He does not mean to claim that a contradiction, for example, is logically impossible but possible for God; he claims instead that contradictions are, in fact, possibly true because it is within God's power to make them true.

What someone says may be unintelligible to us in at least two ways. In the first place, she may utter or write strings of syllables we are unable to construe as words of any language we know. If, for example, she assertively utters "Twas brillig; and the slithy toves did gyre and gymble in the wabe," what she says is thus unintelligible. We may have a similar difficulty if instead she utters in affirmative fashion such a sentence as "The not nothings itself." Here we clearly have words of English, but they are used in such an unfamiliar fashion that we are unable to identify any proposition as the one being expressed and asserted. In both of these cases, the difficulty can sometimes be relieved; she can tell us what she means by these otherwise Delphic utterances. But what Descartes says is not unintelligible in this way. What he says, substantially, is

(21) Since God has infinite power, there are no necessary truths;

and there is no difficulty in construing these words. It's fairly clear which proposition is being asserted.

What someone says may be unintelligible to us in another way: she may employ perfectly ordinary words in a perfectly familiar fashion to express a proposition which we are incapable of grasping or understanding. Perhaps it involves concepts we don't grasp; then it will be unintelligible to us in the way

(22) No particle has both an instantaneous position and an instantaneous velocity

is unintelligible to someone who doesn't have the concepts of instantaneous position and velocity. But Descartes' claim isn't like that either. Most of us have a fairly adequate grasp of the concept it involves. In the passage quoted, Frankfurt suggests that "infinite power" does not express a concept we grasp; but this seems wrong. God has infinite power if and only if every proposition is within his control — if and only if for every proposition p there is an action A he can perform, such that if he did perform A, then p would be true. None of the concepts involved here is beyond our grasp. We can certainly understand (21); what we cannot understand is how it could possibly be *true*. That is, the view looks obviously false or even obviously impossible. And of course Descartes concedes this; he agrees that when we entertain such a proposition as

(23) $2 \times 4 = 7$

it looks obviously impossible. So the claim that no propositions are impossible seems itself clearly false or impossible. But this is not to say that it is unintelligible.

Shall we say that universal possibilism is *incoherent?* Incoherence is a slippery notion. Not just any necessarily false claim is incoherent; a person who holds that, say, every even number is the sum of two primes is not holding an incoherent view, even if it turns out to be necessarily false. After repeated calculations, I may believe that $26 \times 431 = 12,106$; my view is not incoherent, although it is necessarily false. What is incoherence? It may be hard to give a general answer; examples, however, are easy to come by. A theologian under the influence of Tillich or Kant might claim that there is a God, all right, but nothing whatever — not even that he exists — can be said about him. This is clearly incoherent, for here the claimant asserts that no assertions of a certain sort can be made, while his claim is an assertion of that very sort. But what Descartes says is clearly not incoherent in that way. A theologian under the influence might also argue as follows:

(24) God transcends human experience;

therefore

(25) None of our concepts applies to God.

But one who offers this argument is committed to supposing that our concept of transcending human experience applies to God. If so, however, the conclusion of the argument is false. Here the incoherence consists in offering an argument of such a sort that in accepting one of the premises one is committed to denying the conclusion.

In the passage I quoted above, Frankfurt hints that Descartes has fallen into this sort of incoherence: "That there is a deity with infinite power is supposed by Descartes to entail the possibility of what is logically impossible." We could imagine Descartes arguing as follows:

(26) God has infinite power.
(27) That God has infinite power entails that no propositions are necessarily true.

Therefore

(28) No propositions are necessarily true.

If Descartes offered this argument, then he would be guilty of incoherence, at any rate if he understood 'entails' in the usual fashion. For then in asserting (27) he would be committed to

(29) The proposition *if God is infinitely powerful, then there are no necessary truths* is a necessary truth

in which case his acceptance of one of the premises of his argument commits him to the denial of its conclusion. But why construe Descartes this way? Why not give him the benefit of the doubt and see him as arguing

(26) God has infinite power;

(30) If God has infinite power, there are no necessary truths;

therefore

(28) There are no necessary truths?

All Descartes needs for the argument is the *truth* of (30), not its necessity.

But isn't he committed to necessary truth in offering an argument at all? The above argument involves (is a substitution instance of) *modus ponens;* in advancing such an argument and claiming that it is valid, isn't Descartes committed to the necessary truth of the corresponding conditional of the argument? Must he not suppose that

(31) If God has infinite power, and if God has infinite power there are no necessary truths, then there are no necessary truths

is a necessary truth? It is hard to see why. No doubt he is committed to the *truth* of (31); but why should he suppose it is necessary? Of course he cannot explain the validity of this argument in terms of the necessity of its corresponding conditional; but that doesn't mean he cannot explain it at all. He can say, for example, that an argument is valid if it is a substitution instance of an argument form none of whose substitution instances has true premises and a false conclusion. There are problems here; but perhaps they are no more intractable for Descartes than for those contemporary logicians who give this explanation of validity. Descartes' possibilism does not compel him to give up either standard logic (first-order logic with identity) or its ordinary application. He can assert the truth of all its theorems and their instances; he need only refrain from adding that they are *necessarily* true. He can accept as valid all argument proceeding in terms of standard logic; he need only refrain from claiming that their corresponding conditionals are necessary.

But how does he know that such propositions as (31) are true? Well, how do *we* know they are true? Perhaps we think we know them because we just *see* they cannot be false — because, substantially, we see that they are *necessarily* true. Descartes' retort is that what we see is not their necessity, but only their truth; and he sees that as clearly as we. God has constructed us so that we see the truth of (31) and its kin; we are so constituted that we can't help believing (31) when we entertain it. But we confuse this compulsion to believe — a fact about us and our noetic constitution — with a compulsion to be true on the part of the proposition. The fact is, says Descartes, we can't help believing (31); and we do indeed see that it is true. It doesn't follow that it is necessarily true. So he claims to know the truth of (31) in just the way everyone else does. And the rest of us, he thinks, confuse a compulsion on our part to believe such propositions with a compulsion on God's part to make them true. In all this there seems nothing in any straightforward sense incoherent.

Accordingly, Descartes' view is neither unintelligible nor incoherent. The most we can fairly say, here, is that his view is strongly counterintuitive — that we have a strong inclination to believe propositions from which its falsehood follows. This Descartes concedes; but he is unmoved. In a way, Descartes' position has more to be said for it than the view that God is simple. Descartes recognizes that the real issue with respect to God's sovereignty and aseity is *control* — what is or isn't within God's power. He holds that there are propositions, properties, and all the rest of the Platonic swarm. He clearly sees, however, that what counts so far as these things and God's sovereignty is concerned, is the question whether or not they are within his control. He therefore holds that all the truths about these abstract objects *are* within God's control. Failing to see the centrality of control, the partisan of divine simplicity misdiagnoses the situation. Descartes sees the situation clearly; he sees that if we take the sovereignty-aseity intuition with real seriousness, we shall be obliged to suppose that every proposition is within God's control. But then we shall be obliged to accept universal possibilism. According to the Reverend Andrew Mackerel, "It is the final proof of God's omnipotence that he need not exist in order to save us."[11]

V. The Divine Nature

On Descartes' view, then, God has no nature because none of his properties is *essential* to him. There is no property he could not have lacked; if every proposition is within his control, then every proposition predicating a property of him is within his control. But then for every property P he has, there is something he could have done, some action he could have taken, such that if he had taken that action then he would not have had P. And our final question is: should we follow Descartes in giving full sway to the sovereignty-aseity intuition, thus denying that God has a nature?

11. Peter DeVries, *The Mackerel Plaza* (Boston: Little, Brown and Co., 1958), p. 8.

A. A Conflict of Intuitions

The first thing we must note is that this view is indeed wildly counterintuitive. If God has no nature, then there is no property he could not have had and none he could not have lacked. So for any proposition p, God could have had the property of knowing that p. He could have brought it about, made it true, that he was powerless, without knowledge, and wicked. Indeed he could have brought it about that he was powerless, without knowledge, and wicked, but at the same time omnipotent, omniscient, and morally perfect. He could have brought it about that he has a nature; and that he has a nature and furthermore doesn't have a nature. He could have brought it about that he does not exist while serenely continuing as a necessary being. He could have brought it about that we know that he exists but don't believe that he does; that we know that he exists and also know that he doesn't exist. On this view, it is logically possible, as Harry Frankfurt suggests, that God knows that he doesn't exist.

Now of course what Descartes holds is that these outrageous suggestions are possibly true, that is, not necessarily false. God could have caused them to be true. He is not holding that they may be true in the sense that for all we know they *are* true. What he says, in fact, suggests that we know they are *not* true. They are logically but not epistemically possible. Here we must ask the following question: how could we know, on Descartes' view, that these peculiar states of affairs are not actual as well as merely possible? How do we know, for example, that we don't both believe that God loves us and know that he doesn't? True, we don't believe that he doesn't love us, and we know we don't believe that; but why let that prejudice our views as to whether we know it? On the present view these things are quite compatible (since they are compatible with everything) with our both believing and knowing that he doesn't love us. And does the believer, from this point of view, have a reason for rejecting atheism? Of course he believes in God; but God could have brought it about that he both exists and doesn't exist, that theism and atheism are both true. How do we know he hasn't done just that?

It seems we can't appeal, here, to the fact that God has told us much about himself and is not a deceiver. He has told us, for example, that he loves us, and that he wishes us to love one another. On the present view, it could be both that he was entirely truthful in so saying, and that he neither loves us nor desires that we love one another. Perhaps in fact he hates us, and hopes we will follow suit by hating each other. How do we know that he doesn't?

Descartes' answer isn't entirely clear; but perhaps it would go along the following lines. God has in fact made certain propositions true and others false:

> The mathematical truths which you call eternal have been laid down by God. . . . Please do not hesitate to assert and proclaim everywhere that it

is God who has laid down these laws in nature just as a king lays down laws in his kingdom. (To Mersenne, April 15, 1630)

Furthermore, God has so created us that we are compelled or at least impelled to believe some of these truths. The passage continues:

There is no single one that we cannot understand if our mind turns to consider it. They are all *inborn in our minds* just as a king would imprint his laws on the hearts of all his subjects if he had enough power to do so. (To Mersenne, April 15, 1630)

He has so created us that we are impelled to believe that if he exists, then it isn't true that he doesn't exist; and we find ourselves incapable of believing that he knows that he doesn't exist, or both exists and does not exist. When we bring to mind or consider such a proposition as $2 + 1 = 3$, or *God doesn't know that he doesn't exist,* it displays a sort of luminous aura, a "clarity and brightness," to use Locke's phrase, or a sort of clarity and distinctness, as Descartes says. And when we believe a proposition that displays this aura, we may properly be said to know it. So we know that God does not both exist and fail to exist. Even though that proposition is not necessarily true.

But can't the very same question rear its ugly head again? It is *possible,* Descartes says, that both

(32) God has made p true and has created in us a powerful tendency to believe p; we do believe p; and if we believe p we know p,

and

(33) We don't know p and p in fact is false

should be true. So how do we know that they aren't both true? Indeed, no matter what answer Descartes gives, the same question can be raised again. Descartes concedes that on his view, it is possible that

(34) $2 + 1 = 3$

should be false. So we ask: how then do you know it *isn't* false? He responds by citing some reason R. But then comes the rejoinder: you concede that it's possible that R should be true and (34) false. How then do you know that that possibility isn't *actual?*

So this question will always arise. But does that mean that Descartes cannot coherently claim to know that (34) is true? I think not. How do *we* know that

(35) If, if p then q, and p, then q

is true? Not, presumably, by inferring it from other propositions that are more obvious or better known than this one; we simply see that it is true and couldn't be false. And why can't Descartes make the same reply, minus the "couldn't be false"? He doesn't know (34) or (35) on the basis of evidence, just as the rest of us don't. So he does not need an answer to the question "How do you know that those bizarre possibilities aren't actual?" He can claim, quite properly, that he just does know that they aren't. This objection, therefore, is inconclusive.

The first objection, however, remains. If Descartes is right, then every proposition is possibly true. But if we know anything at all about modality, we know that some propositions —

(36) God knows that he does not exist

for example — are impossible. Of course Descartes concedes that "there are contradictions which are so evident, that we cannot put them before our minds without judging them entirely impossible, like the one you suggest: *That God might have made creatures independent of him*" (to Mersenne, May 26, 1630). He simply claims we know on other grounds that those contradictions are *not* impossible; we know this because we know that God is sovereign and omnipotent. Pared to essentials, then, his argument goes like this:

(37) God is omnipotent.
(38) If God is omnipotent, then his power is absolutely unlimited.
(39) If his power is absolutely unlimited, then he could make (36) true.
(40) If he could make (36) true, then (36) could be true and is possible.

Therefore

(41) (36) is possible.

More accurately, taking account of Descartes' seeing God's omnipotence as a consequence of his sovereignty, we could put his argument as follows:

(42) God is sovereign.
(43) If God is sovereign, then everything is dependent upon him.
(44) If everything is dependent upon him, then every truth is within his control.
(45) If every truth is within his control, then (36) could be true and is possible.

Therefore

(41) (36) is possible.

Now (42) is non-negotiable from the point of view of Christian theism; (45) seems utterly obvious; and both (43) and (44) have at least some intuitive support. As has been remarked, however, one man's *modus ponens* is another's *modus tollens;* (43) and (44) have at least some support, but so does

(46) (36) is not possible.

Indeed, (46) seems to have a good deal more intuitive support than either (43) or (44). Descartes' procedure here is like the following. Suppose someone considers the premises of a Russell paradox: that some properties exemplify themselves and others do not; that if so, there is such a property as self-exemplification, that every property has a complement and the like. Suppose he notes, furthermore, that each of these premises has a good deal of intuitive support and that by forms of argument themselves having strong intuitive support they entail

(47) There is a property that both exemplifies itself and does not exemplify itself.

Finally, suppose he concludes (perhaps with an air of baffled bewilderment) that we are obliged to accept (47), despite the fact that it seems self-evidently false. Such a person has forgotten that the argument is reversible. We aren't obliged to accept the conclusion; instead we may reject one of the premises or one of the argument forms by which they entail the conclusion.

But the same goes for Descartes' argument. He thinks we should reject (46), because of (43) and (44). He concedes that we find ourselves strongly inclined to accept (46); we find it hard to see how it could possibly be false; we have a powerful and nearly overwhelming tendency, when considering it, to accept it. Nevertheless, we must reject it, because its denial follows from (43) and (44). But how could the latter have better credentials than the ones just conceded to (46)? How could they possibly have a stronger claim on our belief? It isn't as if we are just *given* (43) and (44) as settled in advance, while other propositions such as (46) have no more than their intuitive support to rely on. Descartes' reason for supposing (43) and (44) true is just that they seem evident upon reflection, in the way in which it may seem evident upon reflection that there are no things that do not exist or that whatever has any properties exists. But of course (46) seems at least as evident upon reflection. The source and motivation for these conflicting suggestions is the same: each seems intuitively plausible. So what we really have here is a conflict of intuitions. The question is: which has stronger intuitive support, (43) and (44) (or (38) and (39)) on the one hand or (46) on the other? I can't speak for Descartes, of course; but as for me and my house, (46) seems about as stable and clear and compelling as any intuition we have — considerably more compelling than either of (43) or (44). We should therefore accept (46) and reject (43) or (44).

Could it be that a person should find herself more strongly inclined to believe (46) than (43) or (44) and nevertheless be rationally permitted or even rationally obliged to reject (46) in favor of (43) and (44)? Suppose I take the Bible as God's speaking to us, thereby teaching us important truths; suppose I believe

(48) Whatever the Bible teaches is true.

Suppose I also believe

(49) The Bible teaches that (46) is false;

and suppose it teaches that this powerful tendency we have to believe (46) is a result of the willfully sinful condition into which mankind has fallen. Finally, suppose that whenever I think about (46), I find myself more strongly impelled to believe it than I am to believe (48) and (49) when I think about *them*. Under those conditions, what should I do? Would I be doing the right thing in believing (48) and (49), even though they conflict with (46), which has more intuitive support than they do? To vary the case, imagine you are exploring mood- and mind-altering drugs; you come upon one that produces an overwhelming tendency to believe that *modus ponens* is invalid and its corresponding conditional false. You experiment widely; in 1,000 out of 1,000 cases the drug produces this ineluctable tendency to find *modus ponens* obviously false. You take the drug yourself. First you notice a shade of doubt creeping in about *modus ponens;* then substantial uneasiness; and after ten minutes you find yourself powerfully impelled to believe it false. It seems as improbable, to you, as any contradiction; and the more you think about it, the more obviously false it appears. Indeed, its falsehood seems much clearer and more evident to you than what you know about the drug. What should you do? I don't have the space to discuss this question (as one says when one doesn't know the answer); let me say that it is by no means obvious that one should reject *modus ponens,* under those conditions. In the same way, it is by no means obvious that one could not sensibly reject (46) on grounds like (48) and (49), even if one has a stronger tendency to accept (46) than to accept (48) and (49).

But of course Descartes does not argue for (43) and (44) in any such fashion as this. He just takes them to be intuitively obvious. The question is: which is *more* intuitively obvious, (46) or (43) and (44)? The conflict is between two intuitions: the intuition that some propositions are impossible and the intuition that if God is genuinely sovereign, then everything is possible. But when the issue is thus baldly stated, so it seems to me, there really isn't any issue. Obviously not everything is possible; obviously, for example, it is impossible that God be omniscient and at the same time not know anything at all. And this is far more obvious than either (43) or (44). So the right course is to reject (43) or (44). We should hold that (36) is not possibly true and its denial is necessarily true. But then God has at least one essential property: not knowing that he does not exist. We should therefore assert forthrightly that God has a nature and that not everything is possible — even for him.

B. *God's Nature and Necessary Beings*

God has essentially the property of not knowing that he does not exist; but of course he has many more. For example, he has *existence* essentially; like everything else, he is such that he exists in every possible world in which he exists. But Christian theists have traditionally said something much stronger. Not only is it not possible that God exist but fail to exist; it is also not possible that he fail to exist. Like all the rest of us, he has existence essentially; unlike the rest of us, he also has necessary existence — the property a thing has if and only if it could not have failed to exist. There is no possible world in which God does not exist. If so, however, then the proposition

(50) God has a nature

is equivalent to

(51) There are some necessary propositions.

For suppose (50) is true; then God has essentially some property P. But then

(52) God has P

will be a necessary truth, so that (51) is true. Suppose on the other hand that (51) is true. Then there is at least one necessary proposition A. But then it follows that God has essentially the property of not knowing that A is false; hence (50) is true. So if God exists necessarily, the question whether he has a nature is equivalent to the question whether there are any necessary truths. Which properties are included in God's nature? If, as most of the Christian tradition affirms, he could not have been powerless, or morally imperfect or without knowledge, then he has the complements of those properties essentially; being knowledgeable, morally perfect, and powerful will be part of his nature. But the tradition has typically gone further; God is not only not possibly powerless; he is essentially omnipotent. And not only is he essentially knowledgeable; he is essentially omniscient. That is, he believes no false propositions, and for any true proposition p, God knows that p; and this is so in every world in which he exists. But suppose he exists in every world; then each proposition p will be equivalent to the proposition that God knows that p, which is equivalent to *God believes that p.*

Furthermore, if the number 7 or the proposition *all men are mortal* exists necessarily, then God has essentially the property of affirming its existence. That property, therefore, will be part of his nature. Indeed, for any necessarily existing abstract object O, the property of affirming the existence of O is part of God's nature. It is thus part of God's nature to say, "Let there be the number 1; let there be 2; let there be 3. . . ." According to Kronecker God created the natural numbers and men created the rest — rational numbers, real numbers, complex numbers, and the like. Kronecker was wrong on two counts. God hasn't *created* the numbers; a thing is created only if its existence has a beginning, and no number ever began to exist. And secondly, other mathematical entities — the reals, for example — stand in the same relation to God and humankind as do the natural numbers. Sequences of natural numbers, for example, are necessary beings and have been created neither by God nor by anyone else. Still, each such sequence is such that it is part of God's nature to affirm its existence.

And of course the same goes for other necessarily existing abstract objects. Though God affirms the truth of only some propositions, he affirms the *existence* of them all; and if no proposition could have failed to exist, then for any proposition p, it is part of God's nature to affirm that p exists. The same holds for states of affairs and possible worlds; each possible world is such that God affirms its existence. If what is possible does not vary from world to world, then each possible world is such that it is part of God's nature to affirm its existence; and there is no world in which it is part of God's nature to affirm the existence of a world distinct from any he does in fact affirm. So in each possible world God affirms the existence of the same possible worlds: the ones that exist in fact, in the actual world. Of course in each possible world W he affirms the *actuality* of just one world: W itself.[12]

From this point of view, then, exploring the realm of abstract objects can be seen as exploring the nature of God. Mathematics thus takes its proper place as one of the *loci* of theology; perhaps this explains the high esteem in which it is held in many quarters. And the same goes for logic, both broadly and narrowly conceived. Of course God neither needs nor uses logic; that is, he never comes to know a proposition A by inferring it from a proposition B. Nevertheless each theorem of logic — first-order logic with identity, let's say — is such that affirming it is part of God's nature. And to determine that a proposition A is equivalent to (i.e., true in the same world as) a proposition B is to determine that it is part of God's nature to believe both A or B or neither A nor B.

By way of conclusion, I wish to ask but not answer the following question. Take any necessary proposition:

(53) $7 + 5 = 12$

for example. (53) is equivalent to

(54) God believes (53);

and

(55) Necessarily $7 + 5 = 12$

12. See my book *The Nature of Necessity,* chapter IV.

is equivalent to

(56) It is part of God's nature to believe that $7 + 5 = 12$.

Can we see (56) as somehow *prior* to (55)? Explanatorily prior, perhaps? Can we explain (55) by appealing to (56)? Can we perhaps answer the question "Why is (55) true?" by citing the fact that believing (53) is part of God's nature? Can we explain the necessary existence of the number 7 by citing the fact that it is part of God's nature to affirm its existence? More exactly, is there a sensible sense of "explain" such that in that sense, (56) is the explanation of (55) but (55) is not the explanation of (56)? Or could we say, perhaps, that what *makes* (55) *true* is the fact that (56) is true? Can we ever say of a pair of necessary propositions A and B that A makes B true or that A is the explanation of the truth of B? Could we say, perhaps, that (55) is *grounded in* (56)? If so, what are the relevant senses of "explains," "makes true," and "grounded in"? These are good questions, and good topics for further study. If we can answer them affirmatively, then perhaps we can point to an important dependence of abstract objects upon God, even though necessary truths about these objects are not within his control.

CHAPTER TEN

On Ockham's Way Out

Two essential teachings of western theistic religions — Christianity, Judaism, and Islam — are that God is omniscient and that human beings are morally responsible for at least some of their actions. The first apparently implies that God has knowledge of the future and thus has foreknowledge of human actions; the second, that some human actions are *free*. But divine foreknowledge and human freedom, as every twelve-year-old Sunday School student knows, can seem to be incompatible; and at least since the fifth century A.D. philosophers and theologians have pondered the question whether these two doctrines really do conflict. There are, I think, substantially two lines of argument for the *incompatibility thesis* — the claim that these doctrines are indeed in conflict; one of these arguments is pretty clearly fallacious, but the other is much more impressive. In Part I, I state these two arguments; in Part II, I explain (and endorse) Ockham's reply to them; in Part III, I point out some startling implications of Ockham's way out; and finally in Part IV, I offer an account of accidental necessity. There is also an appendix on possible worlds explanations of ability.

I. Foreknowledge and the Necessity of the Past

In *De Libero Arbitrio* Augustine puts the first line of argument in the mouth of Evodius:

> That being so, I have a deep desire to know how it can be that God knows all things beforehand and that, nevertheless, we do not sin by necessity. Whoever says that anything can happen otherwise than as God has fore-

258

known it, is attempting to destroy the divine foreknowledge with the most insensate impiety. If God foreknew that the first man would sin — and that anyone must concede who acknowledges with me that God has foreknowledge of all future events — I do not say that God did not make him, for he made good, nor that the sin of the creature whom he made good could be prejudicial to God. On the contrary, God showed his goodness in making man, his justice in punishing his sin, and his mercy in delivering him. I do not say, therefore, that God did not make man. But this I say. Since God foreknew that man would sin, that which God foreknew must necessarily come to pass. How then is the will free when there is apparently this unavoidable necessity?[1]

(Replies Augustine: "You have knocked vigorously.") Evodius's statement of the argument illustrates one parameter of the problem: the conception of freedom in question is such that a person S is free with respect to an action A only if (1) it is within S's power to perform A and within his power to refrain from performing A, and (2) no collection of necessary truths and causal laws — causal laws outside S's control — together with antecedent conditions outside S's control entails that S performs A, and none entails that he refrains from doing so. (I believe that the first of these conditions entails the second, but shall not argue that point here.) Of course if these conditions are rejected, then the alleged problem dissolves.

The essential portion of Evodius's argument may perhaps be put as follows:

(1) If God knows in advance that S will do A, then it must be the case that S will do A.

(2) If it *must* be the case that S will do A, then it is not within the power of S to refrain from doing A.

(3) If it is not within the power of S to refrain from doing A, then S is not free with respect to A.

Hence

(4) If God knows in advance that S will do A, then S is not free with respect to A.

Augustine apparently found this argument perplexing. In some passages he seems to see its proper resolution; but elsewhere he reluctantly accepts it and half-heartedly endorses a compatibilist account of freedom according to which it is possible both that all of a person's actions be determined and that some of them be free.

1. Augustine, *On Free Will in Augustine: Earlier Writings,* tr. J. H. S. Burleigh, vol. VI (Philadelphia: Westminster, 1953), bk. III, ii, 4.

Thomas Aquinas, however, saw the argument for the snare and delusion that it is:

> If each thing is known by God as seen by Him in the present, what is known by God will then have to be. Thus, it is necessary that Socrates be seated from the fact that he is seen seated. But this is not absolutely necessary or, as some say, with the *necessity of the consequent;* it is necessary conditionally, or with the *necessity of the consequence.* For this is a necessary conditional proposition: *if he is seen sitting, he is sitting.*[2]

Aquinas's point may perhaps be put more perspicuously as follows. (1) is ambiguous as between

(1a) Necessarily, if God knows in advance that S will do A, then S will do A.

and

(1b) If God knows in advance that S will do A, then it is necessary that S will do A.

Now consider

(1c) If God knows in advance that S will do A, then S will do A.

(1a), says Aquinas, is a true proposition expressing "the necessity of the consequence"; what it says, sensibly enough, is just that the consequent of (1c) follows with necessity from its antecedent. (1b), on the other hand, is an expression of the necessity of the *consequent;* what *it* says, implausibly, is that the necessity of the consequent of (1c) follows from its antecedent. Aquinas means to point out that (1a) is clearly true but of no use to the argument. (1b), on the other hand, is what the argument requires; but it seems flatly false — or, more modestly, there seems not the slightest reason to endorse it.

If the above argument is unconvincing, there is another, much more powerful, that is also considered by Aquinas.[3] The argument in question has been discussed by a host of philosophers both before and after Aquinas; it received a particularly perspicuous formulation at the hands of Jonathan Edwards:

---

2. Thomas Aquinas, *Summa Contra Gentiles,* book I, chapter 67, 10. The quoted passage involved Aquinas's view that the future is (in a sense hard to make clear) somehow *present* to God. This does not affect my point in quoting it, which is only to show that Aquinas notes the distinction between necessity of the consequent and necessity of the consequence — a distinction that enables us to see just how the argument in question goes wrong.

3. See *Summa Contra Gentiles* I, 67, and *Summa Theologiae* I, Q.14, a.13.

1. I observed before, in explaining the nature of necessity, that in things which are past, their past existence is now necessary . . . : having already made sure of existence, 'tis now impossible, that it should be otherwise than true, that that thing has existed.

2. If there be any such thing as a divine foreknowledge of the volitions of free agents, that foreknowledge, by the supposition, is a thing which already has, and long ago had existence; and so, now its existence is necessary; it is now utterly impossible to be otherwise, than that this foreknowledge should be, or should have been.

3. 'Tis also very manifest, that those things which are indissolubly connected with other things that are necessary, are themselves necessary. As that proposition whose truth is necessarily connected with another proposition, which is necessarily true, is itself necessarily true. To say otherwise, would be a contradiction; it would be in effect to say, that the connection was indissoluble and yet was *not so,* but might be broken. If that, whose existence is indissolubly connected with something whose existence is now necessary, is itself not necessary, then it may possibly not exist, notwithstanding that indissoluble connection of its existence. — Whether the absurdity ben't glaring, let the reader judge.

4. 'Tis no less evident, that if there be a full, certain and infallible foreknowledge of the future existence of the volitions of moral agents, then there is a certain infallible and indissoluble connection between those events and that foreknowledge; and that therefore, by the preceding observations, those events are necessary events; being infallibly and indissolubly connected with that whose existence already is, and so is now necessary, and can't but have been.[4]

Edwards concludes that since "God has a certain and infallible prescience of the acts and will of moral agents," it follows that "these events are necessary" with the same sort of necessity enjoyed by what is now past.

The argument essentially appeals to two intuitions. First, although the past is not necessary in the broadly logical sense (it is possible, in that sense, that Abraham should never have existed), it *is* necessary in *some* sense: it is fixed, unalterable, outside anyone's control. And second, whatever is "necessarily connected" with what is necessary in some sense, is itself necessary in that sense; if a proposition A, necessary in the way in which the past is necessary, entails a proposition B, then B is necessary in that same way. If Edwards's argument is a good one, what it shows is that if at some time in the past God knew that I will do A, then it is necessary that I will do A — necessary in just the way in which

4. Jonathan Edwards, *Freedom of the Will,* 1745, section 12.

the past is necessary. But then it is not within my power to refrain from doing A, so that I will not do A freely. So, says Edwards, suppose God knew, eighty years ago, that I will mow my lawn this afternoon. This foreknowledge is, as he says, a "thing that is past." Such things, however, are now necessary; "'tis now impossible, that it should be otherwise than true, that that thing has existed." So it is now necessary that God had that knowledge eighty years ago; but it is also *logically* necessary that if God knew that I will mow my lawn today, then I will mow my lawn today. It is therefore now necessary that I will mow; it is thus not within my power to refrain from mowing; hence though I will indeed mow, I will not mow freely.

Edwards's argument is for what we might call "theological determinism"; the premise is that God has foreknowledge of the "acts and wills of moral agents" and the conclusion is that these acts are necessary in just the way the past is. Clearly enough the argument can be transformed into an argument for *logical* determinism, which would run as follows. It was true, eighty years ago, that I will mow my lawn this afternoon. Since what is past is now necessary, it is now necessary that it was true eighty years ago that I will mow my lawn today. But it is logically necessary that if it was true eighty years ago that I will mow my lawn today, then I will mow my lawn today. It is therefore necessary that I will mow my lawn — necessary in just the sense in which the past is necessary. But then it is not within my power not to mow; hence I will not mow freely.

Here is where a Boethian bystander might object as follows. Edwards's argument involves divine *fore*knowledge — God's having known at some time in the past, for example, that Paul will mow his lawn in 2005. Many theists, however, hold that God is *eternal*[5] and that his eternity involves at least the following two properties. First, his being eternal means, as Boethius suggested, that everything is *present* for him; for him there is no past or future. But then God does not know any such propositions as *Paul will mow in 2005;* what he knows, since everything is present for him, is just that Paul mows in 2005. And secondly, God's being eternal means that God is atemporal, "outside of time" — outside of time in such a way that it is an error to say of him that he knows some proposition or other *at a time*. We thus cannot properly say that God *now* knows that Paul mows in 2005, or that at some time in the past God knew this; the truth, instead, is that he knows this proposition *eternally.* But then Edwards's argument presupposes the falsehood of a widely accepted thesis about the nature of God and time.

I am inclined to believe that this thesis — the thesis that God is both atemporal and such that everything is present for him — is incoherent. If it

---

5. See E. Stump and N. Kretzmann, "Eternity," *The Journal of Philosophy* (1981): 429-58.

is coherent, however, Edwards's argument can be restated in such a way as not to presuppose its falsehood. For suppose in fact Paul will mow his lawn in 2005. Then the proposition *God (eternally) knows that Paul mows in 2005* is now true. That proposition, furthermore, was true eighty years ago; the proposition *God knows (eternally) that Paul mows in 2005* not only *is* true *now,* but *was* true *then.* Since what is past is necessary, it is now necessary that this proposition was true eighty years ago. But is logically necessary that if this proposition was true eighty years ago, then Paul mows in 2005. Hence his mowing then is necessary in just the way the past is. But, then it neither now is nor in future will be within Paul's power to refrain from mowing.

Of course this argument depends upon the claim that a proposition can be true *at a time* — eighty years ago, for example. Some philosophers argue that it does not so much as make sense to suggest that a proposition *A* is or was or will be true at a time; a proposition is true or false *simpliciter* and no more true at a time than, for example, true in a mail box or a refrigerator.[6] (Even if there is no beer in the refrigerator, the proposition *there is no beer* is not true in the refrigerator.) We need not share their scruples in order to accommodate them; the argument can be suitably modified. Concede for the moment that it makes no sense to say of a *proposition* that it was true at a time; it nonetheless makes good sense, obviously, to say of a sentence that it expressed a certain proposition at a time. But it also makes good sense to say of a sentence that it expressed a truth at a time. Now eighty years ago the sentence

(5) God knows (eternally) that Paul mows in 2005

expressed the proposition that God knows eternally that Paul mows in 2005 (and for simplicity let us suppose that this proposition was the only proposition it expressed then). But if in fact Paul will mow in 2005, then (5) also expressed a truth eighty years ago. So eighty years ago (5) expressed the proposition that Paul will mow in 2005 and expressed a truth; since what is past is now necessary, it is now necessary that eighty years ago (5) expressed that proposition and expressed a truth. But it is necessary in the broadly logical sense that if (5) then expressed that proposition (and only that proposition) and expressed a truth, then Paul will mow in 2005. It is therefore necessary that Paul will mow then; hence his mowing then is necessary in just the way the past is.

---

6. See, for example, Peter van Inwagen, *An Essay on Free Will* (Oxford: Oxford University Press, 1983), pp. 35ff.; and Nelson Pike, *God and Timelessness* (New York: Schocken Books, 1970), pp. 67ff. Pike's objection is not to temporally indexed propositions as such, but to alleged propositions of the sort *It is true at T_1 that S does A at T_2.*

Accordingly, the claim that God is outside of time is essentially irrelevant to Edwardsian arguments. In what follows I shall therefore assume, for the sake of expository simplicity, that God does indeed have foreknowledge and that it is quite proper to speak of him both as holding a belief at a time and as having held beliefs in the past. What I shall say, however, can be restated so as to accommodate those who reject this assumption.

In 1965 Nelson Pike proposed an interesting variant of Edwards's argument for theological determinism from the stability of the past. (Those not interested in a detailed anatomy of Pike's argument are invited to skip to the beginning of section II.) More exactly, what he proposed was an interesting variant of the argument for the conclusion that divine foreknowledge is incompatible with human freedom. What he argued is not that human freedom is incompatible with divine foreknowledge *simpliciter*, but that it is incompatible with the claim that God is *essentially* omniscient and has foreknowledge of human actions. To say that God has the property of being omniscient *essentially* is to say that he is indeed omniscient and furthermore could not have failed to be so. It is to say that God is omniscient and that it is not possible that he should have existed and failed to be omniscient: there is no possible world in which he exists but is not omniscient. It follows that it is impossible that God holds or has held a false belief.

To argue his case, Pike considers the case of Jones, who mowed his lawn at T_2 — last Saturday, let's say. Now suppose God is essentially omniscient. Then at an earlier time T_1 — 80 years ago, for example — God believed that Jones would mow his lawn at T_2. Furthermore, since he is essentially omniscient, it is not possible that God falsely believe something; hence his having believed at T_1 that Jones would mow at T_2 entails that Jones does indeed mow at T_2. The essential premise of the argument, as Pike puts it, goes as follows:

(vi) If God existed at T_1 and if God believed at T_1 that Jones would do X at T_2, then if it was within Jones' power at T_2 to refrain from doing X, then (1) it was within Jones' power at T_2 to do something that would have brought it about that God held a false belief at T_1, or (2) it was within Jones' power at T_2 to do something which would have brought it about that God did not hold the belief He held at T_1, or (3) it was within Jones' power at T_2 to do something that would have brought it about that any person who believed at T_1 that Jones would do X at T_2 (one of whom was, by hypothesis, God) held a false belief and thus was not God — that is, that God (who by hypothesis existed at T_1) did not exist at T_1.[7]

7. Nelson Pike, "Divine Omniscience and Voluntary Action," *The Philosophical Review*, 1965, p. 33.

Another way to put the claim Pike makes in (vi), I think, is to claim that

(6) God existed at T_1 and believed at T_1 that Jones would do X at T_2 and it was within Jones's power at T_2 to refrain from doing X

entails

(7) Either (7.1) it was within Jones's power at T_2 to do something that would have brought it about that God held a false belief at T_1, or (7.2) it was within Jones's power at T_2 to do something which would have brought it about that God did not hold the belief he held at T_1, or (7.3) it was within Jones's power at T_2 to do something that would have brought it about that God did not exist at T_1.

The rest of the argument then consists in suggesting that each of (7.1), (7.2), and (7.3) is necessarily false. If so, however, then (6) is necessarily false and divine foreknowledge is incompatible with human freedom.

Now everyone will concede, I think, that it was not possibly within Jones's power at T_2 to do something that would have brought it about that God did not exist at T_1; nor, if God is essentially omniscient, was it possibly within Jones's power at T_2 to do something that would have brought it about that God held a false belief at T_1.[8] But what about (7.2), the second disjunct of (7): Was it — could it have been — within Jones's power to do something that would have brought it about that God did not hold the belief he held at T_1? We must ask a prior question. How shall we *understand*

(7.2) It was within Jones's power at T_2 to do something that would have brought it about that God did not hold the belief he held at T_1?

If God is essentially omniscient, it is clearly necessary that if Jones had refrained from doing X at T_2, then God would not have believed at T_1 that Jones would do X at T_2. Hence (6) entails that it was within Jones's power at T_2 to do something — namely refrain from doing X — which is such that if he had done it, then God would not have held a belief that in fact he *did* hold. This suggests that Pike intends (7.2) as ascribing to Jones the power to do something that would have brought it about that God would not have held a belief that in fact he did hold. So construed, what (7.2) asserts is that God held a certain belief at T_1, and it was within Jones's power at T_2 so to act that God would not have held that belief then. Presumably, therefore, (7.2) must be understood as

---

8. Of course it does not follow that it was not within Jones's power, at T_1, so to act that a belief God *did* hold at T_1 *would have been false.* See my *God, Freedom, and Evil* (New York: Harper & Row, 1974, and Grand Rapids: William B. Eerdmans, 1977), p. 70.

(7.2*) God held a certain belief B at T_1, and at T_2 it was within Jones's power to perform an action which is such that if he had performed it, then at T_1 God would not have held B.[9]

Accordingly, (7.2) is to be read as (7.2*). Now Pike's strategy here is to claim first that (6) entails (7) and then that each of the disjuncts in (7) is necessarily false. The premise proclaiming the falsehood of (7.2) is

(iv) It is not within one's power at a given time to do something that would bring it about that someone who held a certain belief at a time prior to the time in question did not hold that belief at the time prior to the time in question.[10]

If the argument is to succeed, then of course (iv) must be construed in such a way as to contradict (7.2*) — perhaps as

(iv*) For any persons S and $S*$, if at some time in the past $S*$ held a certain belief, then it is not within the power of S to perform any action which is such that if he were to perform it, then $S*$ would not have held that belief then.

The relevant specification of (iv*) withholds from Jones, not the absurd power of bringing it about that God both did and did not hold a given belief, but the power, at T_2, to do a thing X which is such that if he *had* done it, then God would not have held a belief that as a matter of fact he did hold. But of course the question is, what do (iv*) and its specification have to recommend them? Why should we be inclined to accept them? Perhaps, Pike thinks, because the proposition *God believed at T_1 that Jones would mow at T_2* is a fact about the past relative to T_2; and it is not within anyone's power so to act that what is *in fact* a fact about the past wouldn't have been a fact about the past. That is, for any fact f about the past, it is not within anyone's power to perform an action which is such that if he were to perform it, then f would not have been a fact about the past. More likely, the claim is that there is a certain *kind* of

---

9. In principle, of course, (7.2) is subject to another reading, one in which "it is within Jones's power to do something that would have brought it about that" has wide scope, so that what is expressed could be put more explicitly as

(7.2**) It is within Jones's power at T_2 to do something that would have brought it about that the proposition *God did not hold the belief he held at T_1* would have been true.

The proposition *God did not hold the belief he held at T_1* would have been true if and only if there is a certain belief such that God held that belief at T_1 and furthermore did *not* hold that belief then. The power of (7.2**) ascribed to Jones, therefore, is the absurd power of doing something such that if he had done that thing, then God would have held a certain belief at T_1 and furthermore would *not* have held that belief then. If we read (7.2) as (7.2**), however, then it is easy to show that (6) does not entail (7), so that Pike's claim that it *does* would be false.

10. Pike, "Divine Omniscience and Voluntary Action," p. 32.

proposition about the past such that it is never within anyone's power so to act that a true proposition of *that* kind would have been false; a proposition specifying what someone believed at an earlier time, furthermore, is a proposition of just that sort. In either case Pike's argument for the incompatibility of divine foreknowledge and human freedom is rightly seen as in the company of the argument Aquinas, Ockham, Edwards, and others consider for that conclusion — the argument from the fixedness of the past.

II. Ockham's Way Out

As Edwards (and perhaps Pike) sees things, then, "in things which are past, their past existence is now necessary . . . , 'tis too late for any possibility of alteration in that respect: 'tis now impossible, that it should be otherwise than true, that that thing has existed." Nor is Edwards idiosyncratic in this intuition; we are all inclined to believe that the past, as opposed to the future, is fixed, stable, unalterable, closed. It is outside our control and outside the control even of an omnipotent being. Consider, for example, Peter Damian, often (but mistakenly) cited as holding that the power of God is limited by nothing at all, not even the laws of logic. In *De Divina Omnipotentia,* a letter to Desiderio of Cassino, Damian recalls and discusses a dinner conversation with the latter, a conversation that touched off a centuries-long discussion of the question whether it was within the power of God to restore to virginity someone who was no longer a virgin. The topic is God's power over the past:

> . . . I feel obliged to respond to an objection that many put forward. They say: "If God," as you affirm, "is omnipotent in all things, can he so act that things that are made, are not made? He can certainly destroy all things that have been made, so that they exist no more: but it is impossible to see how he can bring it about that those things which were made should never have been made at all. He can bring it about that from now and henceforth Rome should no longer exist, but how can the opinion be maintained that he can bring it about that it should never have been built of old?"[11]

Damian's response is not entirely clear. In chapter 15, which is substantially his concluding chapter, he suggests that "it is much the same thing to ask 'How can God bring it about that what once happened did not happen?' or 'Can God act in such a way that what he made, he did not make?' as to

11. Peter Damian, *De Divina Omnipotentia,* chapter IV. In Migne's *Patrologia Latina,* vol. 145, 599. The translation of the last two sentences is from Anthony Kenny's *The God of the Philosophers* (Oxford: Clarendon, 1979), p. 101.

assert that what God has made, God did not make."[12] (Damian takes a relatively strong line with respect to this last; anyone who asserts it, he says, is contemptible, not worthy of a reply, and should instead be branded.) Here it isn't clear whether he is holding that the proposition *what has happened is such that God can bring it about that it has not happened* is equivalent to the proposition *God can bring it about that what has happened hasn't happened* and is thus false, or whether he simply fails to distinguish these propositions. He goes on to make heavy weather over the relation of God's eternity to the question under discussion, apparently holding that "relative to God and his unchangeable eternity," it is correct to say that God *can* bring it about that Rome was never founded; "relative to *us*," on the other hand, the right thing to say is that God *could have* brought it about that Rome was never founded.[13]

Damian's views on the matter are not altogether clear; what *is* clear is that he, like the rest of us, saw an important asymmetry between past and future. This asymmetry consists in part in the fact that the past is outside our control in a way in which the future is not. Although I now have the power to raise my arm, I do not have the power to bring it about that I raised my arm five minutes ago. Although it is now within my power to think about Vienna, it is not now within my power to bring it about that five minutes ago I was thinking about Vienna. The past is fixed in a way in which the future is open. It is within my power to help determine how the future shall be; it is too late to do the same with respect to the past.

Edwards, indeed, speaks in this connection of the *unalterability* of the past; and it is surely natural to do so. Strictly speaking, however, it is not alterability that is here relevant; for the future is no more alterable than the past. What after all, would it be to alter the past? To bring it about, obviously, that a temporally indexed proposition which is true and about the past before I act, is false thereafter. On January 1, 1982, I was not visiting New Guinea. For me to change the past with respect to that fact would be for me to perform an action *A* such that prior to my performing the action, it is true that on January 1, 1982, I was not in New Guinea, but after I perform the action, false that I was not in New Guinea then. But of course I can't do anything like that, and neither can God, despite his omnipotence.

But neither can we alter the future. We can imagine someone saying, "Paul will in fact walk out the door at 9:21 A.M.; hence *Paul will walk out at 9:21 A.M.* is true; but Paul has the power to refrain from walking out then; so Paul has the power to alter the future." But the conclusion displays confusion;

---

12. Peter Damian, *De Divina Omnipotentia*, p. 618. The translation is by Owen J. Blum and is taken from John Wippel and Alan Wolter, *Medieval Philosophy* (New York: The Free Press, 1969), p. 147.

13. Peter Damian, *De Divina Omnipotentia*, p. 619.

Paul's not walking out then, were it to occur, would effect no alteration at all in the future. To alter the future, Paul must do something like this: he must perform some action A at a time t before 9:21 such that prior to t it is true that Paul will walk out at 9:21, but after t (after he performs A) false that he will. Neither Paul nor anyone — not even God — can do something like that. So the future is no more alterable than the past.

The interesting asymmetry between past and future, therefore, does not consist in the fact that the past is unalterable in a way in which the future is not; nonetheless this asymmetry remains. Now, before 9:21, it is within Paul's power to make it false that he walks out at 9:21; after he walks out at 9:21 he will no longer have that power. In the same way, in 1995 B.C. God could have brought it about that Abraham did not exist in 1995 B.C.; now that is no longer within his power. As Edwards says, it's too late for that.

Recognizing this asymmetry, Ockham, like several other medieval philosophers, held that the past is indeed in some sense necessary: it is *necessary per accidens:*

> I claim that every necessary proposition is *per se* in either the first mode or the second mode. This is obvious, since I am talking about all propositions that are necessary *simpliciter.* I add this because of propositions that are necessary *per accidens,* as is the case with many past tense propositions. They are necessary *per accidens,* because it was contingent that they be necessary, and because they were not always necessary.[14]

Here Ockham directs our attention to propositions about the past: past tense propositions together with temporally indexed propositions, such as

(8) *Columbus sails the ocean blue* is true in 1492[15]

whose index is prior to the present time. Such propositions, he says, are accidentally necessary if true; they are *accidentally* necessary because they *become* necessary. Past tense propositions become necessary when they become true; temporally indexed propositions such as (8), on the other hand, do not become true — (8) was always true — but they become necessary, being necessary after but not before the date of their index. And once a proposition acquires this status, says Ockham, not even God has the power to make it false.

---

14. William of Ockham, *Ordinatio,* I, Prologue, q.6.

15. I take it that (8) is equivalent to

(8*) *Columbus sails the ocean blue* is, was, or will be true in 1492;

I am here ignoring allegedly tenseless propositions, if indeed there are any such things.

In *Predestination, God's Foreknowledge and Future Contingents,* Ockham goes on to make an interesting distinction:

> Some propositions are about the present as regards both their wording and their subject matter *(secundum vocem et secundum rem).* Where such propositions are concerned, it is universally true that every true proposition about the present has (corresponding to it) a necessary one about the past: — e.g., 'Socrates is seated,' 'Socrates is walking,' 'Socrates is just,' and the like.
>
> Other propositions are about the present as regards their wording only and are equivalently about the future, since their truth depends on the truth of propositions about the future. Where such (propositions) are concerned, the rule that every true proposition about the present has corresponding to it a necessary proposition about the past is not true.[16]

Ockham means to draw the following contrast. Some propositions about the present "are about the present as regards both their wording and their subject matter"; for example,

(9) Paul is seated.

Such propositions, we may say, are *strictly* about the present; and if such a proposition is now true, then a corresponding proposition about the past

(10) Paul was seated

will be accidentally necessary from now on. Other propositions about the present, however, "are about the present as regards their wording only and are equivalently about the future"; for example,

(11) Paul correctly believes that the sun will rise on January 1, 2010.

Such a proposition is "equivalently about the future," and it is not the case that if it is true, then the corresponding proposition about the past

(12) Paul correctly believed that the sun will rise on January 1, 2010

in this case — will be accidentally necessary from now on. (Of course we hope that (12) will be accidentally necessary after January 1, 2010.)

What Ockham says about the present, he would say about the past. Just as some propositions about the present are "about the present as regards their wording only and are equivalently about the future," so some propositions about the past are about the past as regards their wording only and are equivalently about the future; (12) for example, or

---

16. William of Ockham, *Predestination, God's Foreknowledge, and Future Contingents,* tr. with Introduction, Notes, and Appendices by Marilyn Adams and Norman Kretzmann (Ithaca: Cornell University Press, 1969), pp. 46-47.

(13) Eighty years ago, the proposition *Paul will mow his lawn* in 2005 was true

or (to appease those who object to the idea that a proposition can be true at a time)

(14) Eighty years ago, the sentence "Paul will mow his lawn in 2005" expressed the proposition *Paul will mow his lawn in 2005* and expressed a truth.

These propositions are about the past, but they are also equivalently about the future. Furthermore, they are not necessary *per accidens* — not yet, at any rate. We might say that a true proposition like (12)-(14) is a *soft* fact about the past, whereas one like

(15) Paul mowed in 1981

— one *strictly* about the past — is a *hard* fact about the past.[17]

Now of course the notion of aboutness, as Nelson Goodman has reminded us,[18] is at best a frail reed; *a fortiori,* then, the same goes for the notion of being *strictly* about. But we do have *something* of a grasp of this notion, hesitant and infirm though perhaps it is. It may be difficult or even impossible to give a useful criterion for the distinction between hard and soft facts about the past, but we do have *some* grasp of it, and can apply it in many cases. The idea of a hard fact about the past contains two important elements: *genuineness* and *strictness*. In the first place, a hard fact about the past is a genuine fact about the past. This cannot be said, perhaps, for (13). It is at least arguable that if (13) is a fact about the past at all, it is an *ersatz* fact about the past; it tells us nothing about the past except in a Pickwickian, Cantabridgian sort of way. What it really tells us is something about the future: that Paul will mow in 2005. (12) and (14), on the other hand, do genuinely tell us something about the past: (12) tells us that Paul believed something and (14) that a certain sentence expressed a certain proposition. But (12) and (14) aren't *strictly* about the past; they also tell us something about what will happen in 2005. It may be difficult to give criteria, or (informative) necessary and sufficient conditions for either genuineness or strictness; nevertheless we do have at least a partial grasp of these notions.

Accordingly, let us provisionally join Ockham in holding that there is a viable distinction between hard and soft facts about the past. The importance of this distinction, for Ockham, is that it provides him with a way of disarming

17. See Nelson Pike, "Of God and Freedom: A Rejoinder," *The Philosophical Review,* 1966, p. 370, and Marilyn Adams, "Is the Existence of God a 'Hard' Fact?" *The Philosophical Review,* 1966, pp. 493-94.

18. Nelson Goodman, "About," *Mind* (1962).

the arguments for logical and theological determinism from the necessity of the past. Each of those arguments, when made explicit, has as a premise

(16) If p is about the past, then p is necessary

or something similar. Ockham's response is to deny (16); *hard* facts about the past are indeed accidentally necessary, but the same cannot be said for soft facts. Such propositions as (13) and (14) are not hard facts about the past; each entails that Paul will mow his lawn in 2005, and is therefore, as Ockham says, "equivalently about the future." Not all facts about the past, then, are hard facts about the past; and only the hard facts are plausibly thought to be accidentally necessary. (16), therefore, the general claim that all facts about the past are accidentally necessary, is seen to be false — or at any rate there seems to be no reason at all to believe it. And thus dissolves any argument for theological determinism which, like Edwards's, accepts (16) in its full generality.

I believe Ockham is correct here; furthermore, there is no easy way to refurbish Edwards's argument. Given Ockham's distinction between hard and soft facts, what Edwards's argument needs is the premise that such propositions as

(17) God knew eighty years ago that Paul will mow in 2005

are hard facts about the past. Clearly, however, (17) is not a hard fact about the past; for (like (13) and (14)), it entails

(18) Paul will mow his lawn in 2005;

and no proposition that entails (18) is a hard fact about the past.

Let me be entirely clear here; I say that none of (13), (14), and (17) is a hard fact about the past, because each entails (18). In so saying, however, I am not endorsing a *criterion* for hard facthood; in particular I am not adopting an "entailment" criterion, according to which a fact about the past is a hard fact about the past if and only if it entails no proposition about the future. No doubt *every* proposition about the past, hard fact or not, entails *some* proposition about the future; *Socrates was wise,* for example, entails *It will be true from now on that Socrates was wise;* and *Paul played tennis yesterday* entails *Paul will not play tennis for the first time tomorrow.* What I *am* saying is this: No proposition that entails (18) is a hard fact about the past, because no such proposition is *strictly* about the past. We may not be able to give a criterion for being strictly about the past; but we do have at least a rough and intuitive grasp of this notion. Given our intuitive grasp of this notion, I think we can see two things. First, no conjunctive proposition that contains (18) as a conjunct is (now, in 1986) strictly about the past. Thus *Paul will mow his lawn in 2005 and Socrates was wise,* while indeed a proposition about the past, is not *strictly* about the past. And second, hard facthood is closed under logical equivalence: any proposition equivalent (in the broadly logical sense) to a proposition strictly about the past is itself strictly about the past.[19] But any proposition that entails (18) is equivalent, in the broadly logical sense, to a conjunctive proposition one conjunct of which is (18); hence each such proposition is equivalent to a proposition that is not a hard fact about the past and is therefore itself not a hard fact about the past. Thus the Edwardsian argument fails.

Similar comments apply to Pike's argument (above, pp. 264ff.) for the incompatibility of essential divine omniscience with human freedom. Pike puts his argument in terms, not of God's fore*knowledge*, but, so to speak, of God's fore*belief;* and the essential premise of the argument, as you recall, is

(iv*) For any persons S and S^*, if at some time in the past S^* held a certain belief, then it is not within the power of S to perform an action such that if he were to perform it, then S^* would not have held that belief then.

His essential insights, I think, are two: first, it seems natural to think of propositions of the sort *eighty years ago, S believed p* as hard facts about the past (and thus as plausible candidates for accidental necessity); and secondly, if God is essentially omniscient, then such a proposition as *God believed eighty years ago that p* entails *p.* (To these insights he adds the idea, not in my view an insight, that it is not within anyone's power to perform an action which is such that if he were to perform it, then what is *in fact* a hard fact about the past wouldn't have been a fact at all.)

Unfortunately, the second of these insights is incompatible with the first. If God is essentially omniscient, then

(19) Eighty years ago, God believed the proposition that Paul will mow his lawn in 2005

entails that Paul will mow in 2005. By the above argument, then, (19) is not strictly about the past and is therefore not a hard fact about the past. But then we no longer have any reason to accept (iv*). Perhaps it is plausible to accept (iv*) for S^* stipulated not to be essentially omniscient, or stipulated to be such that propositions of the sort S^* *believed that p* are hard facts about the past.[20] But given the possibility of essential divine omniscience, (iv*) in

---

19. I think it is clear that hard facthood *is* closed under broadly logical equivalence; this argument, however, does not require the full generality of that premise. All it requires is that no proposition strictly about the past is equivalent in the broadly logical sense to a conjunction one conjunct of which, like (18), is a contingent proposition paradigmatically about the future.

20. Even so restricted, (iv*) is by no means obviously true: couldn't I know my wife or child so well that, while I correctly believe that she will do A, it is within her power to do B instead; and if she were to do B, then I would have believed that she will do B? It isn't easy to see why not.

its full generality has nothing whatever to recommend it; for if God is essentially omniscient, then such propositions as (19) are not hard facts about the past.

We can see the same point from a slightly different perspective. Pike is assuming, for purposes of argument, that God is essentially omniscient. Suppose we add, as classical theism also affirms, that God is a necessary being. What follows is that God both exists and is omniscient in every possible world; hence in every possible world God believes every true proposition and believes no false propositions. But then *truth* and *being believed by God* are equivalent in the broadly logical sense; it is then necessary that for any proposition p, p is true if and only if God believes p. It follows that

(20) Eighty years ago, God believed that Paul will mow in 2005

is equivalent in the broadly logical sense to

(21) Eighty years ago, it was true that Paul will mow in 2005.

Here again we can accommodate our colleagues ("atemporalists," as we may call them) who do not believe that propositions can be true at times; for (20), given the plausible (but widely disputed) assumption that necessarily, for any time t there is a time t^* eighty years prior to t, is also equivalent to

(22) Paul will mow in 2005.

Even without the "plausible assumption," (20) is equivalent to

(23) There is (i.e., is, was, or will be) such a time as eighty years ago, and Paul will mow in 2005.

Clearly enough none of (21), (22), and (23) is a hard fact about the past; but (20) is equivalent in the broadly logical sense to at least one of them; hence (20) is not a hard fact about the past. Furthermore, (20) is inconsistent with Paul's being free to mow in 2005 only if (23) is; and no one, presumably, except for the most obdurate logical fatalist, will hold that (23) is incompatible with Paul's being free to mow in 2005.[21] So if, as traditional theism affirms, God is both a necessary being and essentially omniscient, then theological determinism is logically equivalent to logical determinism; divine foreknowledge is incompatible with human freedom only if the latter is inconsistent with the existence of true propositions detailing future free actions.

---

21. More exactly, anyone who thinks *both* that such propositions as (23) are either true or false *and* that (23) is incompatible with Paul's being free to mow in 2005, will be a logical fatalist.

Ironically enough, from Ockham's perspective it is the suggestion that God is omniscient but not *essentially* omniscient that is plausibly thought to create a problem. Return, once more, to

(20) Eighty years ago, God believed that Paul will mow in 2005.

If God is not essentially omniscient, then (20) does not entail that Paul will mow in 2005; at any rate we no longer have any reason to suppose that it does. But then we are deprived of our only reason for denying that (20) is strictly about the past. From an Ockhamist perspective, it follows that (20) is accidentally necessary. But an Ockhamist would also certainly hold that even if God is not *essentially* omniscient, nevertheless his omniscience is counter-factually independent of Paul's actions; that is to say, there isn't anything Paul can do such that if he were to do it then God would not have been or would no longer be omniscient. If Paul were to refrain from mowing his lawn in 2005, therefore, God would not have believed, eighty years ago, that Paul will mow then. But Ockham also thinks it is or will be within Paul's power to refrain from mowing then. From Ockham's point of view, then, the facts are these: if God is not essentially omniscient, then there is an accidentally necessary proposition P — (20) as it happens — and an action Paul can perform, such that if he were to perform it, then P would have been false. Ockham is not very explicit about accidental necessity; nevertheless he would have held, I think, that it is not within anyone's power to perform an action which is such that if he were to perform it, then a proposition which is in fact accidentally necessary would have been false. From Ockham's point of view, therefore, divine foreknowledge threatens human freedom only if God is not essentially omniscient.

What I have argued, then, is that Ockham's way out gives us the means of seeing that neither Edwards's nor Pike's argument is successful. Edwards's argument fails because, essentially, God's having *known* a certain proposition is not, in general, a hard fact about the past; but only hard facts about the past are plausibly thought to be accidentally necessary. Pike's argument fails for similar reasons: if God is essentially omniscient, then the facts about what God *believed* are not, in general, hard facts about the past; but then there is no reason to suppose that none of us can act in such a way that God would not have believed what in fact he does believe. In sections III and IV, therefore, I shall assume, with Ockham, that divine foreknowledge and human freedom are not incompatible.

III. On Ockham's Way Out

As we have seen, Ockham responds to the arguments for theological determinism by distinguishing hard facts from the past — facts that are genuinely and strictly about the past — from soft facts about the past; only the former, he says, are necessary *per accidens*. This response is intuitively plausible. It is extremely difficult, however, to say precisely what it is for a proposition to be strictly about the past, and equally difficult to say what it is for a proposition to be accidentally necessary. According to Ockham, a proposition is not strictly about the past if its "truth depends on the truth of propositions about the future" (above, p. 270). This suggests that if a proposition about the past *entails* one about the future, then it isn't strictly about the past; we might therefore think that a proposition is strictly about the past if and only if it does not entail a proposition about the future. We might then concur with Ockham in holding that a proposition about the past is accidentally necessary if it is true and *strictly* about the past. But as John Fischer points out, difficulties immediately rear their ugly heads.[22] I shall mention only two. In the first place, suppose we take 'about the future' in a way that mirrors the way we took 'about the past'; a proposition is then about the future if and only if it is either a future-tense proposition or a temporally indexed proposition whose index is a date later than the present. Then obviously any proposition about the past will entail one about the future;

> (24) Abraham existed a long time ago

and

> (25) Abraham exists in 1995 B.C.

entail, respectively,

> (26) It will be the case from now on that Abraham existed a long time ago

and

> (27) It will always be true that Abraham exists in 1995 B.C.

But then the distinction between propositions strictly about the past and propositions about the past *simpliciter* becomes nugatory.

Perhaps you will reply that propositions like (26) and (27) are at best *ersatz* propositions about the future, despite their future tense or future index; on a less wooden characterization of 'about the future' they wouldn't turn out to be about the future. Perhaps so; I won't here dispute the point. But other and less tractable difficulties remain. First, (24) and (25) both entail that Abraham will not begin

---

22. John Fischer, "Freedom and Foreknowledge," *The Philosophical Review,* 1983, pp. 73-75.

to exist (i.e., exist for the first time) in 2005 (Fischer, p. 75); and that isn't, or isn't obviously, an *ersatz* fact about the future. Second, on that more adequate characterization, whatever exactly it might be, it will no doubt be true that

> (28) It was true eighty years ago either that God knew that Friesland will rule the world in 2010 A.D. or that Paul believed that Friesland will rule the world in 2010 A.D.[23]

entails no non-*ersatz* future propositions and is thus strictly about the past. Now suppose, *per impossible,* that Friesland will indeed rule the world in 2010 A.D. Then (28) (given divine omniscience) will be true by virtue of the truth of the first disjunct; the second disjunct, however, is false (by virtue of Paul's youth). And then on the above account (28) is accidentally necessary; but is it really? Isn't it still within someone's power — God's let's say — to act in such a way that (28) would have been false (Fischer, p. 74)?

Necessary *per accidens* and *being strictly about the past* thus present difficulties when taken in tandem in the way Ockham takes them. The former, furthermore, is baffling and perplexing in its own right; and this is really the fundamental problem here. If, as its proponents claim, accidental necessity isn't any sort of logical or metaphysical or causal necessity, what sort of necessity is it? How shall we understand it? Ockham, Edwards, and their colleagues don't tell us. Furthermore, even if they (or we) had a plausible account of *being strictly about the past,* we couldn't sensibly *define* accidental necessity in terms of being strictly about the past; for the whole point of the argument for theological determinism is just that propositions about the future that are entailed by accidentally necessary propositions about the past will themselves be accidentally necessary. So how shall we understand accidental necessity?

Perhaps we can make some progress as follows. In explaining accidental necessity, one adverts to facts about the power of agents — such facts, for example, as that not even God can now bring it about that Abraham did not exist; it's too late for that. Furthermore, in the arguments for logical and theological determinism, acccidental necessity functions as a sort of middle term. It is alleged that a proposition of some sort or another is about or strictly about the past; but then, so the claim goes, that proposition is accidentally necessary — in which case, according to the argument, it is not now within the power of any agent, not even God, to bring it about that it is false. Why not eliminate the middle man and *define* accidental necessity in terms of the powers of agents? If a proposition p is accidentally necessary, then it is not possible — possible in the broadly logical sense — that there be an agent who has it within his power to bring it about that p is false; why not then define accidental necessity as follows:

---

23. I leave it to the reader to restate (28) in such a way as to accommodate those who hold that propositions are not true at times.

(29) p is accidentally necessary at t if and only if p is true at t and it is not possible both that p is true at t and that there is a being that at t or later has the power to bring it about that p is false?[24]

But how shall we understand this "has the power to bring it about that p is false"? Pike speaks in this connection of "it's being within Jones' power to do something that would have brought it about that" p, and Fischer of "being able so to act that p would have been false." This suggests

(30) S has the power to bring it about that p is false if and only if there is an action it is within S's power to perform such that if he were to perform it, p would have been false.

(30) is perhaps inadequate as a *general* account of what it is to have the power to bring it about that a proposition is false. For one thing, it seems to imply that I have the power with respect to necessarily false propositions (as well as other false propositions whose falsehood is counterfactually independent of my actions) to bring it about that they are false; and this is at best dubious. But here we aren't interested, first of all, in giving an independent account of having the power to bring it about that p is false; even if (30) isn't a satisfactory general account of that notion, it may serve acceptably in (29). Incorporating (30), therefore, (29) becomes

(31) p is accidentally necessary at t if and only if p is true at t and it is not possible both that p is true at t and that there exists an agent S and an action A such that (1) S has the power at t or later to perform A, and (2) if S were to perform A at t or later, then p would have been false.[25]

24. The appropriate atemporalist counterpart of (29) is

(29*) p is accidentally necessary if and only if p is true and it is not possible both that p is true and that there is or will be a being that has or will have the power to bring it about that p is false

of which (29) is a generalization. (31), (39), (42), and (44) below have similar counterparts.

25. (31) can be expressed a bit more precisely (if a bit less felicitously) as

(31) p is accidentally necessary at t if and only if p is true at t and it is not possible both that p is true at t and that there exists a time t^*, an agent S and an action A such that t^* is at least as late as t, at t^* S has the power to perform A, and if S were to perform A at t^*, then p would have been false.

The atemporalist counterpart of (31) is

(31*) p is accidentally necessary if and only if p is true and it is not possible both that p is true and that there exists or will exist an action A such that (1) S has or will have the power to perform A, and (2) if S were to perform A, then p would have been false.

Note that on (31) propositions that are necessary in the broadly logical sense turn out to be accidentally necessary. If this is considered a defect, it can be remedied by adding an appropriate condition to the *definiens*. Similar comments apply to (39), (42), and (44) below.

Now so far as I know, Ockham gave no explicit account or explanation of accidental necessity; nevertheless it is not implausible to see him as embracing something like (31). On this definition, furthermore (given common sense assumptions), many soft facts about the past will not be accidentally necessary: for example

(32) Eighty years ago it was true that Paul would not mow his lawn in 2005.

Even if true, (32) is not accidentally necessary: it is clearly possible that Paul will have the power, in 2005, to mow his lawn; but if he were to do so, then (32) would have been false. The same goes for

(33) God believed eighty years ago that Paul would mow his lawn in 2005

if God is essentially omniscient; for then it is a necessary truth that if Paul were to refrain from mowing his lawn during 2005, God would not have believed, eighty years ago, that he would mow then. (32) and (33), therefore, are not accidentally necessary.

Since (32) and (33) are not hard facts about the past, Ockham would have welcomed this consequence. But our account of accidental necessity has other consequences — consequences Ockham might have found less to his liking. Let's suppose that a colony of carpenter ants moved into Paul's yard last Saturday. Since this colony hasn't yet had a chance to get properly established, its new home is still a bit fragile. In particular, if the ants were to remain and Paul were to mow his lawn this afternoon, the colony would be destroyed. Although nothing remarkable about these ants is visible to the naked eye, God, for reasons of his own, intends that they be preserved. Now as a matter of fact, Paul will not mow his lawn this afternoon. God, who is essentially omniscient, knew in advance, of course, that Paul will not mow his lawn this afternoon; but if he had foreknown instead that Paul *would* mow this afternoon, then he would have prevented the ants from moving in. The facts of the matter, therefore, are these: if Paul would mow this afternoon, then God would have prevented the ants from moving in. So if Paul were to mow his lawn this afternoon, the ants would not have moved in last Saturday. But it is within Paul's power to mow this afternoon. There is therefore an action he can perform such that if he were to perform it, then the proposition

(34) That colony of carpenter ants moved into Paul's yard last Saturday

would have been false. But what I have called "the facts of the matter" certainly seem to be possible; it is therefore possible that there be an agent who has the power to perform an action which is such that if he were to perform it, then (34) would have been false — in which case it is not accidentally necessary. But (34), obviously enough, is strictly about the past; insofar as we have any grasp at all of this notion, (34) is about as good a candidate for being an exemplification of it as any we can easily think of. So, contrary to what Ockham supposed, not all true propositions strictly about the past — not all hard facts — are accidentally necessary — not, at any rate, in the sense of (31).

Another example: a few years ago Robert Nozick called our attention to *Newcomb's Paradox*. You are confronted with two opaque boxes, box A and box B. You know that box B contains $1,000 and that box A contains either $1,000,000 or nothing at all. You can choose to take both boxes or to take just box A; no other action is possible. You know, furthermore, that the money was put there eight years ago by an extremely knowledgeable agent according to the following plan: if she believed that you would take both boxes, she put $1,000 in box B and nothing in box A; if, on the other hand, she believed that you would exercise a decent restraint and take only box A, she put $1,000 in box B and $1,000,000 in box A. You know, finally, that this being has an amazing track record. Many other people have been in just your situation and in at least a vast majority of such cases, if the person in question took both boxes, he found box A empty; but if he took just box A, he found it to contain $1,000,000. Your problem is: given your depleted coffers and acquisitive nature, what should you do? Should you take both boxes, or just box A? And the puzzle is that there seem to be strong arguments on both sides. First, there seems good reason to take just box A. For if you were to take just box A, then the being in question would have known that you'd take just box A, in which case she would have put $1,000,000 in it. So if you were to take just box A, you'd get $1,000,000. If you were to take both boxes, on the other hand, then the being in question would have known that you would take both, in which case she would have put nothing in box A and $1,000 in box B. If you were to take both boxes, therefore, you would get $1,000. So if you were to take just box A you'd get $1,000,000 and if you were to take both boxes you'd get $1,000. Obviously, then, you ought to take just box A.

But there seems an equally plausible argument on the other side. For the money in the boxes has been there for a long time — eighty years, let's say. So if in fact there is $1,001,000 in those boxes, then there is nothing you can do now to alter that fact. So if there is $1,001,000 there, then if you were to take both boxes, you'd get $1,001,000. On the other hand, if there is $1,001,000 there, then if you were to take just box A, you'd get only $1,000,000, thus missing out on the extra $1,000. So if there is $1,001,000 there, you would get more if you took both boxes than if you took only one. But a similar argument shows that the same holds if there is just $1,000 there; in that case you'd get $1,000 if you took both boxes but nothing at all if you took just box A. The only prudent course, then, is to take both boxes.

Now the fact is, as I think, that neither of these arguments is conclusive; each takes as a premise a proposition not obviously true and not entailed by the puzzle conditions. Thus the two boxer appears to argue that if there is $1,001,000 there, then it follows that if you were to take both boxes, there (still) would have been $1,001,000 there. But of course that doesn't follow; the argument form *A: therefore, if P were true A would be true* is invalid. Or perhaps he argues that since it is true that if there were $1,001,000 there and you were to take both boxes, you'd get $1,001,000, it follows that if there were $1,001,000 there, then if you were to take both boxes, you would get $1,001,000. But that doesn't follow either; exportation doesn't hold for counterfactuals. The one boxer, I think, has a better time of it. He does claim, however, that if you were to take both boxes, then the being in question would have known that you'd take both boxes; but of course this isn't entailed by the puzzle conditions. The best we can say is that it is *probable,* relative to the puzzle conditions, that if you were to take both, then she would have known that you would take both. This is the best we can say, but can we say even as much as that? How does one determine the probability of such a counterfactual on the basis of such evidence as the puzzle conditions provide?

But suppose we strengthen the puzzle conditions. Suppose it isn't just some knowledgeable being with a splendid track record that puts the money in the boxes, but God. Suppose furthermore, that God is omniscient; and add one of the following further conditions (in order of decreasing strength): God is *essentially* omniscient; God is omniscient in every world in which you exist; God is omniscient both in the worlds in which you take just box A and the worlds in which you take both; God's being omniscient is counterfactually independent of your decision, so that God would have been omniscient if you were to take box A and would have been omniscient if you were to take both boxes. Add also that the other puzzle conditions are counterfactually independent of your actions. Then there is a knock-down drag-out argument for taking just box A (and no decent argument at all for taking both). For then both

(35) If you were to take both boxes, then God would have believed that you would take both boxes

and

(36) If you were to take both boxes and God had believed that you would take both boxes, then God would have put nothing in box A

follow from the puzzle conditions; from (35) and (36) it follows by counterfactual logic that

(37) If you were to take both boxes, then God would have put nothing in box A;

and from (37) (together with the puzzle conditions) it follows that if you were to take both boxes, then you'd get only $1,000. But a precisely similar argument shows that if you were to take just box A, you'd get $1,000,000. So if you were to take just box A, you would get a lot more money than you would if you were to take both. This argument will be resisted only by those whose intellects are clouded by unseemly greed.

But something further follows. The puzzle conditions, thus strengthened, seem possible. But they entail that there is a true proposition p strictly about the past and an action you can perform such that if you were to perform it, then p would have been false. For suppose in fact that you will take both boxes, so that in fact

(38) There was only $1,000 there eighty years ago

is true. According to the puzzle conditions, it is within your power to take just box A; but they also entail that if you were to take just box A, then (38) would have been false. (38), however, is strictly about the past; hence there is a proposition strictly about the past that is not necessary *per accidens*.

So here are a couple of propositions — (34) and (38) — that are hard facts about the past, but are not accidentally necessary. Of course there will be many more. It is possible (though no doubt unlikely) that there is something you can do such that if you were to do it, then Abraham would never have existed. For perhaps you will be confronted with a decision of great importance — so important that one of the alternatives is such that if you were to choose *it,* then the course of human history would have been quite different from what in fact it is. Furthermore, it is possible that if God had foreseen that you would choose *that* alternative, he would have acted very differently. Perhaps he would have created different persons; perhaps, indeed, he would not have created Abraham. So it is possible that there is an action such that it is within your power to perform it and such that if you were to perform it, then God would not have created Abraham. But if indeed that *is* possible, then not even the proposition *Abraham once existed* is accidentally necessary in the sense of (31). By the same sort of reasoning we can see that it is possible (though no doubt monumentally unlikely) that there is something you can do such that if you were to do it, then the Peloponnesian War would never have occurred.

It follows, then, that even such hard facts about the past as that Abraham once existed and that there was once a war between the Spartans and Athenians are not accidentally necessary in the sense of (31). Indeed, it is not easy to think of *any* contingent facts about the past that are accidentally necessary in that sense. Of course there are limits to the sorts of propositions such that it is possibly within my power so to act that they would have been false. It is not possible, for example, that there be an action I can perform such that if I were to do so, then I would never have existed.[26] But even if it is necessarily not within *my* power so to act that I would not have existed, the same does not go for *you;* perhaps there is an action you can take which is such that if you were to take it, then I would not have existed. (I should therefore like to ask you to tread softly.) Neither of us (nor anyone else) could have the power so to act that there should never have been any (contingently existing) agents; clearly it is not possible that there be an action A some (contingently existing) person could perform such that if he were to do so, then there would never have been any contingent agents. So the proposition *there have been* (contingent) *agents* is accidentally necessary; but it is hard indeed to find any stronger propositions that are both logically and accidentally necessary.

IV. Power over the Past

The notion of accidental necessity explained as in (31) is, I think, a relevant notion for the discussion of the arguments for theological determinism from the necessity of the past; for the question at issue is often, indeed ordinarily, put as the question which propositions about the past are such that their truth entails that it is not within anyone's power so to act that they would have been false. Accidental necessity as thus explained, however, does little to illumine our deep intuitive beliefs about the asymmetry of past and future — the fact that the future is within our control in a way in which the past is not; for far too few propositions turn out to be accidentally necessary.[27] What is the root of these beliefs and what is the relevant asymmetry between past and future; is it just that the scope of our power with respect to the past is vastly more limited than that of our power with respect to the future? That is, is it just that there are far fewer propositions about

---

26. Every action is necessarily such that if I were to perform it, I would have existed; so if there were such an action, it would be such that if I were to perform it, then I would both have existed and not existed.

27. We might be inclined to broaden (31) as follows:

(31*) p is accidentally necessary at t if and only if p is true at t and there is no action A and person S such that if S were to perform A, then p would have been false.

(31*) is indeed broader than (31). First, it is clearly necessary that any proposition satisfying the *definiens* of (31) also satisfies the *definiens* of (31*). Second, it seems possible that there be a true proposition p such that, while indeed it is *possible* that there be a person S and an action A such that S can perform A and such that if S were to perform A, then p would have been true, as a matter of fact there is no such person and action. It is therefore possible that there be a proposition that is accidentally necessary in the sense of (31*) but not in the sense of (31). The problem with (31*), however, is a close relative of the problem with (31); under (31*) there will be far too few (contingent) propositions such that *we have any reason to think* them accidentally necessary.

the past than about the future which are such that I can so act that they would have been false? I doubt that this is an important part of the story, simply because we really know very little about how far our power with respect to either past or future extends. With few exceptions, I do not know which true propositions about the past are such that I can so act that they would have been false; and the same goes for true propositions about the future.

So suppose we look in a different direction. Possibly there is something I can do such that if I were to do it, then Abraham would not have existed; but it is not possible — is it? — that I now *cause* Abraham not to have existed. While it may be within Paul's power so to act that the colony of ants would not have moved in last Saturday, surely it isn't within his power now — or for that matter within God's power now — to *cause* it to be true that the colony didn't move in. Perhaps we should revise our definition of accidental necessity to say that a proposition is (now) accidentally necessary if it is true and also such that it entails that it is not (now) within anyone's power (not even God's) to cause it to be false. And perhaps we could then see the relevant asymmetry between past and future as the fact that true propositions strictly about the past — unlike their counterparts about the future — are accidentally necessary in this new sense.

The right answer, I suspect, lies in this direction; but the suggestion involves a number of profound perplexities — about agent causation, the analysis of causation, whether backwards causation is possible, the relation between causation and counterfactuals — that I cannot explore here. Let us instead briefly explore a related suggestion. In our first sense of accidental necessity, a proposition p is accidentally necessary if and only if p is true and such that it is not possible that p be true and there be an agent and an action such that (1) the agent is now or will in the future be able to perform the action and (2) if he were to do so, p would have been false. Then such propositions as *Abraham existed in 1995 B.C.* turn out not to be accidentally necessary because of the possibility of divine foreknowledge and, so to speak, divine fore-cooperation. Perhaps if I were to do A, then God would have foreseen that I would do A and would not have created Abraham. My doing A, however, isn't by *itself* sufficient for Abraham's not existing; it requires God's previous cooperation. So suppose we strengthen the counterfactual involved in the above definition; suppose we say

> (39) p is accidentally necessary at t if and only if p is true at t and it is not possible both that p is true at t and that there exists an action A and an agent S such that (1) S has the power at t or later to perform A, and (2) *necessarily* if S were to perform A at t or later, then p would have been false.

While it may be within Paul's power to do something — namely, mow his lawn — such that if he were to do so, then that colony of ants would not have moved in, his performing that action does not *entail* the falsehood of the proposition that the ants did move in; and it looks as if there is nothing he or anyone can do that does entail its falsehood.

Permit me a couple of comments on this definition. First, although it involves the idea of a proposition's being true at a time, it is easily revised (as are (42) and (44) below) so as to accommodate our atemporalist friends. Second, I am thinking of the notion of an *agent,* as it enters into the definition, broadly, in such a way as to include agents of all sorts; in particular it is to include God. Third, propositions that are necessary in the broadly logical sense turn out to be accidentally necessary (see footnote 25). Fourth, accidental necessity thus characterized is closed under entailment but not under conjunction; see Appendix, below, pp. 288-92. Fifth, many contingent propositions about the past turn out to be accidentally necessary, but so do some contingent propositions about the future. And finally, Ockham's claim that necessity *per accidens* is connected with what is strictly about the past seems to be vindicated on (39); barring a couple of complications (see below, pp. 285-87), it looks as if a logically contingent proposition about the past is accidentally necessary in the sense of (39) if and only if it is true and strictly about the past. So, for example,

(40) Eighty years ago, the sentence "Paul will mow his lawn in 2005" expressed the proposition *Paul will mow his lawn in 2005* and expressed a truth

is true (let's suppose), but not strictly about the past. Here there is indeed something someone can do that entails its falsehood: Paul can decide not to mow his lawn in 2005. But it's not possible that there be an action Paul (or anyone) can or will be able to perform such that his performing it entails that

(41) Paul didn't mow his lawn in 1984

is false. We may thus say, with Ockham, that propositions strictly about the past are accidentally necessary; and the relevant asymmetry between past and future is just that contingent propositions strictly about the past are accidentally necessary, while their colleagues about the future typically are not.

Unfortunately, there is a residual perplexity. For what shall we count, here, as *actions?* Suppose it is in fact within Paul's power so to act that the ants would not have moved in; isn't there such an action as *bringing it about that the ants would not have moved in* or *so acting that the ants would not have moved in?* If there is (and why not?) then it is both an action he can perform and one such that his performing it entails that the ants did not move in; but then *the ants moved in* is not accidentally necessary after all. Here what we need, clearly enough, is the idea of a *basic* action, what an agent can in some sense do *directly.* Moving my arm, perhaps, would be such an action;

starting a world war or so acting that the ants would not have moved in would not. Let's say that an action is one I can *directly* perform if it is one I can perform without having to perform some other action in order to perform it. Starting a war would not be an action I can directly perform; I cannot start a war without doing something like pushing a button, pulling a trigger, or making a declaration. According to Roderick Chisholm, the only actions I can directly perform are *undertakings*.[28] I can't, for example, raise my arm without trying or endeavoring or undertaking to do so; more exactly (as Chisholm points out, p. 57), I can't raise it without undertaking to do *something* — scratch my ear, for example. I am inclined to think he is right: more generally, I can't perform an action which is not itself an undertaking, without undertaking some action or other. (What I say below, however, does not depend on this claim.) But he is also right in thinking that undertakings are not undertaken. If so, however, it will follow that the only actions I can directly perform are undertakings.

Now some actions I can perform are such that my undertaking to perform them and my body's being in normal conditions are together causally sufficient for my performing them; raising my hand and moving my feet would be an example. "Normal conditions" here, includes, among other things, the absence of pathological conditions as well as the absence of such external hindrances as being locked in a steamer trunk or having my hands tied behind my back. Of course more should be said here, but this will have to suffice for now. Let us say, then, that an action A is a basic action for a person S if and only if there is an action $A*$ that meets two conditions: first, S can directly perform $A*$, and secondly, S's being in normal conditions and his directly performing $A*$ is causally sufficient for his performing A. Then we may revise (39) by appropriately inserting "A is basic for S":

(42) p is accidentally necessary at t if and only if p is true at t and it is not possible both that p is true at t and that there exists an agent S and an action A such that (1) A is basic for S, (2) S has the power at t or later to perform A, and (3) necessarily if S were to perform A at t or later, then p would have been false.

There is one more complication.[29]

28. Roderick Chisholm, *Person and Object* (La Salle: Open Court Publishing Co., 1976), p. 85. Chisholm's powerful discussion of agency (pp. 53-88 and 159-74) should be required reading for anyone interested in that topic. (Chisholm does not use the term "directly perform," and I am not here using the term "basic action" in just the way he does.)

29. Called to my attention by Edward Wierenga, to whom I am especially grateful for penetrating comments on an ancestor of this paper. I am grateful for similar favors to many others, including Lawrence Powers, Alfred Freddoso, Mark Heller, Peter van Inwagen, William Alston, David Vriend, the members of the Calvin College Tuesday Colloquium, and especially Nelson Pike.

(43) God foreknew that Smith and Jones will not freely cooperate in mowing the lawn

should not turn out to be accidentally necessary; but on (42) it does. The problem is that (42) does not properly accommodate cooperative ventures freely undertaken; it must be generalized to take account of multiple agency. This is easily enough accomplished:

(44) p is accidentally necessary at t if and only if p is true at t and it is not possible both that p is true at t and that there exist agents $S_1 \ldots, S_n$ and actions $A_1 \ldots, A_n$ such that (1) A_i is basic for S_i, (2) S_i has the power at t or later to perform A_i, and (3) necessarily, if every S_i were to perform A_i at t or later, than p would have been false.[30]

And now we may say, perhaps, that the way in which the future but not the past is within our control is that contingent propositions strictly about the past are accidentally necessary, while those about the future typically are not.

By way of summary and conclusion, then: the two main arguments for the incompatibility of divine foreknowledge with human freedom are both failures. The Ockhamite claim that not all propositions about the past are hard facts about the past seems correct; among those that are not hard facts would be propositions specifying God's (past) foreknowledge of future human actions, as well as propositions specifying God's past beliefs about future human actions, if God is essentially omniscient. Only hard facts about the past, however, are plausibly thought to be accidentally necessary; hence neither God's foreknowledge nor God's forebelief poses a threat to human freedom. Accidental necessity is a difficult notion, but can be explained in terms of the

---

30. Again, (44) can obviously be recast so as to accommodate our atemporalist colleagues. What I claim for (44) is that propositions strictly about the past are accidentally necessary in the sense of (44), while their colleagues about the future typically are not; I do not claim that (44) is a satisfactory general analysis of our preanalytic notion of accidental necessity. So taken, it is subject to counterexamples of various kinds, including propositions of the form PvQ where P is a false contingent proposition strictly about the past and Q is a future proposition to the effect that some free agent A will perform some action (an action that is within A's power). I think we do indeed *have* a general preanalytic notion of accidental necessity, although there are some hard puzzle cases, and the issues get complicated. Allow me to venture the following as a first approximation: say that p is *past* accidentally necessary if and only if p is a proposition about the past (not necessarily strictly about the past) and p is accidentally necessary in the sense of (44); and let P be a conjunction of the past necessary propositions. Then

(44*) p is accidentally necessary *simpliciter* if and only if p is true and it is not possible that both (a) p but no proposition properly entailing p is past accidentally necessary, and (b) there is a past accidentally necessary proposition q, an agent S, and an action A such that (1) A is basic for S, (2) S can perform A at t or later, and (3) necessarily, if q is true and S were to perform A, then p would have been false.

power of agents. The initially plausible account of accidental necessity ((31)) is defective as an account of the intuitively obvious asymmetry between past and future; for far too few propositions turn out to be accidentally necessary on that account. (44), however, is more satisfying.

Appendix: Ability and Possible Worlds

What is it to have the *ability* to do something — to mow the lawn, for example? What is it for an action to be within my power? Can we get any insight into this question by thinking about it in terms of possible worlds? It is initially obvious that I have the ability to perform an action at a time only if there is a possible world in which I perform that action then. Of course this condition isn't *sufficient;* what it is within my power to do and what it is logically possible that I do, sadly enough, do not coincide. But what would be the right condition? Can we give an illuminating account of ability in terms of possible worlds?

In replying to a criticism made[31] of his argument for the incompatibility of human freedom with essential divine foreknowledge, Nelson Pike ventures such an account. He points out first that "when assessing what is within my power at a given moment, I must take into account the way things are and the way things have been in the past." He continues:

> If we assume that what is within my power at a given moment determines a set of possible worlds, all of the members of that set will have to be worlds in which what has happened in the past relative to the given moment is precisely what has happened in the past relative to that moment in the actual world.[32]

He then applies this account to Jones and the question whether it was within his power to refrain from mowing at T_2 if at T_1 God believed that he would mow at T_2:

> Going back now to the original problem, we have assumed that Jones does X at T_2 and that God exists and is everlasting and essentially omniscient. It follows that God believes at T_1 that Jones does X at T_2. The question before us is whether it is within Jones' power at T_2 to refrain from doing X. Plantinga assumes that this is to ask whether there is a possible world in which Jones refrains from doing S at T_2. His answer is that there is — it is a world in which

---

31. *God, Freedom, and Evil,* pp. 66-73.

32. Nelson Pike, "Divine Foreknowledge, Human Freedom and Possible Worlds," *The Philosophical Review,* 1979, p. 216.

God does not believe at T_1 that Jones does X at T_2. But Plantinga has not formulated the question correctly. He has not taken account of the restrictions that must be respected if one is to employ a possible worlds analysis of what it is for something to be within one's power. The question is not whether there is just some possible world or other in which Jones refrains from doing X at T_2. What must be asked is whether there is a possible world, having *a history prior to T_2 that is indistinguishable from that of the actual world,* in which Jones refrains from doing X at T_2. The answer is that there is not. All such worlds contain an essentially omniscient being who believes at T_1 that Jones does X at T_2. There is no possible world of this description in which Jones refrains from doing X at T_2.[33]

Now on one point Pike is wholly correct: (broadly) logical possibility, as he says, is quite insufficient for ability. There are plenty of actions I cannot perform, despite the fact that there are possible worlds in which I do perform them: composing poetry in Japanese is an example, as is, say, memorizing Kant's *Critique of Pure Reason* in half an hour. Ability and logical possibility do not coincide; and (contrary to what Pike says) I have never assumed or suggested otherwise. Indeed, as I've argued elsewhere, ability and possibility do not coincide even for God. There are many possible worlds God could not have weakly actualized, despite the fact that it is logically possible that he weakly actualize them — despite the fact, that is, that there are possible worlds in which he does weakly actualize them.[34]

Pike's positive proposal as to what it is to have the ability to do or refrain from doing X, however, is vastly more problematic. The suggestion is that

(1) *S* has the power to refrain from doing *X* at *t* if and only if there is a possible world *W* that has a history up to *t* indistinguishable from the actual world and in which *S* refrains from doing *X* at *t*.

And given (1), it follows that at T_2 Jones does not have the power not to mow. For a world in which there is no essentially omniscient being who believes at T_1 that Jones will do X at T_2 does not (given our supposition that God is essentially omniscient and believes at T_1 that Jones will do X at T_2) have a history prior to T_2 that is indistinguishable from that of the actual world; every world in which there is such a being, furthermore, is one in which, clearly enough, Jones does X at T_2. Accordingly, there is no possible world that meets the above two conditions with respect to Jones's doing X; it therefore follows, Pike thinks, that Jones's having the power to refrain from doing X at T_2 is inconsistent with God's being essentially omniscient and believing at T_1 that Jones would do X at T_2.

---

33. Nelson Pike, "Divine Foreknowledge," p. 217.

34. See my *The Nature of Necessity* (Oxford: Oxford University Press, 1974), pp. 169-84, and also my "Which Worlds Could God Have Created?" *Journal of Philosophy,* 1973.

Now it isn't wholly clear what it is for a pair of worlds to have indistinguishable histories prior to t;[35] but (1) seems initially much too strong. First, what is so special about *essential* omniscience? According to Pike, a pair of worlds have distinguishable histories prior to t if one but not the other of which contains an essentially omniscient being who prior to t believes that Jones will mow; but won't the same go for a pair of worlds one but not the other of which contains a being who is omniscient *simpliciter* and believes that proposition prior to t? If so, on Pike's showing human freedom is incompatible with God's being omniscient *simpliciter.* Further, wouldn't a pair of worlds have distinguishable histories prior to t if one but not the other contained a being, omniscient or not, who prior to t *knew* the proposition in question?[36] Or a being who *correctly believed* the proposition, whether or not he knew it? Indeed, wouldn't W and $W*$ have distinguishable histories prior to t if in one but not the other the proposition in question was *true* prior to t, whether or not anyone knew or believed it? Or if one but not the other contained a being who prior to t had the property *mows his lawn at* t? But then on Pike's account it will follow that a person is free with respect to an action A at a time t only if it is not true prior to t that he will perform A then, and only if he doesn't have, prior to t, the property of being such that he performs A at t. And then Pike's account of ability, together with the assumption that propositions about the future have truth value, will imply logical determinism.

An Ockhamite bystander might suggest that what Pike needs here is the distinction between those propositions about the past that are accidentally necessary and those that are not. It is only the former, he says, that are relevant to a pair of worlds having indistinguishable histories prior to t; a pair of worlds have indistinguishable histories prior to t if and only if no proposition is accidentally necessary (in the sense of (44)) at t in one but not the other. Then the fact that, say, in W but not $W*$ Smith knows at $t - n$ that Jones will mow at $t + n$ does not suffice to show that W and $W*$ have distinguishable histories prior to t; for

(2) Smith knows at $t - n$ that Jones will mow at $t + n$

while true in W is not accidentally necessary in W at t.

Sadly enough, however, this suggestion is unsatisfactory; for

(3) Every proposition Paul believed at noon yesterday was true

and

---

35. See my *The Nature of Necessity,* pp. 175-76.

36. See Stephen David, "Divine Omniscience and Human Freedom," *Religious Studies,* 1979, pp. 303-16, and Joshua Hoffman, "Pike on Possible Worlds, Divine Foreknowledge, and Human Freedom," *The Philosophical Review,* 1979, pp. 433-42.

(4) At noon yesterday Paul believed that Jones will not mow his lawn for the next three days

are both true (let's suppose). If so, they are also accidentally necessary; each is such that there is nothing anyone can now do that entails its falsehood. (Their conjunction, however, is another matter; accidental necessity is not closed under conjunction, as this example shows.) Clearly enough, however, there is no possible world in which (3) and (4) are both true and in which Jones mows his lawn tomorrow; but surely this does not imply that it is not or will not be within his power to mow then.

Here the Ockhamite bystander might make another suggestion: what Pike needs here, he might say, is not the idea of accidental necessity, but the distinction between hard and soft facts about the past. What we should say, he suggests, is that I have the ability to do X if and only if there is a possible world that shares its hard facts about the past with the actual world and in which I do X. This suggestion, however, is doubly deficient. First it is of no use to Pike. For on this suggestion a pair of worlds can have histories that are indistinguishable prior to t even if the one but not the other contains an essentially omniscient God who prior to t believes that Jones will mow at t; as we have already noted, if God is essentially omniscient, then *God believed at t_1 that Jones will mow at t_2* is not strictly about the past. Secondly, the suggestion is dubious in its own right. The fact that there is a possible world that shares its hard facts with the actual world and in which I do X, does not, I think, suffice to show that it is within my power to do X. Return to the Newcomb situation; and suppose that the knowledgeable agent involved is extremely knowledgeable but not essentially omniscient. Suppose this person (call him Michael) knows whether you will take one box or two, and suppose his knowledge is counterfactually independent of your action: it is true (but not necessarily true) that if you were to take both boxes, then Michael would have known that, but if you were to take just one, then he would have known *that*. More generally, it is true (but not necessarily true) that there is nothing you can do which is such that if you were to do it, then Michael would have held a false belief as to what you would do. I take it the case as so far set out entails that it is not within your power to bring it about that Michael holds a false belief on the topic in question. It is consistent with these conditions, I think, to add that the conjunction of all the hard facts about the past with the proposition that Michael believes that you will take both boxes, does not entail that you will in fact take both. It is therefore possible that this conjunction be true but you take just one box. If this conjunction were true and you took only one box, however, then in so doing you would bring it about that Michael had a false belief. Now I am inclined to think that all this is possible; but if it is, then there is a possible world that shares its hard facts about the past with the actual world and in which you bring it about that Michael held a false belief — and this despite the truth that it is not in fact within your power to bring it about that Michael held a false belief. I am therefore inclined to think that this suggestion — the suggestion that S has the power to do X if and only if there is a possible world that shares its hard facts about the past with the actual world and in which he does X — is at best dubious.

What I can do depends upon what I can *directly* do, together with the facts, with respect to each of the actions $A*$ I can directly perform, as to what would happen if I were to perform $A*$. What I can do depends (among other things) on two things: (a) my repertoire of direct actions, and (b) the question which counterfactuals are true — which counterfactuals whose antecedents specify that I perform some action or series of actions that are direct for me. Now of course possible world thought has been abundantly illuminating and clarifying with respect to the second. It is hard to see, however, how it can help us with the first; it is hard to see, that is, how to give an illuminating account in terms of possible worlds of what it is within a person's power to do directly.

SECTION IV

Christian Philosophy

Introduction

In the final essay in this collection, Plantinga identifies four essential divisions to the category "Christian philosophy": "apologetics, both negative and positive, philosophical theology, Christian philosophical criticism, and constructive Christian philosophy." As he goes on to describe these, it becomes apparent that each is adequately represented in the essays of this volume and throughout Plantinga's work in general. So it is a bit misleading to title one section "Christian Philosophy." However, in addition to *doing* Christian philosophy, Plantinga has distinguished himself as the primary voice calling others to do it as well. The essays in this section represent that call. Here Plantinga stops doing Christian philosophy long enough to talk about doing it — about what needs to be done and about how to do it right.

Chapter 11 is "Advice to Christian Philosophers" — that essay the publication of which Kelly James Clark labeled one of the two significant events contributing to the current resurgence in Christian philosophy. Here Plantinga issues a call for Christian philosophers to form a community of their own, one that recognizes and encourages philosophical inquiry undertaken from a Christian perspective and with Christian concerns and presuppositions guiding the tasks. Plantinga warns Christian philosophers against being misdirected by current philosophical trends and fashions, which are invariably set by the unbelieving philosophical community, guided and directed by non-Christian presuppositions and worldviews. He shows how Christian philosophers have been misled by such trends in the past, and have thus abandoned traditional and perfectly legitimate Christian approaches to problems in favor of those approaches sanctioned by the unbelieving majority.

Chapter 12, "Sheehan's Shenanigans," is unique in this collection for

293

a variety of reasons. First, it is not taken from an academic philosophical journal or collection. Rather, it is a reprint from the theological/ecclesiastical magazine *The Reformed Journal*. Second, it is not a freestanding paper, but a book review. Third, it deals not so much with traditional philosophy of religion issues as with theological and biblical studies issues. Nonetheless, it is a vital addition to the collection, and one that is here by Plantinga's own urging. In this paper Plantinga confronts contemporary theology and biblical studies with the same challenge with which he confronts Christian philosophy in chapter 11. He charges that believing theologians and biblical scholars should not be driven or motivated by the agendas, programs, and presuppositions of the unbelieving community. Nor should they feel compelled to accept naturalistic or humanistic approaches to theology and the Bible. Plantinga uses Thomas Sheehan's book *The First Coming: How the Kingdom of God Became Christianity* to illustrate the dangers and the total uselessness of this approach.

This chapter illustrates one of Plantinga's most refreshing (some might say infuriating!) tendencies. Plantinga is forever bringing the light of analysis to corners that theology has often been more than content to leave dark and murky. He raises questions and makes claims that the current climate in academic theology often won't allow, and demonstrates that widely accepted assumptions in the field are not only baseless, but also block innovative (and traditional) approaches to theological issues.

With the title "Christian Philosophy at the End of the Twentieth Century," chapter 13 provides a ready-made exit point for this collection. In this essay Plantinga identifies two dominant contemporary worldviews with which the Christian philosopher must contend: naturalism and what he calls "creative anti-realism."[1] Together these worldviews represent the starting points of the lion's share of non-Christian scholarship and creativity. From the context of the challenge these worldviews present, Plantinga then rehearses what is being done and what remains to be done in the four major areas of Christian philosophy mentioned in the first paragraph of this introduction. He contends that contemporary Christian philosophy has fared well recently in apologetics and philosophical theology, though there is (of course!) still plenty to be done. He is not, however, as complimentary in his assessment of our performance in Christian philosophical criticism and constructive Christian philosophy. Here he reiterates and expands on the challenges of chapters 11 and 12.

In "Advice to Christian Philosophers," Plantinga quips, " 'Who are you,' you say, 'to give the rest of us advice?' That's a good question. I shall

---

1. Plantinga introduces and fully explicates the concept of creative anti-realism in his American Philosophical Association presidential address, "How to Be an Anti-Realist" (Bibliography #70).

deal with it as one properly deals with good questions to which one doesn't know the answer: I shall ignore it" (p. 297 below). His characteristic graciousness and modesty prevent Plantinga from offering the real answer to this question, so I will answer it here in his stead. Who is he? He is the founder of the modern resurgence in Christian philosophy. He is the most influential and perhaps the boldest of all Christian philosophers working today. He is the one who has blazed the trails the rest of us currently follow. He is the mentor and philosophical father of many of the most influential Christian philosophers of the present day. He is, as my students might put it, The Man. The essays in this section offer counsel that anyone who considers himself a philosopher and a Christian will do well to ponder.

CHAPTER ELEVEN

Advice to Christian Philosophers

I. Introduction

Christianity, these days, and in our part of the world, is on the move. There are many signs pointing in this direction: the growth of Christian schools, of the serious conservative Christian denominations, the furor over prayer in public schools, the creationism/evolution controversy, and others.

There is also powerful evidence for this contention in philosophy. Thirty or thirty-five years ago, the public temper of mainline establishment philosophy in the English-speaking world was deeply non-Christian. Few establishment philosophers were Christian; even fewer were willing to admit in public that they were, and still fewer thought of their being Christian as making a real difference to their practice as philosophers. The most popular question of philosophical theology, at that time, was not whether Christianity or theism is *true;* the question, instead, was whether it even *makes sense* to *say* that there is such a person as God. According to the logical positivism then running riot, the sentence "there is such a person as God" literally makes no sense: it is disguised nonsense; it altogether fails to express a thought or a proposition. The central question wasn't whether theism is *true;* it was whether there *is* such a thing as theism — a genuine factual claim that is either true or false — *at all.* But things have changed. There are now many more Christians and many more unabashed Christians in the professional mainstream of American philosophical life. For example, the foundation of the Society for Christian Philosophers, an organization to promote fellowship and exchange of ideas among Christian philosophers, is both evidence and a consequence of that fact. Founded in 1977, it is now a thriving organization with regional meetings in every part of the country; its members are deeply involved in American professional philosophical life. So Chris-

296

tianity is on the move, and on the move in philosophy, as well as in other areas of intellectual life.

But even if Christianity is on the move, it has taken only a few brief steps; and it is marching through largely alien territory. For the intellectual culture of our day is for the most part profoundly non-theistic and hence non-Christian — more than that, it is anti-theistic. Most of the so-called human sciences, much of the non-human sciences, most of non-scientific intellectual endeavor, and even a good bit of allegedly Christian theology is animated by a spirit wholly foreign to that of Christian theism. I don't have the space here to elaborate and develop this point; but I don't have to, for it is familiar to you all. To return to philosophy: most of the major philosophy departments in America have next to nothing to offer the student intent on coming to see how to be a Christian in philosophy — how to assess and develop the bearing of Christianity on matters of current philosophical concern, and how to think about those philosophical matters of interest to the Christian community. In the typical graduate philosophy department there will be little more, along these lines, than a course in philosophy of religion in which it is suggested that the evidence for the existence of God — the classical theistic proofs, say — is at least counterbalanced by the evidence against the existence of God — the problem of evil, perhaps; and it may then be added that the wisest course in view of such maxims as Ockham's Razor, is to dispense with the whole idea of God, at least for philosophical purposes.

My aim, in this talk, is to give some advice to philosophers who are Christians. And although my advice is directed specifically to Christian philosophers, it is relevant to all philosophers who believe in God, whether Christian, Jewish, or Moslem. I propose to give some advice to the Christian or theistic philosophical community: some advice relevant to the situation in which in fact we find ourselves. "Who are you," you say, "to give the rest of us advice?" That's a good question. I shall deal with it as one properly deals with good questions to which one doesn't know the answer: I shall ignore it. My counsel can be summed up on two connected suggestions, along with a codicil. First, Christian philosophers and Christian intellectuals generally must display more autonomy — more independence of the rest of the philosophical world. Second, Christian philosophers must display more integrity — integrity in the sense of integral wholeness, or oneness, or unity, being all of one piece. Perhaps 'integrality' would be the better word here. And necessary to these two is a third: Christian courage, or boldness, or strength, or perhaps Christian self-confidence. We Christian philosophers must display more faith, more trust in the Lord; we must put on the whole armor of God. Let me explain in a brief and preliminary way what I have in mind; then I shall go on to consider some examples in more detail.

Consider a Christian college student — from Grand Rapids, Michigan, say, or Arkadelphia, Arkansas — who decides philosophy is the subject for her. Naturally enough, she will go to graduate school to learn how to become a philosopher. Perhaps she goes to Princeton, or Berkeley, or Pittsburgh, or Arizona; it doesn't much matter which. Here she learns how philosophy is presently practiced. The burning questions of the day are such topics as the new theory of reference; the realism/anti-realism controversy; the problems with probability; Quine's claims about the radical indeterminacy of translation; Rawls on justice; the causal theory of knowledge; Gettier problems; the artificial intelligence model for the understanding of what it is to be a person; the question of the ontological status of unobservable entities in science; whether there is genuine objectivity in science or anywhere else; whether mathematics can be reduced to set theory and whether abstract entities generally — numbers, propositions, properties — can be, as we quaintly say, "dispensed with"; whether possible worlds are abstract or concrete; whether our assertions are best seen as mere moves in a language game or as attempts to state the sober truth about the world; whether the rational egoist can be shown to be irrational, and all the rest. It is then natural for her, after she gets her Ph.D., to continue to think about and work on these topics. And it is natural, furthermore, for her to work on them in the way she was taught to, thinking about them in the light of the assumptions made by her mentors and in terms of currently accepted ideas as to what a philosopher should start from or take for granted, what requires argument and defense, and what a satisfying philosophical explanation or a proper resolution to a philosophical question is like. She will be uneasy about departing widely from these topics and assumptions, feeling instinctively that any such departures are at best marginally respectable. Philosophy is a social enterprise; and our standards and assumptions — the parameters within which we practice our craft — are set by our mentors and by the great contemporary centers of philosophy.

From one point of view this is natural and proper; from another, however, it is profoundly unsatisfactory. The questions I mentioned are important and interesting. Christian philosophers, however, are the philosophers of the Christian community; and it is part of their task as *Christian* philosophers to serve the Christian community. But the Christian community has its own questions, its own concerns, its own topics for investigation, its own agenda, and its own research program. Christian philosophers ought not merely take their inspiration from what's going on at Princeton or Berkeley or Harvard, attractive and scintillating as that may be; for perhaps those questions and topics are not the ones, or not the only ones, they should be thinking about as the philosophers of the Christian community. There are other philosophical topics the Christian community must work at, and other topics the Christian community must work at philosophically. And obviously, Christian philosophers are the ones who must do the philosophical work involved. If they devote their best efforts to the topics fashionable in the non-Christian philosophical world, they will neglect a crucial and central part of their task as Christian philosophers. What is needed here is more independence, more autonomy with respect to the projects and concerns of the non-theistic philosophical world.

But something else is at least as important here. Suppose the student I mentioned above goes to Harvard; she studies with Willard van Orman Quine. She finds herself attracted to Quine's programs and procedures: his radical empiricism, his allegiance to natural science, his inclination towards behaviorism, his uncompromising naturalism, and his taste for desert landscapes and ontological parsimony. It would be wholly natural for her to become totally involved in these projects and programs, to come to think of fruitful and worthwhile philosophy as substantially circumscribed by them. Of course she will note certain tensions between her Christian belief and her way of practicing philosophy; and she may then bend her efforts to putting the two together, to harmonizing them. She may devote her time and energy to seeing how one might understand or reinterpret Christian belief in such a way as to be palatable to the Quinian. One philosopher I know, embarking on just such a project, suggested that Christians should think of God as a *set* (Quine is prepared to countenance sets): the set of all true propositions, perhaps, or the set of right actions, or the union of those sets, or perhaps their Cartesian product. This is understandable; but it is also profoundly misdirected. Quine is a marvelously gifted philosopher: a subtle, original, and powerful philosophical force. But his fundamental commitments, his fundamental projects and concerns, are wholly different from those of the Christian community — wholly different and, indeed, antithetical to them. And the result of attempting to graft Christian thought onto his basic view of the world will be at best an unintegral *pastiche;* at worst it will seriously compromise, or distort, or trivialize the claims of Christian theism. What is needed here is more wholeness, more integrality.

So the Christian philosopher has his own topics and projects to think about; and when he thinks about the topics of current concern in the broader philosophical world, he will think about them in his own way, which may be a *different* way. He may have to reject certain currently fashionable assumptions about the philosophic enterprise — he may have to reject widely accepted assumptions as to what are the proper starting points and procedures for philosophical endeavor. And — and this is crucially important — the Christian philosopher has a perfect right to the point of view and pre-philosophical assumptions he brings to philosophic work; the fact that these are not widely shared outside the Christian or theistic community is interesting but fundamentally irrelevant. I can best explain what I mean by way of example; so I shall descend from the level of lofty generality to specific examples.

II. Theism and Verifiability

First, the dreaded "Verifiability Criterion of Meaning." During the palmy days of logical positivism, some thirty or forty years ago, the positivists claimed that most of the sentences Christians characteristically utter — "God loves us," for example, or "God created the heavens and the earth" — don't even have the grace to be false; they are, said the positivists, literally meaningless. It is not that they express *false* propositions; they don't express any propositions at all. Like that lovely line from *Through the Looking Glass,* " 'Twas brillig, and the slithy toves did gyre and gimbol in the wabe," they say nothing false, but only because they say nothing at all; they are "cognitively meaningless," to use the positivist's charming phrase. The sorts of things theists and others had been saying for centuries, they said, were now shown to be without sense; we theists had all been the victims, it seems, of a cruel hoax — perpetrated, perhaps, by ambitious priests and foisted upon us by our own credulous natures.

Now if this is true, it is indeed important. How had the positivists come by this startling piece of intelligence? They inferred it from the Verifiability Criterion of Meaning, which said, roughly, that a sentence is meaningful only if either it is analytic, or its truth or falsehood can be determined by empirical or scientific investigation — by the methods of the empirical sciences. On these grounds not only theism and theology, but most of traditional metaphysics and philosophy and much else besides was declared nonsense, without any literal sense at all. Some positivists conceded that metaphysics and theology, though strictly meaningless, might still have a certain limited value. Carnap, for example, thought they might be a kind of *music*. It isn't known whether he expected theology and metaphysics to supplant Bach and Mozart, or even Wagner; I myself, however, think they could nicely supersede *rock*. Hegel could take the place of The Talking Heads; Immanuel Kant could replace The Beach Boys; and instead of The Grateful Dead we could have, say, Arthur Schopenhauer.

Positivism had a delicious air of being *avant-garde* and with-it; and many philosophers found it extremely attractive. Furthermore, many who didn't endorse it nonetheless entertained it with great hospitality as at the least extremely plausible. As a consequence many philosophers — both Christians and non-Christians — saw here a real challenge and an important danger to Christianity: "The main danger to theism today," said J. J. C. Smart in 1955, "comes from people who want to say that 'God exists' and 'God does not exist' are equally absurd." In 1955 *New Essays in Philosophical Theology* appeared, a volume of essays that was to set the tone and topics for philosophy of religion for the next decade or more; and most of this volume was given over to a discussion of the impact of Verificationism on theism. Many philosophically inclined Christians were disturbed and perplexed and felt deeply threatened; could it really be true that linguistic philosophers had somehow discovered that the Christian's most cherished convictions were, in fact, just meaningless? There was a great deal of anxious hand wringing among philosophers, either themselves theists or sympathetic to theism. Some suggested, in the face of positivistic onslaught, that the thing for the Christian community to do was to fold up its tents and silently slink away, admitting that the verifiability criterion was probably true. Others conceded that strictly speaking, theism really *is* nonsense, but is *important* nonsense. Still others suggested that the sentences in question should be reinterpreted in such a way as not to give offense to the positivists; someone seriously suggested, for example, that Christians resolve, henceforth, to use the sentence "God exists" to mean "some men and women have had, and all may have, experiences called 'meeting God' "; he added that when we say "God created the world from nothing" what we should mean is "everything we call 'material' can be used in such a way that it contributes to the well-being of men." In a different context but the same spirit, Rudolph Bultmann embarked upon his program of demythologizing Christianity. Traditional supernaturalistic Christian belief, he said, is "impossible in this age of electric light and the wireless." (One can perhaps imagine an earlier village skeptic taking a similar view of, say, the tallow candle and the printing press, or perhaps the pine torch and the papyrus scroll.)

By now, of course, Verificationism has retreated into the obscurity it so richly deserves; but the moral remains. This hand wringing and those attempts to accommodate the positivist were wholly inappropriate. I realize that hindsight is clearer than foresight and I do not recount this bit of recent intellectual history in order to be critical of my elders or to claim that we are wiser than our fathers: what I want to point out is that we can *learn* something from the whole nasty incident. For Christian philosophers should have adopted a quite different attitude towards positivism and its verifiability criterion. What they should have said to the positivists is: "Your criterion is mistaken: for such statements as 'God loves us' and 'God created the heavens and the earth' are clearly meaningful; so if they aren't verifiable in your sense, then it is false that all and only statements verifiable in that sense are meaningful." What was needed here was less accommodation to current fashion and more Christian self-confidence: Christian theism is true; if Christian theism is true, then the verifiability criterion is false; so the verifiability criterion is false. Of course, if the verificationists had given cogent *arguments* for their criterion, from premises that had some legitimate claim on Christian or theistic thinkers, then perhaps there would have been a problem here for the Christian philosopher; then we would have been obliged either to agree that Christian theism is cognitively meaningless, or else revise or reject those premises. But the Verificationists never gave any cogent arguments; indeed, they seldom gave any arguments at all. Some simply trumpeted this principle as a great discovery, and when challenged, repeated it loudly and slowly; but why should *that* disturb anyone? Others proposed it as a *definition*

— a definition of the term "meaningful." Now of course the positivists had a right to use this term in any way they chose; it's a free country. But how could their decision to use that term in a particular way show anything so momentous as that all those who took themselves to be believers in God were wholly deluded? If I propose to use the term 'Democrat' to mean 'unmitigated scoundrel,' would it follow that Democrats everywhere should hang their heads in shame? And my point, to repeat myself, is that Christian philosophers should have displayed more integrity, more independence, less readiness to trim their sails to the prevailing philosophical winds of doctrine, and more Christian self-confidence.

III. Theism and Theory of Knowledge

I can best approach my second example by indirection. Many philosophers have claimed to find a serious problem for theism in the existence of *evil,* or of the amount and kinds of evil we do in fact find. Many who claim to find a problem here for theists have urged the *deductive argument from evil:* they have claimed that the existence of an omnipotent, omniscient, and wholly good God is *logically incompatible* with the presence of evil in the world — a presence conceded and indeed insisted upon by Christian theists. For their part, theists have argued that there is no inconsistency here. I think the present consensus, even among those who urge some form of the argument from evil, is that the deductive form of the argument from evil is unsuccessful.

More recently, philosophers have claimed that the existence of God, while perhaps not actually *inconsistent* with the existence of the amount and kinds of evil we do in fact find, is at any rate *unlikely* or *improbable* with respect to it; that is, the probability of the existence of God with respect to the evil we find, is less than the probability, with respect to that same evidence, that there is no God — no omnipotent, omniscient, and wholly good Creator. Hence the existence of God is improbable with respect to what we know. But if theistic belief *is* improbable with respect to what we know, then, so goes the claim, it is irrational or in any event intellectually second-rate to accept it.

Now suppose we briefly examine this claim. The objector holds that

(1) God is the omnipotent, omniscient, and wholly good creator of the world

is improbable or unlikely with respect to

(2) There are 10^{13} turps of evil

(where the *turp* is the basic unit of evil).

I've argued elsewhere[1] that enormous difficulties beset the claim that (1) is unlikely or improbable given (2). Call that response "the low road reply." Here I want to pursue what I shall call the *high road* reply. Suppose we stipulate, for purposes of argument, that (1) *is,* in fact, improbable on (2). Let's agree that it is unlikely, given the existence of 10^{13} turps of evil, that the world has been created by a God who is perfect in power, knowledge, and goodness. What is supposed to follow from that? How is that to be construed as an objection to theistic belief? How does the objector's argument go from there? It doesn't follow, of course, that theism is false. Nor does it follow that one who accepts both (1) and (2) (and let's add, recognizes that (1) is improbable with respect to (2)) has an irrational system of belief or is in any way guilty of noetic impropriety; obviously there might be pairs of propositions A and $B,$ such that we *know* both A and $B,$ despite the fact that A is improbable on $B.$ I might know, for example, both that Feike is a Frisian and 9 out of 10 Frisians can't swim, and also that Feike can swim; then I am obviously within my intellectual rights in accepting both these propositions, even though the latter is improbable with respect to the former. So even if it were a fact that (1) is improbable with respect to (2), that fact, so far, wouldn't be of much consequence. How, therefore, can this objection be developed?

Presumably what the objector means to hold is that (1) is improbable, not just on (2) but on some appropriate body of *total evidence* — perhaps all the evidence the theist has, or perhaps the body of evidence he is rationally obliged to have. The objector must be supposing that the theist has a relevant body of total evidence here, a body of evidence that includes (2); and his claim is that (1) is improbable with respect to this relevant body of total evidence. Suppose we say that T_s is the relevant body of total evidence for a given theist T; and suppose we agree that a belief is rationally acceptable for him only if it is not improbable with respect to T_s. Now what sorts of propositions are to be found in T_s? Perhaps the propositions he *knows* to be true, or perhaps the largest subset of his beliefs that he can rationally accept without evidence from other propositions, or perhaps the propositions he knows *immediately* — knows, but does not know on the basis of other propositions. However exactly we characterize this set T_s, the question I mean to press is this: why can't belief in God be itself a member of T_s? Perhaps for the theist — for many theists, at any rate — belief in God is a member of T_s, in which case it obviously won't be improbable with respect to T_s. Perhaps the theist has a right to *start from* belief in God, taking that proposition to be one of the ones probability with respect to which determines the rational propriety of *other* beliefs he holds. But if so, then the Christian *philosopher* is entirely within his rights in starting from belief in God to his philosophizing.

1. "The Probabilistic Argument from Evil," *Philosophical Studies,* 1979, pp. 1-53.

He has a right to take the existence of God for granted and go on from there in his philosophical work — just as other philosophers take for granted the existence of the past, say, or of other persons, or the basic claims of contemporary physics.

And this leads me to my point here. Many Christian philosophers appear to think of themselves *qua* philosophers as engaged with the atheist and agnostic philosopher in a common search for the correct philosophical position *vis-à-vis* the question whether there is such a person as God. Of course the Christian philosopher will have his own private conviction on the point; he will believe, of course, that indeed there is such a person as God. But he will think, or be inclined to think, or half inclined to think that as a *philosopher* he has no right to this position unless he is able to show that it follows from, or is probable, or justified with respect to, premises accepted by all parties to the discussion — theist, agnostic, and atheist alike. Furthermore, he will be half inclined to think he has no right, as a philosopher, to positions that presuppose the existence of God, if he can't show that belief to be justified in this way. What I want to urge is that the Christian philosophical community ought *not* to think of itself as engaged in this common effort to determine the probability or philosophical plausibility of belief in God. The Christian philosopher quite properly *starts from* the existence of God, and presupposes it in philosophical work, whether or not he can show it to be probable or plausible with respect to premises accepted by all philosophers, or most philosophers, or most philosophers at the great contemporary centers of philosophy.

Taking it for granted, for example, that there is such a person as God and that we are indeed within our epistemic rights (are in that sense justified) in believing that there is, the Christian epistemologist might ask what it is that confers justification here: by virtue of what is the theist justified? Perhaps there are several sensible responses. One answer he might give and try to develop is that of John Calvin (and before him, of the Augustinian, Anselmian, Bonaventurian tradition of the middle ages): God, said Calvin, has implanted in humankind a tendency or nisus or disposition to believe in him:

> "There is within the human mind, and indeed by natural instinct, an awareness of divinity." This we take to be beyond controversy. To prevent anyone from taking refuge in the pretence of ignorance, God himself has implanted in all men a certain understanding of his divine majesty. . . . Therefore, since from the beginning of the world there has been no region, no city, in short, no household, that could do without religion, there lies in this a tacit confession of a sense of deity inscribed in the hearts of all.[2]

2. *Institutes of the Christian Religion,* tr. Ford Lewis Battles (Philadelphia: Westminster, 1960), bk. 1, chap. III, pp. 43-44.

Calvin's claim, then, is that God has so created us that we have by nature a strong tendency or inclination or disposition towards belief in him.

Although this disposition to believe in God has been in part smothered or suppressed by *sin,* it is nevertheless universally present. And it is triggered or actuated by widely realized conditions:

> Lest anyone, then, be excluded from access to happiness, he not only sowed in men's minds that seed of religion of which we have spoken, but revealed himself and daily disclosed himself in the whole workmanship of the universe. As a consequence, men cannot open their eyes without being compelled to see him. (p. 51)

Like Kant, Calvin is especially impressed in this connection, by the marvelous compages of the starry heavens above:

> Even common folk and the most untutored, who have been taught only by the aid of the eyes, cannot be unaware of the excellence of divine art, for it reveals itself in this innumerable and yet distinct and well-ordered variety of the heavenly host. (p. 52)

And now what Calvin says suggests that one who accedes to this tendency and in these circumstances accepts the belief that God has created the world — perhaps upon beholding the starry heavens, or the splendid majesty of the mountains, or the intricate, articulate beauty of a tiny flower — is quite as rational and quite as justified as one who believes that he sees a tree upon having that characteristic being-appeared-to-treely kind of experience.

No doubt this suggestion won't convince the skeptic; taken as an attempt to convince the skeptic it is circular. My point is just this: the Christian has his own questions to answer, and his own projects; these projects may not mesh with those of the skeptical or unbelieving philosopher. He has his own questions and his own starting point in investigating these questions. Of course, I don't mean to suggest that the Christian philosopher must accept Calvin's answer to the question I mentioned above; but I do say it is entirely fitting for him to give to this question an answer that presupposes precisely that of which the skeptic is skeptical — even if this skepticism is nearly unanimous in most of the prestigious philosophy departments of our day. The Christian philosopher does indeed have a responsibility to the philosophical world at large; but his fundamental responsibility is to the Christian community, and finally to God.

Again a Christian philosopher may be interested in the relation between faith and reason, and faith and knowledge: granted that we hold some things by faith and know other things; granted that we believe that there is such a person as God and that this belief is true; do we also *know* that God exists?

Do we accept this belief by faith or by reason? A theist may be inclined towards a *reliabilist* theory of knowledge; he may be inclined to think that a true belief constitutes knowledge if it is produced by a reliable belief-producing mechanism. (There are hard problems here, but suppose for now we ignore them.) If the theist thinks God has created us with the *sensus divinitatis* Calvin speaks of, he will hold that indeed there is a reliable belief-producing mechanism that produces theistic belief; he will thus hold that we *know* that God exists. One who follows Calvin here will also hold that a capacity to apprehend God's existence is as much part of our natural noetic or intellectual equipment as is the capacity to apprehend truths of logic, perceptual truths, truths about the past, and truths about other minds. Belief in the existence of God is then in the same boat as belief in truths of logic, other minds, the past, and perceptual objects; in each case God has so constructed us that in the right circumstances we acquire the belief in question. But then the belief that there is such a person as God is as much among the deliverances of our natural noetic faculties as are those other beliefs. Hence we *know* that there is such a person as God, and don't merely believe it; and it isn't by *faith* that we apprehend the existence of God, but by reason; and this whether or not any of the classical theistic arguments is successful.

Now my point is not that Christian philosophers must follow Calvin here. My point is that the Christian philosopher has a right (I should say a duty) to work at his own projects — projects set by the beliefs of the Christian community of which he is a part. The Christian philosophical community must work out the answer to *its* questions; and both the questions and the appropriate ways of working out their answers may presuppose beliefs rejected at most of the leading centers of philosophy. But the Christian is proceeding quite properly in starting from these beliefs, even if they are so rejected. He is under no obligation to confine his research projects to those pursued at those centers, or to pursue his own projects on the basis of the assumptions that prevail there.

Perhaps I can clarify what I want to say by contrasting it with a wholly different view. According to the theologian David Tracy,

> In fact the modern Christian theologian cannot ethically do other than challenge the traditional self-understanding of the theologian. He no longer sees his task as a simple defense of or even as an orthodox reinterpretation of traditional belief. Rather, he finds that his ethical commitment to the morality of scientific knowledge forces him to assume a critical posture towards his own and his tradition's beliefs. . . . In principle, the fundamental loyalty of the theologian *qua* theologian is to that morality of scientific knowledge which he shares with his colleagues, the philosophers, historians, and social scientists. No more than they can he allow his own — or his

tradition's — beliefs to serve as warrants for his arguments. In fact, in all properly theological inquiry, the analysis should be characterized by those same ethical stances of autonomous judgment, critical judgment and properly skeptical hard-mindedness that characterize analysis in other fields.[3]

Furthermore, this "morality of scientific knowledge insists that each inquirer start with the present methods and knowledge of the field in question, unless one has evidence of the same logical type for rejecting those methods and that knowledge." Still further, "for the new scientific morality, one's fundamental loyalty as an analyst of any and all cognitive claims is solely to those methodological procedures which the particular scientific community in question has developed" (p. 6).

I say *caveat lector.* I'm prepared to bet that this "new scientific morality" is like the Holy Roman Empire: it is neither new nor scientific nor morally obligatory. Furthermore the "new scientific morality" looks to me to be monumentally inauspicious as a stance for a Christian theologian, modern or otherwise. Even if there were a set of methodological procedures held in common by most philosophers, historians, and social scientists, or most secular philosophers, historians, and social scientists, why should a Christian theologian give ultimate allegiance to them rather than, say, to God, or to the fundamental truths of Christianity? Tracy's suggestion as to how Christian theologians should proceed seems at best wholly unpromising. Of course I am only a philosopher, not a modern theologian; no doubt I am venturing beyond my depths. So I don't presume to speak for modern theologians; but however things stand for them, the modern Christian *philosopher* has a perfect right, as a philosopher, to start from his belief in God. He has a right to assume it, take it for granted, in his philosophical work — whether or not he can convince his unbelieving colleagues either that this belief is true or that it is sanctioned by those "methodological procedures" Tracy mentions.

And the Christian philosophical community ought to get on with the philosophical questions of importance to the Christian community. It ought to get on with the project of exploring and developing the implications of Christian theism for the whole range of questions philosophers ask and answer. It ought to do this whether or not it can convince the philosophical community at large either that there really is such a person as God, or that it is rational or reasonable to believe that there is. Perhaps the Christian philosopher *can* convince the skeptic or the unbelieving philosopher that indeed there is such a person as God. Perhaps this is possible in at least some instances. In other instances, of course, it may be impossible; even if the skeptic in fact accepts premises from which theistic belief follows by argument forms he also accepts,

3. *Blessed Rage for Order* (New York: Seabury Press, 1978), p. 7.

he may, when apprised of this situation, give up those premises rather than his unbelief. (In this way it is possible to reduce someone from knowledge to ignorance by giving him an argument he sees to be valid from premises he knows to be true.)

But whether or not this is possible, the Christian philosopher has other fish to fry and other questions to think about. Of course he must listen to, understand, and learn from the broader philosophical community and he must take his place in it; but his work as a philosopher is not circumscribed by what either the skeptic or the rest of the philosophical world thinks of theism. Justifying or trying to justify theistic belief in the eyes of the broader philosophical community is not the only task of the Christian philosophical community; perhaps it isn't even among its most important tasks. Philosophy is a communal enterprise. The Christian philosopher who looks exclusively to the philosophical world at large, who thinks of himself as belonging primarily to *that* world, runs a twofold risk. He may neglect an essential part of his task as a Christian philosopher; and he may find himself adopting principles and procedures that don't comport well with his beliefs as a Christian. What is needed, once more, is autonomy and integrality.

IV. Theism and Persons

My third example has to do with philosophical anthropology: how should we think about human persons? What sorts of things, fundamentally, *are* they? What is it to be a person, what is it to be a *human* person, and how shall we think about personhood? How, in particular, should Christians, Christian philosophers, think about these things? The first point to note is that in the Christian scheme of things, *God* is the premier person, the first and chief exemplar of personhood. God, furthermore, has created man in his own image; we men and women are image bearers of God, and the properties most important for an understanding of our personhood are properties we share with him. How we think about God, then, will have an immediate and direct bearing on how we think about humankind. Of course we learn much about ourselves from other sources — from everyday observation, from introspection and self-observation, from scientific investigation and the like. But it is also perfectly proper to start from what we know as Christians. It is not the case that rationality, or proper philosophical method, or intellectual responsibility, or the new scientific morality, or whatever, require that we start from beliefs we share with everyone else — what common sense and current science teach, e.g., and attempt to reason to or justify those beliefs we hold as Christians. In trying to give a satisfying philosophical account of some area or phenomenon, we may properly appeal, in our account or explanation, to anything else we already rationally believe — whether it be current science or Christian doctrine.

Let me proceed again to specific examples. There is a fundamental watershed, in philosophical anthropology, between those who think of human beings as *free* — free in the libertarian sense — and those who espouse determinism. According to determinists, every human action is a consequence of initial conditions outside our control by way of causal laws that are also outside our control. Sometimes underlying this claim is a picture of the universe as a vast machine where, at any rate at the macroscopic level, all events, including human actions, are determined by previous events and causal laws. On this view every action I have in fact performed was such that it wasn't within my power to refrain from performing it; and if, on a given occasion I did *not* perform a given action, then it wasn't then within my power to perform it. If I now raise my arm, then, on the view in question, it wasn't within my power just then not to raise it. Now the Christian thinker has a stake in this controversy just by virtue of being a Christian. For she will no doubt believe that God holds us human beings responsible for much of what we do — responsible, and thus properly subject to praise or blame, approval or disapproval. But how can I be responsible for my actions, if it was never within my power to perform any action I didn't in fact perform, and never within my power to refrain from performing any I did perform? If my actions are thus determined, then I am not rightly or justly held accountable for them; but God does nothing improper or unjust, and he holds me accountable for some of my actions; hence it is not the case that all of my actions are thus determined. The Christian has an initially strong reason to reject the claim that all of our actions are causally determined — a reason much stronger than the meager and anemic arguments the determinist can muster on the other side. Of course if there *were* powerful arguments on the other side, then there might be a problem here. But there aren't; so there isn't.

Now the determinist may reply that freedom and causal determinism are, contrary to initial appearances, in fact compatible. He may argue that my being free with respect to an action I performed at a time *t*, for example, doesn't entail that it was then within my power to refrain from performing it, but only something weaker — perhaps something like *if I had chosen not to perform it, I would not have performed it.* Indeed, the clearheaded compatibilist will go further. He will maintain, not only that freedom is compatible with determinism, but that freedom *requires* determinism. He will hold with Hume that the proposition *S is free with respect to action A* or *S does A freely* entails that *S* is causally determined with respect to *A* — that there are causal laws and antecedent conditions that together entail either that *S* performs *A* or that *S* does not perform *A*. And he will back up this claim by insisting that if S is not thus determined with respect to A, then it's merely a matter of *chance* — due, perhaps, to quantum effects in S's brain — that S does A. But if it is just a matter of chance that S does A, then either S doesn't really do A at all, or at any rate S is not responsible for doing A. If S's doing A is just a matter of chance, then S's doing A is something that just *happens* to him; but then it is not really the case that he *performs A* — at any rate it is not the case that he is *responsible* for performing A. And hence freedom, in the sense that is required for responsibility, itself requires determinism.

But the Christian thinker will find this claim monumentally implausible. Presumably the determinist means to hold that what he says characterizes actions generally, not just those of human beings. He will hold that it is a *necessary* truth that if an agent isn't caused to perform an action then it is a mere matter of chance that the agent in question performs the action in question. From a Christian perspective, however, this is wholly incredible. For God performs actions, and performs free actions; and surely it is not the case that there are causal laws and antecedent conditions outside his control that determine what he does. On the contrary: God is the author of the causal laws that do in fact obtain; indeed, perhaps the best way to think of these causal laws is as records of the ways in which God ordinarily treats the beings he has created. But of course it is not simply a matter of *chance* that God does what he does — creates and upholds the world, let's say, and offers redemption and renewal to his children. So a Christian philosopher has an extremely good reason for rejecting this premise, along with the determinism and compatibilism it supports.

What is really at stake in this discussion is the notion of agent causation: the notion of a person as an ultimate source of action. According to the friends of agent causation, some events are caused, not by other events, but by substances, objects — typically personal agents. And at least since the time of David Hume, the idea of agent causation has been languishing. It is fair to say, I think, that most contemporary philosophers who work in this area either reject agent causation outright or are at the least extremely suspicious of it. They see causation as a relation among *events;* they can understand how one event can cause another event, or how events of one kind can cause events of another kind. But the idea of a *person,* say, causing an event, seems to them unintelligible, unless it can be analyzed, somehow, in terms of event causation. It is this devotion to event causation, of course, that explains the claim that if you perform an action but are not caused to do so, then your performing that action is a matter of chance. For if I hold that all causation is ultimately event causation, then I will suppose that if you perform an action but are not caused to do so by previous events, then your performing that action isn't caused at all and is therefore a mere matter of chance. The devotee of event causation, furthermore, will perhaps argue for his position as follows.

If such agents as persons cause effects that take place in the physical world — my body's moving in a certain way, for example — then these effects must ultimately be caused by volitions or *undertakings* — which, apparently, are immaterial, unphysical events. He will then claim that the idea of an immaterial event's having causal efficacy in the physical world is puzzling or dubious or worse.

But a Christian philosopher will find this argument unimpressive and this devotion to event causation uncongenial. As for the argument, the Christian already and independently believes that acts of volition have causal efficacy; he believes, indeed, that the physical universe owes its very existence to just such volitional acts — God's undertaking to create it. And as for the devotion to event causation, the Christian will be, initially, at any rate, strongly inclined to reject the idea that event causation is primary and agent causation to be explained in terms of it. For he believes that God does and has done many things: he has created the world; he sustains it in being; he communicates with his children. But it is extraordinarily hard to see how these truths can be analyzed in terms of causal relations among events. What events could possibly cause God's creating the world or his undertaking to create the world? God himself institutes or establishes the causal laws that do in fact hold; how, then, can we see all the events constituted by his actions as related by causal laws to earlier events? How could it be that propositions ascribing actions to him are to be explained in terms of event causation?

Some theistic thinkers have noted that problem and reacted by soft-pedaling God's causal activity, or by impetuously following Kant in declaring that it is of a wholly different order from that in which we engage, an order beyond our comprehension. I believe that is the wrong response. Why should a Christian philosopher join in the general obeisance to event causation? It is not as if there are cogent *arguments* here. The real force behind this claim is a certain philosophical way of looking at persons and the world; but this view has no initial plausibility from a Christian perspective and no compelling argument in its favor.

So on all these disputed points in philosophical anthropology the theist will have a strong initial predilection for resolving the dispute in one way rather than another. He will be inclined to reject compatibilism, to hold that event causation (if indeed there is such a thing) is to be explained in terms of agent causation, to reject the idea that if an event isn't caused by other events then its occurrence is a matter of chance, and to reject the idea that events in the physical world can't be caused by an agent's undertaking to do something. And my point here is this. The Christian philosopher is within his right in holding these positions, whether or not he can convince the rest of a philosophical world and whatever the current philosophical consensus is, if there is a consensus. But isn't such an appeal to God and his properties, in this philosophical context, a shameless appeal to a *deus ex machina?* Surely not. "Philosophy," as Hegel once exclaimed in a rare fit of lucidity, "is thinking things over." Philosophy is in large part a clarification, systematization, articulation, relating, and deepening of pre-philosophical opinion. We come to philosophy with a range of opinions about the world and humankind and the place of the latter in the former; and in philosophy we think about these matters, systematically articulate our views, put together and relate our views on diverse topics, and deepen our views by finding unexpected interconnections and by discovering and answering unanticipated questions. Of course we may come to change our minds by virtue of philosophical endeavor; we may discover incompatibilities or other infelicities. But we come to philosophy with pre-philosophical opinions; we can do no other. And the point is: the Christian has as much right to his pre-philosophical opinions as others have to theirs. He needn't try first to 'prove' them from propositions accepted by, say, the bulk of the non-Christian philosophical community; and if they are widely rejected as naïve, or pre-scientific, or primitive, or unworthy of "man come of age," that is nothing whatever against them. Of course if there were genuine and substantial arguments against them from premises that have some legitimate claim on the Christian philosopher, then he would have a problem; he would have to make some kind of change somewhere. But in the absence of such arguments — and the absence of such arguments is evident — the Christian philosophical community quite properly starts, in philosophy, from what it believes.

But this means that the Christian philosophical community need not devote all of its efforts to attempting to refute opposing claims and/or to arguing for its own claims, in each case from premises accepted by the bulk of the philosophical community at large. It ought to do this, indeed, but it ought to do more. For if it does only this, it will neglect a pressing philosophical task: systematizing, deepening, clarifying Christian thought on these topics. So here again: my plea is for the Christian philosopher, the Christian philosophical community, to display, first, more independence and autonomy: we needn't take as our research projects just those projects that currently enjoy widespread popularity; we have our own questions to think about. Secondly, we must display more integrity. We must not automatically assimilate what is current or fashionable or popular by way of philosophical opinion and procedures; for much of it comports ill with Christian ways of thinking. And finally, we must display more Christian self-confidence or courage or boldness. We have a perfect right to our pre-philosophical views: why, therefore, should we be intimidated by what the rest of the philosophical world thinks plausible or implausible?

These, then, are my examples; I could have chosen others. In ethics, for example: perhaps the chief theoretical concern, from the theistic perspective, is the question How are right and wrong, good and bad, duty, permission, and obligation related to God and to his will and to his creative activity? This question doesn't arise, naturally enough, from a non-theistic perspective; and so, naturally enough, non-theist ethicists do not address it. But it is perhaps the most important question for a Christian ethicist to tackle. I have already spoken about epistemology; let me mention another example from this area. Epistemologists sometimes worry about the confluence or lack thereof of epistemic *justification,* on the one hand, and *truth,* or *reliability,* on the other. Suppose we do the best that can be expected of us, noetically speaking; suppose we do our intellectual duties and satisfy our intellectual obligations: what guarantee is there that in so doing we shall arrive at the truth? Is there even any reason for supposing that if we thus satisfy our obligations, we shall have a better chance of arriving at the truth than if we brazenly flout them? And where do these intellectual obligations come from? How does it happen that we have them? Here the theist has, if not a clear set of answers, at any rate clear suggestions towards a set of answers. Another example: creative anti-realism is presently popular among philosophers; this is the view that it is human behavior — in particular, human thought and language — that is somehow responsible for the fundamental structure of the world and for the fundamental kinds of entities there are. From a theistic point of view, however, universal creative anti-realism is at best a mere impertinence, a piece of laughable bravado. For *God,* of course, owes neither his existence nor his properties to us and our ways of thinking; the truth is just the reverse. And so far as the created universe is concerned, while it indeed owes its existence and character to activity on the part of a person, that person is certainly not a *human* person.

One final example, this time from philosophy of mathematics. Many who think about *sets* and their nature are inclined to accept the following ideas. First, no set is a member of itself. Second, whereas a property has its extension contingently, a set has *its* membership essentially. This means that no set could have existed if one of its members had not, and that no set could have had fewer or different members from the ones it in fact has. It means, furthermore, that sets are contingent beings; if Ronald Reagan had not existed, then his unit set would not have existed. And thirdly, sets form a sort of iterated structure: at the first level there are sets whose members are non-sets, at the second level sets whose members are non-sets or first level sets; at the third level, sets whose members are non-sets or sets of the first two levels, and so on. Many are also inclined, with Georg Cantor, to regard sets as *collections* — as objects whose existence is dependent upon a certain sort of intellectual activity — a collecting or "thinking together" as Cantor put it. If sets were collections of this sort, that would explain their displaying the first three features I mentioned. But if the collecting or thinking together had to be done by *human* thinkers, or any finite thinkers, there wouldn't be nearly enough sets — not nearly as many as we think in fact there are. From a theistic point of view, the natural conclusion is that sets owe their existence to *God's* thinking things together. The natural explanation of those three features is just that sets are indeed collections — collections collected by God; they are or result from God's thinking things together. This idea may not be popular at contemporary centers of set-theoretical activity; but that is neither here nor there. Christians, theists, ought to understand sets from a *Christian* and *theistic* point of view. What they believe as theists affords a resource for understanding sets not available to the non-theist; and why shouldn't they employ it? Perhaps here we *could* proceed without appealing to what we believe as theists; but why *should* we, if these beliefs are useful and explanatory? I could probably get home this evening by hopping on one leg; and conceivably I could climb Devil's Tower with my feet tied together. But why should I want to?

The Christian or theistic philosopher, therefore, has his own way of working at his craft. In some cases there are items on his agenda — pressing items — not to be found on the agenda of the non-theistic philosophical community. In others, items that are currently fashionable appear of relatively minor interest from a Christian perspective. In still others, the theist will reject common assumptions and views about how to start, how to proceed, and what constitutes a good or satisfying answer. In still others the Christian will take for granted and will start from assumptions and premises rejected by the philosophical community at large. Of course I don't mean for a moment to suggest that Christian philosophers have nothing to learn from their non-Christian and non-theist colleagues: that would be a piece of foolish arrogance, utterly belied by the fact of the matter. Nor do I mean to suggest that Christian philosophers should retreat into their own isolated enclave, having as little as possible to do with non-theistic philosophers. Of course not! Christians have much to learn and much of enormous importance to learn by way of dialogue and discussion with their non-theistic colleagues. Christian philosophers must be intimately involved in the professional life of the philosophical community at large, both because of what they can learn and because of what they can contribute. Furthermore, while Christian philosophers need not and ought not to see themselves as involved, for example, in a common effort to determine whether there is such a person as God, we are all, theist and non-theist alike, engaged in the common human project of understanding ourselves and the world in which we find ourselves. If the Christian philosophical community is doing its job properly, it will be engaged in a complicated, many-sided dialectical discussion, making its own contribution to that common human project. It may pay careful attention to other contributions; it must gain a deep understanding of them; it must learn what it can from them and it must take unbelief with profound seriousness.

All of this is true and all of this is important; but none of it runs counter to what I have been saying. Philosophy is many things. I said earlier that it is a matter of systematizing, developing, and deepening one's pre-philosophical opinions. It is that; but it is also an arena for the articulation and interplay of commitments and allegiances fundamentally religious in nature; it is an expression of deep and fundamental perspectives, ways of viewing ourselves and the world and God. The Christian philosophical community, by virtue of being Christian, is committed to a broad but specific way of looking at humankind and the world and God. Among its most important and pressing projects are systemizing, deepening, exploring, articulating this perspective, and exploring its bearing on the rest of what we think and do. But then the Christian philosophical community has its own agenda; it need not and should not automatically take its projects from the list of those currently in favor at the leading contemporary centers of philosophy. Furthermore, Christian philosophers must be wary about assimilating or accepting presently popular philosophical ideas and procedures; for many of these have roots that are deeply anti-Christian. And finally the Christian philosophical community has a right to its perspectives; it is under no obligation first to show that this perspective is plausible with respect to what is taken for granted by all philosophers, or most philosophers, or the leading philosophers of our day.

In sum, we who are Christians and propose to be philosophers must not rest content with being philosophers who happen, incidentally, to be Christians; we must strive to be Christian philosophers. We must therefore pursue our projects with integrity, independence, and Christian boldness.[4]

---

4. Delivered November 4, 1983, as the author's inaugural address as the John A. O'Brien Professor of Philosophy at the University of Notre Dame.

CHAPTER TWELVE

Sheehan's Shenanigans:
How Theology Becomes Tomfoolery

I

Higher criticism — source criticism, form criticism, redaction criticism, various contemporary amalgams — has been with us now for at least a century and a half. To the layman it can easily seem that higher critics disparage what they see as the naiveté of the ordinary Christian's belief in the events reported in the New Testament: Christ's virgin birth, his miracles, his death, his (literal and physical) resurrection, his being seen by "more than five hundred of the brethren," his ascension into heaven, and the like. Thus David Strauss, in his *Life of Jesus, Critically Examined,* published in 1835: "Nay, if we would be candid with ourselves, that which was once sacred history for the Christian believer is, for the enlightened portion of our contemporaries, only fable." To the layman it can also seem that the grounds for this disparagement are sometimes extremely slender — so gossamer thin as to be nearly nonexistent. There is much confident assertion but little compelling evidence, abundant speculation but next to nothing of real solidity.

Protestants have had to deal with "higher criticism" for a good long time; but Catholic scholars have been discovering (or at any rate employing) it only over the last quarter-century or so. The result has been a spate of books of biblical criticism by Catholic scholars, some of them, I am sorry to say, running to sizeable excess. Thomas Sheehan's much publicized *The First Coming: How the Kingdom of God Became Christianity* (New York: Random House, 1986) is a case in point. Sheehan is professor of philosophy at Loyola University in Chicago.

Sheehan begins his book by claiming that the Christian church is undergoing a crisis in what she thinks and believes about Jesus: "The crisis grows out of the fact now freely admitted by both Protestant and Catholic theologians

316

and exegetes: that as far as can be discerned from the available historical data, Jesus of Nazareth did not think he was divine [and] did not assert any of the messianic claims that the New Testament attributes to him . . ." (p. 9). Sheehan's project is apparently fourfold: (a) to try once more to determine the actual content of Jesus' preaching (as opposed to what Christians have thought it was); (b) to determine how the idea that Jesus arose from the dead developed in the early church; (c) to do the same for the idea that Jesus was the Christ, the Messiah, and the divine Son of God; and (d) to discover what is the *actual* significance of the preaching and life and death of Jesus. The project is to try to accomplish (a), (b), and (c) "from below": without making such theological assumptions as, for example, that Jesus is the incarnate Son of God, or that the Bible is in any special sense the word of God, or that there is such a thing as the testimony of the Holy Spirit, enabling us to grasp scriptural truths we would otherwise miss. Sheehan hopes to accomplish (a)-(c) by using the sorts of methods that would be employed by a historian confronting any ancient text: "I adopt the viewpoint of the historian, not that of the believer. I take the word 'history' in the context of the original Greek verb that underlies it: *historein,* to search and inquire, using only the light of natural, empirical reason" (p. 9). So the idea is to try to discover what Jesus preached, and how the belief in the resurrection developed, and how the early Christologies developed "using only the light of the natural, empirical reason."

On (b) and (c) Sheehan adopts what is by now a very familiar line: none of the apparent testimony to Jesus' resurrection from the dead and his being literally and physically seen by his disciples ("by more than five hundred of the brothers at the same time"; 1 Cor. 15:6) is to be taken seriously. The nature miracles are

> simply legends which arose among early Christians and which were projected backward, under the impact of faith, into the life of the historical Jesus. (p. 74)

> The reason for the patent inconsistencies and the physical unrecordability of these miraculous "events" comes down to one thing: The gospel stories about Easter are not historical accounts but religious myths. (p. 97)

> To counter the climate of doubt aroused by Jesus' failure to return, some gospel accounts embellished the Easter experience with elaborate apocalyptic stories that concretized the "resurrection" of Jesus by providing him with a preternatural body that was physically seen, touched and elevated into heaven. (p. 293)

The addition of mythical elements was due to a sort of failure of nerve on the part of Peter and others; as a result of this failure there developed in the early church these myths about angels at the tomb, Jesus' being literally seen by many, and the like. Similarly for the development of Christology culminating in the Prologue to the Gospel of John, the Philippians hymn, and Paul's letter to the Colossians: Jesus himself made none of these claims for himself; they were invented later on by a church intent on buttressing a theological point.

Now taken in its own terms Sheehan's case for these claims is at best tenuous, speculative, and fanciful. However, I shall mostly neglect what he says about (b) and (c) and concentrate on what he says under rubrics (a) and (d); then I'll turn to a brief examination of the sorts of reasons scholars sometimes give for supposing that Christology "from below" — attempting to understand the relevant texts without recourse to theological beliefs about Christ or the Bible — is in fact correct and *de rigueur* for Scripture scholarship.

Well then, what does "natural, empirical reason" reveal about what Jesus actually preached? Sheehan's answer may strike an ordinary Christian as indeed amazing, not to say preposterous. Jesus, for example, did not claim to be the Messiah or even a messiah, let alone the divine Son of God:

> What then have the post-Bultmannian critics discovered about the historical Jesus . . . ? Negatively, they have established that Jesus did not express his self-understanding in any Christological titles — certainly not in the so-called higher titles (such as "God" or "Lord") in the full divine sense and not even in the so-called lower titles (for example "messiah," . . . and "Son of Man"). (p. 25)

What did he claim then? What was his positive message? It isn't easy to understand Sheehan's answer. It all began, however, when Jesus came under the spell of John the Baptist; upon hearing the latter, says Sheehan, "Jesus, we may imagine, was pierced to the heart. He repented and was baptized" (p. 53). "Jesus was impressed by the fact that John, unlike the apocalyptic preachers so popular in those days, preached no messiah, proclaimed no end of the world, and promised no future aeon of bliss" (p. 52). Following suit, Jesus too proclaimed no end of the world, preached neither that he nor some other was the messiah. He followed John in "the reduction of apocalypse to its existential core" (p. 55); this means, as far as I can make out, that Jesus had no apocalyptic message, but did enjoin justice and mercy. Further:

> The immediate presence of God as a loving Father is what Jesus meant by the "kingdom. . . ." As Jesus preached it, the kingdom of God had nothing to do with the fanciful geopolitics of the apocalyptists and messianists — a kingdom up above or up ahead. . . . Rather, it meant God's act of reigning, and this meant — here lay the revolutionary force of Jesus' message — that God, as God, had *identified himself without remainder with his people* [Sheehan's italics]. The reign of God meant the *incarnation* of God. (p. 60)

That is, Jesus destroyed the notion of "God-in-Himself" and put in its place the experience of "God-with-mankind." Henceforth, according to the prophet from Galilee, the Father was not to be found in a distant heaven but was entirely identified with the cause of men and women. Jesus' doctrine of the kingdom meant that God had become incarnate: He had poured himself out, had disappeared into mankind and could be found nowhere else but there. . . . The doctrine of the kingdom meant that henceforth and forever God was present only in and as one's neighbor. Jesus dissolved the fanciful speculations of apocalyptic eschatology into the call to justice and charity. (p. 61)

[Jesus'] proclamation marked the death of religion and religion's God and heralded the beginning of the post-religious experience: the abdication of "God" in favor of his hidden presence among human beings. (pp. 61-62)

So Jesus did not proclaim that he was the Messiah, let alone the Son of God; what he preached is not "Believe on me and thou shalt be saved," but something quite different: "God has disappeared into mankind." But what could *that* mean? "God, as God, had *identified himself without remainder with his people*"; "God has disappeared into mankind"; "the abdication of 'God' in favor of his hidden presence among human beings": how are we to understand these dark sayings?

It isn't easy to tell, but I *think* what Sheehan means here is that according to Jesus, there simply *is* no all-powerful being who has, say, created the world and to whom we owe worship and obedience. There is nothing at all like the sort of being Christians and other theists believe in: a transcendent, all-powerful, all-knowing person who has created the heavens and the earth and sustains them in being. And although Sheehan speaks of God's *disappearing into* mankind, *becoming* incarnate without remainder, and the like, the idea is not, I gather, that previously there was such a being, but then later on he somehow disappeared into humanity: the idea is that there never was any such person at all. All there had ever been to God, we might say, was his incarnation in his people: "All Jesus did was bring to light in a fresh way what had always been the case, but what had been forgotten or obscured by religion. His role was simply to end religion — that temporary governess who had turned into a tyrant . . ." (p. 68). So Jesus' message, according to Sheehan, was that theism is false and there is no God. It isn't that theism is at best *approximately* true (as with the nineteenth-century liberals with leanings towards absolute idealism); it isn't true *at all.* Jesus was really an atheist; he preached the end of religion and religion's God, dissolving all this into the recommendation of justice and mercy.

Among liberal theologians of a certain stripe there appears to be a kind of desperate quest for novelty; those who take part in this derby seem to vie with each other to see who can make the most outrageous pronouncements. To understand Sheehan and his claims about Jesus, we must see him and them in their historical context. Twenty years ago when "Death of God Theology" burst (or perhaps dribbled) upon the scene, many of us thought that heights of theological tomfoolery had been achieved that could never be exceeded. One of their number, Paul Van Buren, suggested that logical positivism with its Verifiability Criterion of Meaning — according to which most of what Christians say about God is literally nonsense — was really the proper foundation of Christian theology. Another, Thomas Altizer, seems to have claimed that God died when Christ was born, that he died again in the nineteenth century, and that he has also died in human history generally. He then went on to say that atheism is in fact the final flower and purest form of Christianity (neglecting to add the obvious corollary that bigotry is the final flower and purest form of chastity).

What we had here, many thought, was theological foolishness than which none greater could be conceived. And indeed, Altizer's achievement along these lines is truly formidable. But credit where credit is due: Sheehan, it seems, has topped it. According to Altizer, the real Christian recognizes that atheism is the truth; and now Sheehan adds, in a spectacular burst of insight, that this is the gospel Jesus Christ himself brought! Colossal! There is only one way to go beyond this: to hold that God himself, eternal, omnipotent, and omniscient as he is, was an atheist even before Jesus, and has suffered from a distressing inability to get the message across. (Using terminology in the confusing, vaguely dishonest way characteristic of such theology, one could support this view by pointing out that God worships no one and does not acknowledge a superior being, both of which are characteristic of the atheist.) But even this suggestion, logically impossible though it is, doesn't have quite the sheer bite and panache of Sheehan's preposterous claim.

Sheehan's own message — what *he* sees as the real meaning of the empty tomb, as opposed to the meaning ascribed to it by Christians — is of a piece with the message he puts in the mouth of Jesus. (The tailless fox, as R. G. Collingwood says, preaches taillessness.) According to Sheehan, the real meaning:

> As we peer into that emptiness [of the tomb, with no resurrection], the absence of the living Jesus and even of his dead body allows us to identify a unique form of seeking: the desire for that which can never be had. This unique kind of seeking is the experience that makes human beings different from any other kind of entity, and we see it exemplified in the women who actually found the tomb empty on that first Easter Sunday. Such seeking is not something we occasionally get caught up in; rather, it is what makes us human, constitutes us as the futile passion, the unfulfilled and presumably unfulfillable desire that we are. (p. 172)

Taking Jesus *as (sic)* his word means understanding that he is what everyone else is: a finite fallible, mortal act of interpretation. Every human being is just that and no more: a hermeneusis, a lived interpretation (in action, in play, in language and thought) of what one's existence is and is about. (p. 225)

All of us, including Jesus, are inevitably and forever a question to which there is no answer. Taking Jesus *as* his word means understanding and accepting that. (p. 226)

Taking Jesus *as* his word? This is already enough to make one a bit nervous; how are we to do a thing like that? Would it be to believe that Jesus (contrary to what we have always thought) was really a *proposition* or an assertion? As I say, this is enough to make one a bit nervous; but it is only the tip of the iceberg. Easter, for the Christian, is a time of joy and celebration, a time of profound gratitude for the unthinkable splendor of God's gift of salvation through the death and resurrection of his Son. But according to Sheehan, the *real* meaning of Easter, the real meaning of the empty tomb, is not the glad Easter cry "He is risen" with the declaration that Christ is the firstfruits and the earnest of our own resurrection, so that death has been swallowed up in victory. Not at all; what it really means, he says, is that we are all futile and unfulfillable passions, questions to which there are no answers.

Being a question without an answer certainly sounds like a depressing condition, and no doubt something of a comedown; but what could it *mean?* What is it to be a futile passion, or a question without an answer? You meet some unusual people nowadays, but hardly ever anyone who is a question, let alone a question without an answer. Shorn of excessive pathetic rhetoric, what Sheehan means, I think, is that it is very hard to be sure of anything; no matter what you believe there are always equally satisfactory alternatives. This fits in with Sheehan's claim earlier on in the introduction that

Christianity is a "hermeneusis," or interpretation. Its beliefs and doctrines are but one of many possible and equally valid ways of understanding the universally available empirical data about Jesus of Nazareth. Christians may claim that their faith is based on revelation, but as far as one can tell empirically, such revelation is a name for the historically relative and culturally determined hermeneutical process in which Christians, confronting the humanly available information about Jesus of Nazareth, choose to interpret him as their savior who reigns with God in heaven. (p. 7)

There is much to be said about this (most of it not flattering), but I won't take the time to say it. The basic idea here seems to be the notion, familiar in some varieties of continental philosophy, that whatever we think or believe is only a hermeneusis or interpretation, to which there are equally satisfactory alternatives. No matter what you believe on any important matter, there are alternatives to your belief that are quite as valid and acceptable. Indeed, for any belief you hold, its *denial* will be just as valid or satisfactory as it is.

Of course if this is true, then Christianity, despite Sheehan's confident pronouncements, is as good an interpretation as any other. Thus Sheehan winds up (p. 223) having to concede that Christianity is as acceptable an interpretation or hermeneusis as any other, and, indeed, as *true* as any other — Sheehan's own interpretation, for example. (How we are to understand that is a bit puzzling, since Christianity and what Sheehan proposes are clearly inconsistent; but then Sheehan neither says nor suggests that ordinary logic is part of *his* interpretation.) Self-referential problems loom here. The fundamental claim seems to be that all we can ever have are equally acceptable if conflicting interpretations. But then, of course, if this claim is true, then it is itself just one more interpretation, and it is no better or closer to the truth than alternatives — for example, its denial. If all is interpretation, then this idea itself has no more to be said for it than the contrary idea that some interpretations are vastly preferable and vastly closer to the truth than others. If all is interpretation to which there are equally satisfactory alternatives, then this very claim is an interpretation to which there are equally satisfactory alternatives: one can take it or leave it. As for me and my house, I think we'll leave it.

II

How does Sheehan reach these startling claims as to what Jesus taught? By starting from what he sees as the agreed-upon results of New Testament scholarship and extrapolating: "I depend upon (and hope that I am faithful to) the scientifically controllable results of modern biblical scholarship; but then I go beyond that scholarship, by using its scientific results as data for my own theories" (p. 9). Sheehan draws upon source criticism, form criticism, redaction criticism, and some hitherto unclassified similar criticisms; and his introduction contains a clear and readable account of some of these developments.

To the uninitiate, it can easily seem that much that is tenuous lies at the very foundations of some of these methods. Thus, for example, Sheehan reports that the post-Bultmannian form critics

> make use of at least four criteria for determining whether elements of the gospel material are authentically historical, that is, traceable to Jesus himself. First, the criterion of dissimilarity allows the exegete to attribute to

Jesus at least those sayings which can be shown to be probably unique to him insofar as they are notably dissimilar from sayings that are provably typical either of the early church or ancient Judaism. Secondly, the criterion of coherence allows these exegetes to attribute to Jesus those sayings that are coherent with the material that has already been established to be "unique because dissimilar." Thirdly, the criterion of multiple attestation permits the exegete, within limits, to attribute to Jesus those deeds or kinds of behavior which are attested in all or many of the distinct gospel sources (for example, Mark and Q). Finally, according to the criterion of language and environment, any authentic saying of Jesus would have to reflect Aramaic speech and, in general, the cultural patterns of early Palestine — although it is possible that such characteristics might reflect only the earliest Palestinian churches. (p. 25)

But there is a clear tension here between the first and the fourth criterion: only those sayings that are dissimilar from what was current will be certified by the first criterion, while if the saying does not reflect the cultural patterns of early Palestine then it will be decertified by the fourth. (And of course if you think that Jesus is indeed the divine Son of God, you will no doubt hesitate to assume that any authentic saying of Jesus would have to reflect the cultural patterns of early Palestine.) Further, these methods seem to display an alarming degree of flexibility or flaccidity, permitting an astoundingly wide range of conclusions. Sheehan's own conclusions require, as you can imagine, a good bit of picking and choosing among texts. Using these methods, this is always easy enough: you simply demote any text that doesn't fit your interpretation; you claim that it is a later addition by the Christian community intent on making a theological point. Does Mark 14 or Matthew 26 say Jesus says he is the Son of God and will return in glory? No problem: simply declare that it was added later on and is not a report of anything Jesus actually said.

I shall leave it to the experts to decide how much of value there is in these methods; what concerns me here is Sheehan's tendentious use of them. For example, he regularly speaks of what has been *confirmed* by these methods, or *shown* (p. 12) by them, or *discovered* by them (p. 13), or *established* by them (p. 15); in nearly all of these cases there is scholarly opinion on both sides of the question. (Of course there is also the fact that, from Sheehan's perspective, nothing can really be shown or established; all we have are interpretations to which there are always equally acceptable alternatives.) Further, there is a great deal of dogmatic and unsupported assertion. For example, speaking of John's "leaping in the womb" when his mother Elizabeth met Mary: "But that legend, like the inspiring but unhistorical story about the miraculous virginal conception of Jesus, is a theological interpretation created some decades after the death of Jesus to express Christianity's faith in his special status" (p. 55). Again: "And in any case the words the Gospels put into Jesus' mouth at his [Sanhedrin] hearing (for example, his claim to being the Messiah; Mark 14:62) are later theological interpolations of the early church and cannot be credited as historical statements" (p. 86). And: ". . . it is not true that the Jewish crowds shouted out that Jesus should be crucified (Mark 15:12) or that they took his blood upon themselves and their children (Matt. 27:25). . . . These sentences, which were later written into the accounts of Jesus' passion, are the product of a bitter polemic between early Christianity and Judaism . . ." (p. 87). Here one wonders at the source of Sheehan's information, and here, as in many other places, the footnotes reveal that the matter in question is very much a topic of scholarly debate.

Frequently the text contains a bland assertion to the effect that such and such is the case, and a footnote contradicting the assertion. Thus Sheehan claims that "There is no evidence that Jesus himself forgave sinners in his own name"; in a footnote he gives the evidence, adding that while some take the saying in question to be authentic, others do not. Again, "Jesus had not fainted. He was dead. And in the spirit of the New Testament we may add: He never came back to life" (p. 101). Here there is a footnote, directing us, not as you might expect, to the New Testament, but to Thomas Aquinas — who, of course, does not say that Jesus never came back to life: what he does say is that upon his resurrection Jesus entered a life that was immortal and Godlike.

Sheehan also displays a certain distressing inability to distinguish the assertion that not-p from the failure to assert p. Thus, for example, he says that according to Matthew, "He does not ascend into heaven" (p. 97), giving as a reference Matthew 28:16-20. But of course Matthew 28:16-20 does not say that Jesus did not ascend into heaven; it simply doesn't say that he did. Again, there is often a certain lack of balance between the plausibility of a claim and the weight of its documentation. For example: "For Simon and the others," he says, " 'resurrection' was simply one way of articulating their conviction that God had vindicated Jesus and was coming soon to dwell among his people. And this interpretation would have held true for the early believers, even if an exhumation of Jesus' grave had discovered his rotting flesh and bones" (p. 109). The evidence for this astonishing claim is the fact that there is at least one Scripture scholar who says so. Finally, as Sheehan interprets 1 Corinthians 15:3-8, Paul did not mean to say that Christ had physically risen from the dead: "The raising of Jesus has nothing to do with a spatio-temporal resuscitation, a coming back to life . . ." (p. 112). But here he completely neglects the remainder of the chapter, where Paul relates Jesus' resurrection to our own coming resurrection, which he clearly sees as literal, physical, and spatio-temporal.

III

The most interesting issues raised by this book, I think, have less to do with Sheehan's dubious claims than with the enterprises of Christology "from below" and "objective" biblical scholarship — i.e., scholarship in which one does not assume or take for granted what one knows or believes by faith about (say) Jesus, but instead treats the Bible as one would any ancient text and Jesus as any character in such a text. The idea is to see what can be established (or at least made plausible) using only the light of "natural, empirical reason," ignoring anything one may know by faith. The idea is that a proper Scripture scholar will be "objective." Objectivity is sometimes represented as a matter of sticking to the objective facts, not bringing in any theological interpretation. What is really meant in this context, however, is that the objective scholar will not use any theological assumptions or knowledge in the attempt to determine what the objective facts are. Thus, for example, Barnabas Lindars, a well-known New Testament scholar, seems to suggest that it is somehow wrong or improper to rely upon what one knows or believes by faith in biblical interpretation:

> There are in fact two reasons why many scholars are very cautious about miracle stories. . . . The second reason is historical. The religious literature of the ancient world is full of miracle stories, and we cannot believe them all. It is not open to a scholar to decide that, just because he is a believing Christian, he will accept all the Gospel miracles at their face value, but at the same time he will repudiate miracles attributed to Isis. All such accounts have to be scrutinized with equal detachment. (*Theology,* March 1986, p. 91)

Why think this? Why *isn't* it open to a scholar to accept the Gospel accounts of miracles, but reject others? Because, thinks Lindars, proceeding that way wouldn't be properly detached or objective; there would be something merely arbitrary about it. The real question here is this: is it legitimate for a Christian scholar — a Christian Scripture scholar, for example — to employ assumptions or beliefs the source of which is her Christian faith? Can one properly employ, in scholarship, assumptions that aren't shared by all members of the scholarly community? Can you properly employ what you know by faith? Thus, for example, the Christian, thinking that Jesus is indeed the divine Son of God, might be inclined to credit certain miracle stories as sober historical accounts of what Jesus did (the raising of Lazarus, e.g., or his own resurrection). If you don't think Jesus was divine, however, you would plausibly think it very unlikely that these are accounts of what actually happened; it might be more plausible to see them as added by the early church to make a theological point of one sort or another. So whether you think Christ was (is) in fact divine could certainly make a big difference to how you proceed in Scripture scholarship.

And isn't it simple common sense to think that a Christian scholar (or the Christian scholarly community) should use everything she knows in pursuing her discipline? Suppose you (or the Christian community) do in fact believe that Jesus was divine. If what you want, in scholarship, is to reach the truth about the matters at hand, then why not use all that you know, regardless of its particular source? Isn't it merely perverse to limit yourself to only *some* of what you know, or only *some* sources of knowledge, if your aim is to reach the truth about the phenomenon in question? That would be like trying to do physics, say, without in any way relying upon your own memory or the memory of anyone else. (Any proposition accepted in part by virtue of reliance upon memory, you declare, is not to be taken as part of the evidence.) You might be able to do a bit of physics that way, but it would be pretty limited, a poor, paltry, truncated thing. And why would you want to do it? (Perhaps I could climb Devil's Tower with my feet tied together, but why would I want to?) If your aim is to reach as much as you can of the full-fledged, full-orbed truth about the matter at hand, then presumably the right way to proceed is to use all of your resources, everything you know, including what you know by faith.

But, says Lindars, isn't it just arbitrary to treat miracle stories about Jesus differently from miracle stories about Isis? Well, no; for you think that Jesus was divine but Isis was not — or perhaps you think that "Isis," in this use, doesn't name anything at all, so that there simply wasn't any such person or thing as Isis. So there is a great difference between the two, a difference which requires that they be treated differently. (Objectivity requires that we treat similar things similarly; it doesn't require that we ignore important differences.)

But then isn't it arbitrary to have *that* belief — that Jesus was Christ, and the Son of God, and hence special? What makes you think that is true? How could you sensibly come to *that* belief, except upon the basis of historical investigation — investigation that does not start by presupposing the truth of the belief in question? The suggestion is that any appropriately justified belief about Jesus must be based entirely upon ordinary historical investigation. But why should we believe a thing like that? Christians don't typically come to their beliefs about Jesus in that way; and I know of no good reason to think that this is the way they *would* do it, if they did it properly. This claim — that one ought not to employ the view that Jesus was (is) divine in scholarship — rests on the assumption that the only way in which we could properly come to characteristically Christian beliefs is by way of ordinary scientific or historical investigation. But this assumption is dubious *in excelsis;* it is part and parcel of classical Foundationalism and shares its liabilities (see, for example, my "Reason and Belief in God," chapter 5 of the present volume). Further, it fits poorly with Christian ideas as to the sources of our Christian belief. Reformed Christians, for example, will be likely to follow John Calvin in holding that there is such a thing as the internal testimony of the Holy Spirit; and they will add that this testimony is a source of reliable and perfectly acceptable beliefs about what is communicated in Scripture. Other Christian traditions have other suggestions for sources of belief that play the same role; but nearly all the major Christian traditions unite in rejecting the idea that the only acceptable source of beliefs about Jesus is ordinary scientific investigation. So why should we accept it in Scripture scholarship?

What is really at issue here is a philosophical (epistemological) view about what constitutes correct or reasonable belief, about what constitutes proper or real knowledge. The objectivist thinks that the only sources of knowledge or acceptable scholarly belief are perception, memory, mathematico-logical intuition, and the like — i.e., "natural empirical reason"; he rejects any such alleged sources of belief as the testimony of the Holy Spirit. But there is no good reason for the Christian to join him here; and of course objectivism is an entirely unnatural position for a Christian to adopt. A more natural position is that if we employ all that we know (not just natural empirical reason), we stand a much better chance of getting close to the actual full-orbed truth. And isn't that what we are after in scholarship? So why should we handicap ourselves in the fashion suggested by the objectivist?

CHAPTER THIRTEEN

Christian Philosophy
at the End of the Twentieth Century

My assignment is to reflect on the condition and prospects of Christian philosophy at the end of the twentieth century. Now most philosophers don't even get to comment, prophetically, on the turn of a *century;* we get to comment on the turn of a *millennium!* The last philosopher to be able to do that was probably Gerbert Aurillac, who died in 1003. (Unfortunately, or maybe fortunately, his views on the turn of the millennium have not been preserved.) So why wasn't our symposium given a grander title: "Christian Philosophy at the End of the Second Millennium!", or "Christian Philosophy at the Dawn of the Third Millennium!"? Of course I realize that my paper will be just one more in a flurry of speeches, papers, and declarations greeting the new millennium. We will no doubt hear much about how man (and woman) has finally come of age, or since we have already been hearing that for the last 60 years or so, *really* come of age. There will be strident claptrap about how third millennial men and women can no longer believe this or that, how various items of the Christian faith belong to an earlier and simpler time, and so on. There will be earnest calls to take up our responsibilities as third-millennial people: given what science or Rorty have taught us we must whip our noetic structures into proper third-millennial shape. In American philosophy we have a technical term for all such declarations and calls: we call them 'baloney.'

I shall not take part in this man-has-now-come-of-ageism, or as-we-now-knowism, or other baloney. Still, one hopes we do learn things as we go along; and we can sensibly ask how things stand with Christian philosophy now, on the threshold of a new century, and even a new millennium. I want to ask first what this century has brought for Christian philosophy; then I will propose a sort of typology for Christian philosophy, briefly evaluating our present condition with respect to each of the main areas of the typology; and

328

along the way I shall issue an occasional *obiter dictum* as to what, as it seems to me, we Christian philosophers ought to do next.

I. Christian Philosophy and the Twentieth Century

Well, how *has* the twentieth century treated Christian philosophy? As you may have noticed, the twentieth century includes many different temporal segments and has occurred at many different places; and things have gone differently in these different place-times. I write mainly of Christian philosophy in the Anglophone world; I just don't know enough about how it has gone in German, French, and Dutch philosophy to speak at all authoritatively. I shall also leave out of account twentieth-century developments in Catholic and Thomist philosophy; otherwise my subject would be genuinely unmanageable.

The main positive development in Christian philosophy during the first half of our century must surely be the work of the man whose 100th birthday we are presently celebrating. Dooyeweerd's work was comprehensive, insightful, profound, courageous, and quite properly influential. It isn't necessary, however, for me to sing the praises of Dooyeweerd to this audience; that would be carrying coals to Newcastle, or perhaps corn to Iowa, or maybe cheese to Gouda. Let us simply note the sheer size of Dooyeweerd's accomplishment, remembering that it took place in a context going back to Abraham Kuyper and indeed back all the way to Bonaventura, Augustine, and Tertullian.

On the other hand, the main negative development during that same period, and in Anglo-American philosophy, would certainly be logical positivism and allied streams of thought. According to positivism, characteristically Christian utterances do not so much as have the grace to be false: they are "cognitively meaningless," sheer nonsense — *disguised* nonsense, to be sure, but nonsense nonetheless. The harrowing vicissitudes of positivism and its verifiability criterion of meaning are an instructive and oft-told story; I will not add another telling; but I am afraid it must be admitted that the response of Christian thinkers to it was not, on the whole, an edifying spectacle.

By now logical positivism has retreated into well-earned obscurity; but what has taken its place? Not one, but rather, in hydra fashion, *two* equally nasty phenomena. Out of the frying pan into the fire. First, note that logical positivism is just a special if specially noxious case of a broader positivism — a line of thought that elevates science and scientific knowledge at the expense of more important kinds of knowledge such as knowledge of God and knowledge of how to live properly before him. But that broader positivism is itself a manifestation of a still broader perspective we can call "perennial naturalism." Christian philosophers since Augustine's great work *De Civitas Dei* have seen human history as a sort of arena for a contest or struggle: a struggle, says Augustine, between the *Civitas Dei,* on the one hand, and the *Civitas Mundi* on the other. I think Augustine is right; but at present, at the end of the second millennium, the *Civitas Mundi* is divided into two dukedoms — or since we are talking cities and not kingdoms, two precincts or boroughs. One of these is the perennial naturalism I just mentioned. This is a basic perspective on the world, a fundamental way of thought that goes back to Epicurus, Lucretius, Democritus, and others in the ancient world, but finds much more powerful and explicit expression in the modern and contemporary world. Naturalism is perhaps the dominant perspective or picture among contemporary Western intellectuals; its central tenet is that there is no God and nothing beyond nature. Human beings, therefore, must be understood, not in terms of their being image bearers of God, but in terms of their commonality with the rest of nature, i.e., nonhuman nature. The things we think distinctive about ourselves — religion, morality, love, scholarship, humor, adventure, politics — all must be understood in natural terms, which in our day means evolutionary terms. An astonishing number of contemporary scholarly projects, both inside and outside philosophy, are explicit or implicit attempts to understand one or another area of human life in naturalistic terms: think, for example, of sociobiology, and think of contemporary materialistic cognitive science — a many-sided, far-flung project involving many different disciplines and thousands of scholars all over the Western world.

Perennial naturalism, while it has been present for quite some time in English-speaking philosophy, has in the last quarter century or so taken an increasingly aggressive and explicit stance. And what we have in philosophy, as one head of the post-positivistic hydra, is a proliferation of efforts to give naturalistic accounts of various philosophical topics and phenomena: there is naturalist epistemology, conceived as the attempt to understand knowledge from a naturalistic point of view; there are naturalist accounts of intentionality and aboutness, of morality, of teleology, and proper function; of language, of meaning, of thought, of much more. The naturalism that underlies and gives birth to these projects is quite as opposed to Christian ways of thinking as was logical positivism, and perhaps more dangerous because more plausible.

But the *Civitas Mundi* is divided into two precincts. The second head of that post-positivistic hydra is connected with the second precinct of the *Civitas Mundi:* I shall call it 'creative anti-realism.' Here the basic claim or idea is not that we human beings are just one more kind of animal with a rather unusual means of survival, but that we are actually responsible for the basic lineaments, the fundamental structure and framework of the world itself. Like perennial naturalism, creative anti-realism goes back to the ancient world, back at least to Protagoras's dictum "Man is the measure of all things, of the existence of things that are, and of the nonexistence of things that are not . . ." (*Theaetetus* 152 A). But, also, like perennial naturalism, creative anti-realism has received much more compelling formulation in the modern and contemporary world.

The story begins with Immanuel Kant. His basic idea, in his monumental first *Critique,* the *Critique of Pure Reason,* is that the fundamental categories that characterize the world in which we live are imposed upon that world by *our* noetic activity: they do not characterize that world as it is in itself. Such features of the world as space and time, substance-property structure, number, modality, and even truth and existence are not to be found in things in themselves. They are rather to be found in the "things for us"; they are *contributed* to the world; these structures are there as a result of our noetic or intellective activity. According to an older way of thinking, *God's* knowledge is creative: according to this more recent Kantian way of thinking, it is *our* knowledge that is creative. I realize that it is extremely difficult to give a clear but accurate summary of Kant's thought here in three sentences. Indeed it is extremely difficult to give a clear but accurate summary of Kant's thought in three hundred sentences, or three hundred pages. That is because Kant's thought, in the first critique, does not lend itself to clear and accurate summary at *any* length; as far as I can see it contains deep ambiguities and confusions. Still, the understanding of Kant just outlined has been both historically influential, and intimately connected with the second precinct of the *Civitas Mundi.*

I believe that the thought of the first *Critique,* at least understood as above, is incompatible with Christianity. For the things we know are *essentially* such that they display subject-property structure; it is not as if a horse, say, or the sun, could have existed but not been an object with properties. There really isn't any alternative available to horses or stars. If so, however, then the horse in question, as well as the sun, owes its existence to *us:* it could not have existed apart from our noetic activity. From this perspective, then, it is not *God* who has created the heavens and the earth, but we ourselves — or at any rate God could not have done it without our help. We can reach the same conclusion by a much quicker route: *existence* is one of the categories of the understanding, a structure we human beings impose on things. But if so, then if it weren't for our noetic activity, there wouldn't be any things that exist. Indeed, since the things that exist are the only things there are, if it weren't for us and our conceptual activity, there wouldn't be or have been anything at all, no dinosaurs, stars, mountains, trees, or electrons. In fact, on this way of thinking, we owe our own existence to our categorizing activity, a thought that can easily induce a sort of intellectual vertigo. But then an implication of this way of thinking is that it is we who have created the heavens and the earth, not God. As a matter of fact, taken strictly, this strand of Kant's thought would apply to God as well; if the category of existence is a merely human category we impose upon things, if things fall under or into this category only because of our noetic activity, then the same would be true of God himself. He, too, in a stunning reversal of roles, would owe his existence to us.

Creative anti-realism, taken neat and globally, is clearly incompatible with Christianity. Indeed, taken neat it is, I think, incompatible with every-thing, because incompatible with itself, inconsistent. Of course Kant himself did not take creative anti-realism globally and neat. Neatness is not a Kantian category; no doubt that is part of his charm. And no doubt there are restrictions of Kantian creative anti-realism that are compatible with Christianity, and that ought to be explored as among the possibilities as to how things are. But the second head of the post-positivistic hydra is not creative anti-realism taken neat: it is instead a spin-off or dialectical consequence of it. For suppose we begin by thinking that it is we human beings who are responsible for the way the world is; it is we ourselves who form or structure the world in which we live. Then it is an easy step to the thought that we do not all live in the same world. The *Lebenswelt* of Richard Rorty or Jacques Derrida is quite different from that of Herman Dooyeweerd or C. S. Lewis; and each of those is wholly different from that of Bertrand Russell or Carl Sagan.

It is then tempting to take the next step: that we live in different worlds, that there simply isn't any such thing as *the* way the world is, the same for each of us. Instead, there is my way of structuring reality (by choice or language, or whatever), your way, and in fact many different ways. There is no such thing as *the* way the world is, and no such thing as *truth,* objective truth, the same for each of us whether we know it or not. Instead, there is what is true from my perspective, in my version, in the world as I've structured it, what is true from *your* perspective, in *your* version, in the world as *you've* structured it, and so on. My beginning students at Calvin used to tell me, sometimes, after I proposed an absolutely conclusive and apodictically certain argument for some thesis or other, that while my thesis was certainly true *for me,* it wasn't true *for them.* At the time I thought that a peculiarly sophomoric confusion: the very idea of "truth for you" as opposed to "truth for me," I thought, if it is not just an inept way of speaking of what you believe as opposed to what I believe, makes no sense. But the fact is this confusion, as I then thought of it, is an expression of contemporary relativism, a way of thought as widespread as it is lamentable.

There is another and very contemporary way to arrive at this same relativism. As we are often told nowadays, we live in a postmodern era; and postmodernists pride themselves on rejecting the classical foundationalism that we all learned at our mother's knee. Classical foundationalism has enjoyed a hegemony, a near consensus in the West from the Enlightenment to the very recent past. And according to the classical foundationalist, our beliefs, at least when properly founded, are objective in a double sense. The first sense is a Kantian sense: what is objective in this sense is what is not merely subjective, and what is subjective is what is private or peculiar to just some persons. According to classical foundationalism, well-founded belief is objective in this sense; at least in principle, any properly functioning human beings who think together about a disputed question with care and good will, can be expected to come to agreement. Well-founded belief is objective in another sense as well: it has to do with, is successfully aimed at, *objects,* things, things in themselves, to borrow a phrase. Well-founded belief is often or usually adequate to the thing; it has an *adequatio ad rem.* There are horses, in the world, and my thought of a given horse is indeed a thought of that horse. Furthermore, it is *adequate* to the horse, in the sense that the properties I take the horse to have are properties it really has. That it has those properties — the ones I take it to have — furthermore, does not depend upon me or upon how I think of it: the horse has those properties on its own account, independent of me or anyone else. My thought and belief is therefore objective in that it is centered upon an object independent of me; it is not directed to something I, as subject, have constructed or in some other way created.

Now what is characteristic of much postmodern thought is the rejection of objectivity in this second sense — often in the name of rejecting objectivity in the first sense. The typical argument for postmodern relativism leaps lightly from the claim that there is no objectivity of the first sort, to the claim that there is none of the second. As you have no doubt noticed, this is a whopping non sequitur; that hasn't curbed its popularity in the least. Classical foundationalism, so the argument runs, has failed: we now see that there is no rational procedure guaranteed to settle all disputes among people of good will; we do not necessarily share starting points for thought, together with forms of argument that are sufficient to settle all differences of opinion. That's the premise. The conclusion is that therefore we can't really think about objects independent of us, but only about something else, perhaps constructs we ourselves have brought into being. Put thus baldly, the argument does not inspire confidence; but even if we put it less baldly, is there really anything of substance here? In any event, by this route too we arrive at the thought that there isn't any such thing as a truth that is independent of us and our thoughts. The idea seems to be that objectivity in the first, Kantian sense, necessarily goes with objectivity in the second, external sense, so that if our thought isn't objective in the first sense, then it isn't objective in the second sense either. And what has happened within at least some of so-called postmodernisms is that the quite proper rejection of the one — a rejection that would of course have received the enthusiastic support of Kuyper and Dooyeweerd — has been confused with the rejection, the demise of the other — an idea that Kuyper and Dooyeweerd would have utterly rejected.

However arrived at, it is this relativism that is the second head of the post-positivistic hydra. Clearly this head of the hydra is no more receptive to Christian thought than the positivistic head it replaced. Contrary to what I used to think, it is vastly more than a mere confusion; it is instead a more or less willful rejection of something that lies very deep in Christian thought. Clearly one of the deepest impulses in Christian thought is the idea that there really is such a person as God, who has established the world a certain way: there really is a correct or right way of looking at things; this is the way God looks at things. Furthermore, things are the way God sees them for everyone, quite independently of what they might think, say, or wish. It is not the case that people can escape being desperately and irremediably wrong about God just by virtue of failing to believe the truth about him.

An example of relativism is the sort of thought associated with Richard Rorty, who apparently thinks of truth as what our peers will let us get away with saying. This thought exemplifies the sort of relativism I'm speaking of. The reason is that my peers might not let me get away with saying what your peers let you get away with. For in the first place we might have different peers, and there is no reason to think your peers coordinate and synchronize their activities with mine. But even if we had the same peers, there is no reason to think they would have to let you and me get away with saying the same things: perhaps they think I am a bit unduly prickly and are consequently more indulgent towards you than towards me. Therefore what is true "for you" need not be true "for me." Presumably, furthermore, the truth can change: what my peers will let me get away with saying about the Peloponnesian War today, for example, might be different from what they let me get away with saying about it yesterday.

This way of thinking has real possibilities for dealing with war, poverty, disease, and the other ills our flesh is heir to. Take AIDS, for example, about which there has been great recent concern: if we all let each other get away with saying that there just isn't any such thing as AIDS, then on this Rorty-esque view it would be *true* that there isn't any such thing as AIDS; and if it were *true* that there is no such thing as AIDS, then there would *be* no such thing. So all we have to do to get rid of AIDS, or cancer, or poverty is let each other get away with saying there is no such thing. That seems a much easier way of dealing with them than the more conventional methods, which involve all that money, energy, and time.

Similarly, consider the Chinese authorities who murdered those students at Tiananmen Square and then compounded their wickedness by bald-faced lies, claiming they'd done no such thing. From a Rortian point of view, this is a most uncharitable way to think about it. For in denying it ever happened, they were merely trying to bring it about that their peers would let them get away with saying it had never happened, in which case it would have been true that it never happened, in which case it would never have happened. So the charitable thought here, from a Rortian point of view, is that the Chinese authorities were only trying to bring it about that this terrible thing had never happened: and who can fault them for a thing like that? The same goes for those Nazi skinhead types who claim there was no holocaust and that Hitler and his cohorts were as gentle as lambs and never harmed anyone; they too should charitably be seen as trying to see to it that those terrible things never did happen. And in your own personal life, if you have done something wrong, lie about it, try to get your peers to let you get away with saying you didn't do it. If you succeed, then in fact you won't have done it; furthermore, as an added bonus then you won't have lied about it either.

So these are the hydra heads that have sprung up to replace logical positivism. The first, perennial naturalism, is particularly rampant in the sciences and among those who nail their banners to the mast of science. The second runs riot in the humanities, in literary studies, film studies, law, history, and to some degree in the human sciences. But both are dead opposed to Christian thought; both are wholly inimical to it; both are its sworn enemies. And one important task of the Christian philosopher — that is, of the Christian philosophical community — is consciousness-raising: pointing out that there is this conflict, and testing the spirits. There are a thousand intellectual projects that find their roots in these ways of thinking; we Christians and our children are often heavily influenced by these projects; they are unavoidable because of their widespread dominance; and they often corrupt and compromise the intellectual and spiritual life of the Christian community. It is our task as Christian philosophers to pay careful and determined attention to the way in which such projects are related to Christian thought.

II. Christian Philosophy

But in waxing thus hortatory, I am getting a bit ahead of myself. I should like now to turn more directly to my assignment, which was to make some remarks about how I see the accomplishments and tasks of Christian philosophy at this point in our history; this will be connected with the above exhortation. The first thing to note, of course, is that there are several different parts, several different divisions to Christian philosophy. As I see it, there are essentially four different divisions: apologetics, both negative and positive, philosophical theology, Christian philosophical criticism, and constructive Christian philosophy. The philosophers of the Christian community have done better by some of these, during our century, than by others. Suppose we briefly take them each in turn.

A. Negative Apologetics

Roughly speaking, negative apologetics is the attempt to defend Christian belief against the various sorts of attacks that have been brought against it: the argument from evil, for example, or the claim that science has somehow shown Christian belief wanting. But isn't the very idea of apologetics, whether negative or positive, contrary to the basic Reformed insight of Kuyper and Dooyeweerd? If all thought has religious roots, then the thing to say about attacks on Christianity is just that they too have religious roots — *non-Christian* religious roots; thus they do not require an answer. Faith cannot reason with unbelief: it can only preach to it.

Perhaps in a world where the wheat and the tares were more clearly separated and more thoroughly articulated, something like this would be right. But our world is not such a world. In our world there are people who are moving in opposite directions, but nevertheless occupying some of the same places. And the places they occupy are not abstract types. It is the part of Calvinism to hold that Christians are not complete; they are in process. John Calvin, himself no mean Calvinist, points out that believers are constantly beset by doubts, disquietude, spiritual difficulty, and turmoil. "It never goes so well with us," he says, "that we are wholly cured of the disease of unbelief and entirely filled and possessed by faith" (*Institutes,* III, ii, par. 18). It never goes that well with us, and it often goes a good deal worse. There is an unbeliever within the breast of every Christian; in the believing mind, says Calvin, "certainty is mixed with doubt." (No doubt the proportions differ for different people and for the same person at different times.) But then objections brought by the atheologians — the Freuds, Marxes, and Nietzsches, the Flews, Mackies, and Nielsens — these objections can and do trouble the Christian community and need to be answered. And that is, in part, the function of negative apologetics: to refute such objections, thus removing one kind of obstacle to the spiritual peace and wholeness of the Christian community.

Of course negative apologetics can also be useful for those who are not in the Christian community, but perhaps on its edges, perhaps thinking about joining it. And it can also be useful for those who are not on the edges but adamantly opposed to the Christian truth; perhaps once they really see just how weak their arguments really are, they will be moved closer to it.

Well, how has negative apologetics fared during our century? Reasonably well, I think, but not as well as one might hope. What sorts of considerations and objections really do trouble thoughtful Christians — students and others? No doubt several, but among the more important, during our century, I think, have been (1) the positivistic claim that Christianity really makes no sense; (2) the argument from evil, which is a sort of perennial concern of Christian apologetics; (3) the heady brew served up by Freud, Marx, Nietzsche, and other masters of suspicion; and (4) pluralistic considerations: given that there are all these different religions in the world, isn't there something at least naïve and probably worse, in doggedly sticking with Christianity? Positivism, the first of these four, has by now crawled back into the woodwork; but I am sorry to say Christian apologetics cannot claim much of the credit. Far too many Christian philosophers were thoroughly intimidated by the positivistic onslaught, suspecting that there must be much truth to it, and suggesting various unlikely courses of action. Some thought we should just give up; others said, for example, that we should concede that Christianity is in fact nonsense, but insist that it is important nonsense; still others proposed that we continue to make characteristically Christian utterances, but mean something wholly different by them, something that would not attract the wrath of the positivists. This was not a proud chapter in our history, but since positivism is no longer with us, we shall avert our eyes from the unhappy spectacle and move on.

Turning to the second item on the list, there has been a good deal of work on the argument from evil, and in fact it is now, as opposed to forty years ago, rather rare for an atheologian to claim that there is a contradiction between the claim that there is a wholly good, all-powerful, all-knowing God, on the one hand, and the existence of evil on the other. This is due in large part to the efforts of Christian philosophers. Those atheologians who now press the argument from evil must resort to the *probabilistic* argument from evil: given all the evil the world contains, it is unlikely, improbable, that there is a wholly good, all-powerful, and all-knowing God. This argument is much messier, much more complicated, and much less satisfactory from the point of view of the objector. In other ways, however, this probabilistic argument is more realistic and perhaps more disturbing. Christian philosophers — William Alston and Peter van Inwagen, for example — have done good work here, but much remains to be done.[1]

Christian philosophers haven't done as well, I think, in defusing the sorts of objections offered by those masters of suspicion — Freud, with his claim that religious belief stems from a cognitive process aimed at psychological comfort rather than the truth, Marx and his claim that religious belief

---

1. William Alston, "The Inductive Argument from Evil and the Human Cognitive Condition," and Peter van Inwagen, "The Problem of Evil, the Problem of Air, and the Problem of Silence," both in *Philosophical Perspectives #5: Philosophy of Religion, 1991*. Alston, pp. 29-67; van Inwagen, pp. 135-65. [Editor's Note: These two papers have recently been reprinted, along with several other recent, significant works on the subject, in Daniel Howard-Snyder, editor, *The Evidential Argument from Evil* (Bloomington: Indiana University Press, 1996).]

really results from cognitive malfunction consequent upon social malfunction, and Nietzsche with his shrilly strident claims to the effect that Christianity arises from and results in a sort of weak, sniveling, envious, and thoroughly disgusting sort of character. There are many who do not accept the details of what any of these three say, but nonetheless entertain the sneaking suspicion that there is something to these charges and that something like them might be true. Christian apologists must forthrightly and honestly address these doubts and these arguments, although in fact argument is hard to find in these thinkers.

Finally, pluralist objections too trouble many Christians, especially Christian academics and others who are acutely aware of some of the other major religions of the world. This is something of a new or revitalized worry for the Christian community; as a result we have just begun to work at it and think about it. But I venture to predict that these pluralist objections will loom large in the next segment of our adventure as Christians.

B. Positive Apologetics

The twentieth century in the West has not been hospitable to positive apologetics. Reformed thought has concurred in this lack of hospitality: it is rather characteristic of Reformed Christian philosophy to view theistic arguments with suspicion, and to some degree with good cause. But as my minister said the other day, everything is context. One may offer theistic arguments because you think that without them belief in God would be unjustified or unwarranted; this is what Reformed thought has always adamantly opposed. But it doesn't follow that theistic argument is without value, or that the Christian thinker shouldn't engage in it. After all, John Calvin himself was not always inhospitable to rational arguments on these topics. Consider his attitude towards rational arguments for the reliability of Scripture. He argues first that our confidence in the Scripture ought not to depend upon such arguments, even though good arguments of this sort, he thinks, are available. Rather, our confidence, when things are going as they should, will depend upon the internal testimony of the Holy Spirit. Still there remains a role for those arguments to play:

> Conversely, once we have embraced it [Scripture] devoutly as its dignity deserves, and have recognized it to be above the common sort of things, those arguments — not strong enough before to engraft and fix the certainty of Scripture in our minds — become very useful aids. (*Institutes*, I, viii, par. 1).

This topic of course deserves a paper all to itself: but perhaps what Calvin has in mind, put briefly, is this. First, theistic arguments can obviously be of value for those who don't already believe; they can move them closer to belief, and can bring it about that belief in God is at any rate among the live options for them. Only God bestows saving faith, of course, but his way of doing so can certainly involve cooperation with his children, as in preaching and even argumentation. But second, theistic arguments can also be useful for *believers*. Calvin notes that believers struggle constantly with doubts; in this life, he says (as we saw above), "faith is always mixed with unbelief" and ". . . in the believing mind certainty is mixed with doubt . . ." (*Institutes*, III, ii, par. 18). At times the truth of the main lines of the gospel seems as certain and sure that there is such a country as the Netherlands; at other times you wake up in the middle of the night and find yourself wondering whether this whole wonderful Christian story is really anything more than just that: a wonderful story. Theistic arguments can be helpful here. Perhaps you accept (as I do) an argument to the effect that there could be no such thing as genuine moral obligation, if naturalism were true and there were no such person as God; perhaps it is also obvious to you that moral obligation is real and important; these thoughts can help dispel the doubt. Perhaps you think, as I do, that there could be no such thing as genuinely horrifying evil if there were no God; but you are also convinced that the world is full of horrifying evil; again, these thoughts can dispel the doubt. Perhaps, more abstractly, you think there could be no such thing as propositions, the things that are true or false, that stand in logical relations and that can be believed or disbelieved, if there were no such person as God; but you also find yourself convinced that there are such things as propositions; again, this thought can dispel the doubt, increase your confidence and repose.

How has positive apologetics (which I shall think of as just the effort to develop and provide theistic arguments) fared in the twentieth century? On the whole, I think, not well. Some Thomists have thought themselves committed to Thomas's view that the existence of God is provable, but they haven't for the most part thought that they could produce the arguments. Perhaps the major work of natural theology of the century is contained in the first two volumes of Richard Swinburne's trilogy: his books *The Coherence of Theism* (Oxford: Clarendon Press, 1977) and *The Existence of God* (Oxford: Clarendon Press, 1979). These have been influential, and there is much to be said for them. There have also been other arguments: for example, a contemporary version of the moral argument has been developed by George Mavrodes and Robert Adams.

But much more can and should be done. There are really a whole host of good theistic arguments, all patiently waiting to be developed in penetrating and profound detail. This is one area where contemporary Christian philosophers have a great deal of work to do. There are arguments from the existence of good and evil, right and wrong, moral obligation; there is an argument from the existence of horrifying evil, from intentionality and the nature of propositions and properties, from the nature of sets and numbers, from counterfactuals, and from the apparent fine-tuning of the universe. There is the onto-logical argument, but also the more convincing teleological argument, which can be developed in many ways. There is an argument from the existence of contingent beings, and even an argument from colors and flavors. There are arguments from simplicity, from induction, and from the falsehood of general skepticism. There is a general argument from the reliability of intuition, and also one from Kripke's Wittgenstein. There is an argument from the existence of *a priori* knowledge, and one from the causal requirement in knowledge. There are arguments from love, beauty, play and enjoyment, and from the perceived meaning of life. There are arguments from the confluence of justi-fication and warrant, from the confluence of proper function and reliability, and from the existence, in nature, of organs and systems that function properly. (So far as I can see, there is no naturalistic account or analysis of proper function.) These arguments are not apodictic or certain; nevertheless they all deserve to be developed in loving detail; and each of them will be of value both as a theistic argument, and also as a way of thinking about the relation between God and the specific sort of phenomenon in question. I believe Christian philosophers of the next century (not to mention the remainder of this one) should pay a great deal more attention to theistic argument.

C. Philosophical Theology

A second element of Christian philosophy: *philosophical theology.* This is a matter of thinking about the central doctrines of the Christian faith from a philosophical perspective; it is a matter of employing the resources of philos-ophy to deepen our grasp and understanding of them. Philosophical theology, of course, has been the stock-in-trade of Christian philosophers and theolo-gians from the very beginning; think of Augustine's great work on the Trinity, for example. At present, this enterprise is faring rather well, perhaps even flourishing; the last few years have seen a remarkable flurry of activity in philosophical theology as pursued by Christian philosophers. There is impor-tant work on the divine attributes: for example, the classic Stump-Kretzmann work on God's eternity and Nicholas Wolterstorff's work on God's everlast-ingness and his arguments against divine impassability. There is Brian Lef-tow's fine pair of books *Time and Eternity* and *Divine Ideas,* and Edward

2. Eleonore Stump and Norman Kretzmann, "Eternity," *Journal of Philosophy* 78 (1981): 492-58; Nicholas Wolterstorff, "God Everlasting," in C. Orlebeke and L. Smedes, editors, *God and the Good* (Grand Rapids: Eerdmans, 1975); Brian Leftow, *Time and Eternity* (Ithaca: Cornell University Press, 1991) and *Divine Ideas* (Ithaca: Cornell University Press, 1994); Edward Wierenga, *The Nature of God: An Inquiry into Divine Attributes* (Ithaca: Cornell University Press, 1989).

Wierenga's *The Nature of God.*[2] There has been excellent work on divine simplicity over the last 15 years — probably more work, in Anglo-American philosophy, at any rate, than there had been during the preceding 150 years — as well as on God's action in the world and the central doctrines of Original Sin, Incarnation, and Atonement. There has been fine work on freedom, foreknowledge, and middle knowledge. Of course not everyone is unreservedly enthusiastic about this work; some theologians seem to harbor the impression that philosophical theology as pursued by contemporary philosophers is often unduly ahistorical and uncontextual. Sometimes this arises from the thought that *any* concern with the above topics is ahistorical; those topics belong to another age and can't properly be discussed now. That seems to me historicism run amok; but no doubt some of this work could profit from closer contact with what theologians know. Still, the theologians don't seem to be doing the work in question. I therefore hope I will not be accused of interdisciplinary chauvinism if I point out that the best work in philosophical theology — in the English-speaking world and over the last quarter century — has been done not by theologians but by philosophers.

D. Christian Philosophical Criticism

We come now to Augustinian Christian philosophy more precisely and narrowly so-called. This has two parts: Christian philosophical criticism, on the one hand, and, on the other, constructive Christian philosophy. That isn't a good name for it; I shall call it instead "positive Christian philosophy." First, Christian cultural criticism. There is a great deal to be said here, and little space to say it; fortunately I have already said some of what needs to be said in pointing to Augustine's view of human history as an arena for a contest between the *Civitas Dei* and the *Civitas Mundi.*

In our day and in the West, the second comes in two divisions; so in our day there are fundamentally three basic pictures, three fundamental and fundamentally religious perspectives on ourselves and our world: Christian theism, perennial naturalism, and creative anti-realism with its attendant relativism. But Augustine added another profound and seminal idea, an idea that flowered much later in the work of Kuyper, Dooyeweerd, Harry Jellema, and others: scholarship, intellectual endeavor, science in the sense of *Wetenschap* is inevitably involved in these perspectives. Intellectual activity has religious roots. Science and philosophy are not neutral with respect to the contest between these perspectives: they are ordinarily expressions of them. Most sizeable scholarly projects, to the extent that they are pursued with depth and insight and fullness, are in the service of one or another of these perspectives.

Here we need to emphasize two things: (1) these perspectives, these ways of thinking, are indeed contrary to Christian thought, and (2) they dominate much of the intellectual culture we all live in. But this brings in its train real problems for the Christian community. For it is inevitable that our thought, our spiritual life, our responses to the world and to God should be influenced, colored, perhaps corrupted by these ways of thinking. To the extent that this is so, our intellectual and spiritual lives will be characterized by a lack of integrality, of wholeness, of being all of one piece. We ourselves and our students and our children will be pulled in different directions, will be inclined to take for granted, unthinkingly assume, ways of thought and ways of looking at the world that don't fit at all well with the Christian faith to which we are committed.

It is therefore of the first importance that Christian philosophers engage in Christian philosophical and cultural criticism. This is true, of course, not just for philosophers, but for Christian intellectuals generally and especially for Christian intellectuals working in the humanities and the human sciences. But here we are concerned specifically with philosophy. We must take a careful look at the various projects and research programs we encounter: how are they related to Christianity? And we find, I think, that an astonishing proportion of them, when we examine them closely, spring out of the soil of perennial naturalism or creative anti-realism. I don't have the space here to give anything like a properly representative sample: let me just call your attention, then, to contemporary philosophy of mind. In the United States, philosophy of mind is really one part of a larger project that includes cognitive science, in particular certain parts of psychology, computer science, artificial intelligence, certain developments in epistemology, and more. It is thus an enormous project that involves several different disciplines and thousands of scholars. And it is fundamentally materialist in origin: its aim is to understand the basic phenomena of mind — intentionality or aboutness, consciousness, qualia, affect, and the like — in materialistic and naturalistic terms.

Now how should the Christian community think about this project? How does it fit in with the fact that God, who is *not* a material object, has knowledge (knows each of us), intentionality (he thinks about his creatures), affect (he loved the world so much that he sent his only begotten son to suffer and die, thereby redeeming us), and so on? Can Christian philosophers properly and in good conscience join these projects? What, if anything, can we learn from them? What stance should we take towards them? To continue with the example, in contemporary philosophy of mind there is what is called 'the problem of intentionality.' Well, what is this problem? *Intentionality* is *aboutness;* and our thought, obviously enough, is fundamentally characterized by intentionality or aboutness. We can think about things of a thousand different sorts; we can think about things far removed from us in space and time; we can think about the Big Bang, quarks, the parting of the Red Sea, and God himself. The so-called problem of intentionality is really the question of how to understand this, how to make sense of it, from a materialist perspective. If this way of thinking is fundamentally right, then a belief or thought will have to be a material process of some sort, that being the only kind there is. But how can a material process, a transaction among a group of neurons, say, be *about* something? How could it be about the Big Bang, or dinosaurs, or quarks, or the parting of the Red Sea, or God? What in those neurons or in what happens to them would make it the case that they are about those things?

This is a tough problem, and my guess is that there really isn't much of anything to say here. The serious materialist, in the long run, will just have to say, with John Searle, "Well, some material objects or processes just do have this mysterious property of aboutness and that's all there's too it. Case closed." As Darwin's bulldog, T. H. Huxley, once said, the brain secretes thought like the liver secretes bile. The only alternative I can see is to follow the *eliminative materialists:* According to them there really isn't any such thing as aboutness, intentionality, at all. Thinking in terms of aboutness or intentionality, so they say, is an error; it is really a relic of prescientific ways of thought, or perhaps of an early and very primitive kind of science. These are the alternatives, and a pretty grim pair they are. But is this "problem of intentionality" a problem for the Christian thinker? Should she join in on this project, writing her dissertation on it, and taking for granted the way the problem is put? I suggest not, or at least normally not. She should instead point out that this is a problem only for someone who is a materialist about minds; the Christian needn't be, and in my opinion shouldn't be. But then the very appellation "the problem of intentionality," like in another context the appellation "the problem of other minds," is not a neutral label; it betrays a materialist perspective. This is not a problem from just any perspective, and in particular not from a Christian perspective.

This is of course just one example, and a clear and unambiguous example. There will be dozens of other examples (and many of them will not be unambiguous). There are many projects in philosophy of language that have naturalistic roots, and others that have their roots in creative anti-realism. There are attempts to understand all the various varieties of human phenomena — morality, religion, love, humor, knowledge, and the like — from a naturalistic point of view; there are also attempts to come to terms with mathematical reality and numbers, propositions, properties, and states of affairs from a naturalistic perspective. Similarly, there are an enormous number of projects in philosophy that originate in creative anti-realism; and of course there are many projects of mixed parentage. It is the job of the Christian philosophical community to carefully study these projects, claims, and positions, so that their relationship to Christian ways of thought is made evident. And this is not important just for Christian philosophers, but for the spiritual health and welfare of the Christian community.

E. Constructive Christian Philosophy

I come finally to the fourth and last division of Christian philosophy, constructive Christian philosophy. This is, I think, clearly the most difficult of the four; it requires more creativity and intellectual suppleness, more insight and discernment than we can easily muster. But it is also in some ways the most important, and I'd like to emphasize that it is important to *do* this, not merely talk about how we ought to do it, how we might do it, what the best way of doing it might be, what will happen if we do it, what will happen if we don't, what the various theories of doing it are, and so on. An occupational hazard of academics is just that: *talking about* things, even things that themselves are essentially a matter of thinking and talking, instead of actually getting in there and doing them. That would be serious error: we must do it, and not merely talk about it. But what is it I say we must do? Here the aim is to consider the various questions philosophers ask and answer, and to answer these questions from an explicitly Christian or theistic perspective, taking advantage, in attempting to answer them, of all that we know, including what we know as Christians.

I said above that there are philosophical problems Christians won't be attracted to: the problem of how to understand intentionality from a naturalistic perspective, for example. On the other hand, and at another level of generality, there are questions that philosophers of all persuasions try to answer: how shall we understand morality, art, religion, humor, abstract objects, science? What is knowledge? What is meaning; how do terms get meaning, and what do they have when they have it? Do we think in terms of properties that we predicate of objects, or does thought and speech go on in some other way? How far does human freedom extend? What *is* freedom? These and a thousand other topics are among the topics the Christian philosophical community should address, and address from a distinctively and unabashedly Christian point of view. At one level, therefore, the Christian philosopher shares concerns, questions, and topics with his non-Christian colleagues. But he answers those questions differently, and, at another level, answers different questions. We might say (to borrow another phrase) that the Christian philosopher must be *in* the world, but not *of* the world. And this can be a cause of perplexity; it makes it hard to know just how to proceed; it gives us a hard row to hoe, or to change the metaphor, a faint trail to follow, with many opportunities for going wrong and winding up in a thicket. We are to be *in* the world: what this means, in this context, is that at certain levels we are engaged in the same philosophical projects as everyone else. We want to know how to understand ourselves and our world; this means we want to understand the topics just listed. But we are not to be *of* the world; this means that our way of understanding these things will inevitably differ from that of those who don't share our basic commitment to the Lord. These differences may sometimes be subtle, and of course may vary widely from area to area.

Let me give an example. (This example, embarrassingly, is from my own work; I cite it only because I am rather familiar with it, not because I am prepared to make claims as to its importance.) A question that has been with us since Plato's *Theaetetus* is this: how shall we think about knowledge? What property or quality is it that distinguishes knowledge from mere true belief? Whatever it is, suppose we call it "warrant." In twentieth-century Anglo-American epistemology, the dominant answer to the question "What is warrant?" has been in terms of *justification;* and justification, in turn, has been construed deontologically, in terms of rights and obligations, permission and duties. On this tradition, what distinguishes knowledge from mere true belief, from a lucky guess, e.g., is the believer's being *justified,* being within her epistemic rights, having fulfilled her cognitive or epistemic duties, having flouted no noetic obligations. This idea gets it inspiration in an Enlightenment conviction that we have an epistemic duty to think critically about the traditional beliefs we have inherited. Perhaps we do have such a duty (and then again perhaps not); but it is easy to see that construing warrant as justification can't possibly be right. That is just because you might be doing your best, be doing your duty to the uttermost, but still, by virtue, e.g., of cognitive malfunction, be forming beliefs in such a way that they have little or no warrant for you. Descartes' madmen thought they were gourds: pumpkins, perhaps, or summer squash. These beliefs of theirs had no warrant; but there is no reason to think they were moral delinquents. Perhaps, morally speaking, they were doing their level best. Clearly this is the wrong place to look for warrant.

Where should we look instead? We should begin, so I suggest, with creation: the idea that we have been created by God and created in his image. This image consists in several properties, but one way in which he made us like him is our ability to have true belief and knowledge. We know much: we know about our immediate environment, about the past, about the far reaches of the universe, about our own interior lives, about morality, about modality, and about God himself. If he has created us to know these things, then he has given us the means to do so — powers or faculties that are employed and exercised in our knowing. And the basic way to think about knowledge, I suggest, is this: a belief constitutes knowledge when it is produced by those faculties *functioning properly* in us, when they are subject to no dysfunction, are not diseased, are working the way God designed them to work. This is a first approximation: further conditions are needed. In particular, we must add that the production of the belief in question is governed by a bit of the design plan that is aimed at the production of *true* beliefs, rather than the production of beliefs aimed at, for example, survival, or comfort, or the possibility of loyalty and friendship. We must also add, finally, that the design plan is a good one, and that it is functioning in an environment sufficiently similar to the environment for which our faculties were designed.

I believe this account of knowledge (properly fleshed out) is closer to the truth than any of the others currently on offer. And it is closer to the truth in part because of features that are not really available to nontheistic views. In particular, the notion of proper function, I believe, can't be accommodated within a naturalistic way of thinking about the world; that is because it essentially involves teleology, and at bottom, teleology in nature requires a creator who intends to accomplish certain ends or aims, and fashions his creation accordingly. Despite this incompatibility with unbelief, however, it might be that such an account will be attractive not just to Christians but to others as well. Perhaps the fact is, for example, that no account of knowledge that doesn't involve the notion of proper function will in fact be successful. By this I don't mean merely that no such account will commend itself to believers in God; I mean no such account will be satisfactory from *anybody's* perspective.

Suppose we stop a moment and illustrate this a bit more fully. Those who don't share our commitment to the Lord are in transition, just as we are. As Calvin says, there is unbelief within the breast of every Christian; but isn't there also belief within the breast of every non-Christian? The antithesis is of course real; but at any time in history it is also less than fully articulated and developed. The City of God stands opposed to the City of the World: sure enough; but we all live in God's world, and those in the City of the World are subject to the promptings and blandishments of our God-given natures, of the Sensus Divinitatis, and of the Holy Spirit. Were the two cities completely formed and articulated, they could have little intellectual commerce or contact with each other. The believer would see the world a certain way, or perhaps in one of a certain range of ways; the unbeliever would see it quite differently, and feel no unease or discomfort in seeing it his way.

But the cities, and the citizens therein, are not completely formed and developed. Thus, for example, in the final analysis (so it seems to me) current forms of anti-theism have no place for the notion of truth. Naturalism does not, because naturalism has no room for the sorts of things that fundamentally are true: propositions and thoughts. And creative anti-realism doesn't either, since it has no room for the notion of a way things are independent of our cognitive and linguistic activities. Still, there is such a thing as truth, and it is intimately connected with God. There is such a thing as the way the world is; there are such things as thoughts and propositions, and these things are true or false. Furthermore, we are all, believer and unbeliever alike, created by the Lord. Despite the ravages of sin, we are all still in epistemic touch with the world for which he created us, still oriented towards the reality he has designed us for. It is therefore extremely difficult for any human being to give up such notions as truth and knowledge; it takes great energy and determination. Consequently there is a constant internal tension in unbelieving thought. It is at this very point that our contributions to the philosophical conversation can be attractive and useful to those who don't share our commitments: attractive, because of these fundamental human inclinations towards the notion of truth (and knowledge, and a host of other notions), and useful, because such an account, insofar as it really does depend upon notions not available to the naturalist, can serve as a sort of implicit theistic argument, perhaps creating the very sort of confusion and turmoil in which the Holy Spirit works.

So we contribute to the human philosophical conversation, but make our own distinctive contribution, a contribution that must be integral in the sense that it does not compromise basic Christian commitments, and does not compromise with ways of thinking that comport ill with Christian thought. But there is another way in which we are in but not of the world. A Christian epistemologist will of course give an account of the basic cognitive faculties with which the Lord has created us: perception, memory, moral knowledge, reason (the faculty of *a priori* knowledge and belief), sympathy or *Einfühlung* (whereby we understand the thoughts and feelings of another), testimony (whereby we learn from others), induction (whereby we learn from experience), the ensemble of processes involved in scientific knowledge, and all the rest. So far, we might say, our account is in the world, in that the naturalist will want to give an account — perhaps a very different account — of all or some of the very same things. And, as I say, I think the resources of the Christian scheme of things provide the means for a good account of many departments of this capacious establishment for which satisfying accounts are not available in naturalistic ways of thinking.

But there is still more, and by virtue of this more a Christian epistemologist will not be of the world. For of course she will also want to think about *other* kinds of knowledge, kinds of knowledge that are of great, indeed maximal importance to us as Christians: knowledge of God, knowledge of the great truths of the gospel, as Jonathan Edwards calls them, knowledge of how we can have access to our only comfort in life and in death, and knowledge of how we can achieve our chief end of glorifying God and enjoying him forever. A Christian epistemologist will keep her eye on these things as she develops her epistemology. She will want to develop an epistemology that fits these things especially well; she won't be satisfied with an account onto which these things have to be grafted as ill-fitting afterthoughts. Here she may, once more, diverge from her unbelieving colleagues, who will see all of this as a manifestation not of knowledge but of superstition and error; here she is not of the world.

A main feature of the epistemology just sketched is that it involves *faculties* or *powers* or *cognitive processes.* We have these faculties or processes by virtue of creation, and it is by virtue of their operation that we form beliefs and acquire knowledge. As I say, an account of this kind essentially involves teleology, and hence essentially involves our being creatures, created and designed by the Lord. But it also enables us to see both that our knowledge of God and of the great truths of the gospel is really just a special case of knowledge generally, and how that knowledge is integrated with the rest of our knowledge. We have two distinct kinds of knowledge to consider here: our knowledge of God, on the one hand, and our knowledge of the great truths of the gospel on the other. There is the knowledge of God we have by virtue of our created nature, and also the knowledge of God and his special work of salvation that we get from Scripture, from God's speaking to us. There is what we know by general revelation, and also what we know by special revelation. Of course there will be deep and intimate connections between these two: after all, the God we know by nature is the principal actor in the sublime drama of salvation. They are nonetheless distinct kinds of knowledge. Had Adam and Eve not sinned, they would have had knowledge of God, but no knowledge of the great truths of the gospel. This knowledge of God would have come by way of a faculty or process whereby they formed the relevant beliefs. That process or power or faculty was part of their increased cognitive equipment, in this way on a par with memory, perception, reason, and sympathy; it remains a part of *our* cognitive economy, although it has been dimmed and distorted by sin. Since we (or at any rate some of us) are Calvinists, we might as well call this process by its right name: the Sensus Divinitatis.

But our original parents did indeed fall into sin. By a process of which we have no clear grasp, this led to a kind of corruption of our nature, including our cognitive nature. But it also led to an epistemic gift of magnificent proportions. In the first place, their sin plunged them and their posterity into a different epistemic state, one in which our natural, increased knowledge of God, while still present, was wounded; this knowledge was obscured by the smoke of our wrongdoing, both the smoke resulting from my own personal sin, and from the wound the Sensus Divinitatis itself sustained. Here we confront the noetic or epistemic effects of sin at their most radical and harmful. But secondly, the Lord took dramatic action to enable us to be reborn, regenerated, to regain our lost relationship with him, to live once more the way he intended us to. He both provided this way back to health, and also *speaks* of it to us, telling us about it, enabling us to learn about it and to know what we need to know to gain its benefits. How does this speaking work? By way of the Scriptures and the church, of course: but how does it happen that we *believe* the Scriptures? Here too, then, there is something like a faculty or process at work; only this time the process in question is not part of our natural, increated epistemic equipment. It is instead a special and supernatural work of God. Once again we must call this work by its proper Calvinist name: it is the internal testimony of the Holy Spirit. I say we should call these things by their proper Calvinist names; but the fact is that here and elsewhere Calvin, despite his fulminations against what he calls the "Papists" with their "Popery" and "Popish Idolatry," is not far at all from Thomas Aquinas.

And here I must make a parenthetical remark. Calvin and his eighteenth-century follower Jonathan Edwards are among my highest-ranking heroes; but their attitude towards Catholics is far from emulable. Detesting the Anabaptists, furthermore, was always a really bad idea; it disfigures the otherwise warm and gracious character of the Belgic Confession. Fortunately, in my communion, anyway, we are no longer enjoined to take that hateful stance. We Christians have *real* enemies in the contemporary world; we do not need to fight each other. Indeed, the unedifying spectacle of Christians at each other's throats is in part responsible for our present enemies, by being in part the cause of modern apostasy. Close parenthesis.

According to Calvin, the chief work of the Holy Spirit in us is the production of faith. And faith, he says, is a kind of knowledge: "a firm and certain knowledge of God's benevolence toward us, founded upon the truth of the freely given promise in Christ . . ." (*Institutes,* III, ii, par. 7). Return to the epistemology I briefly sketched above: from that vantage point, calling faith a kind of *knowledge* need be neither merely figurative nor hyperbole. For this belief in God's benevolence towards us, in his sacrificial activity on our behalf, is produced in us by a cognitive process functioning properly in the kind of environment for which God designed both it and us; the production of this belief, furthermore, is according to a design plan successfully aimed at truth. The conditions for warrant are therefore met; if the belief in question is indeed firm and certain, this belief will constitute knowledge in the original and univocal sense.

Of course what remains to be worked out here is enormous. How exactly is the internal testimony of the Holy Spirit related to the Sensus Divinitatis? Does it restore the latter to its pristine function? If so, does this occur suddenly, or via a long process? And doesn't it also do much more, in convincing us of the great truths of the gospel? What other cognitive or epistemic consequences result from the work of the Holy Spirit? And exactly how does sin fit in? The account of knowledge speaks of faculties functioning properly; can faculties damaged by sin function properly? If not, is there any knowledge? Or, if the workings of some of these faculties is at least partly restored through regeneration, is there any merely natural knowledge? Are all damaged, or only some?

Are all those damaged, damaged to the same extent? Consider, for example, epistemic probability. Epistemic probability, as opposed to objective probability, is a matter of what a rational, i.e., properly functioning person would think in certain circumstances. More precisely, the epistemic probability of a proposition or belief, relative to an epistemic situation (roughly speaking, other beliefs together with current experience), is a matter of how firmly the belief in question would be held by a rational, properly functioning person in the epistemic situation in question.

But of course sin and its effects throw a monkey wrench into this machinery. We are inclined to gauge the rationality of a given belief relative to a given set of circumstances by thinking about what we or someone wiser than we would think in those circumstances; but if the operation of our faculties is compromised by sin, this procedure is at best tenuous and chancy. In this connection we circle back to an item of apologetics: the probabilistic argument from evil. According to the best versions of this argument, a properly functioning human being who is fully aware of the horrifying evils the world contains will be disinclined, or less inclined, to believe that the world is in fact under the control of a wholly good, all-powerful, and all-knowing person. It is therefore a defeater, and a powerful defeater, for theistic belief. But is this correct? What, in fact, would a wholly rational person, i.e., someone with a properly functioning Sensus Divinitatis, think, confronted with the evils our world contains? Presumably she would have an intimate, detailed, vivid, and explicit knowledge of God; she would have an intense awareness of his presence, glory, goodness, power, perfection; she would be as convinced of God's existence as of her own. She might therefore be *puzzled* by the existence of this evil in God's world, but the idea that perhaps there just *wasn't* any such person as God would no doubt not so much as cross her mind. Does it follow that the existence of horrifying evil is not for us a defeater, not even a defeated defeater, not even a defeater at all, of theistic belief?

A second set of questions: according to Calvin, faith is this sure and certain knowledge of God's benevolence towards us, ". . . both revealed to our minds and sealed to our hearts by the Holy Spirit." Revealing and sealing: what is the difference between these two? Mere belief is not enough; it must be sealed to the heart. Is this sealing a matter of religious affections, as Jonathan Edwards suggests? If it is, do these affections themselves contain a cognitive, intentional element? According to the epistle of James, the devils believe, and they tremble. Is the difference between the redeemed Christian and the devils a matter simply of affections, in that the Christian loves the Lord, is heartily thankful for these gracious truths, and commits himself to living in and for the Lord, while the devils take a very different affective stance? Or does the believer know something the devils don't, something of the loveliness, graciousness, beauty, holiness, amiability of the Lord, none of which the devils grasp? What *is* the relation between cognitive processes and affective processes, in an older terminology, between intellect and will, in knowledge of God?

Another set of questions in the same neighborhood: William James, that cultured, sophisticated, New England Victorian gentleman, notes the throbbing elements of longing, yearning, desire, and eros in the writings of Teresa of Avila, looks down his cultivated nose, and finds all that a bit, well, *tasteless,* a bit *déclassé.* Sniffs James, ". . . in the main her idea of religion seems to have been that of an endless amatory flirtation . . . between the devotee and the deity. . . ."[3] But here the joke is on James. The Bible, in particular the Psalms but not only the Psalms, is full of expressions of that longing, yearning, *Sehnsucht.* This erotic element in true religion is deep, obvious, and often noted. How is this kind of eros related to other kinds of eros? Freud thought religious eroticism a distorted and illusory reflection of sexual eros, which he thought the basic driving force in human nature. But here (as elsewhere) perhaps Freud had things just reversed. Perhaps it is *sexual* desire and longing that is a sign of something deeper: perhaps it is a sign of this longing, yearning for God we human beings achieve when we are graciously enabled to reach a certain level of the Christian life. Bernard Williams scoffs that heaven would be pretty boring; and Michael Levine suggests that friendship with God could be fairly interesting, but doubts that it would be "supremely worthwhile." But perhaps these reactions are as spiritually immature as that of a 10-year-old child upon first hearing of the pleasures of sex: could it really match marbles, or chocolate? And here too, what we need to know is how affect and intellect work together; is this longing, this yearning for God, a *knowledge* of God? Or merely a desire for a knowledge of God? Does affect add something cognitive or epistemic to intellect here? How is affect related to intellect in knowledge of God? Is sin at bottom a disorder of affect? Is it a sort of affective psychosis, a madness of the will?

These are some of the questions: of course there are many more. My point has not been to catalog all the questions, but to illustrate a way in which the Christian philosopher is in but not of the world. The Christian epistemologist offers an account of knowledge, thus joining a human project with roots that antedate Christianity. But if she does things right, she will not automatically accept currently popular accounts; she will offer one of her own, one that arises naturally out of her Christian way of thinking about the world. This account should be superior to those offered by naturalists, and may also seem so to others, even to nontheists, thus serving as something like a theistic argument. Her account will of course be designed to fit and illuminate the

3. William James, *Varieties of Religious Experience* (New York: Longman, Green, and Co., 1902), p. 340.

kinds of knowledge we all have in common: perception, memory, reason, and the like; she is thus in the world. But it will also be designed and perhaps specially designed to fit and illuminate kinds of knowledge her unbelieving compatriot will dismiss: our knowledge of God, of the great truths of the gospel, and of how to appropriate the latter for our own lives; she is thus not of the world.

These are some of the ways in which the Christian philosopher will be in but not of the world. There is still another way, perhaps the most important way, one that a Christian philosopher neglects at great peril. For a Christian philosopher is first of all a Christian and only secondarily a philosopher. Her philosophy is her specific way of working out her vocation as a Christian; but then to be a proper Christian philosopher, she must be a proper Christian. This means that all of her thought and activity will be shaped and formed by the traditional ways in which we Christians try to make progress in the Christian life: prayer, Bible reading, taking part in the sacraments, associating with other Christians for fellowship and edification. Those who neglect these things are cutting off the source and root of their being as Christian philosophers.

III. Conclusion

Christian philosophy at the end of the twentieth century is doing rather well along some dimensions, less well along others. And of course its work of properly relating to the *Civitas Mundi* is never done: as the latter constantly changes, so must the Christian response. But the Christian philosophical community must also offer its own accounts of the main philosophical topics and concerns. Herman Dooyeweerd made a determined and powerful effort to do precisely this: for that we are thankful. We must continue in the spirit of his work, offering our own accounts of these areas. This task is challenging, formidable, difficult, frustrating; it is also fascinating, beguiling, fulfilling. Most of all, it is the service we Christian philosophers owe to the Lord and our community. I commend it to you.

Afterword

First, my gratitude to James Sennett for collecting and putting together these essays. He chose wisely, and it does indeed seem to me that they make a pretty good snapshot of my work (so far) in philosophy of religion.

Two concerns have largely dominated that work. First, there is negative apologetics, the attempt to defend the Christian faith against the various sorts of attacks that have been launched against it. Since the Enlightenment, such objections have taken two forms.[1] First, there are *de facto* objections: arguments or claims to the effect that elements of Christian or theistic belief are simply false: there is no such person as God, or Jesus Christ was not in fact the incarnate second person of the Trinity, or he didn't suffer and die as an atonement for our sins, and so on. (The argument that the existence of God is incompatible with the existence of evil is of this sort.) And second (and perhaps more common), there are *de jure* objections: arguments for the conclusion that Christian belief, whether or not true, suffers from some serious epistemic defect: it is irrational, or rationally unjustified, or unwarranted, or something else of the same unhappy sort. A central *de jure* objection has been the *evidentialist* objection to theistic belief, i.e., the claim that belief in God is epistemically defective because there is insufficient evidence for it. In *God and Other Minds,* my first book, I was trying to address this objection — *trying* to address it, because I didn't then understand it very well. From my present vantage point, *God and Other Minds* looks like a promising attempt by someone a little long on chutzpah but a little short on epistemology; I hope to do a better job in *Warranted Christian Belief.*

The latter will differ in two ways from *God and Other Minds.* First, it

---

1. And indeed since long before the Enlightenment: Origen wrote an eight-volume reply to Celsus in which both forms of objection are to be found.

will defend specifically *Christian* belief, not just belief in God. What is of first importance here is not just minimal theism, but the whole panoply of Christian belief, including sin, Trinity, incarnation, atonement, Christ's resurrection, and eternal life. My excuse for confining attention just to theism in *God and Other Minds* and much of my subsequent work can only be that I was reacting to various atheological arguments and claims; these claims were focused, for the most part, on belief in God rather than more specifically Christian belief. And secondly, in *God and Other Minds* I didn't really see what the evidentialist objection amounts to: does the objector claim that theistic belief is *unjustified?* If so, is this to be understood in the original deontological sense, i.e., as contrary to epistemic duty or obligation? Or must it be understood in some analogically extended sense?[2] Or is the claim that theistic belief is *irrational?* But in which sense of that protean term?[3] Or the claim that theistic belief lacks warrant, i.e., that property, whatever exactly it is, that distinguishes knowledge from mere true belief? Or what? The objector doesn't tell us, so we shall have to help him by figuring it out ourselves. That is part of the project of *Warranted Christian Belief.*

It was a short step from *God and Other Minds* to so-called "Reformed Epistemology."[4] The basic idea of the former was that neither belief in other minds nor belief in God has much by way of propositional evidence, but neither seems any the worse for that. The basic idea of the latter is that belief in God can be perfectly rational even if not accepted on the basis of propositional evidence. I developed this idea in "Reason and Belief in God" and elsewhere.[5] In this work I was perhaps mainly concerned with *justification,* and in particular justification in its original and basic form: *deontological* justification. This was in part because the atheological objections to which I was replying seemed to be arguments to the effect that the theist without propositional evidence is (deontologically) unjustified: she doesn't have an intellectual or epistemic *right* to hold her theistic beliefs. It soon became clear, however, that deontological justification, whether or not it was what the atheologians had in mind, can't really be the issue. That is because it is entirely

2. For an account of some of these analogical extensions, see chapter 1 of my *Warrant: The Current Debate* (New York: Oxford University Press, 1993).

3. For some of these senses, see *Warrant: The Current Debate,* pp. 132-37.

4. I'm inclined to regret the choice of the name: some have apparently thought the idea was to cast a gauntlet at the feet of Roman Catholic philosophers. Nothing could be further from the truth. As a matter of fact I think Calvin and Thomas Aquinas are very close on matters epistemological, in particular on matters concerning the epistemology of Christian belief. In *Warranted Christian Belief* I propose a model under which specifically Christian belief can have warrant, and (to note that concord) call it the "Aquinas-Calvin model."

5. The same idea was also being developed by William Alston in a powerful series of articles defending the idea that it is possible to perceive God, and perceive that he has such properties as love, wisdom, graciousness, and the like; this series culminated in his magisterial *Perceiving God* (Ithaca: Cornell University Press, 1991).

too easy for Christian belief to be justified in that deontological sense. Consider someone who does her epistemic best, thinks about objections and difficulties, reflects long and hard, but still finds Christian belief or belief in God overwhelmingly obvious: such a person is clearly within her epistemic rights, whether or not she is aware of any propositional evidence for theism. She may be deceived, or confused, or irrational, or intellectually challenged, but there aren't any duties she's flouting.

So the real question, if there is a real question, must lie somewhere else. Thinking along these lines led me to the idea of *warrant* as developed in *Warrant and Proper Function.*[6] The real question, so it seems to me, is whether Christian and theistic belief can have warrant. But a little reflection reveals that if Christian or theistic belief is in fact *true,* then, very likely, anyway, it does have warrant. So the upshot is that a *de jure* objection like the evidentialist objection — an objection according to which there is something seriously wrong with Christian or theistic belief, whether or not it is true — can't be maintained. The only sensible kind of objection to Christian belief will have to be a *de facto* objection — an argument for the claim that it isn't true. That sort of argument is unfashionable in these postmodern days, when the whole notion of truth is viewed with considerable suspicion, but it is also the atheologian's only hope.

The second main objection with which I've been concerned is the argument from evil. When I began thinking about these matters in the 1950s, the atheologians almost[7] to a man (or woman) declared that the existence of a wholly good, all-powerful, and all-knowing God was flatly inconsistent with the existence of evil in the world. It was in response to this claim that I developed the free will defense — or rather, since it can be found (at least in embryonic form) as far back as Augustine, redeveloped and restated it in a contemporary idiom.

Atheologians now seem to have given up the claim that God and evil are logically incompatible; the usual claim nowadays is that theism is *improbable* given all the evil the world contains, or that the existence of evil is a *defeater* for theistic belief. This is messier and less elegant than the austere allegation of logical incompatibility. Furthermore, a convincing argument of this sort will be hard to mount; what is important is not just the probability of the existence of God on *evil,* but its probability on our *total* evidence, whatever exactly that comes to. It will therefore have to involve an inquiry into nonpropositional evidence for the existence of God as well as propositional evidence; hence a satisfactory argument of this sort will involve nothing less than an entire epistemology of religious belief. But if these nondeductive

6. *Warrant and Proper Function* (New York: Oxford University Press, 1993).
7. The exception was John Wisdom in "God and Evil," *Mind* 44 (1935).

arguments from evil present the atheologian with a problem, they perhaps also present believers with something of a problem: they are more realistic, and (perhaps in part just because they are messier) harder to dismiss, and perhaps more troubling than the earlier claims of incompatibility. I'm not at all satisfied with what I have so far said in response to these nondeductive versions of the objection (and will try again in *Warranted Christian Belief*), but there are powerful responses by William Alston,[8] Peter van Inwagen,[9] Stephen Wykstra,[10] and others. I also believe Christian philosophers should follow the lead of Eleonore Stump and Marilyn Adams in going beyond a *defensive* strategy. They shouldn't just reply to atheological arguments against theistic belief; they should also try to figure out how to think about evil from a Christian perspective.

And this brings me to my last point. For the last 50 years or so, Christians in philosophy of religion have been for the most part on the defensive; they have typically tried to defend Christian belief against attacks of various sorts. This is of course a fine thing to do (since a great deal of my own work has been aimed in this direction, this opinion is more or less *de rigueur* for me). But Christians should do more, and do more in two quite different directions. First, they shouldn't merely defend Christian theism: they should also point out problems with the prominent contemporary alternatives, and point out advantages (advantages in addition to truth) Christian theism enjoys with respect to these alternatives. In "Christian Philosophy at the End of the Twentieth Century" and elsewhere I identify these alternatives as *naturalism* and *creative anti-realism*.

Naturalism, it seems to me, is eminently attackable. Its Achilles' heel (in addition to its deplorable falsehood) is that it has no room for *normativity*. There is no room, within naturalism, for right or wrong, or good or bad. (I realize this may be a little abrupt, and also that is a large and controversial claim, and [as one says in these contexts] I don't have the space here to justify it.) Naturalism also lacks room for the notion of *proper function* for non-artifacts, and hence lacks room for the notion of proper function for our cognitive faculties. It therefore has no room for the notion of knowledge, at least if the account of warrant given in *Warrant and Proper Function* is anywhere nearly correct. There is another way in which naturalism has no

8. "The Inductive Argument from Evil," *Philosophical Perspectives 5: Philosophy of Religion, 1991.*

9. "The Problem of Evil, the Problem of Air, and the Problem of Silence," *Philosophical Perspectives 5: Philosophy of Religion, 1991,* and "The Magnitude, Duration, and Distribution of Evil: A Theodicy," in *Philosophical Topics* 16, no. 2 (1988). Both reprinted in van Inwagen's *God, Knowledge, and Mystery* (Ithaca: Cornell University Press, 1995).

10. "The Humean Obstacle to Evidential Arguments from Suffering: On Avoiding the Evil of 'Appearance,' " *International Journal for Philosophy of Religion* 16 (1984): 73-93, 95-100.

room for knowledge. If you think naturalism is true and also accept current evolutionary accounts of the origins of ourselves and our cognitive faculties (and also grasp a certain cogent argument[11]), then you have a defeater for the proposition that your cognitive faculties are reliable, hence for any belief that is a product of those faculties, and hence for the conjunction of naturalism with these evolutionary accounts. But if you accept naturalism, you will also, no doubt, accept those evolutionary accounts; hence you have a defeater for naturalism. This is "An Evolutionary Argument Against Naturalism." On inductive grounds I doubt that I have the argument exactly right, but I believe it is fundamentally correct, and that the truth lies somewhere in its neighborhood; and I invite others to join in getting the argument right.

The other way in which the Christian philosophical community needs to go beyond negative apologetics is in the direction of specifically Christian philosophy. Here I have little to say in addition to what I've already said in "Advice to Christian Philosophers" and "Christian Philosophy at the End of the Twentieth Century." But note that this second way is connected with the first. According to the first way, Christians shouldn't be content to defend Christian belief against the various sorts of attacks brought against it; they should also analyze and examine the main current alternatives to Christian theism, revealing their deficiencies. Among the deficiencies of naturalism, for example, is the inability to find room for normativity; among the deficiencies of creative anti-realism is an inability to find room for truth and objectivity. Creative anti-realists can ridicule, posture, and write 'Truth' with a capital 'T' and sneering quotes all they like: we all really know (unless thoroughly corrupted) that there really is such a thing as truth ('objective' truth, that being the only kind there is) and that it is of fundamental importance to us and foundational to our noetic structures. Christian philosophers must reveal the deficiencies of the opposing views, thus going on the offensive; but they must also give their own accounts of these areas — truth, objectivity, normativity, and so on.

Indeed, they must give their own accounts of the whole sweep of topics and questions with which philosophers concern themselves: knowledge (as I tried to do in *Warrant and Proper Function*), morality, responsibility, freedom, ethics, the nature of human beings, the nature of abstract objects, the nature of causation, the way to understand science, the way in which Scripture is a special word from the Lord, the sort of warrant enjoyed by Christian belief, and a thousand other topics. Now of course a philosopher hopes that others will be interested in what she comes up with, and perhaps even agree with it. But the Christian philosopher shouldn't think of herself as first of all address-

---

11. To be found in chapter 12 of *Warrant and Proper Function* [Ed. note: chapter 4 above] and in "Naturalism Defeated" (not yet published), a sequel to chapter 12.

ing the philosophical world *überhaupt;* what she wants (in pursuing this project) is to develop ways of thinking that recommend themselves from the point of view of Christian theism. Those who don't share that point of view may not be impressed; but that is not a serious problem. For one important task of the community of Christian philosophers (though not its only important task) is broadly *internal;* in working at this task the Christian faces towards the Christian community. Here the criterion of success is not influence on the non-Christian philosophical world; that is not directly a part of this task, although of course it is to be welcomed if it happens. Here the Christian thinks of herself first of all as a member of the Christian community, and only secondarily as a member of the philosophical community at large. But I fear I begin to repeat myself.

Alvin Plantinga

Alvin Plantinga: A Bibliography

EDITOR'S NOTE: I do not pretend that this bibliography is complete or even completely accurate. In fact, there are several places where the information included is incomplete because my best efforts could not fill in the blanks. A corpus as large as Plantinga's is invariably impossible to catalog fully. Nonetheless, I include here all information my research uncovered, and trust that it will be useful to those desiring in-depth study of his work.

Forthcoming
1. "Arguments for the Existence of God," and "Religion and Epistemology." *Routledge Encyclopedia of Philosophy.*
2. "Essence and Essentialism," "Haecceity," "Natural Theology," and "Pantheism." Ernest Sosa and Jaegwon Kim, editors. *A Companion to Metaphysics.* Oxford: Blackwell.
3. "Preface." Francisco S. Conesa Ferrer. *Dios Y el Mal; La Defensa del Teísmo Frente al problema del mal según Alvin Plantinga.* Pamplona: University of Navarre Press.
4. *Warranted Christian Belief.*

1998
5. *The Analytic Theist: An Alvin Plantinga Reader.* James F. Sennett, editor. Grand Rapids: William B. Eerdmans.

1997
6. "*Ad* Hick." *Faith and Philosophy* 14.30: 295-98.
7. "Warrant and Accidentally True Belief." *Analysis* 57.2: 140-45.

1996

8. "A Defense of Religious Exclusivism." Louis Pojman, editor. *Philosophy of Religion: An Anthology.* Belmont, Calif.: Wadsworth Publishing Company. (Reprinted from #17 below)
9. "Dennett's Dangerous Idea." *Books and Culture,* May-June.
10. "Epistemic Probability and Evil." Daniel Howard-Snyder, editor. *The Evidential Argument from Evil.* Bloomington: Indiana University Press. Pages 69-96. (Reprinted from #46 below.)
11. *Essays in Ontology.* New York: Oxford University Press.
12. "Methodological Naturalism?" J. van der Meer, editor. *Facets of Faith and Science.* Lanham, Md.: University Press of America.
13. "On Being Evidentially Challenged." Daniel Howard-Snyder, editor. *The Evidential Argument from Evil.* Bloomington: Indiana University Press. Pages 244-61.
14. "Respondeo." Jonathan Kvanvig, editor. *Warrant and Epistemology: Essays in Honor of Alvin Plantinga's Theory of Knowledge.*
15. "Science: Augustinian or Duhemian?" *Faith and Philosophy* 13.3 368-94.

1995

16. "Christian Philosophy at the End of the 20th Century." Sander Griffioen and Bert Balk, editors. *Christian Philosophy at the Close of the Twentieth Century.* Kampen: Kok. Pages 29-53.
17. "Pluralism: A Defense of Religious Exclusivism." Thomas D. Senor, editor. *The Rationality of Belief and the Plurality of Faith: Essays in Honor of William P. Alston.* Ithaca: Cornell University Press. Pages 191-215.
18. *"Précis* of *Warrant: The Current Debate* and *Warrant and Proper Function." Philosophy and Phenomenological Research* 55.2: 393-96.
19. "Reliabilism, Analyses, and Defeaters." *Philosophy and Phenomenological Research* 55.2: 427-64.
20. "What's the Question?" *Journal of Philosophical Research* 20: 19-43.

1994

21. "A Christian Life Partly Live." Kelly James Clark, editor. *Philosophers Who Believe.* Downers Grove, Ill.: InterVarsity Press. Pages 45-82.
22. "On Christian Scholarship." Theodore Hesburgh, editor. *The Challenge and Promise of a Catholic University.* Notre Dame, Ind.: University of Notre Dame Press.

1993

23. "Agnosticism," "Dogmatism," and "Epistemology of Religious Be-

lief." Ernest Sosa and Jonathan Dancy, editors. *A Companion to Epistemology.* Oxford: Blackwell.

24. "An Evolutionary Argument Against Naturalism." Carol White and Elizabeth Radcliff, editors. *Faith in Theory and Practice: Essays on Justifying Religious Belief.* Chicago: Open Court. Pages 35-65. (Reprinted from #37 below.)

25. "Divine Knowledge." C. Stephen Evans and Merold Westphal, editors. *Christian Perspectives on Religious Knowledge.* Pages 40-65.

26. "Evolution and the Catholic Character." *Common Sense,* April.

27. "Truth, Omniscience, and Cantorian Arguments: An Exchange" (with Patrick Grim). *Philosophical Studies* 71.3: 267-306.

28. *Warrant and Proper Function.* New York: Oxford University Press.

29. *Warrant: The Current Debate.* New York: Oxford University Press.

30. "Why We Need Proper Function." *Nous* 27.1: 66-82.

1992

31. "Augustinian Christian Philosophy." *Monist* 75.3: 291-320.

32. "Belief in God." R. Boylan, editor. *Introduction to Philosophy.* New York: Harcourt, Brace, Jovanovich.

33. "Epistemic Probability and Evil." Kelly James Clark, editor. *Our Knowledge of God.* Dordrecht: Kluwer. (Reprinted from #45 below.)

34. "Justification in the 20th Century." Enrique Villanueva, editor. *Rationality in Epistemology.* Atascadero, Calif.: Ridgeview. (Reprinted from #42 below.)

1991

35. *"Ad* Walls." *Philosophy and Phenomenological Research* 51.4: 621-24.

36. *Ad* Robbins." *Journal of the American Academy of Religion.*

37. "An Evolutionary Argument Against Naturalism." *Logos* 12: 27-49.

38. "The Prospects for Natural Theology," James E. Tomberlin, editor. *Philosophical Perspectives 5: Philosophy of Religion.* Atascadero, Calif.: Ridgeview.

39. "Warrant and Designing Agents: A Reply to James Taylor." *Philosophical Studies* 64.2: 203-15.

40. "When Faith and Reason Clash: Evolution and the Bible." *The Christian Scholar's Review* 21: 8-32.

41. "Science, Neutrality, and Biblical Scholarship: A Reply to McMullin, Pun, and Van Till." *The Christian Scholar's Review* 21: 80-109.

1990

42. "Justification in the 20th Century." *Philosophy and Phenomenological Research* 50 (supplement): 45-71.

1989

43. *"Ad* de Vries." *The Christian Scholar's Review.*
44. *The Nature of Necessity.* New York: Clarendon Press. (Reprinted from #95 below.)
45. *The Twin Pillars of Christian Scholarship: The Henry Stob Lectures.* Grand Rapids: Calvin College pamphlet.

1988

46. "Chisholmian Internalism." David Austin, editor. *Philosophical Analysis: A Defense by Example.* Dordrecht: D. Reidel. Pages 127-51.
47. "Epistemic Probability and Evil." *Archivio di Filosofia* 56: 557-84.
48. "Method in Christian Philosophy: A Reply." *Faith and Philosophy* 5: 159-64.
49. "Positive Epistemic Status and Proper Function." James E. Tomberlin, editor. *Philosophical Perspectives 2: Epistemology.* Pages 1-50.

1987

50. "Justification and Theism." *Faith and Philosophy* 4: 403-26.
51. "Reply to Timmer." *Reformed Journal,* September.
52. "Sheehan's Shenanigans: How Theology Becomes Tomfoolery." *Reformed Journal* (April): 19-25.
53. "Two Concepts of Modality: Modal Realism and Modal Reductionism." James E. Tomberlin, editor. *Philosophical Perspectives 1: Metaphysics.* Atascadero, Calif.: Ridgeview.

1986

54. "Coherentism and the Evidentialist Objection to Belief in God." Robert Audi and William Wainwright, editors. *Rationality, Religious Belief, and Moral Commitment.* Ithaca: Cornell University Press. Pages 109-38.
55. "Epistemic Justification." *Nous* 20: 3-18.
56. "Is Theism Really a Miracle?" *Faith and Philosophy* 3: 109-34.
57. "On Ockham's Way Out." *Faith and Philosophy* 3: 235-69.
58. "On Taking Belief in God as Basic." Joseph Runzo and Craig Ihara, editors. *Religious Experience and Religious Belief.* Lanham, Md.: University Press of America. Pages 1-17.
59. "The Foundations of Theism: A Reply." *Faith and Philosophy* 3: 292-313.

1985

60. "Alvin Plantinga: Self-Profile." James E. Tomberlin and Peter van Inwagen, editors. *Alvin Plantinga.* Dordrecht: D. Reidel. Pages 3-97.
61. "Replies to Articles." James E. Tomberlin and Peter van Inwagen, editors. *Alvin Plantinga.* Dordrecht: D. Reidel. Pages 313-96.

1984
62. "Advice to Christian Philosophers." *Faith and Philosophy* 1: 253-71.
63. "Modern Philosophy and the Turn to Belief in God." Roy Varghese, editor. *The Intellectuals Speak Out About God.* New York: Regnery.

1983
64. *Faith and Rationality: Reason and Belief in God* (editor, with Nicholas Wolterstorff). Notre Dame, Ind.: University of Notre Dame Press.
65. "Guise Theory." James E. Tomberlin, editor. *Agent, Language and the Structure of the World.* Indianapolis: Hackett. Pages 43-78.
66. "Hector-Neri Castañeda: A Personal Statement." James E. Tomberlin, editor. *Agent, Language and the Structure of the World.* Indianapolis: Hackett. Pages 7-13.
67. "On Existentialism." *Philosophical Studies* 44: 1-20.
68. "Reason and Belief in God." Alvin Plantinga and Nicholas Wolterstorff, editors. *Faith and Rationality.* Notre Dame, Ind.: University of Notre Dame Press. Pages 16-93.
69. "The Reformed Objection Revisited." *Christian Scholar's Review* 12: 57-61.

1982
70. "How to Be an Anti-Realist." *Proceedings of the American Philosophical Association* 56.1: 47-70.
71. "On Reformed Epistemology." *Reformed Journal* 32 (January): 13-17.
72. "Reformed Epistemology Again." *Reformed Journal* 32 (July): 7-8.
73. "Tooley and Evil: A Reply." *Australasian Journal of Philosophy* 60: 66-75.

1981
74. "Is Belief in God Properly Basic?" *Nous* 15: 41-51.
75. "Rationality and Religious Belief." S. Cahn and D. Shatz, editors. *Contemporary Philosophy of Religion.* New York: Oxford University Press. Pages 255-77.
76. "Reply to the Basingers on Divine Omnipotence." *Process Studies* 11: 25-29.
77. "The Case of Kant." Jack Rogers, editor. *Introduction to Philosophy.*

1980
78. *Does God Have a Nature?* Milwaukee: Marquette University Press.
79. "The Reformed Objection to Natural Theology." *Proceedings of the American Catholic Philosophical Association* 15: 49-63.

1979

80. "De Essentia." E. Sosa, editor. *Essays on the Philosophy of Roderick M. Chisholm.* Amsterdam: Rodopi. Pages 101-21.
81. "Is Belief in God Rational?" C. Delaney, editor. *Rationality and Religious Belief.* Notre Dame, Ind.: University of Notre Dame Press. Pages 7-27.
82. "The Probabilistic Argument from Evil." *Philosophical Studies* 35: 1-53.
83. "Transworld Depravity or Worldbound Individuals?" Michael Loux, editor. *The Possible and the Actual.* Ithaca: Cornell University Press. (Reprinted from #97 below.)

1978

84. "The Boethian Compromise." *American Philosophical Quarterly* 15: 129-38.

1977

85. "Reply to Henry." *Philosophical Books* 16.3: 8-10.

1976

86. "Actualism and Possible Worlds." *Theoria* 42: 139-60.
87. "Existence, Necessity and God." *The New Scholasticism* 50: 61-72.
88. "Necessary Existence: A Reply to Carter." *Canadian Journal of Philosophy* 6: 105-11.
89. "Possible Worlds." *The Listener* 95 (June 30).

1975

90. "Aquinas on Anselm." C. Orlebeke and L. Smedes, editors. *God and the Good.* Grand Rapids: Wm. B. Eerdmans.
91. "On Mereological Essentialism." *Review of Metaphysics* 28: 468-76.

1974

92. "Aquinas — 700 Years Later." *Reformed Journal* 24: 5-7.
93. "God and Rationality." *Reformed Journal* 24: 28-29.
94. *God, Freedom and Evil.* New York: Harper Torchbook. (Also published by William B. Eerdmans, Grand Rapids.)
95. *The Nature of Necessity.* Oxford: Clarendon Press.
96. "Our Reasonable Service." *The Banner* 109 (October 18): 6-8.

1973

97. "Transworld Identity or Worldbound Individuals?" Milton Munitz, editor. *Logic and Ontology.* New York: New York University Press. Pages 193-212.

98. "Which Worlds Could God Have Created?" *Journal of Philosophy* 70: 539-52.

1971
99. "Christians, Scholars, and Christian Scholars." *The Banner* 106 (June 18): 4-7.
100. "What George Could Not Have Been." *Nous* 5: 227-32.

1970
101. "The Incompatibility of Freedom with Determinism: A Reply." *Philosophical Forum* 2: 141-48.
102. "Why Climb Mountains?" *Reformed Journal* 20: 6-8.
103. "World and Essence." *Philosophical Review* 79: 461-92.

1969
104. *"De Re et De Dicto." Nous* 3: 235-58.

1968
105. "Induction and Other Minds II." *Review of Metaphysics* 21: 524-33.

1967
106. *God and Other Minds: A Study of the Rational Justification of Belief in God.* Ithaca: Cornell University Press.
107. "Norman Malcolm." Paul Edwards, editor. *Encyclopedia of Philosophy.* New York: Macmillan. 5: 139-40.
108. "Radical Theology." *Reformed Journal* 17 (May/June): 7-10.
109. "The Death of God." *Reformed Journal.*

1966
110. "Comments (on Hillary Putnam's 'The Mental Life of Some Machines')." Henri N. Castañeda, editor. *Intentionality, Minds, and Perception.* Detroit: Wayne State University Press. Pages 201-5.
111. "Induction and Other Minds." *Review of Metaphysics* 19: 441-61.
112. "Kant's Objection to the Ontological Argument." *Journal of Philosophy* 63: 537-45.
113. "On Being Honest to God." *Reformed Journal.*
114. "Pike and Possible Persons." *Journal of Philosophy* 63: 104-8.
115. "Radical Theology and the Death of God." *Reformed Journal.*

1965
116. "Comment on Paul Ziff's 'The Simplicity of Other Minds.'" *Journal of Philosophy* 62: 585-86.

117. "The Free Will Defense." Max Black, editor. *Philosophy in America.* Ithaca: Cornell University Press. Pages 204-20.
118. *The Ontological Argument: From St. Anselm to Contemporary Philosophers* (editor). Garden City, N.Y.: Anchor Books (Doubleday).

1964

119. "A Comment on the Strategy of the Skeptic." John Hick, editor. *Faith and the Philosophers.* London: Macmillan. Pages 226-27.
120. *Faith and Philosophy: Philosophical Studies in Religion and Ethics* (editor). Grand Rapids: William B. Eerdmans.
121. "Necessary Being." Alvin Plantinga, editor. *Faith and Philosophy.* Grand Rapids: William B. Eerdmans. Pages 97-110.

1963

122. "Analytic Philosophy and Christianity." *Christianity Today* 8.2: 17-20.

1962

123. "The Perfect Goodness of God." *Australasian Journal of Philosophy* 40: 70-75.

1961

124. "A Valid Ontological Argument?" *Philosophical Review* 70: 93-101.
125. "It's Actual, so It Must Be Possible." *Philosophical Studies* 12: 61-64.

1960

126. "Things and Persons." *Review of Metaphysics* 14: 493-519.

1958

127. "An Existentialist's Ethics." *Review of Metaphysics* 12: 235-56.
128. "Dooyeweerd on Meaning and Being." *Reformed Journal* 8 (October): 10-15.

SOURCES

Alvin Plantinga: Curriculum Vitae. World Wide Web Page. (URL: id-www.ucsb.edu/fscf/library/plantinga/cv.html).

Loathian's Wall. *Alvin Plantinga: Bibliography.* World Wide Web Page (URL: www.nauticom.net/www/loathian/Biblio.html).

Sennett, James. *Modality, Probability, and Rationality: A Critical Examination of Alvin Plantinga's Philosophy.* New York: Peter Lang, 1992.

The Philosopher's Index Online. Bowling Green, Ohio: Philosophy Documentation Center, 1997.

Tomberlin, James E., and Peter van Inwagen, "Bibliography of Alvin Plantinga." *Alvin Plantinga.* Dordrecht: D. Reidel, 1985. Pages 399-404.

Reprint Permission Acknowledgments

Chapter One: "God and Analogy"
Reprinted from chapter 10 of Alvin Plantinga, *God and Other Minds: A Study of the Rational Justification of Belief in God*, © 1967 by Cornell University Press; used by permission of the publisher.

Chapter Two: "The Free Will Defense"
Reprinted from pp. 29-59 of Alvin Plantinga, *God, Freedom, and Evil* © 1974 by William B. Eerdmans Publishing Co.

Chapter Three: "The Ontological Argument"
Reprinted from pp. 85-112 of Alvin Plantinga, *God, Freedom, and Evil*, © 1974 by William B. Eerdmans Publishing Co.

Chapter Four: "Is Naturalism Irrational?"
Reprinted from chapter 12 of Alvin Plantinga, *Warrant and Proper Function*, © 1993 by Oxford University Press; used by permission of the publisher.

Chapter Five: "Reason and Belief in God"
Excerpted and reprinted from pp. 17-93 of Alvin Plantinga and Nicholas Wolterstorff, editors, *Faith and Rationality: Reason and Belief in God*, © 1983 by the University of Notre Dame Press; used by permission of the publisher.

Chapter Six: "Justification and Theism"
Reprinted from *Faith and Philosophy* 4 (1987), pp. 403-26; used by permission of the editor.

Chapter Seven: "A Defense of Religious Exclusivism"
Previously appeared both in Thomas D. Senor, editor, *The Rationality of Belief and the Plurality of Faith: Essays in Honor of William P. Alston* (Cornell, 1995), pp. 191-215, and in Louis Pojman, editor, *Philosophy of Religion: An Anthology* (Wadsworth, 1996); © 1995 by Alvin Plantinga; used by permission of the author.

Chapter Eight: "Necessary Being"
Reprinted from pp. 97-108 of Alvin Plantinga, editor, *Faith and Philosophy: Philosophical Studies in Religion and Ethics;* © 1964 by William B. Eerdmans Publishing Co.

Chapter Nine: "Does God Have a Nature?"
Excerpted and reprinted from Alvin Plantinga, *Does God Have a Nature?* © 1980 by Marquette University Press; used by permission of the publisher.

Chapter Ten: "On Ockham's Way Out"
Reprinted from *Faith and Philosophy* 3 (1986), pp. 235-69; used by permission of the editor.

Chapter Eleven: "Advice to Christian Philosophers"
Reprinted from *Faith and Philosophy* 1 (1984), pp. 253-71; used by permission of the editor.

Chapter Twelve: "Sheehan's Shenanigans: How Theology Becomes Tomfoolery"
Reprinted from *The Reformed Journal,* April 1987, pp. 19-25.

Chapter Thirteen: "Christian Philosophy at the End of the Twentieth Century"
Reprinted from pp. 29-53 of Sander Griffioen and Bert Balk, editors, *Christian Philosophy at the Close of the Twentieth Century* (Kampen: Kok, 1995); used by permission of the publisher.